Notwithstanding their relevance to the development of collective identities, as well as for the image and narrative of contentious politics, festivals or parades have not received much attention in social movement studies. This volume fills this gap through an in-depth comparative analysis of Pride Parades that uncovers the polyvocal manifestations of LGBT communities in different countries and periods. A brilliant contribution!
Donatella della Porta, Director of Centre of Social Movements Studies, Scuola Normale Superiore, Italy

Pride parades emerged across the globe as routine performances of LGBT collective identity. This book draws on survey and qualitative data to examine parades in seven European countries and Mexico. By exploring who participates and why, how participants are mobilized, and how the parades vary depending on political context, the authors argue that Pride parades are more than celebratory performances. Rather, they are highly political, challenging not only gender and cultural norms but also larger political conditions.
Verta Taylor, Distinguished Professor of Sociology, University of California, Santa Barbara

Pride Parades and LGBT Movements

Today, Pride parades are staged in countries and localities across the globe, providing the most visible manifestations of lesbian, gay, bisexual, trans, queer and intersex movements and politics.

Pride Parades and LGBT Movements contributes to a better understanding of LGBT protest dynamics through a comparative study of eleven Pride parades in seven European countries – Czech Republic, Italy, Netherlands, Poland, Sweden, Switzerland, the UK – and Mexico. Peterson, Wahlström and Wennerhag uncover the dynamics producing similarities and differences between Pride parades, using unique data from surveys of Pride participants and qualitative interviews with parade organizers and key LGBT activists. In addition to outlining the histories of Pride in the respective countries, the authors explore how the different political and cultural contexts influence: *Who* participates, in terms of socio-demographic characteristics and political orientations; *what* Pride parades mean for their participants; *how* participants were mobilized; *how* Pride organizers relate to allies and what strategies they employ for their performances of Pride.

This book will be of interest to political scientists and sociologists with an interest in LGBT studies, social movements, comparative politics and political behavior and participation.

Abby Peterson is Professor Emerita of Sociology at the Department of Sociology and Work Science, University of Gothenburg, Sweden. She has published extensively within the fields of social movement research, cultural sociology and criminology.

Mattias Wahlström is Associate Professor at the Department of Sociology and Work Science, University of Gothenburg, Sweden. He has a PhD in Sociology from the University of Gothenburg. His research mainly concerns social movements, protest and the policing of social protest.

Magnus Wennerhag is Associate Professor in Sociology at the School of Social Sciences, Södertörn University, Sweden. He has a PhD in Sociology from Lund University. His research mainly concerns social movements, political participation, social stratification and theories of modernity.

Gender and Comparative Politics

Edited by Karen Celis (Vrije Universiteit Brussel) and Isabelle Engeli (University of Bath)

The comparative research conducted in the field of gender and politics today is more than ever resulting in innovative theory building, applying novel research designs and engaging with mainstream political science. Gender & Politics has moved from the margins of political science to the center. Given the highly critical and activist roots of the gender and politics scholarship, it quasi naturally embraces intersectionality. The *Routledge Gender and Comparative Politics* book series aims to reflect this rich, critical and broad scholarship covering the main political science sub-disciplines with, for instance, gender focused research on political economy, civil society, citizenship, political participation and representation, governance and policy making.

1. Feminist Activism at War
Belgrade and Zagreb Feminists in the 1990s
Ana Miškovska Kajevska

2. Making Gender Equality Happen
Knowledge, Change and Resistance in EU Gender Mainstreaming
Rosalind Cavaghan

3. The Gender Politics of Domestic Violence
Feminists Engaging the State in Central and Eastern Europe
Andrea Krizsán and Conny Roggeband, with contributions from Raluca Maria Popa

4. Varieties of Opposition to Gender Equality in Europe
Edited by Mieke Verloo

5. Pride Parades and LGBT Movements
Political Participation in an International Comparative Perspective
Abby Peterson, Mattias Wahlström and Magnus Wennerhag

Pride Parades and LGBT Movements
Political Participation in an International Comparative Perspective

Abby Peterson, Mattias Wahlström and Magnus Wennerhag

NEW YORK AND LONDON

First published 2018
by Routledge
711 Third Avenue, New York, NY 10017

and by Routledge
2 Park Square, Milton Park, Abingdon, Oxon OX14 4RN

Routledge is an imprint of the Taylor & Francis Group, an informa business

© 2018 Taylor & Francis

The right of Abby Peterson, Mattias Wahlström and Magnus Wennerhag to be identified as authors of this work has been asserted by them in accordance with sections 77 and 78 of the Copyright, Designs and Patents Act 1988.

All rights reserved. No part of this book may be reprinted or reproduced or utilized in any form or by any electronic, mechanical, or other means, now known or hereafter invented, including photocopying and recording, or in any information storage or retrieval system, without permission in writing from the publishers.

Trademark notice: Product or corporate names may be trademarks or registered trademarks, and are used only for identification and explanation without intent to infringe.

Library of Congress Cataloging in Publication Data
Names: Peterson, Abby, author. |Wahlström, Mattias, author. | Wennerhag, Magnus, 1973- author.
Title: Pride parades and LGBT movements political participation in an international comparative perspective / Abby Peterson, Mattias Wahlström and Magnus Wennerhag.
Description: 1 Edition. | New York : Routledge, 2018. | Series: Gender and comparative politics ; 5 | Includes bibliographical references and index.
Identifiers: LCCN 2018000654| ISBN 9781138202399 (hardback) | ISBN 9781315474052 (Master) | ISBN 9781315474045 (webpdf) | ISBN 9781315474038 (epub) | ISBN 9781315474021 (mobipocket/kindle)
Subjects: LCSH: Gay pride parades–History. | Gay liberation movement–History. | Gays–History.
Classification: LCC HQ76.96 .P478 2018 | DDC 306.76/609–dc23
LC record available at https://lccn.loc.gov/2018000654

ISBN: 9781138202399 (hbk)
ISBN: 9781315474052 (ebk)

Typeset in Times New Roman
by Taylor & Francis Books

Contents

List of illustrations viii
Preface and Acknowledgments x
Abbreviations xii

1 Introduction: "Coming Out All Over" 1
2 The Histories of Pride 18
3 Context Matters 71
4 Who Participates? 88
5 Pride Parade Mobilizing and the Barrier of Stigma 124
6 Friends of Pride: Challenges, Conflicts and Dilemmas 144
7 Performances of Party and Politics 170
8 The Meanings of Pride Parades for their Participants 190
9 Between Politics and Party 211

List of Interviews 227
Appendix 230
Index 249

List of illustrations

Figures

3.1	Homosexuality always or never justifiable, attitudes in eight countries	76
4.1	Political orientations amongst LGBT groups in Pride parades in four countries	114
A.1	Example of how an ideal-typical demonstration can be sampled	233

Tables

3.1	Contextual factors that influence Pride parades	83
4.1	The socio-demographic composition of Pride parades in eight countries, compared to national populations	94
4.2	The composition of gender identities in Pride parades in eight countries	98
4.3	The composition of sexual orientations in Pride parades in four countries	100
4.4	Socio-demographic characteristics in different LGBT groups in Pride parades in four countries.	100
4.5	Participants' political engagement in Pride parades in eight countries	104
4.6	Political engagement among LGBT groups in Pride parades in four countries	107
4.7	Participants' political orientation in Pride parades in eight countries	110
4.8	Political orientations amongst LGBT groups in Pride parades in four countries	113
4.9	Attitudes regarding LGBT movement strategies in Pride parades in four countries	116
4.10	Regression for attitudes regarding LGBT movement strategies in Pride parades in four countries	118
5.1	Types of information channels about the parade (%)	134

List of illustrations ix

5.2	Proportions of participants asked to join and asking others to participate (%)	137
5.3	Most important information channels, first-timers vs. returnees (%)	139
8.1	Motive types compared with previous studies	195
8.2	Prevalence of different motive types in the demonstrations studied (%)	205
A.1	Surveyed demonstrations, distributed questionnaires and response rates	231
A.2	Cases of significant non-response bias in the dataset	236
A.3	Survey question wordings and response alternatives.	240

Preface and Acknowledgments

This book has a long history. It all began in May 2009, with our first meeting in Antwerp with the country teams in the collaborative research project, the European Science Foundation, EUROSCORES Program, "Caught in the act of protest: Contextualizing contestation (CCC)" led by Professors Bert Klandermans, Jacqueline van Stekelenburg, and Stefaan Walgrave. Our Swedish team's participation was made possible by generous support from the Swedish Council for Working Life and Social Research (FAS 2008–1799). At least Peterson was unmercifully thrown into the jaws of hypotheses, regressions, and not least, disciplined and highly standardized data collection. In regards to the latter, Wennerhag and Wahlström picked up the slack and we would like to especially thank Stefaan Walgrave for his patient tutelage. The country teams, the numbers of which grew over the four years of the collaboration, were encouraged to survey between ten and twelve demonstrations with more than 3,000 participants. In Sweden we solved the logistics of this condition by focusing on annual ritual parades – May Day demonstrations and later Pride parades. The latter kind of protest events gave rise to some controversy among the international research teams of CCC, and some colleagues expressed doubts about whether Pride parades would properly count as political demonstrations. We insisted that this is a legitimate, but ultimately empirical, question, which we try to answer in this book. Of course, we are very thankful that the country teams from the Czech Republic, Mexico, Netherlands, Italy, Switzerland, and the UK agreed with us on this point and prioritized Pride parades in their domestic selection of cases.

In addition to our research on labor, anti-austerity, and climate protests the former focus resulted in a collaboration with labor historians and the book, *The Ritual of May Day in Western Europe: Past, Present and Future* (Abby Peterson and Herbert Reiter, Eds. 2016. Oxon, UK: Routledge). Our interest in ritual parades was piqued and at the conclusion of our CCC project we applied for, and were awarded, funding to use and extend this database for the study of Pride parades. We acknowledge the support from the Bank of Sweden Tercentenary Foundation (P2013–0861:1). Throughout this research Wennerhag and Wahlström have carried the brunt of the work

Preface and Acknowledgments xi

with the quantitative data collection and analysis. We wish to thank the CCC teams for conducting the protest surveys at the Pride parades in Prague, Bologna, Haarlem, Geneva, Zurich, London, and Mexico City and students, colleagues, and other persons for helping us conduct the protest surveys at the Pride parades in Warsaw, Gothenburg, and Stockholm (special thanks to Jan Orzechowski for observation of the Warsaw Equality parade). We would also like to thank Anders Hylmö for manually classifying the occupation of all cases in the CCC dataset, as well as managing all the coding of the data into Oesch's class categories for both CCC and ESS data. Henrik Schedin assisted with gathering data on organizers, organizing visual data on Pride parades, and double-coding the motive codes for Chapter 8. We all took equal part in the qualitative data collection. We received valuable help from our CCC colleagues and others in forging contacts with Pride organizers and key LGBT activists. We wish to thank Lorenzo Bosi, Ondřej Císař, Nina Eggert, Ron Holzhacker, Maria Inclán, Jiří Navrátil, Igor Petrovic, Petr Tomas, and Anouk van Leeuwen. Cristiana Olcese conducted the interviews in the UK and one in Italy. Diego Dominguez Cardona, together with Peterson, carried out the interviews in Mexico City. Grzegorz Piotrowski helped with translating the survey to Polish, organizing the survey in Warsaw, and with tips regarding Polish interviewees. We would like to thank Magda Muszel for coding the Polish surveys and transcribing Polish interviews and Graeme Hodgson for several of the interview transcriptions.

Our interviewees have been an invaluable resource for our research (see the List of Interviews). They have all patiently reflected over our questions, which has provided us with the information to "fill in the gaps" and the tools, which helped us interpret our quantitative analyses. By breathing life into our research questions they have been indeed a source of inspiration.

While this has been a joint venture, there has been a division of labor in writing the book. We all authored Chapter 2, with Diego Dominguez Cardona writing the section on the Pride history in Mexico. Peterson has authored Chapters 1, 3, and 7 and co-authored Chapters 5, 6, and 9 with Wahlström. Wahlström has written Chapter 8 and co-authored the Appendix with Wennerhag. Wennerhag has written Chapter 4.

Gothenburg, September 2017

Abbreviations

ARCI	*Associazione Ricreativa e Culturale Italiana*, Italian Recreational and Cultural Association.
BDSMF	Bondage, Discipline/Dominance, Submission/Sadism, Masochism and Fetishism
BDP/PBD	*Bürgerlich-Demokratische Partei Schweiz/Parti Bourgeois Démocratique Suisse*, Conservative Democratic Party of Switzerland
CCC	Caught in the Act of Protest: Contextualizing Contestation
CGH	*Coordinadora de Grupos Homosexuales,* Coordinators of Homosexual Groups (Mexico)
CHE	Campaign for Homosexual Equality (UK)
CoC	*Cultuur en Ontspanningscentrum*, Center for Culture and Leisure (Netherlands)
CONAPRED	*Consejo Nacional para Prevenir La Discriminación*, National Council to Prevent Discrimination (Mexico)
CSD	Christopher Street Day (Switzerland)
ECtHR	European Court of Human Rights
ERCHO	Eastern Regional Conference of Homophile Organizations
EPOA	European Pride Organizers Association
ESS	European Social Survey
EU	European Union
FAHR	*Frente Homosexual de Liberatión Revolutionaria*, Homosexual Front of Revolutionary Action (Mexico)
FNF	*Frente Nacional por la Familia*, National Front for the Family (Mexico)
F.U.O.R.I.	*Fronte Unitario Omosessuale Rivoluzionario Italiano*, Italian Revolutionary Homosexual United Front
GBTQ	Gay, Bisexual, Trans and Queer (preferred Italian moniker)
GLF	Gay Liberation Front (US and UK)

HACH	*Homosexuellen Arbeitsgruppen Schweiz*, Swiss Homosexual Working Groups
HBTQ	Homosexual, Bisexual, Trans and Queer (preferred Swedish moniker)
HFG	*Homosexuelle Frauengruppe Zürich*, Homosexual Women's Group Zurich (Switzerland)
HLRS	Homosexual Law Reform Society (UK)
IAL/GPC	International Association of Lesbian and Gay Pride Coordinators
ICSE	International Committee for Sexual Equality
ILGA	International Lesbian, Gay, Trans and Intersex Association
ILGA-Europe	The European Region of the International Lesbian, Gay, Trans and Intersex Association
ILGNC	International Lesbian and Gay Cultural Network
ILGCN-Polska	International Lesbian and Gay Cultural Network Poland
ISSP	International Social Survey Programme
KDU-ČSL	*Křesťanská a demokratická unie – Československá strana lidová*, Christian and Democratic Union – Czechoslovak People's Party (Czech Republic)
KPH	*Kampania Przeciw Homofobia*, Campaign Against Homophobia (Poland)
LAPOP	Latin American Public Opinion Project
LGBT	Lesbian, Gay, Bisexual and Trans
LGBTQ	Lesbian, Gay, Bisexual, Trans and Queer
LGBTQI	Lesbian, Gay, Bisexual, Trans, Queer and Intersex
LGSM	Lesbian and Gays Support the Miners (UK)
LOS	*Lesbenorganisation Schweiz*, Swiss Lesbian Organization
LPR	*Liga Polskich Rodzin*, League of Polish Families
NAL/GPC	National Association of Lesbian and Gay Pride Coordinators
NGO	Non-Governmental Organization
NWHLRC	North Western Homosexual Law Reform Society (UK)
ODS	*Občanská demokratická strana*, Civic Democratic Party (Czech Republic)
PiS	*Prawo i Sprawiedliwosc*, Law and Justice Party (Poland)
PO	*Platforma Obywatelska*, Civic Platform (Poland)
PRI	*Partido Revolucionario Institucional*, Institutional Revolutionary Party (Mexico)
PROUD	*Platforma pro Rovnoprávnost Uznáni a Diverzitu*, Platform for Equality, Recognition and Diversity (Czech Republic)

RFSL	*Riksförbundet för homosexuellas, bisexuellas, transpersoners och queeras rättigheter*, The Swedish Federation for Lesbian, Gay, Bisexual, Transgender and Queer Rights, formerly *Riksförbundet för sexuellt likaberättigande*, The Swedish Federation for Sexual Equality.
SGL	*Stowarzyszeie Grup Lambda*, Association of Lambda Groups (Poland)
SDPL	*Socjaldemokracja Polska*, Social Democracy of Poland
SOH	*Schweizerische Organisation der Homophilen*, Swiss Organization of Homophiles
SOHO	*Sdružení organizací homosexuálních občanů*, Association of Organizations of Homosexual Citizens (Czechoslovakia/Czech Republic)
SMO	Social Movement Organization
UK	United Kingdom
UKIP	UK Independence Party
US	United States of America
WRH	*Warszawski Ruch Homoseksualny*, Warsaw Homosexual Movement (Poland)
WUNC	Worthiness, unity, numbers, commitment (Tilly 2003)

1 Introduction
"Coming Out All Over"[1]

Pride parades are today staged in countries and localities across the globe, providing the most visible manifestation of lesbian, gay, bisexual, transgender, queer and intersex (LGBT)[2] movements and politics. While Pride parades are the most visible manifestations of LGBT movements, we want to make clear for the reader that our study is not a generalist account of LGBT movements in the countries included in our study. We analyze Pride events in a strategic selection of European countries and Mexico. Our analyses are confined to the parades, even if our analyses can provide (partial) snapshots of LGBT movements in these countries. The main aim of our book is to contribute to a better understanding of LGBT protest dynamics through a comparative study of Pride parades in seven European countries – Czech Republic (Prague), Italy (Bologna), Netherlands (Haarlem), Poland (Warsaw), Sweden (Stockholm and Gothenburg), Switzerland (Geneva and Zurich), the UK (London) – and Mexico (Mexico City), countries which display variation in national level context, while sharing some central characteristics.

As outlined in Chapter 3 our sample includes countries which can be placed into the categories of LGBT friendly, less friendly, and unfriendly political and cultural contexts. We have only included democratic countries and regions where Pride parades are generally permitted and are typically not violently repressed by counterdemonstrators. Hence, our study does not have a global reach, but is empirically confined to the countries included in our sample cases. Nonetheless, the range of political and cultural contexts covered in our study allows us to make generalizations that can extend to Pride events staged in similar contexts. Our central focus is on European countries, but Mexico is included as an outlier, largely to enable us to discuss the analytical generalizability of the European cases (Snow and Trom 2002; Flyvbjerg 2006).

During the post-war period until approximately 1970, homophile organizations in the Netherlands, Switzerland, Sweden, UK, Italy and Mexico worked largely behind the scenes lobbying for legislation to improve the situation for homosexuals and working toward providing the lesbian and gay community with social venues (in the former Eastern Bloc members Poland and Czechoslovakia organizations similar to Western homophile groups emerged alongside more radical gay and lesbian liberation organizations shortly before and after the events of 1989). The homophile movements were confronted with the vigor of new social movements and the new left in the late 1960s and early 1970s. Young lesbian and gay activists, fostered in these movements, challenged the more reformist tactics and goals of the homophile organizations and either contributed to radicalizing these organizations and/or formed new radical organizations. Homophile organizations and their tactics and goals were far from abandoned, but the movements had irrevocably entered a new phase. It is during this phase that "liberation," "gay power" and "coming out" emerged in the rhetoric of the movements – the "Gay Liberation movement" was born. And during this phase lesbians and gays "came out" in the streets to publically celebrate "LGBT life and culture and raise the demand for LGBT liberation, including the abolition of discriminatory laws" (Tatchell 2017). The lesbian and gay movements had entered the era of Pride demonstrations.

Since the first Pride demonstrations in 1970 in New York, Los Angeles and Chicago the tradition has travelled globally. Despite its origins in the US, the tradition has become translated into new contexts to suit different national and local settings. Pride parades today provide sites of tension and ambivalence – between commercialization and politicization, festivity and protest, normalization and contention, "liberation and legitimation" (Rayside 2001, p. 25) – and have assumed different dynamics in different cultural, political and social settings (Browne 2007; Ross 2008; Enguix 2009; Duggan 2010; Calvo and Trujillo 2011; Binnie and Klesse 2011; McFarland 2012; McFarland Bruce 2016). We explore how variation in mobilizing contexts influences the expressions of these tensions and how these tensions impact on who participates in the Pride parades and the kinds of strategies that the organizations staging the parades employ in their political performances of pride.

Despite the still severely restricted rights of LGBT people in many states worldwide, LGBT movements have had considerable success in many democracies resulting in rising levels of tolerance toward lesbians, gay men, bisexuals and transgender individuals, anti-discrimination laws, and in many European countries, recognition of same-sex relationships (registered partnerships and/or same-sex marriage). However, these successes have been unevenly distributed between countries. In many countries LGBT movements are still struggling for basic rights that are fully recognized in other countries. The successes have also created concomitant dilemmas for the national movements with regards to their collective identities and future goals, creating tensions between more counter-cultural and radical factions and those who appear to be relatively content with the increasing normalization of LGBT persons and homosexual relationships. In order to increase our understanding of the conditions for LGBT movements to gain recognition and how national and local factors shape the composition and strategies of LGBT movements, we conducted a comparative study.

Our book focuses on Pride parades, which we argue is one way to capture differences (and even similarities) in LGBT movements from an international comparative perspective studying a shared manifest expression of the movement – the Pride parade and its performances of LGBT collective identity, its organizers and, unique for our study, Pride parade participants.

Across the world LGBT movements are creating political identities based on sexuality, gender identity and community. And at first glance the parallels in the development of different national LGBT movements may seem striking. Such similarities are, however, only on the surface. We have found fundamental disparities between the countries. Processes of transnational diffusion of ideas, strategies, symbols and slogans will be investigated, as will the way in which LGBT movements in different places influence and learn from one another. At the same time, movements are also strongly influenced by local, national and regional political and social structures. All LGBT movements show a clear national or regional imprint, manifesting what Adam, Duyvendak and Krouwel (1999) have called a national "paradigm." Pride mobilizing strategies vary based on national/local cultural, political/legal, and institutional contexts (McFarland 2012, p. 630). Pride parades have travelled to different political and cultural contexts in which the events have been strategically translated – framed – by organizers to adapt to these differing contexts. As Johnston and Waitt (2015, p. 117) point out, "the politics of gay pride festivals and parades is always located; place matters." The politics of gay Pride parades are "dynamic, changing with audiences, participants, sponsors and organizers."

We have sought to uncover the dynamics producing similarities and differences between Pride parades, using a unique individual protest data-set and qualitative interviews with protest organizers and key LGBT activists – combining quantitative survey data from our CCC research collaboration ("Caught in the Act of Protest: Contextualizing Contestation" [see www.protestsurvey.eu]) with qualitative data in part collected in the CCC collaboration and some collected specifically for this book. By using our CCC database we capture participation in specific Pride demonstrations in the study's seven European countries and Mexico; rather than measuring intentions we have comprehensive data on the individuals who actually participated in these Pride demonstrations. This survey data is unique as it provides answers to the following questions: *Who* are the Pride demonstrators, what are their socio-demographic characteristics, what are their political orientations? *Why* do they demonstrate? *What* are the attitudes, motives and beliefs driving them? *How* were they mobilized, through what channels, by which techniques? These are among the focal questions in our book. (For a description and discussion of our methods and empirical materials we refer the reader to the Appendix in this volume.)

Previous research

The US lesbian and gay movement(s) has been dominant on the world scene. There has been a noticeable "Americanization" of homosexualities, especially in its cultural manifestations, for example, in the appropriation of the symbols and language of the American LGBT movement (including rainbow flags, certain clothing styles, the words "pride," "coming out," "Stonewall" and "gay"). Subsequently, much of the research on lesbian and gay politics has a US focus (e.g. Blasius 1994; Ghaziani and Baldassarri 2011; McFarland 2012; McFarland Bruce 2016), however this body of work is complemented by an increasing number of country case studies (e.g. Hallgren [2008] on Sweden and Fojtová [2011] on the Czech Republic).

In addition to these national case studies we find a growing body of work with a comparative focus. Katherine McFarland Bruce (2016) sketches the early establishment of Pride events as a parade during the early 1970s before moving on to her comparative study of Pride parades in New York, Atlanta, San Diego, Salt Lake City, Fargo, ND and Burlington, VT. While McFarland Bruce's (2012, 2016) study is confined to the US, she captures the widely varying cultural climates and political preconditions for the cultural challenges posed by the parades. In all of the parades she studied, participants communicated both a message of defiance emphasizing difference with the heterosexual majority and a message of education, performing sameness with the heterosexual majority. However how these two strategies were combined and performed differed across the contextual variation in her analysis. She uncovers how LGBT movements in these cities adapt their performances to their contexts.

Adam (1995) offers a global perspective on the emergence of gay and lesbian movements. In focus for Adam's book and the later work of Chabot and Duyvendak (2002; see even Swiebel 2009) are processes of transnationalization in gay and lesbian politics that can occur by groups deliberately working together and coordinating activities across national borders (for example the formation of the International Lesbian and Gay Association – Europe [ILGA-Europe]), and/or through a process of diffusion of ideas and action repertoires. These latter researchers point out that the processes of Europeanization and transnationalization are highly linked and influence the strategies pursued by LGBT movements. An additional number of important studies have emerged which interrogate similarities and differences in gay and lesbian movements. Adam, Duyvendak and Krouwel's (1999) anthology offers a comprehensive study of the impact of national contexts on the formation of gay and lesbian politics. The anthology edited by Tremblay, Paternotte and Johnson (2011) includes fifteen countries, where the authors were asked to address whether the LGBT movement had been influenced by the state and whether the state had in turn been influenced by the movement. Engel (2001) compares the post–Second World War histories of the American and British gay and lesbian movements with an eye toward understanding how distinct political institutional environments affect the development, strategies, goals and outcomes of a social movement. Using a similar institutional perspective Ross and Landström (1999) compare the lesbian movements in Canada and Sweden and Smith (2008) assesses the lesbian and gay movements in the US and Canada. Holzhacker (2007) compares the Lesbian and Gay movements in Italy and the Netherlands. Perhaps the most important comparative study of LGBT movements is Omar G. Encarnación's (2016) ground-breaking work on the interaction between global influences and domestic factors in shaping LGBT movements and gay rights policies in Latin America. What all of the comparative studies mentioned above have in common is that they are all qualitative case studies relying on observations, interviews and/or printed materials. Our study complements this work by combining qualitative data with quantitative survey data on grassroots participants in the Pride events included in our study.

The collective performances of pride

Benjamin Shepard (2005) points out that the gestures of one set of participants in a demonstration influence other participants and others whose opinion they seek to influence.

> Thus, social movements and protests are essentially constructions of countless performances. ... With its emphasis on spontaneity and improvisation, protest as performance breaks through barriers to change public opinion and create change.
> (ibid., pp. 452–453)

McFarland Bruce (2016) emphasizes the element of fun for instigating social and cultural change. Having fun in new ways is a tactic, she argues, that urges societies to change. Fun "acts out the world that activists hope to make a reality" (ibid., p. 21). In short, Pride performances seek to represent the idea that another world really is possible. The annual parade format has proved to be the ideal vehicle for mobilizing the LGBT community to culturally challenge the hetero-normative norms that pervade societies, to make demands for citizen rights, and for building collective identity. Pride parades as annual ritual celebratory events focuses the LGBT movements struggles. Encarnación (2016) explains Latin America's enthusiastic embrace of Pride parades:

> Like good old lefties, LGBT groups understand the power of mass protest, especially in the streets. But their approach to taking the streets is not to go on strike, interrupt traffic during rush hour, shut

> down schools and hospitals, or vandalize private property, but rather, throw an annual gay pride march.
>
> (p. 30, citing Javier Corrales)

The underlying script for Pride parades is the idea of coming out (Ghaziani 2008; Chabot and Duyvendak 2002; Herdt 1992, p. 54), that is, the individual and collective processes of publically performing pride – acts of self-affirmation in which Pride participants declare their presence openly and without apology to claim their rights of citizenship. Coming out performances have the explicit intention of increasing the visibility of the LGBT community. "Demonstrating that 'We are everywhere'" (Murray 1996, p. 133) was central to the early gay liberation marches as it is today. "Impatience with closetry has mounted" (ibid.). The pioneers of Pride events were no longer content to seek comfort and support in underground subcultures, nor are Pride participants today content to remain in the closet (Humphreys 1972). They are "coming out all over, not in acts of confession, but rather to profess and advocate the lives they live and the values that those lives express" (Kitsuse 1980, p. 8). John d'Emilio (1998) forcefully argues that gay liberation transformed the meaning of "coming out." During the 1950s and 1960s coming out meant the private decision to accept one's homosexual desires and to acknowledge one's sexual identity to other gay men and women. Gay liberationists:

> recast coming out as a profoundly political act that could offer enormous personal benefits to an individual. The open avowal of one's sexual identity, whether at work, at school, at home, or before television cameras, symbolized the shedding of self-hatred that gay men and women internalized, and consequently it promised an immediate improvement in one's life. To come out of the "closet" quintessentially expressed the fusion of the personal and the political that the late 1960s exalted. ... The exhilaration and anger that surfaced when men and women stepped through the fear of discovery propelled them into political activity.
>
> (pp. 235–236)

Pride parades have been, and are, the polyvocal manifestations of LGBT communities. Hence, we are confronted with multiple performances that do not fit neatly in binary categories of politics and party. Indeed, politics and party or the carnivalesque glide often seamlessly into one another – they are not discrete categories. Furthermore, neither political performances nor performances of the carnivalesque are in themselves uniform categories. The political messages performed in the parades vary. Some of their messages are more accomodationist: "two, four, six, eight, gay is just as good as straight," seeking a normalization of their sexual identities. Other performances are more politically confrontational. Pride participants are also publically proclaiming: "I'm here, I'm queer, get used to it," thereby defying the cultural imperative of heterosexual normativity. Steve, a longtime UK activist, remembered his first Pride parade in London in the mid-1970s. The Chief Constable of Manchester had been quoted as saying "homosexuals are swirling in a cesspool of their own creation." "So I remember going to Pride and they had this banner over the stage, 'A Cesspool of Our Own Creation', and you think that's perfect, it's yes, that is it. ... For him [the Chief Constable] it was the end of civilization as we know it. For us it was just our lives."

Also, carnivalesque performances differ. We can observe some performances as more or less exclusively carnivalesque, for example, joyous dancing in the streets or on floats. Some performers provocatively flaunt their stigma, notably the drag queens and drag kings. Through "camp" performances, which synthesize incongruity, theatricality, and humor, the cultural foundations of hetero-normativity and the masculine–feminine binary can be challenged head on. Esther Newton (1979) points out that incongruity is the subject matter of camp, since to be a feminine man or a masculine woman is by definition incongruous; and if incongruity is the subject matter of camp, theatricality is its style, and humor its strategy (pp. 9–10; Rupp and Taylor 2003). These are powerful tools for political theater. Other performances are more titillating, sending the message: "this is who I am, look at me and think about how I fascinate you!" (Kitsuse 1980, p. 10). These performances are more concerned with making visible different sexual fetishes and subcultures; for example, the floats with BDSM enthusiasts, "puppies" – gay men dressed in rubber or leather dog suits – led down the parade route by their "handlers," or the contingents of "Bear" communities – larger, hairy men conveying their rugged masculinity. However, despite the differences, the coming out performances of LGBT communities are declarations that they will no longer allow the state, the heterosexual majority, or their antagonists to cast them in the shadows.

Coming out is not only an act of making visible previously hidden identities. As Shane Phelan (1993) argues, coming out is just as much a matter of "becoming." The LGBT community fashions itself as a collective political actor through the performances of Pride parades. Bringing together the diversity embraced in the wider LGBT community under the ephemeral umbrella of Pride parades, the movement emerges as a political and cultural force. LGBT politics are inevitably coalitional politics bringing together lesbians, gays, bisexuals, queer, trans, intersex and asexual groups and activists, and even non-LGBT allies, in uneasy alliances. What do lesbian feminists, socialist and conservative gays, queer activists, drag queens, Dykes on bikes, trans persons, bisexuals, leather gays and lipstick lesbians share? However, as Phelan points out, "the problem for coalition politics is not What do we share? But rather, What might we share as we develop our identities through the process of coalition? Who might we become?" (1993, p. 779). Pride parades are performances of a collective becoming – the construction of a temporary collective identity – a sense of community – bridging the diversity of LGBT communities (see also Blasius 2001, pp. 155ff).

We questioned Enrique, a young gay activist and Pride organizer, as to what Pride parades mean for the LGBT community in Mexico City:

> I think there's people, like myself, who see Pride as a mix of party and politics. But also as a really good, positive space to come across people and really feel this sense of community, even if it's just for a little while and for just that moment. That's what I experience, I experience that sense of community because we have something in common, even if we cannot name it, and even if it's just temporary, but there's something here.

LGBT identity strategies

Mary Bernstein's work on "identity politics" has been crucial for our analyses (Bernstein 1997, 2002, 2003, 2005). As Bernstein (2002, p. 532) points out, LGBT movements "alternately and even simultaneously emphasize both cultural and political goals." The challenge is for the researcher to untangle the structural and contextual factors that influence how, in interactions with the state and other institutions, LGBT movements strategically deploy identities. In Bernstein's conceptual framework,

> Identities may be deployed strategically to criticize dominant categories, values, and practices (*for critique*) or to put forth a view of the minority that challenges dominant perceptions (*for education*).
> (Bernstein 2002, p. 539, emphasis in original; McFarland [2012, 2016] uses the same notions, just changing "identity strategy for critique" to "visibility for defiance")

A strategy for critique stresses difference from the majority to confront cultural norms, and even, for that matter, dominant political structures and practices. In contrast, a strategy for education accentuates sameness with the dominant majority, thereby proving their worthiness to enter the polity. In our sample of countries, we find both strategies; nonetheless, we can identify cultural and political contexts where the one or the other strategy dominates.

In addition to identity as strategy, Bernstein (1997) offers two other analytical dimensions of identity: "identity for empowerment" and "identity as goal," both also relevant for our study. The former refers to drawing on an existent identity, or constructing a new collective identity, in order to mobilize a constituency for political action. The latter refers to when activists challenge stigmatized identities, "seek recognition for new identities, or deconstruct restrictive social categories as goals of collective action" (1997, p. 537). How Pride organizers, and participants alike, adapt to their mobilizing contexts by strategically choosing identities and/or suppressing any identities that challenge dominant hetero-normativity and the masculine/feminine binary is a central focus for our study. What we find in our study is that the strategies deployed are not necessarily mutually exclusive. We have not found strict boundaries between assimilationists working for a place at the neoliberal table and liberationists working for profound cultural transformation. LGBT movements in our study seek both change in the political arena for LBGT friendly legislation and policy *and* challenge and confront hetero-normative cultural norms, values and practices.

Diversity and infighting

The LGBT movement is often recognized as "the quintessential identity movement" (Melucci 1989). But the quintessential identity movement harbors a vast diversity of identities or communities: gay men, lesbians, bisexuals, gays of color, transgender, queer, lesbian feminists, gay conservatives, lesbian socialists, liberal homosexuals, lesbian librarians, Social Democratic gays, "Bears," gay military, union gays, and the list goes on, and on. The celebratory parade format proved to be the form that could blend that diversity and temporarily smooth over the differences, into an ephemeral show of unity. Elizabeth Armstrong (2002) argues that,

> the fit between the parade and the message displayed was perfect. ... The parade demanded the display of both shared gay identities and secondary, modifying identities. That everyone needed a contingent, a secondary identity, constructed diversity as a point of commonality.
> (p. 108)

In this way, according to Armstrong, the movement developed "a unity through diversity" (ibid.).

Dissent is endemic for diversity. "Diversity drives dissent" (Ghaziani 2008, p. 7). Amin Ghaziani, together with Steven Epstein (1999), underscore the importance of infighting for shaping the identities, strategies and tactics, and goals for lesbian and gay organizing. Pride parade organizing in our sample of countries has not been without often-rife conflict. While the Pride parade format could (most often) tame diversity, dissent simmers nonetheless under the surface (also Rimmerman 2014). According to Chasin (2000), Pride parades act as a "battleground of sorts for competing strategies" (p. 211) and competing definitions of what the LGBT community is. Like Ghaziani we will seek to tease out the role of infighting, in our case, the tensions involved in organizing Pride parades, for the formations of the LGBT movements' culture, solidarity, strategies and identities – across the cultural and political contexts included in our study.

According to some scholars, the traditional controversies between lesbian women and gay men have become decreasingly salient since the early days of the Lesbian and Gay movement in the 1970s and early 1980s when lesbian separatists rejected the gay rights movement on the grounds of misogyny and sexism (Rimmerman 2014, p. 46; Adam, Duyvendak and Krouwel 1999). Steve, a UK Pride organizer, elaborated on the long-standing discord between lesbians and gay men, which still appears to be entrenched.

> The point I'm making here is, even within the gay community we can't always see eye to eye. We're always arguing amongst ourselves, especially lesbians and gay men and that sort of thing. There was always this, it's almost as if we didn't have anything in common and of course we didn't. We didn't cruise each other, there was no sexual chemistry between mmm, the women and the men, just the opposite in fact in many instances. So that was always an issue. So how we're going to make it work for the broader, for everybody, I've no idea.

Tasso, a West Pride organizer in Gothenburg, Sweden, claimed that the city, Sweden's second largest, was late to host a Pride event because of the deep historical schism between lesbians and gay men. Pride came to Gothenburg first in 2007 upon the initiative of five cultural institutions in the city, not from a gender divided local LGBT movement; the first parade took place first in 2010.

> There is a generation here of older lesbian women and gay men who hate each other. The gay men, these gay groups, thought that lesbian women were the most horrible people around, and the same was true for the lesbians who hated gay men. ... That created these separatist streams that built walls between activists. That isn't the case today of course, but back then, well. So that is the pre-history for why we are so late.

We will return to the question as to whether the conflict between lesbian and gay men has become decreasingly salient as some scholars suggest. However, new conflicts have arisen. Egan and Sherrill (2005) identify a conflict between the traditional focus on "liberty," that is, the right to be left alone to live one's life how one desires and the new rallying cry for "equality," that is, demanding the right to be recognized and respected as equals. They claim that the post-Stonewall period witnesses a dividing line between those seeking a rights-based integrationist approach and those advocating a more radical (often leftist) and confrontational approach. This conflict is related to a political tension within many LGBT movements, pitting equality activists advocating same-sex marriage, adoption rights, etc., against more radical left-wing elements pursuing a struggle against hetero-normativity and patriarchal structures. Margot D. Weiss (2008, p. 89) has described this tension as that between "equality as sameness with normativity (hetero- or homo-) and equality as freedom for difference from the norm."

According to Matthew Waites (2003), since the 1990s a rights-orientated assimilationist agenda has dominated LGBT political discourses. Within the equality normalization discourse lesbians and gay men are represented as oppressed minorities seeking access to core institutions such as marriage, family and the military, as "good" citizens who want to be included and share in the same rights and responsibilities as heterosexuals. "Social acceptance is sought through emphasizing the continuity of lesbian, gay and heterosexual lifestyles and values" (Richardson 2005, p. 392). Underpinning this political discourse is "the idea of lesbians and gay men as being normal, good citizens who are deserving of inclusion and integration into mainstream society" (ibid.). Demands for equality are couched in arguments of "sameness" with the heterosexual majority (Egan and Sherrill 2005). This is a far cry from the political discourses of the 1970s' Gay Liberation Movements and lesbian feminism's arguments on "equality in difference" – the movements from which Gay Pride originally emerged (Chasin 2000; d'Emilio 1998). The early Gay Pride demonstrations, while they protested against discriminatory laws, policies and practices, were above all a celebration of difference and a radical challenge to normative heterosexuality. This rift in the LBGT movement's ideologies lives on today, however, the equal rights-oriented assimilationist agenda of mainstream LGBT organizations dominates, not least because of the discourse's political exigency, and has successfully marginalized other more radical forms of lesbian/gay/transsexual/queer politics (Waites 2003). Schuyf and Krouwel (1999, p. 166) note that with the rise of the human rights discourse and after the organizational and ideological decline of radical gay liberation in the Netherlands during the 1980s, "the number of participants in Gay Pride parades increased sharply over the years." It appears that the equality normalization discourse contributes (at least in part) toward an auspicious situation, at least numerically, for Pride mobilization.

This conflict is in turn related to a political tension within many LGBT movements, pitting equality activists advocating same-sex marriage, adoption rights, etc., against more radical left-wing elements pursuing a broader struggle against patriarchy, hetero-normativity and capitalism *per se*. This point of dissent reveals itself in part in infighting around the question of single-issue parades and multi-issue events. Proponents of the former advocate that the movement should focus solely on LGBT issues, while the latter encourages engagement in a host of other struggles and forging coalitions with other aggrieved groups and social movements "to foster more progressive social change" (Rimmerman 2014, p. 27). The single-issue/multi-issue divide has been a bone of contention throughout Pride history (Ghaziani 2008, p. 103), and it remains a bone of contention particularly for organizers of more politically inclusive Pride events.

Lastly, we have observed the tension between commercialization and politicization. Conflicts have arisen between what is perceived by many organizers as the commercial imperatives of Pride events, on the one hand, and on the other, the political ambitions of LGBT movements. Alexandra Chasin (2000) traced the increasing commercialization of Pride in the US and how this has resulted in an increasing professionalization of organizers' staffs, with paid employees whose role was to secure further commercial funding. This is a development we find not only in the US but elsewhere. Infighting centers on discussions as to whether Pride organizers are "selling out" to commercial interests thereby transforming the parade "from a place of protest to a marketplace" (McFarland Bruce 2016, p. 158).

In conclusion, the apparent shift in the LGBT movement's political discourse can be understood as a sign of the times. Central to neoliberal modes of governance is normalization, the means by which norms of behavior are identified, encouraged and (re)produced within populations. Subsequently, as Diane Richardson (2005) observes, we can see a convergence between LGBT politics and neoliberal state practices. The convergence might also contribute to explaining the political successes of LGBT movements in some countries in attaining many of its goals (Cooper 2006), as well as the support (both economic and organizational) that Pride parades enjoy in many countries. For example, government support for Pride parades in Sweden and the Netherlands is substantial, as is corporate/business support. In both countries local governments have taken organizational initiative to the Pride celebrations. In both countries the parades mobilize a broad cross-section of the LGBT movement with tens of thousands of participants and the carnival-like performances draw hundreds of thousands of amused and bemused tourist onlookers. The success of Stockholm Pride and Amsterdam's Canal Pride, with their incorporation into city promotions and mainstream media, may be understood as, according to Lynda Johnston (2007, p. 1): "'being proud', out and visible, can be politically transgressive as well as about being accepted in neoliberal forms of sexual citizenship."

The historical development of Pride parades continues to be hotly debated in academia as well as amongst LGBT activists.

Outline of the book

On the basis of our interviews and secondary sources, in Chapter 2 we trace the historical trajectories and ritual traditions of Pride events in the countries/cities included in our study. The Pride events we have studied all bear their unique histories. The original impetus may have come from the US, but the notion of an annual ritual parade has been translated within the specific cultural and political contexts where they have been adopted. For sure there are similarities, but also distinctive variations. Pride celebrations adapt to their contexts, hence in Chapter 3 we provide the reader with a model of factors that impact upon the political context and the cultural context, as well as the dynamics between the two, for the Pride events in our study. On the basis of our model we can group the countries in three categories (given variation within the categories): LGBT unfriendly contexts (Poland and Italy), less LGBT friendly contexts (Mexico, Czech Republic and Switzerland), and LGBT friendly contexts (the Netherlands, Sweden and the UK).

In Chapter 4 we analyze who participates in Pride parades in terms of gender identity, sexual orientation, age, education, social class, political attitudes and political participation. The discussion centers on similarities and differences between the Pride participant population and the general population in the respective countries. Which LGBT communities are represented in Pride parades, do they differ in their political attitudes and degree of involvement in LGBT activism, and how does the cultural and political context impact upon which communities participate?

The main focus for Chapter 5 is on the practical aspects of Pride mobilizing in different contexts and how that is linked to different mobilization patterns. The chapter is a comparative analysis of the transcribed interviews, together with the data regarding individual avenues for participation from our questionnaires. There are many pathways to mobilization and we can distinguish contextual variation, but central to our analysis is that potential Pride participants must be targeted, motivated, and encouraged to overcome the barrier of stigmatization.

In Chapter 6 we focus on how and why Pride organizers mobilize what we call "friends of Pride," and the opportunities as well as challenges, conflicts and dilemmas associated with allies. For LGBT movements that seek allies – both individual and collective friends – there are two types of challenges. First, how are (potential) friends mobilized? Second, how do LGBT movements deal with the opportunities – and risks – that are associated with different friendships? Is there a risk that the participation of friends can potentially "de-gay" Pride events as many queer scholars warn?

Pride parades are, we argue, inherently political performances that challenge the dominant sexual and gender norms in society emphasizing the LGBT communities' position outside the cultural structure of heteronormativity. At the same time Pride organizers direct participants to perform in ways that will communicate that they are worthy, committed and determined to achieve acceptance and inclusion in the wider political and cultural community (Alexander and Mast 2006, p. 1). In Chapter 7 we will look more closely at this paradox and analyze the performances of Pride in the different political and cultural contexts included in our study.

Chapter 8 poses the question: "What are the meanings of Pride parades today?" In order to fully answer this question we argue that one needs to turn to the Pride participants and the meanings that they confer to the parades and to their own participation. Thirteen participant motives were identified, which reflects the heterogeneous and multifaceted meanings that Pride parades hold for their participation. We found that Pride participants, more or less across the board, attach explicitly political or protest-oriented meanings to their participation. Only in Haarlem, Netherlands and in London, less than 30 percent of the participants expressed this type of motive. But even in regards to motives, context matters. In the LGBT unfriendly contexts of Poland and Italy, participants had the most explicitly politicized motives.

In our concluding Chapter 9 we will return to the question raised in this introduction: how are the inherent tensions within LGBT movements provisionally smoothed over in Pride parades in a temporary show of unity? Is indeed "the fit between the parade and the message displayed perfect" as Armstrong (2002) argues? We will reflect upon the conflicts that we nonetheless observed, in particular those between lesbians and gay men, and how they were resolved or, for that matter, left unresolved, as well as the conflict between commercialization and politicization.

We concluded our interviews with Pride organizers and activists asking them to reflect over the future of Pride in their countries. Here we found that the cultural and political context appears to also impact upon their visions of how Pride will develop in their countries.

The year 2020 will mark Pride parades' fiftieth anniversary, fifty years after the first parades were held in New York, Los Angeles and Chicago. And indeed Pride parades and LGBT politics in general have come a long way since their inauspicious beginnings. The parades now attract tens of thousands and even hundreds of thousands participants and have proliferated across the globe. But perhaps most remarkably, Pride parades in Europe, as in Latin America, have become a container of Western liberal values; a "litmus test" that the country hosting them shares neoliberalism's highly touted values of human rights, tolerance and freedom. In conclusion, we will discuss the geopolitical role, as well as the domestic political role, of Pride parades and LGBT politics – roles that were probably inconceivable for the Pride pioneers.

Notes

1 The title of John Kitsuse's (1980) article in *Social Problems*.
2 We have chosen to use the acronym LGBT throughout this book. LGBT is the most globally widespread portmanteau acronym for the lesbian, gay, bisexual, and transgender movement. Although the movement's world federation ILGA (which has more than 1200 member organizations) since 2007 has used the acronym LGBTI (for lesbian, gay, bisexual, and trans, and intersex), LGBT is still more commonly used in scholarly texts, policy making and public debates. Sometimes the use of variations of the LGBT acronym also mirrors differences in priorities between the groups of the movement, which at times make the decision to use a specific acronym a contested issue. In some countries, other acronyms are more common. In Sweden the initials are HBTQ (homosexual, bisexual, trans, queer) and in Italy the acronym is GLBT. Where appropriate we will refer to the movements in these countries with their preferred acronyms.

References

Adam, B.D. (1995). *The rise of a gay and lesbian movement*. Boston, MA: Twayne Publisher.

Adam, B.D., Duyvendak, J.W., and Krouwel, A. (1999). Gay and lesbian movements beyond borders? In Adam, B.D., Duyvendak, J.W., and Krouwel, A. (Eds) *The global emergence of gay and lesbian politics* (pp. 344–371). Philadelphia, PA: Temple University Press.

Alexander, J.C., and Mast, J.L. (2006). Introduction: Symbolic action in theory and practice: the cultural pragmatics of symbolic action. In Alexander, J.C., Giesen, B., and Mast, J.L. (Eds) *Social performance: Symbolic action, cultural pragmatics, and ritual* (pp. 1–28). Cambridge: Cambridge University Press.

Armstrong, E.A. (2002). *Forging gay identities: Organizing sexuality in San Francisco, 1950–1994*. Chicago, IL: University of Chicago Press.

Bernstein, M. (1997). Celebration and suppression: The strategic uses of identity by the lesbian and gay movement. *American Journal of Sociology*, 103(3), 531–565.

Bernstein, M. (2002). Identities and politics. *Social Science History*, 26(3), 531–581.

Bernstein, M. (2003). Nothing ventured nothing gained? Conceptualizing social movement "success" in the lesbian and gay movement. *Sociological Perspectives*, 46(3), 353–379.

Bernstein, M. (2005). Identity politics. *Annual Review of Sociology*, 31, 47–74.

Binnie, J., and Klesse, C. (2011). "Because it was a bit like going to an adventure park": The politics of hospitality in transnational lesbian, gay, bisexual, transgender and queer activist networks. *Tourist Studies*, 11(2), 157–174.

Blasius, M. (1994). *Gay and lesbian politics: Sexuality and the emergence of a new ethic*. Philadelphia, PA: Temple University Press.

Blasius, M. (2001). An ethos of lesbian and gay existence. In M. Blasius (Ed.) *Sexual identities, queer politics.* (pp. 143–177). Princeton, NJ: Princeton University Press.

Browne, K. (2007). A party with politics? (Re)making LGBTQ Pride spaces in Dublin and Brighton. *Social and Cultural Geography*, 8(1), 63–87.

Calvo, K., and Trujillo, G. (2011). Fighting for love rights: Claims and strategies of the LGBT movement in Spain. *Sexualities*, 14(5), 562–579.

Chabot, S., and Duyvendak, J.W. (2002). Globalization and transnational diffusion between social movements: Reconceptualizing the dissemination of the Gandhian repertoire and the "coming out" routine. *Theory and Society*, 31(6), 697–740.

Chasin, A. (2000). *Selling out: The gay and lesbian movement goes to market*. New York: Palgrave.

Cooper, D. (2006). Active citizenship and the governmentality of local lesbian and gay politics. *Political Geography*, 25(8), 921–943.

d'Emilio, J. (1998 [1983]). *Sexual politics, sexual communities. The making of a homosexual minority in the United States, 1940–1970*. 2nd edition. Chicago and London: The University of Chicago Press.

Duggan, M. (2010). Politics of Pride: Representing relegated sexual identities in Northern Ireland. *The Northern Ireland Legal Quarterly*, 61, 163–179.

Egan, P.J., and Sherrill, K. (2005). Marriage and the shifting priorities of a new generation of lesbians and gays. *PS: Political Science & Politics*, 38(2), 229–232.

Encarnación, O.G. (2016). *Out in the periphery: Latin America's gay rights revolution*. Oxford: Oxford University Press.

Engel, S.M. (2001). *The unfinished revolution: Social movement theory and the gay and lesbian movement.* Cambridge: Cambridge University Press.
Enguix, B. (2009). Identities, sexualities and commemorations: Pride parades, public space and sexual dissidence. *Anthropological Notebooks,* 15(2), 15–33.
Epstein, S. (1999). Gay and lesbian movements in the United States: Dilemmas of identity, diversity, and political strategy. In Adam, B.D., Duyvendak, J.W., and Krouwel, A. (Eds) *The global emergence of gay and lesbian politics* (pp. 30–90). Philadelphia, PA: Temple University Press.
Flyvbjerg, B. (2006). Five misunderstandings about case-study research. *Qualitative Inquiry,* 12(2), 219–245.
Fojtová, S. (2011). Czech lesbian activism: Gay and lesbian parental rights as a challenge to patriarchal marriage. *Journal of Lesbian Studies,* 15(3), 356–383.
Ghaziani, A. (2008). *The dividends of dissent. How conflict and culture work in lesbian and gay marches on Washington.* Chicago, IL: University of Chicago Press.
Ghaziani, A., and Baldassarri, D. (2011). Cultural anchors and the organization of differences: a multi-method analysis of LGBT marches on Washington. *American Sociological Review,* 76(2), 179–206.
Hallgren, H. (2008). *När lesbiska blev kvinnor: Lesbiskfeministiska kvinnors diskursproduktion rörande kön, sexualitet, kropp och identitet under 1970- och 1980-talen i Sverige.* Göteborg: Kabusa böcker.
Herdt, G.H. (1992). "Coming Out" as a rite of passage: A Chicago study. In Herdt, G.H. (Ed.) *Gay culture in America: Essays from the field* (pp. 29–69). Boston, MA: Beacon Press.
Holzhacker, R. (2007). *The Europeanization and transnationalization of civil society—Organizations striving for equality: Goals and strategies of gay and lesbian groups in Italy and the Netherlands.* Florence: EUI RSCAS Working Papers 2007/36.
Humphreys, L. (1972). *Out of the closets.* Engelwood Cliffs, NJ: Prentice-Hall.
Johnston, L. (2007). *Queering tourism: Paradoxical performances of gay pride parades.* New York: Routledge.
Johnston, L., and Waitt, G. (2015) The spatial politics of gay Pride parades and festivals: Emotional activism. In Paternotte, D., and Tremblay, M. (Eds) *The Ashgate research companion to lesbian and gay activism* (pp. 105–120). Farnham: Ashgate.
Kitsuse, J.I. (1980). Coming out all over: Deviants and the politics of social problems. *Social Problems,* 28(1), 1–13.
McFarland, K. (2012). *Cultural contestation and community building at LGBT Pride parades* (Unpublished doctoral dissertation): Chapel Hill, South Carolina.
McFarland Bruce, K. (2016). *Pride Parades: How a parade changed the world.* New York: NYU Press.
Melucci, A. (1989). *Nomads of the present: Social movements and individual needs in contemporary society.* New York: Vintage.
Murray, S.O. (1996). *American gay.* Chicago, IL: University of Chicago Press.
Newton, E. (1979). *Mother camp, female impersonators in America.* Chicago, IL: University of Chicago Press.
Phelan, S. (1993). (Be)coming Out: Lesbian identity and politics. *Signs,* 18(4), 765–790.
Rayside, D. (2001). The structuring of sexual minority activist opportunities in the political mainstream: Britain, Canada, and the United States. In Blasius, M.

(Ed.) *Sexual identities, queer politics* (pp. 23–55). Princeton, NJ: Princeton University Press.
Richardson, D. (2005). Desiring sameness: The rise of a neoliberal politics of normalization. *Antipode*, 37(3), 515–553.
Rimmerman, C.A. (2014). *The lesbian and gay movements: Assimilation or liberation?* Boulder, CO: Westview Press.
Ross, B.L., and Landström, C. (1999). Normalization versus diversity: Lesbian identity and organizing in Sweden and Canada. In Briskin, L., and Eliasson, M. (Eds) *Women's organizing and public policy in Canada and Sweden* (pp. 310–346). Montreal and Kingston, London: McGill-Queen's University Press.
Ross, C. (2008). Visions of visibility: LGBT communities in Turin. *Modern Italy*, 13(3), 241–260.
Rupp, L.J., and Taylor, V.A. (2003). *Drag queens at the 801 Cabaret*. Chicago, IL: University of Chicago Press.
Schuyf, J., and Krouwel, A. (1999). The Dutch lesbian and gay movement: The politics of accommodation. In Adam, B.D., Duyvendak, J.M., and Krouwel, A. (Eds) *The global emergence of gay and lesbian politics* (pp. 158–183). Philadelphia, PA: Temple University Press.
Shepard, B. (2005). Play, creativity, and the new community organizing. *Journal of Progressive Human Services*, 16(2), 47–69.
Smith, M. (2008). *Political institutions and lesbian and gay rights in the United States and Canada*. New York: Routledge.
Snow, D.A., and Trom, D. (2002). The case study and the study of social movements. In Klandermans, B., and Staggenborg, S. (Eds) *Methods of social movement research* (pp. 146–172). Minneapolis, MN: University of Minnesota Press.
Swiebel, J. (2009). Lesbian, gay, bisexual and transgender human rights: the search for an international strategy. *Contemporary Politics*, 15(1), 19–35.
Tatchell, P. (2017). LGBT+ Pride parade – Time for a rethink? Back to first principles. www.petertatchellfoundation.org (accessed August 31, 2017).
Taylor, V., and Rupp, L.J. (1993). Women's culture and lesbian feminist activism: A reconsideration of cultural feminism. *Signs: Journal of Women in Culture and Society*, 19(1), 32–61.
Tremblay, M., Paternotte, D., and Johnson, C. (Eds) (2011). *The lesbian and gay movement and the state: Comparative insights into a transformed relationship*. Farnham: Ashgate Publishing, Ltd.
Waites, M. (2003). Equality at last? Homosexuality, heterosexuality and the age of consent in the United Kingdom. *Sociology*, 37(4), 637–655.
Weiss, M.D. (2008). Gay shame and BDSM pride: Neoliberalism, privacy, and sexual politics. *Radical History Review* 100, 87–101.

2 The Histories of Pride

The Stonewall myth and gay liberation

Just before midnight on June 27, 1969, New York police raided the Stonewall Inn, a gay bar on Christopher Street in Greenwich Village. Instead of dispersing to avoid arrest, patrons and those who quickly gathered outside fought back, throwing paving stones, cans, bottles and uprooted parking meters at the police. Reinforced by gays and lesbians living in the area, the raid turned into a full-blown riot, which continued the following two nights (Duberman 1993; Humphreys 1972; d'Emilio 1998; Murray 1996; McFarland 2012). Interpreted by activists as a major turning point in the history of the lesbian and gay movement, the "Stonewall myth" was born. The Stonewall riot in New York City in 1969 was regarded as *the* watershed event in the history of gay life in the United States leading John d'Emilio (1992) to divide gay history into two epochs – "before Stonewall" and "after Stonewall" (also Carter 2004; Tiemeyer 2013; Rimmerman 2015). While similar events had occurred elsewhere in the US during the 1960s it was the Stonewall riots which galvanized the imagination of gay liberation activists.[1] Jill Johnston (1994, p. ix), a *Village Voice* journalist and prominent lesbian activist, claimed that Stonewall

> was the event that catalyzed the modern gay and lesbian political movement. It changed the ways thousands, ultimately millions, of men and women thought of themselves ... It represented the birth of an identity unprecedented in society.

Certainly equally, if not more, important gay resistance events had occurred prior to Stonewall from the mid-1960s onwards. For just one example: in Los Angeles the raid of the Black Cat bar and other Silver Lake bars led to the formation in 1967 of the organization called Personal Rights in Defense and Education (PRIDE). "PRIDE organized a protest march, and, when the march was not covered in the news media, began publication of a weekly newspaper, *The Advocate*" (Murray 1996, p. 62). Nonetheless, it was the Stonewall riots that galvanized a nationwide lesbian and gay movement that celebrated the event in annual ritual parades. Armstrong and Crage (2006, p. 724) point out that the Stonewall riots are remembered "because they were the first to meet two conditions: activists considered the event commemorable and had the mnemonic capacity to create a commemorative vehicle." The "Stonewall myth" is, according to Armstrong and Crage, an achievement of gay liberation and it is remembered, "because it is marked by an international commemorative ritual – an annual gay pride parade" (p. 725). Murray (1996, pp. 63–64) suggests that New York's position as the media capital of the US more than anything else explains why an occurrence there, *sic* the Stonewall riots, became a generalized symbol for lesbian and gay defiance. The myth of Stonewall, according to Murray, was elevated to being a universal drama through a media hype.

But was the Stonewall riot such a big deal? d'Emilio (1998, p. 260) reinterprets Stonewall not as an "event of great historic significance but as a kind of queer shorthand for a larger historic phenomenon: 'the sixties'." In the late 1960s and early 1970s the time was ripe for a new style of lesbian and gay activism in the wake of the 1960s' New Left, Anti-Vietnam War, and not least, the Women's and Civil Rights movements (d'Emilio 1998, pp. 223ff). Departing from the more moderate, accomodationist and discrete tactics of the homophile phase, lesbian and gay movements were now ready to "take to the streets" entering into a more militant confrontational phase (Bernstein 2002, pp. 541ff; Rimmerman 2015, pp. 19ff) – gays and lesbians in the US would take their first steps out from the "closet." New York gay liberation activists took the initiative to a national Stonewall commemorative event by sending a call at the Eastern Regional Conference of Homophile Organizations (ERCHO) in Philadelphia on November 2, 1969 to homophile organizations across the country to host a demonstration on the last Saturday in June.

> We propose that a demonstration be held annually on the last Saturday in June in New York City to commemorate the 1969 spontaneous demonstrations on Christopher Street and this demonstration to be called Christopher Street Liberation Day. No dress or age regulations shall be made for this demonstration.
> We also propose that we contact Homophile organizations throughout the country and suggest that they hold parallel demonstrations on that day. We propose a nationwide show of support.
> (Carter 2004, pp. 230, 247)

Activists intended this first demonstration to be a protest against discrimination, police raids on gay bars, and anti-gay violence (Ghaziani 2008, p. 27). However, even at this initial stage conflicts emerged as to the form the event should take. On the one side, the more radical activists argued that:

> a march would display the community's political power and confront repressive politicians and public officials. Others championed cultural concerns of celebrating [the] gay community.
>
> (ibid.)

The solution was to do both. A weeklong series of cultural events was organized in conjunction with the march. From the very beginning these events combined politics with celebration and party. The New York march as well as the Los Angeles event combined elements of traditional protest politics with celebratory festive elements. But the events were different. McFarland (2012, pp. 52–56) describes the differences between the first Christopher Street Liberation parade in New York and the Christopher Street Freedom march in Los Angeles. The New York activists were more intent on emphasizing the political messages of the march. While there were festive elements of celebration, brightly colored pennants and Day-Glo signs everywhere proclaiming "Gay Pride," "Lesbians are Lovable," "Gay is Good," there were no floats, amplified music or go-go boys. "Instead marchers chanted slogans like '2, 4, 6, 8, Gay is just as good as straight!' and held signs to 'smash imperialism'" (p. 52). She reports that the New York "organizers were concerned to keep the march from becoming a carnivalesque parade, thinking that would take away from the seriousness of the event" (ibid.). Disco music and flamboyant costumes, it was felt, would detract from the contentious message of the march. Organizers in Los Angeles did not share these concerns. McFarland cites the coverage of the event by the *Advocate,* the largest nation-wide homosexual periodical at that time.

> Over 1000 homosexuals and their friends staged, not just a protest march, but a full-blown parade down world-famous Hollywood Boulevard. [...] Flags and banners floated in the chill sunlight of late afternoon; a bright red sound truck blared martial music; drummers strutted; a horse pranced; clowns cavorted; "vice cops" chased screaming "fairies" with paper wings; the Metropolitan Community Church choir sang "Onward Christian Soldiers"; a bronzed and muscular male model flaunted a 7 1/2 foot live python. ... Sensational Hollywood had never seen anything like it.
>
> (*The Advocate*, July 22–August 4, 1970, cited in McFarland 2012, p. 54)

According to McFarland, the *Advocate* "reported that there were five floats, one with a confrontational display of a gay man 'nailed' to a cross and another with an equally provocative large jar of Vaseline" (p. 54).

The Los Angeles event, with its official title "Christopher Street West: A Freedom Revival in Lavender" (p. 50), confronted head-on the dominant cultural mores and hetero-normative norms, but both events and the Pride

Week held at the same time in Chicago, were dramatic challenges to the homophile movement's accomodationist strategy of respectability and behind the scenes lobbying. According to McFarland what the events had in common was:

> the open display of gays and lesbians without regard to making the image palatable to mainstream society. In New York, that took the form of a protest march with festive elements to celebrate gay identity; in Los Angeles participants put on a parade to make this identity visible.
>
> (p. 58)

Armstrong (2002) highlights the historical importance of these first Pride marches in that they ushered in the lesbian and gay identity movement. These events in 1970 were unique in that they were the first time in history that large numbers of gays and lesbians expressed their sexuality openly in public, without "dialing down the gay" (Encarnación 2016, p. 18) – a collective "coming out." And according to Armstrong and Crage (2006), the 1970 Christopher Street Liberation Day demonstration in New York, Christopher Street West demonstration in Los Angeles, and Gay Pride week in Chicago were regarded as huge successes, which inspired and prompted activists in other cities to follow their lead. In 1971 larger events were arranged in the original three cities, and Dallas, Boston, Milwaukee and San Jose hosted their first celebrations. In 1972 even the reluctant gay liberation activists in San Francisco, "ambivalent about ceding vanguard status to New York" (p. 742), relented and staged their first commemorative parade. That year Ann Arbor, Atlanta, Buffalo, Detroit, Washington, D.C., Miami and Philadelphia also joined the ranks of cities commemorating Stonewall.

Pride goes nationwide across the US

Throughout the 1970s parades both grew in size and spread geographically across the United States, making Gay Pride celebrations a truly national event. Forty years after the first Pride events in 1970, McFarland (2012, p. 69) reports that Pride parades and marches are held in more than 100 cities across the country; not restricted to major urban centers with large and visible lesbian and gay communities, but spread across the spectrum of city size with the largest growth in cities with populations less than 500,000. She concludes that while the parades in the original founding cities and other major metropolitan centers garner the most media attention, Pride parades are now more often held in smaller cities such as Birmingham, Alabama and Las Cruces, New Mexico (p. 121).

Early in the development and geographical diffusion of Gay Pride celebrations it became evident that activists had discovered a form of collective action that blended unity and diversity.

> The language of *celebration* and *pride* emerged at this historical moment, with leaders committed to unifying the community, feeling a parade would be broadly palatable. A non-political Gay Pride celebration, activists argued, would be able to unite all spectrums of the community.
>
> (Ghaziani 2008, p. 27; emphasis in original)

The parade as a commemorative vehicle proved to be the solution for the US Lesbian and Gay Movement's diversification, division and fragmentation. Under the umbrella of the parade and its expression of an (ephemeral) all-embracing gay identity, and during this one day each year, lesbians could march with gay men, gays of color could participate under their banners, radical liberationist groups could march with more moderate activist organizations, etc. (Ghaziani 2008, p. 149). Armstrong (2002, p. 110; emphasis in original) argues, "by participating in the same parade, the contingents appeared unified. ... *Everyone* brought one or more additional identities into the community with them." Subgroup challenges to the lesbian and gay movement could be (most often) temporarily diffused. Nonetheless, fissures in this symbolic show of unity bubbled under the surface as early as 1973 in the New York Christopher Street Liberation march when a transgender activist was denied the right to speak (Shepard 2010 p. 5). Only gradually over the next decades was the original lesbian and gay movement expanded to formally include first in 1993 bisexuals in conjunction with that year's "March on Washington for Lesbian, Gay, and Bi Equal Rights and Liberation," and later in the 1990s transsexuals, transgender and non-gender conforming persons began to be accepted in the movement (Ghaziani 2008). With the subsequent inclusion of queer and intersex as separate categories, the moniker now in the 2010s is frequently an inclusive LGBTQI catalog of identities.

During the 1980s and 1990s, at least in the more lesbian and gay friendly cities, political challenges took a step back and festive celebration took center stage. Gradually the names "gay liberation" and "gay freedom" were dropped in favor of the more politically ambiguous "gay pride," or just "pride." Marches in San Francisco and New York, for example, by the mid-1990s gathered hundreds of thousands of participants. In the large parades floats, dancers, drag queens and amplified music appeared. As the Gay Pride celebrations grew in size they became more attractive to corporate sponsoring. But these developments did not go without challenges. According to Benjamin Shepard (2010, p. 5), "demonstrations of ideological fissures had become a common fixture of the theater of the parade." In New York queer activists were arrested in 1998 while attempting to stop the participation of the mayor. In 1999,

> a float dubbed "Rudy's Sex Police" cruised down the parade route in a 1970s hotrod come blue squad car adorned with a papier-mâché

replica of the major's face and a sign declaring, "Because Rudy Hates You". SexPanic members led the crowd in chants of "More Boody, Less Rudy! Keep New York Sexy!" until police ordered their hotrod off the parade route.

(ibid.)

Innovative challenges to the Pride parades were played out within the parades, but also alternative events, which were sometimes complementary events, were launched in the 1990s. Lesbian Avengers in Washington, D.C. organized the first Dyke March in conjunction with the 1993 "March on Washington for Lesbian, Gay and Bi Equal Rights and Liberation." While separatist lesbian marches had been held in San Francisco during the 1970s they had not become a tradition. After the success of the Dyke March in Washington D.C. local chapters of Lesbian Avengers launched Dyke Marches in June 1993 in San Francisco and New York, a week before the Pride parade. The tradition lives on today and has spread across the US. The Dyke Marches are staged to increase the visibility of lesbians and a critique of what lesbians perceive as the dominance of white gay men in Pride celebrations. Less robust than the tradition of Dyke Marches were the alternative events staged by Gay Shame in direct critique of what these activists perceived as the commercialization and mainstreaming of Gay Pride events. In Brooklyn 1998 queer activists boycotted the Gay Pride parade, which they saw as too commercial, by organizing their own Gay Shame festival. Gay Shame manifestations were later adopted in San Francisco.

Pride is exported

As we will see below, in some countries, most notably the UK, Pride-like events appeared already in the early 1970s. A few were partly in direct response to the Stonewall events but they were all broadly connected with the cultural changes linked to the 1968 protests and the "new social movements." The rhetoric of liberation sent powerful echoes across Western Europe in the 1970s. Initially, there seem to have been little or no active attempts to disseminate the concept of the Pride parade outside the United States. However, in a second phase of the spread of Pride events, an element of direct promotion was also introduced in the 1980s. A major vehicle for exporting the format of Pride celebrations across the globe is a non-profit organization – the US-dominated InterPride. In the fall of 1982 representatives from about half a dozen US Pride organizations gathered together in Boston to network and there founded the National Association of Lesbian and Gay Pride Coordinators (NAL/GPC), and in 1985 changed its name to the International Association of Lesbian and Gay Pride Coordinators (IAL/GPC). An annual conference has been held in different cities each year and attendance has steadily grown. At the 1999 conference in Glasgow,

Scotland the organization again changed its name to InterPride to consolidate and better reflect its international structure. InterPride licenses the title WorldPride, the first of which was held in Rome in July 2000 and the second in Jerusalem in 2006. In 2012, WorldPride was held in London, then it occurred in Toronto, Canada in 2014 and Madrid, Spain hosted a WorldPride in 2017.[2] In 2019, WorldPride will be held in New York, celebrating the fiftieth anniversary of the Stonewall uprising in 1969.[3]

For the diffusion and standardization of Pride parades in Europe, EuroPride and the association European Pride Organisers Association (EPOA), have furthermore been crucial. The initiative for the first EuroPride in London 1992 came from local Pride organizers in London and Berlin, and it was supported by both ILGA-Europe and IAL/GPC. In 1993, EPOA was founded as a separate association with the purpose of bringing together European Pride organizers and licensing an annual EuroPride event.[4] Since 1992, EuroPride has been held almost every year, and when WorldPride has been organized in Europe they have been regarded by EPOA as EuroPride events.

Despite this later development in Europe, it is important to stress that the tradition of staging annual Pride parades originated in the US; it was from the US that the background script – "coming out" – was exported, as well as the format of an annual Pride parade and the means for symbolic projections to be made, such as the rainbow flag. To be sure, the rainbow flag, designed by San Francisco artist Gilbert Baker in 1978, has become the symbol *par excellence* worldwide representing the unity in diversity communicated in Pride parades. The ritual-like performances of the LGBT movements studied in this book were indeed influenced by impulses emanating from the US, *but* both the background scripts, as well as the foreground scripts, were translated by activists embedded in their specific national and local contexts. Local Pride organizers constructed the *mise-en-scène*, the choreography of the actors so they could walk and talk the texts on the public stage. Just as comparative studies of US Pride events found significant differences in their ritual-like performances (see McFarland 2012; McFarland Bruce 2016), it is the differences (and similarities) that will be in focus in our study of Pride parades in seven European countries and Mexico. In the following pages we will briefly sketch the history of Pride celebrations in the countries and cities covered in our study, approximately in the order of when the first Pride-like march took place.

Pride parades in the United Kingdom

Inauspicious beginnings

The first UK Pride parades were organized during a period of significant tactical and strategic shifts in the British LGBT movement. The activities during the 1950s and 1960s were dominated by prudent and predominantly backstage lobbying activities in London by the Homosexual Law Reform Society (HLRS) and somewhat more open but nevertheless rather cautious promotional work in the North of England by the North Western Homosexual Law Reform Committee (NWHLRC) (Lent 2001). This work led up to the Labour Government's passing of a new Sexual Offences Act in 1967, which legalized gay sex by consenting adults over 21 years of age. The legalization of homosexual sex did not extend to Scotland and Northern Ireland, and the Act still prohibited, for example, public displays of homosexual affection. Nevertheless, the victory led to reduced activity and the eventual decline of these organizations.

Around this time, however, British society, along with other Western democracies, went through rapid cultural changes, and British gay activists started to look across the Atlantic to the increasingly open and transgressive tactics starting to be used by their US peers. Two key figures, Aubrey Walter and Bob Mellors, travelled in the US during the summer of 1970 and returned to found the Gay Liberation Front (GLF) on October 13th the same year, inspired by the newly established American organization with the same name. The following month, in November, it organized its first demonstration, located in Highbury Fields, in support of a man facing charges for indecency (Adam 1995).

On August 28th, 1971, the GLF organized a march through London, and on July 1st, 1972 in London, the first British Gay Pride march to be organized close to the correct date (June 28th) in commemoration of the Stonewall events (Weeks 1990 [1977]). GLF was the main initiator, but several other emerging LGBT groups were part of the organizing committee. Peter Tatchell, one of the around 40 co-organizers of the event, says that the participants,

> didn't know what to expect. In those days most LGBT people were very closeted. They would never ever dare show their faces in public and identify with those persons. Many, many aspects of gay male life were still criminalized despite the partial de-criminalization in 1967. [...] We were very gratified when between 700 and 1,000 people turned up. It began in Trafalgar Square and marched to Hyde Park where we held an impromptu gay day. Sort of a gay picnic in the park. People bought their own food drink and dope, and we played queer versions of traditional party games like oranges and lemons and spin the bottle. The march itself was very heavily policed. There was virtually one police officer for every single marcher. We were hemmed in quite tightly. Some police were openly abusive, calling us "queers, poofs, faggots, dykes." They treated us like criminals, which of course in many respects we still were. [...]
>
> The response from the public was very interesting. [...] About a third of the public were overtly hostile. They shouted abuse, threw coins, cans and bottles at us. Another third were more curious and

bewildered. They were sort of shocked to see gay people dare showing their faces and they just wondered who we were and why we were doing it. But you couldn't really sense what their opinion was. They were gawping in disbelief that gay people would dare show their faces but they weren't hostile nor were they supportive. The other third did applaud and cheer us and smile and gave us thumbs up. That was quite surprising. [...] When we got to the park the police ringed around one section of where we were, and stood in very aggressive poses with their arms folded and glaring at us clearly very hostile. But they didn't ... You know, we thought they may try and arrest us when people kissed and cuddled but they didn't.

The march was part of a Gay Pride Week, and only one of numerous protest actions organized by the GLF. However, by this time GLF was already starting to dissolve. Weeks (1990 [1977]) outlines various internal tensions between factions in the diverse group, perhaps most pronounced around the relations between women and men, between feminists and those emphasizing "gay issues," as well as around socialism and the relation to the labor movement (also Plummer 1999). As the revolutionary imagination of 1968 lost its immediate force, GLF lost further momentum and by the end of 1973 it had practically disappeared. By then the organization of the London Pride week had been taken over by the less militant organization Campaign for Homosexual Equality (CHE) (Hughes 2006).

HIV and the Thatcher Government bring new impetus to Pride

Annual Pride parades continued, while the surrounding movement moved into a somewhat less energetic phase in the mid- to late 1970s. The beginning of the 1980s introduced two factors that changed the mobilizing context of the LGBT movement and, by extension, the Pride parades. First, the HIV epidemic emerged, which had direct disastrous effects and brought about increased hostility among the UK population toward gays. However, it had the side effect of contributing to a re-politicization of the movement and increased mobilization of straight allies (Engel 2001). Second, the election of the conservative government led by Prime Minister Margaret Thatcher represented both a power shift in labor market relations away from the trade unions, and a political turn toward the promotion of conservative values. Meanwhile, in the early 1980s the Labour Party took a more explicitly supportive stance on gay rights issues, notably manifested by Labour controlled local governments, including London and Manchester.

During the extensive pit closures, vigorously resisted by the miners' unions, a number of lesbian and gay activists decided to organize in solidarity with the unions, which they regarded as fellow victims of the Thatcher Government's political agenda. In 1984 they founded the organization

Lesbians and Gays Support the Miners (LGSM), which raised funds from the LGBT community in support of the miners' strikes. (The story of this campaign was later transformed into the motion picture *Pride*, released in 2014.) Mike Jackson, who was part of the LGSM core group, described for us how the fundraising basically started at the 1984 Pride parade in London.

> The response we got from the lesbians and gays was astonishing, it was really, really supportive. Not only the money that the people put in the buckets but what people were saying was, because for a lot of people it wasn't just about the miners, it was about Thatcher, people hated Thatcher, and Thatcher had chosen fights with the miners. [...] The miners were standing up against Thatcher, and that's what it was about, we wanted to get rid of Thatcher.

Apart from acting as brokers between different social movements, the activities of the LGSM also raised issues of class *within* the LGBT community that, according to Mike Jackson, had hardly been present before. The 1985 Gay Pride became perhaps the prime symbol of the alliance with a large number of miners attending the march. Mike Jackson remembers:

> Then in 1985 the miners came and led the Gay Pride march in London, which was astonishing really. You know nobody, nobody had anticipated that would happen and it was incredible. [...] LGSM were a contingent on the march so we took our banners and we took our supporters and we took the miners and we were the largest single group on the march that year, it was huge, well over 1,000 people.

While the Thatcher Government represented a broad range of conservative values, it did not initially focus on implementing policies targeting on sexual minorities. However, in 1987–1988 the new anti-gay law "Section 28" was prepared, and eventually passed, which prohibited the promotion of homosexuality by schools and local authorities. According to Weeks (1990 [1977]), the law was an attempt by the national government to circumscribe the independence of local authorities in Labour dominated areas, such as London and Manchester, which in various policies supported lesbian and gay rights. Whereas the concrete impact of the law may have been limited, it sent a strong symbolic message against acceptance for sexual minorities. The conflicts around Section 28 also point to the predominance of two parties in British politics – Labour and Conservatives – which shapes the conditions for alliances between movements and political parties. Although the Labour Party temporarily became somewhat ambivalent on lesbian and gay issues toward the late 1980s, for fear of putting off traditional working-class voters, it has remained a crucial political ally for the LGBT movement. The Conservative Party long remained largely anti-LGBT, although it has gone through a shift toward acceptance of gay and lesbian families, most pronounced under former Prime Minister David Cameron (Hayton 2010).

Pride goes commercial

Section 28 led to dramatically increased mobilization of the LGBT community and new organizations were founded, including in 1989 the campaigning and lobby organization Stonewall and the direct action group OutRage!. Peter Tatchell describes how the London Pride march grew dramatically from the late 1980s until 1997, peaking at around 100,000 participants. This highpoint in popular mobilization paradoxically led to a takeover of the event by commercial interests, since it became too expensive for the organizers to pay for the bill for stewarding, policing, cleanup and fencing.

> Well, 1997 was the high point, but the organizers, because of its huge size, did lose I think about £60,000, and this was used by gay business people to say that the community was unfit to run LGBT Pride and that they should take it over. And that is what they did. [...] So they began charging to go to the festival after the parade, which never happened before. The combination of commercialization and charging resulted in the numbers participating plummeting maybe down to 20,000 in the march and maybe 50,000 for the festival.

A sign of the increasing commercialization of London Pride was the decision by the local gay business consortia organizing the event to drop the term "Pride"; for three years, between 1999 and 2002, the event was called "London Mardi Gras" (a generic term for festival and carnival; Hughes 2006, p. 243). However, in 2003, London Pride was again taken back by civil society organizers and gradually regained legitimacy within the community. Apparently, however, the economy has remained a challenge for the organizers; the 2012 WorldPride (the one included in our statistical analyses in Chapters 4, 5 and 8) became a great disappointment for many after the organizers had to cancel several side events due to failure to raise sufficient funds to pay a number of key subcontractors for the event.[5] The authorities also banned all vehicles and floats since the organizers could not ensure the necessary safety precautions. After this debacle a new organizer took over Pride London: London LGBT+ Community Pride.

Regardless of the formal level of commercialism of its organizers, since the 1970s and early 1980s the London Pride parade has been criticized over the years for its increased level of commercialization. From a feminist position, some critics have also pointed to the dominance of a sexually hedonistic theme in the march – primarily expressed by gay men – at the expense of both the parade's critical edge as well as misrepresenting the political interests of its female participants (Laughland 2012).

UK Pride parades proliferate

Smaller Pride events also occurred in other locations in the UK from 1972 onwards. A week after the London Gay Pride Week in 1972, the local GLF in Birmingham organized a Pride Weekend, which included a small march of 20 people through the city (Knowles 2009). Pride weekends, including Pride parades, were organized annually for a few years, after which they disappeared. Pride festivals were again organized from 1983 onwards, but not including a parade until the year 2000. In Brighton, the first Pride parade was organized in 1973. In 1992, the parade was reintroduced as the Brighton Pride March and Brighton is today considered one of the main UK Pride events. Similar to the dissatisfaction expressed by some about the gay dominance in London, Brighton Pride has been ridden by internal struggles between women and, allegedly, a small number of powerful gay men blocking changes in the way the festival was organized (Browne and Bakshi 2013).

Manchester Pride is also considered to be one of the main Pride events in the UK. It started as a fundraising event for local AIDS organizations in 1985 (Williams 2016), which developed into Manchester Mardi Gras, run by the Village Charity since 1991. In its early years it was explicitly not a Pride event and the festival established close ties to the business community (Hughes 2006). The festival developed in an ambiguous context with a new generation of supportive Labour politicians in the 1980s, while police repression of gay people remained considerable far into the 1990s. In 2003 Manchester hosted the EuroPride event, and only after that changed its name into Manchester Pride.

In some regions of the UK it took a long time before any Pride parades were organized. For example, the Northern Ireland regional capital Belfast did not have its first Pride parade until 1991. Not unlike the Polish Pride parades, Belfast Pride is characterized by Nagle (2013) as expanding its scope beyond LGBT issues. "Pride has developed as a celebration of all forms of diversity to contest ethno-national polarization" (p. 86). In the still divided city, Pride bridges the nationalist/unionist split and, according to Nagle, may contribute to making city spaces more inclusive and even to reducing ethnic conflict. As noted by Drissel (2016), the Belfast Pride parade manifests as a clear counterpoint to the many sectarian parades in the region.

Since the early 2000s, Pride parades have cropped up in several UK cities, and the organization InterPride lists 60 different UK Pride events in its 2016/17 Pride Radar, including Black Pride in London, and the Sparkle Weekend in Manchester for transgender people (InterPride 2016).

History of Pride in Sweden

In Sweden, same-sex activities were decriminalized in 1944. However, as in other Western countries, post-war Sweden witnessed a surge in homophobic public sentiments, through hostile media anti-gay campaigns, and an increase in prosecutions for homosexual acts with persons younger than 18 years (Rydström 2007b). It was during this period that the first association for homosexuals in Sweden was created, in 1950, as the Swedish section of the Danish *Forbundet af 1948* (The Federation of 1948). In 1952, this association was renamed *Riksförbundet för sexuellt likaberättigande*, RFSL (The Swedish Federation for Sexual Equality; today it is called The Swedish Federation for Lesbian, Gay, Bisexual, Transgender and Queer Rights), which has since then been the dominant organization for LGBT persons in Sweden. Until the early 1970s, RFSL was the only association that organized and represented gays and lesbians in Sweden, even though its members were predominantly male (Söderström 1999; Petersson 2000).

Activism within RFSL during the 1950s and 1960s had the same characteristics as the post-war homophile movement of most other Western countries. During the 1950s, the movement was engaged in a few public debates, but mostly it lobbied politicians and authorities behind the scenes. For example, RFSL demanded same-sex marriage (or, "homophile marriage") already in 1953 (Petersson 2000, p. 29). During the 1960s, political advocacy became less prioritized within the movement, and arranging social activities within the community became a more central activity.

Swedish gay and lesbian activists begin to take to the streets

Between 1969 and 1971, some contingents within RFSL were radicalized politically. The main inspiration was drawn from American "Gay Liberation" activism, but also from the general ideas of sexual liberation characterizing public debates and activism at the time. Important for this development in Sweden was the start of the gay magazine *Viking* in 1969, which in 1971 was renamed *Revolt mot sexuella fördomar* (Revolt against sexual prejudices). In the magazine, pornographic pictures and short stories were combined with political debates and reports from protests and activism in other countries. In 1970 an association independent from the RFSL was formed in the mid-size city of Örebro, calling itself the Gay Power Club. Together with the more radical activists within RFSL, these actors were central for pushing RFSL to a more radical analysis and the use of protest as a political means (Söderström 1999; Petersson 2000; Rydström 2007a; interviews with Stig-Åke and Jan-Eric).

The first demonstration staged by the gay and lesbian movement in Sweden was organized by the Gay Power Club in Örebro on May 15th, 1971. Even though the founder of this association was highly inspired by American "Gay Liberation" activism, this first demonstration (which attracted around 15 participants) was not staged as a Stonewall commemorative event. A second demonstration (attracting 30 participants) was staged a week later in Uppsala during a national conference of RFSL. The first Stonewall commemorative demonstration was staged yet a few weeks later, organized by Gay Power Club but held in central Stockholm as "Christopher Street Liberation Day" on June 27th, 1971 (Wennerhag 2017).

In the reports from this demonstration in the subsequent issue of *Revolt*, it is claimed that "16 brave persons marched in Stockholm's first homosexual demonstration on Christopher Street Liberation day on the last Sunday of June." The author complained about the low turnout, which is ascribed to both inactivity on the part of the local RFSL groups and the fact that the event coincided with Midsummer, one of the major Swedish holidays (Wennerhag 2017). When interviewing Stig-Åke Petersson, one of the activists advocating a more radical approach within RFSL (and president of the federation in 1972–1973 and 1984–1988), he recalls the feelings of failure after the first Stonewall commemoration in Sweden. "There were so few people in the parade, only sixteen, so our enthusiasm dampened a little."

No new efforts to organize a gay liberation event were made in Sweden until September 3rd, 1977, when the first *Homosexuella frigörelsedagen* (Homosexual Liberation Day) took place in Stockholm. Since then, there has been an unbroken series of annual homosexual liberation demonstrations in Stockholm (the event after EuroPride 1998 was called Stockholm Pride).

In 1977 the Swedish gay and lesbian movement had grown and become more diversified. Alongside RFSL, new groups had been formed. Lesbian groups that were part of the left-wing oriented feminist movement were created in the mid-1970s in the major cities, under the name *Lesbisk Front* (Lesbian Front), critical to what was perceived as male dominance in RFSL. Radical left groups for gay men were also created during this time, for example *Homosexuella Socialister* (Homosexual Socialists). The main organizers of the first Homosexual Liberation Day in 1977 were RFSL Stockholm, *Lesbisk Front*, and *Homosexuella Socialister*. Especially the two latter groups were important for the movement's use of protest as a means to bring attention to their political agenda. Despite the previous years of radicalization, the movement had not staged any joint protests after the first attempts in 1971. The more left-wing oriented gay and lesbian groups had more experience staging protests, and brought their skills when organizing the Homosexual Liberation Day (Rydström 2007a; Hallgren 2008; interview with Stig-Åke).

Stig-Åke reflects over why the demonstration was called the Homosexual Liberation Day, and why the word "Pride" wasn't used:

> In 1977, "Pride" didn't exist as a concept [in Sweden]. [...] At that time, we talked about "Gay Liberation." Maybe we sometimes talked about "Gay Pride" in very specific contexts, but overall it was "Gay Liberation." That's the reason why we choose to translate the "Gay Liberation" concept [...]. When we began talking about the Homosexual Liberation Day, it was part of a strategy to make people use the word homosexual in a positive way.

The first Homosexual Liberation Day in Stockholm attracted 300–400 participants. From the very beginning, the demonstrations focused the situation for gays and lesbians in other countries, for instance in Finland, Greece, Austria, Chile and the Soviet Union. In 1979, the event was renamed as "the Homosexual Liberation Week," as it was broadened to not only be a demonstration, but a week full of other activities such as seminars, political debates and cultural activities. Representatives from all parliamentary parties were invited to a debate concerning gay and lesbian issues, which since then has been a standing feature. Gay and lesbian associations connected to some of the political parties were also created during this time, for example, *Homosexuella liberaler* (Homosexual Liberals) and *Gaymoderaterna* (the Gay Conservatives). Meanwhile, *Homosexuella Socialister* became more focused on lobbying the Social Democrats and the Left Party. RFSL primarily regarded the Left Party and the Liberal Party as easiest to work with. The attempts to create alliances with influential groups in society were, however, not limited to the main political parties; also, key individuals within religious institutions were addressed. For instance, in 1980, the first "homosexual divine service" was held during the Homosexual Liberation Week, which was organized by a pastor from the Swedish Lutheran state church (Rydström 2007a; interview with Stig-Åke; Wennerhag 2017).

During the 1980s, the number of participants in the demonstration in the Homosexual Liberation Week grew steadily; 2,400 participated in 1980 and 5,000 in 1985 (Wennerhag 2017). The activities of the gay and lesbian movement during the 1980s was, as in other countries, much affected by the AIDS epidemic, but it was also a time when the movement's strengthened connections with both political and cultural elites led to a few political gains, for instance anti-discrimination legislation. The early 1990s were characterized by campaigns for a civil partnership law, which was passed by the Parliament in 1995 (Rydström 2007a).

Pride consolidates in Stockholm

In 1998 EuroPride was held for the first time in Stockholm. In the preceding years, individual activists had made contacts with the European umbrella organization for Pride organizers, EPOA, and as a result it was decided that a separate association only working with EuroPride 1998 should be founded. From the beginning RFSL Stockholm had been the main organizer for the Homosexual Liberation Week (which in 1995–1997 had been renamed *Stockholms Homofestival*, Stockholm's Homo Festival), but a separate association was founded when EuroPride was organized. EuroPride in Stockholm 1998 was deemed a success, and around 10,000 people participated in the march. Shortly thereafter, a new association was founded for arranging Stockholm Pride in subsequent years, which consisted of LGBT organizations (e.g. RFSL), individual activists, and other organizations (e.g. political parties and prominent civil society organizations). The experiences of EuroPride in 1998 thus led to both a permanent renaming of the Stockholm Homosexual Liberation Week into Stockholm Pride, and a new way of organizing the event (Wennerhag 2017).

Since 1998 Stockholm Pride has developed into one of Europe's largest Pride parades. In 2016, around 45,000 participants took part in the march, and around 10 times as many were reported as bystanders (Wennerhag 2017). In comparison to the first Homosexual Liberation Days during the late 1970s, which looked like other protest marches at the time and primarily featured activists holding political placards and banners, today's Stockholm Pride also contains carnivalesque elements with some participants dressed in colorful and extravagant costumes, and floats sponsored by organizations and companies. The main organizing principle of the parade, nevertheless, remains that participants march in specific sections, as members of various LGBT groups, civil society organizations, trade unions and professions, public authorities, and political parties. Victor, one of the organizers of Stockholm Pride in recent years, who has also taken part in EPOA meetings at the European level, stresses the significant presence of politicians and political parties as a feature that distinguishes the parade in the Swedish capital from parades elsewhere:

> I would say that half of the national parliament is walking in the Pride parade, more or less, and that turnout you probably wouldn't find in any other country. [...] We have chosen to include the politicians, while others maybe only choose to make demands on politicians.

One important part of today's Stockholm Pride is "Pride House," which the week before the parade hosts around 200 events including everything from political debates and seminars to theater and movies. Here, LGBT organizations, trade unions, political parties and other civil society organizations arrange discussions regarding LGBT-relevant issues. Sandra, President of the Association Stockholm Pride in 2014–2016, believes that this distinguishes the Stockholm Pride from Pride events in many other countries. "We kind of invented Pride House. [Stockholm Pride] is something more, it is not only a parade, and it's not only clubs."

For the parade organizers and the LGBT organizations, Stockholm Pride is thus about combining the parade with both LGBT community-oriented social activities and political advocacy aimed at political parties and other influential actors. Ulrika, past President of the main Swedish LGBT organization RFSL and President of the Stockholm Pride association in 2005–2006, sees the opportunities for having political impact during Stockholm Pride as a crucial part of the event. She compares it to the Almedalen Week, the main annual gathering for politicians, journalists, interest organizations and lobbyists in Sweden held during a week in the beginning of July, where a host of actors launch political demands and campaigns.

> Stockholm Pride has grown tremendously. It's the biggest event in Stockholm, and that generates a lot of media attention. […] It's the Almedalen Week of the LGBTQ movement, one could say. We never launch anything during the Almedalen Week. We know it's no use because there we compete with a lot of moneyed actors that pay a lot when launching campaigns, which we are not able to do. We know that if we only wait three weeks and launch our demands during Stockholm Pride, then the newspapers will write about it anyhow and give our issues attention, without us having spent any extra money on it. This is because Stockholm Pride is such a large common manifestation that is regarded as a big common united front from a large group in society, and then the politicians want to be there.

The active use of the Pride parades in Stockholm as a vehicle for political advocacy could perhaps be seen in light of Sweden's relatively centralized and traditionally corporativist political system, where movements and interest groups have often cultivated strong ties to political parties and other influential actors. And it is in Stockholm that most political power is centered.

Pride travels nationwide

Despite Stockholm's role as national capital and politico-administrative center, later years have witnessed a major diffusion of Pride parades to other cities and towns in Sweden. The first Pride event outside of Stockholm was *Regnbågsfestivalen* (the Rainbow Festival), first held in 1995 in Sweden's third largest city Malmö (today called Malmö Pride).

In Gothenburg, the second largest city in the country, it wasn't until 2007 that the first *HBT-festivalen* (the LGBT Festival) was organized as a collaboration between five local cultural institutions (two museums and three theatres). The city previously had had numerous lesbian and gay protests, but all had been separate and no LGBT organization was at the time in a position to unify the disparate gay and lesbian organizations. According to Tasso, formerly the festival coordinator (and a former MP for the Left Party), the Gothenburg LGBT Festival initially distanced itself from the name "Pride" which was associated with Stockholm and commercialization. Nevertheless, the festival later renamed itself West Pride. The Gothenburg Rainbow Parade (surveyed in our study in 2012) was not organized until 2010. West Pride has developed in close collaboration with the City of Gothenburg and the festival has a prominent presence in the city space with a massive number of rainbow flags on public buildings, along the main boulevard, and on every vehicle running in local public transports. Gothenburg and Stockholm are the joint organizers of 2018 EuroPride.

In 2007 parades also started to be held in Eskilstuna and Sundsvall, and in 2008 in Uppsala and Karlstad. Since 2010 annual Pride parades have been established in an increasing number of cities. In 2016 Pride parades or other types of events celebrating LGBT Pride were held in around 50 places in Sweden (RFSL 2016). Judging from InterPride's figures over where Pride events are held today globally, this would make Sweden the country having the most Pride events per capita today (InterPride 2016, p. 12). Furthermore, many Pride parades are staged in towns with smaller populations than 10,000 inhabitants, for example, Åmål, Mellerud, Ånge, Älmhult and Arvidsjaur.

The former President of RSFL, Ulrika, says that local RFSL chapters have initiated only around half of these Pride events:

> Sometimes it can be independent activists and sometimes a co-operation between RFSL and other organizations. Sometimes it is the local municipality, sometimes the local business association. [...] The only thing we have said about this development is that it is great, but we think that it is important that it is based in the local LGBTQ movement. So that it is not something that a local business association or a local municipality does without co-operating with local LGBTQ persons. Because the purpose should be, one must hope, to improve the situation for LGBTQ persons in this specific location, or make visible their situation.

This development has not, however, taken place without conflicts within the movement. Some of these conflicts have been about the role, or even presence, of commercial business actors, while others have been about the presence of political parties that some activists deem to be unsuitable allies for the LBGT movement. For example in Stockholm, parts of the radical left have organized a small AnarchoPride some years, where neither companies nor politicians were welcome. Another case was the Uppsala Pride in 2012, which denied the Liberal Party to participate in the parade since it was framed as a socialist and queer feminist Pride festival. There have also been radical left "pink-black" sections at the parades in Malmö, Gothenburg and Stockholm, which sometimes have disturbed other participants from the police, military, migration authorities and moderate-right parties for being allegedly "anti-LGBTQ."

The Dutch Pink Saturday parades

Early tolerance

Pink Saturday parades appeared in an internationally unique political context for the Gay and Lesbian movement. The Netherlands did not only allow for same-sex sexual acts very early, already in 1811 (Hildebrandt 2014), the country has had a more or less continuous homosexual emancipation movement since 1911 with the founding of a Dutch division of the German *Wissenschaftlich-humanitäre Komitee* (Scientific Humanitarian

Committee). The motto of the organization, "through science to justice," exemplifies the Dutch movement's pre–World War II, as well as post-war, political strategy. Its early pre-war emphasis on human rights, reinforced by the Universal Declaration of Human Rights (1949) and its strategic use of academic information to convince influential people in society of the normality of homosexuality, has pervaded its history. The new organization for homosexual emancipation, CoC (a code name, Center for Recreation and Culture), was established in 1946. Reflecting the organization's "coming out process" it was renamed the Dutch Society for Homophiles in 1964 and in 1971 the Dutch Society for the Integration of Homosexuals (Hekma and Duyvendak 2011a; Hekma 2014). Its activities were internally centered on providing members with social meeting spaces and externally only its leaders lobbied for equal rights, together with taking a lead in starting international cooperation with the formation of the International Committee for Sexual Equality (ICSE). Interestingly, this international committee was strictly a European collaboration, mainly between three groups in West Germany, CoC and Der Kreis from Switzerland, but with connections to organizations and individuals in Sweden, Norway, Denmark, France, Belgium and Britain. Working tenaciously behind the scenes during the early 1960s, in a more liberalized and secularized political climate, CoC's efforts were beginning to pay off. "Almost ten years before 'Stonewall' in the United States, the bud of Dutch tolerance towards homosexuality started to develop" (Schuyf and Krouwel 1999).

Dutch gays and lesbians reluctantly take to the streets

Within this solidly entrenched reformist political context in a country, which was beginning to accept homosexuality and the human rights of homosexuals, CoC was initially negative to Dutch Pride parades; they found no reason for homosexuals to demonstrate – "homosexuals are just normal people."[6] However, in the late 1960s and early 1970s a more radical wing in the gay and lesbian movement emerged, demanding "integration" of homosexuality in Dutch society – first the Federation of Student Working Groups on Homosexuality and later the lesbian groups Purple September and Lesbian Nation, and the male group Red Faggots (Hekma and Duyvendak 2007). This early radicalism, what Gert Hekma (2014, p. 67) calls a "Queer fire," burned out in the early 1980s when "gays and lesbians began the long march through the institutions."

CoC distanced itself from the first public homosexual demonstration near the Dutch Parliament in The Hague, January 1969 as well as the march in May 1970 in Amsterdam to commemorate the homosexual victims of World War II. However, after mounting pressure from within and challenged by radical groups outside of the organization, CoC slowly changed course to a more radical, albeit modest, left-wing direction. CoC gave its tacit support for an International Day of Liberation and Solidarity demonstration in Amsterdam in June 1977. The initiative for this march came from Lesbian Nation (Hekma and Duyvendak 2011b). It was homosexual repression in the US, and not domestic developments, which prompted the first large public manifestation of the Dutch gay and lesbian movement. It was in reaction to Anita Bryant's anti-homosexual campaign against a newly passed antidiscrimination law in Dade County, Florida, and its subsequent rejection in a popular referendum.[7] A second International Liberation and Solidarity march was held in 1978 (Schuyf and Krouwel 1999). In the most LGBT friendly countries – the Netherlands, as in Sweden and the UK in our sample – international solidarity has often taken center-stage on their Pride parades' political agendas; in contemporary parades solidarity with homosexuals in "places where we cannot march" is often a dominant theme. In the Netherlands the historical first Pride demonstrations were manifestations against repression in the US. The Dutch Gay and Lesbian Movement paradoxically adopted and adapted the Pride ritual in the late 1970s as manifestations of their support for their "oppressed sisters and brothers" in the US.

In 1979 the more radical political groups within the movement decided that the Netherlands should also have an annual Pride Parade and The Pink Front, a coalition of lesbian and gay groups and organizations, was founded in 1979 primarily to organize Pink Saturday following the "Stonewall riot tradition."[8] Pink Saturday was initially the most visible expression of homosexuality in Dutch society (Schuyf and Krouwel 1999). This more radical wing fought no longer for acceptance and normality, they now demanded the right to be different embracing a more confrontational politics. The first two Pink Saturday Parades in 1979 and 1980, both in Amsterdam, mobilized more than 5,000 demonstrators. In order to focus the political relevance of the event, in 1981 the Front decided that the Pink Saturday should ambulate between the provincial cities in the country and held a demonstration in a town in the Catholic south. In 1982 in the city of Amersfoort, also a city in the Dutch "bible belt," the event was met with severe and unprecedented violence. While police stood passively by, local youths confronted the demonstration with 4,000 participants resulting in 15 people injured. Amersfoort led to a new dialogue between the movement and the government, leading to the plans for the Equal Treatment Law (Schuyf and Krouwel 1999; Hekma 2000), which in 1993 "extended equal legal, social security, housing, pension, legacy, and asylum rights to gays and lesbians" (Hekma and Duyvendak 2007, p. 413; Hekma and Duyvendak 2011b).

From politics to party

Throughout the 1980s the more political wing of the movement prevailed over the more social – in the Pink Front's organization and in the annual parades – which attracted increasing numbers of participants. But this was an uneasy tension between party and politics resulting in internal conflicts peaking in 1985 and the eventual demise of the Pink Front and its disintegration in 1995 (Schuyf and Krouwel 1999, p. 165). The Pink Saturday held in 1992 in Zoetermeer, upon the initiative of the city council and with local government subsidizing, to celebrate the city's famous flower exhibition, marked a definite shift in emphasis in following Pink Saturday events – party rather than politics now dominated. Pink Saturday from the mid-1990s to today became more and more a social event for the LGBT communities. Erwina, who had organized the Pink Saturdays in Haarlem in 1989, 1997 and 2011, explained his view of the meaning of the events.

> I think that the gay movement should not be too political. It should be about equality, and you need everybody behind you. ... there was a time when our movement was kidnapped by the lefties, and I don't think that is a good thing to do. It is not in the benefit of our people who are from everywhere across the political spectrum.

In 1994 Amsterdam won the bid to host the third EuroPride and the Pink Saturday event was subsequently incorporated in Amsterdam EuroPride that year. From 1996 the Gay Business Amsterdam organized Gay Pride Amsterdam with its Canal Pride culminating the events. After some controversy, the city granted permission for organizing the Pride to a new foundation in 2006 and since 2014 with a new board. Since its very beginnings, and in contrast with Pink Saturday, Amsterdam Pride "was solely meant to be a celebration of freedom and diversity in Amsterdam, and not as a political demonstration for equal rights or against discrimination."[9] Also in 1996 the first Amsterdam Leather Pride was held in October and the tradition continues to this day (ibid.).

Smaller Pride events are staged in seven other Dutch cities, with Rotterdam Pride in September the largest. Meanwhile Pink Saturday events continue to ambulate between provincial cities in the Netherlands, some events attracting more participants than others, but its future is uncertain (interviews, gay organizer and lesbian organizer). According to a spokesperson from CoC, Pink Saturday's waning existence is in part a result of organizational discontinuity. "The organization of Pink Saturday each year, in a different town or city, takes little learning and input from previous events. Instead of coordinating their experiences, 'they reinvent the wheel each and every year'." In 2016 Amsterdam again hosted the EuroPride and Pink Saturday returned to Amsterdam after 22 years and kicked off the two-week event under the theme "Join our Freedom" with a "freedom" party in Vondelpark and a walk to Dam Square under the banner "jump out of the closet on Pink Saturday." With stages in the park and in the square and countless entertainers, this was a decidedly social event, even if the "walk" included a few politicized messages. Dutch scholars have long lamented the demise of politics in the Dutch LGBT movement, its "de-politicization" and orientation toward "normalization" (e.g. Schuyf and Krouwel 1999; Hekma and Duyvendak 2011a and 2011b; Hekma 2014). They point out that social rights have not followed the changes in legal rights, violence against LGBT persons still persists, acceptance of LGBT lifestyles is but superficial in the Netherlands, and Hekma and Duyvendak (2011a, p. 629) warn that LGBT rights have become vulnerable to opportunistic appropriation by radical right parties. Nonetheless few radical activists remain: "Dutch gays maintain a low profile and are definitely not queer" (Hekma and Duyvendak 2011b, p. 113). Normalization of homosexuality in the Netherlands, according to Hekma and Duyvendak (2011a, p. 629), has led to the fact that "many gay men and lesbians share, for example, the ambivalent feelings of straight, Dutch people regarding Amsterdam's annual Canal Pride due to its ostentatious semi-nudity, drag and leather."

Pink Saturday parades in provincial cities across the Netherlands are primarily organized as "social events for lesbians and their children and friends" (group interview with male organizers; interview with lesbian organizer). The Pink Saturday in Haarlem included in our database was in stark contrast with Pride Parades elsewhere. The parade was dominated by middle-class (74 percent), women (61 percent) – lesbians and non-LGBT women – the age group 50–64 years was most prevalent, only 12 percent of the Dutch participants were under the age of 30 and only 1 percent were students (not working). Furthermore, this Pride event had the by far lowest number of participants with experience of extra-parliamentary activism (Peterson, Wahlström and Wennerhag 2017; Chapter 4 this volume) and the smallest share with political motives for their participation (Chapter 8 this volume) – indications of the de-politicization of Dutch Pink Saturday parades.

Pride in Switzerland

From homophile to gay liberation

Switzerland was one of the first countries in which same-sex activities were decriminalized, due to the adoption of the Napoleonic Code in 1798. This legislation was soon revoked in most Swiss cantons, apart from in a few French- and Italian-speaking cantons. After the Swiss Confederation's adoption of a common criminal code in 1942, homosexuality was decriminalized in all parts of the country (schwulengeschichte.ch; Delessert and Voegtli 2012).

The first association for homosexuals in Switzerland, the *Schweizer Freundschaftsbund* (The Swiss Friendship Association), was founded in 1922 with inspiration from Germany (schwulengeschichte.ch; Tamagne 2006, p. 73). German influences were also important for the founding in 1932 of the first homosexual journal in Switzerland, the Zurich-based *Freundschafts-Banner*, which in 1943 was renamed *Der Kreis* (Kennedy 1999).

When the Nazi government in Germany shut down all homosexual periodicals and associations, Switzerland and in particular Zurich became one of the few safe havens for gay men in continental Europe. Many activities evolved around the journal *Der Kreis*. Between 1940 and 1945, *Der Kreis* was the only homosexual periodical in the world (Jackson 2015).

During the decades following World War II, *Der Kreis* played a central role for homosexuals in other European countries, where same-sex activities were still criminal or homosexual periodicals censored. The journal had texts written in German, French and English, and almost half of its readership was outside Switzerland. Until it was discontinued in 1967, *Der Kreis* played an important role in the post-war "homophile movement" emerging in several Western countries during the 1950s and 1960s, for both inspiring and connecting activists across borders (Kennedy 1999; Whisnant 2012; Tremblay 2015). As noted in the section on the Netherlands, the people around *Der Kreis* were – together with Dutch and West German groups – the most crucial actors for creating the International Committee for Sexual Equality (ICSE) in 1951.

Despite Switzerland's comparatively liberal laws on same-sex activities, the late 1950s and 1960s was a period when homosexuals and homophile activists increasingly experienced police repression and hostile public debates (schwulengeschichte.ch). Activism was mainly centered in a few larger cities (in particular Zurich), and focused on social and cultural activities and more moderate forms of advocacy.

As in other Western countries, new and more radical forms of homosexual activism however took root in the early 1970s. Already in 1967, young activists around *Der Kreis* formed a new journal and association, *Club68*, and activists from these circles were in 1971 central for creating *Schweizerische Organisation der Homophilen* (SOH, Swiss Organization of Homophiles) (schwulengeschichte.ch). This national umbrella organization was however more grounded in the pre-1968 tradition of moderate homophile activism. Amongst the more radical groups founded during this period, we in particular find *Homosexuellen Arbeitsgruppen* (Homosexual Working Groups), originally founded in Zurich 1972; but soon it spread to other cities, and in 1974 the national umbrella organization *Homosexuellen Arbeitsgruppen Schweiz* (HACH) was created. HACH was inspired by the new ideas about "gay liberation," and clearly left leaning in their analysis and strategy (schwulengeschichte.ch; Delessert and Voegtli 2012). As part of the new radical women's movement, lesbian groups were also created; in particular *Homosexuelle Frauengruppe Zürich* (HFG), which was founded in 1974 (Marti 2000).

Christopher Street Days

These three organizations – SOH, HACH and HFG – were the main organizers of the first Swiss manifestation commemorating the Stonewall riots, in Zurich, June 24th, 1978. The manifestation was called "Christopher Street Day" and abbreviated CSD. This abbreviation has since then been used to name Stonewall commemorations both in the German-speaking parts of Switzerland and in Germany. The first Swiss CSD took the form of a sit-in, in the Platzspitz Park in central Zurich, where speeches were held and signatures collected for a petition. Apart from commemorating Stonewall, a main objective with the manifestation was to demand a stop to the Zurich police's registration of homosexuals, a goal that was accomplished half a year later (schwulengeschichte.ch; Delessert and Voegtli 2012).

The following year, 1979, the "first national gay liberation day" in Switzerland was organized in Bern, an event that was also framed as a 10-year anniversary of Stonewall. The primary political demand was the same as the previous year, but this time aimed at the police in Bern. In contrast to the year before, the CSD in Bern was a demonstration which attracted around 300 participants (schwulengeschichte.ch). In the following years, national CSD demonstrations were organized in different Swiss cities: Basel (1980, 1985), Lausanne (1981), Zurich (1982, 1986), Lucerne (1983), and Bern (1984, 1987) (schwulengeschichte.ch). Apart from the demonstrations, evening parties and other festivities were often part of the CSD.

During the 1980s, CSD demonstrations were given less priority, and some organizations stopped taking part in the organizing efforts. More moderate groups (such as SOH) saw the CSDs as too focused on protest and radical critique. Another reason was the AIDS epidemic, which forced many organizations to prioritize information and solidarity work, at the same time as the deaths of friends and central activists created anxiety within the community. Despite this, a CSD was organized every year until 1989, when it was once again held in Zurich. After that, there was a five-year break until the next CSD (schwulengeschichte.ch).

In 1994, Christopher Street Day was once again organized in Zurich as a 25-year commemoration of Stonewall. A film festival, lectures, discussions and parties, were also organized the weeks before the CSD demonstration. In 1995 the organization CSD Zürich was founded, and since then it has been the organizer of the event in Zurich. The same year, the demonstration was called "CSD Gay Parade," and drew around 3,000 participants. Earlier the CSDs had been touring between different cities, but since 1994 the Zurich CSD has been the sole annual Pride parade held in the German-speaking part of Switzerland (apart from a three-country CSD organized in 2003 in Basel and its two bordering cities in France and Germany, and since 2009 a bi-annual CSD parade that starts in the Swiss city of Kreuzlingen and ends in the adjoining German city Konstanz) (schwulengeschichte.ch).

In 2009, Zurich hosted the country's first EuroPride, and nearly 50,000 people took part in the parade (Zurich Pride 2016). The following year both the annual event and its organizer were renamed Zurich Pride Festival. In comparison with the CSDs of the 1980s, the CSDs/Pride Festivals in

Zurich since 1994 have been more focused on festivities, but most of the parades have still had an annual theme that addressed specific LGBT issues and on-going national political debates. For instance, the CSD Zürich in 2005 was organized the day before the national referendum on June 5th on registered partnership for same-sex couples, and at the CSD prominent politicians gave speeches (schwulengeschichte.ch; interview with David). In the referendum 58 percent of the Swiss voters supported this proposal.

Pride in the Romandy region

The only CSD organized in a French-speaking canton was in Lausanne in 1981, where the local authorities at first had tried to prevent the demonstration from taking place (schwulengeschichte.ch). Overall, the activities of the movement were relatively loosely connected between Romandy, e.g. the country's French-speaking part, and the German-speaking part (today 64 percent of the population is German-speaking, 23 percent French-speaking, and 8 percent Italian-speaking, out of a population of 8 million). The main impetus for the 1970s "Gay Liberation" groups in Romandy (in particular in Geneva and Lausanne) instead came from radical groups in Paris, and they were in general politically close to HACH (schwulengeschichte.ch; Delessert and Voegtli 2012).

During the late 1980s and early 1990s, the divisions within the movement were increasingly overcome. Through the creation of Pink Cross in 1993, a national umbrella organization for gay men, groups that earlier belonged to the more moderate SOH and the more radical HACH were brought together, and the main groups from the French-speaking cantons also became members (schwulengeschichte.ch). A national umbrella organization for lesbian groups, *Lesbenorganisation Schweiz* (LOS), had been founded a few years earlier, in 1990 (Marti 2000). Pink Cross and LOS have since then been the main gay and lesbian organizations in Switzerland.

Following the pattern of the touring CSDs during the 1980s, the first Lesbian and Gay Pride of the Romandy region – *la Pride romande* – was organized in Geneva in 1997. Since then, Pride parades have been organized almost annually in different cities in Romandy: Lausanne (1998, 2006), Fribourg (1999, 2013, 2016), Bern (2000, 2017), Sion (2001, 2015), Neuchâtel (2002), Delémont (2003, 2012), Geneva (2004, 2011), Lucerne (2005) and Biel/Bienne (2008) (schwulengeschichte.ch).

Yves, one of the activists who took part in organizing the political side of Pride Romandy during the first years, explains the main reasons behind ambulating Pride events:

> The aim was really to spread, to show that there were gays, lesbians, bisexuals and trans not only in Geneva and Lausanne but also in Jura, in Fribourg, in Neuchâtel, in all the other regions, in Valais, and also to show the support of all the other cantons, with gays, lesbians,

bisexuals and trans or intersex from those regions, which were maybe less vulnerable to the issue, so that was a solidarity issue actually. [...] Another reason that we wanted the Pride to go to many places was that here in Geneva we could not organize a Pride every year: that would be far too exhausting. [...] Of course in Zurich it's a bit different because it's really the biggest city so they have more people and more strength.

While the same association has always organized the Zurich Pride Festival, the Pride parades in Romandy have been mainly organized by local LGBT organizations in the different cantons. In one of the most conservative cantons, Jura, there were initially no LGBT organizations, but the organization of the 2003 Pride in the canton's capital Delémont became pivotal for establishing a local organization. In this way, the touring Pride parades also contributed to strengthening the LGBT community in the cities where it was least visible. This model with locally based organizing and mobilization from other parts of Romandy has, however, not always been without tensions. The same activist recalls a dispute between the local organizers of the Pride parade in Sion, the capital of the conservative canton Valais, about the slogan of the parade.

> The organizers didn't want to have a slogan that was a political demand that was actually asking too much from politicians. The slogan was something like "I like Valais" – I like my region, the canton, something like that. But it was not saying that we want partnership, we want marriage, or that we want rights for rainbow families, or that we want political rights, these types of things. And of course, the organizations in some other cantons said we disagree: "Okay it's your Pride, but if you want other people to come, if you want our solidarity, we need to have solidarity with something. We can't show solidarity with a slogan that says, 'oh, we like our canton'. I mean, why should we like your canton, since your canton is the most homophobic maybe in the whole of Switzerland?"

One of the other interviewees, who worked with Geneva Pride in 2004 and 2011 (and who is active in *Dialogai*, the main organization for gay men in Romandy), emphasized that the Swiss political system's regular use of referendums has made it important to use Pride parades as an occasion to reach out to the people, since it is the people who finally decide on specific political issues, not the political elites.

> Switzerland was the first country that accepted partnership with a referendum. It was not the parliament, but the people ... Between the first and second Pride in Geneva [in 1997 and 2004], there was this big

campaign for partnership in Switzerland. [...] The second Pride in Geneva was in this way: we have to go to the people and explain and explain and they are going to understand and change their mind. [...] Pride is part of this thing to change the minds of people, I think. [...] It is part of the action of the movement. [...] We have to take the votes one by one.

When discussing the differences between Pride Romandy and Zurich Pride with the president of the Zurich Pride association, he stresses that on the one hand, Zurich's traditional role as the Swiss center of gay life makes it relatively easier to organize Pride parades there. For instance, the LGBT bars of the city take care of selling drinks at the festival field, and it is easier to get continuity and stability when it is always the same organization that runs the Zurich Pride. At the same time, he sees advantages with the Pride Romandy model.

I would say that Zurich Pride is like a big, probably elegant, elderly ship, like a cruise ship and Pride in Romandy is like a pirate boat that is fast and can turn around really quick. [...] In Zurich Pride we have our plans, we have always the same place, and demonstrations run just the same. We have not had any big changes in the committee or the whole team during the last few years and you feel that there are strong connections, people know what they have to do. [But regarding impact on society], I would say Zurich Pride has less influence than Pride in Romandy because it is in smaller cities, they are mostly a bit more conservative, so the Pride in Romandy has a bigger impact, and bigger presence in the newspapers than Zurich Pride has. [...] In Zurich we won't move anybody anymore, because in Zurich it is open, you can be gay at work, in the city.

In terms of size, the parade during Zurich Pride has about 12,000 participants each year, but still the organization is run by volunteers, and the main income is from membership fees in the association and advertisements in a magazine printed before the parade. The Zurich Pride festival does not receive any direct financial support from the local municipality, and only about one-third of its budget comes from commercial sponsors. Even if Zurich Pride has a more established organization than Pride Romandy, it still does not match Europe's larger and more professionalized Pride parades.

Mexico City gay and lesbian Pride history[10]

The Mexican lesbian and gay and lesbian movement emerged, against all odds, in 1971 in a society wrought by harsh government repression. The killing of hundreds of students in the *Plaza de las Tres Culturas* in

Tlatelolco by military and police forces on October 2nd, 1968, and the Corpus Christi massacre against student demonstrators on June 10th, 1971, are two of the most emblematic events of the Mexican political regime's so-called "dirty war" against all oppositional voices. Even if Mexico had formally decriminalized same-sex sexual acts already in 1872 (Hildebrandt 2014), gays, lesbians and trans people were nevertheless subject to persecution and imprisonment. "Being gay in the 1930s and still at the end of the 1970s, when the sexual liberation movement began, was a crime" (El Universal 2016). Police forces regularly carried out raids on gay bars and arrested homosexuals with the permission of the authorities. In this context, the first group of homosexuals in Mexico and Latin America established in 1971 the *Movimiento de Liberación Homosexual*, but out of fear for the lives of its members, it was a secret association aimed at sharing individual experiences about their sexualities and promoting homosexuality as a legitimate expression of sexuality (González Pérez 2005, pp. 91–92).

Lesbian and gay liberation emerges

However, this situation changed drastically in the second half of the 1970s, when homosexual men and women in Mexico, inspired by the discourses of sexual liberation that had emerged in the US and Europe, began to identify themselves as a repressed social group. Based on the liberationist approach of lesbian and gay movements in other countries, Mexico witnessed the creation of three homosexual organizations in 1978: the Homosexual Front of Revolutionary Action (*Frente Homosexual de Liberación Revolucionaria*, FAHR), the Lambda Group of Homosexual Liberation (*Grupo Lambda de Liberación Homosexual*) and Okiabeth.[11] The members of FHAR were mainly homosexual men who sympathized with communism and anarchism. The Lambda Group was made up of middle-class men and women who supported feminist ideas and advocated for an end to homophobia in newspapers, magazines and other publications. Finally, Okiabeth was a women-only group that embraced lesbian-feminist ideas (Diez 2011, p. 695; Figueroa 2003). The creation of these three groups with distinctive ideologies, along with a political regime that was facing increasing democratization pressures from below, allowed the lesbian and gay movement to leave the closet for the first time. On July 26th, 1978, the FHAR joined a demonstration to support the Cuban Revolution. Around 30 homosexuals came out of the social closet for the first time in Mexican history to publicly express their demands for sexual liberation (Hernández and Manrique 1989, p. 68).

The positive impact of this event led the other two organizations – the Lambda Group and Okiabeth – to join the FAHR and create the "Coordinator of Homosexual Groups" (*Coordinadora de Grupos Homosexuales*, CGH) soon after (Figueroa 2003). The CGH formed its own contingent and participated in the demonstration convened on October 2nd, 1978, to observe the tenth anniversary of the Tlatelolco massacre. Homosexual men and women from the three groups marched and chanted slogans such as "Not sick, not criminals, but simply homosexuals!" (*Ni enfermos, ni criminales, simplemente homosexuales!*), and "There is no political freedom without sexual freedom!" (*No hay libertad política sin libertad sexual!*) (Peralta 2006, p. 114).

The time was now ripe for the lesbian and gay movement to stage its first collective manifestation of its newfound identity. Mexico City held Latin America's first gay Pride parade in late June 1979 (Encarnación 2016, p. 29). The demonstrators demanded the recognition of sexual freedom as a political right (Mogrovejo 1996). The Pride parade was meant to take place in *Paseo de la Reforma*, the most important, and politically significant, avenue in Mexico City. However, due to the outcries from large sectors of society about the "celebration" of homosexuality in public places, the Mexico City government did not allow the parade to go through *Reforma* and, instead, it took place on a secondary street (Lumsden 1991).

However, as a result of negotiations undertaken by the various homosexual groups, the Mexico City government authorized a Pride parade to take place in *Reforma* in 1980 (Figueroa 2003) It is estimated that nearly seven thousand people attended this second Pride parade in Mexico City, which started at the *Ángel de la Independencia*, a monument built in 1910 to commemorate the 100th anniversary of Mexican independence, and the starting point for all major demonstrations in the city. That same year, one contingent of the Pride parade joined a procession to the Basilica of Our Lady of Guadalupe – possibly the most important Catholic Church in Mexico – in memory of Monsignor Óscar Romero, a Catholic priest from El Salvador, who was assassinated on March 24th, 1980 (González Pérez 2005, p. 96).

LGBT movement experiences a decline in visibility

Notwithstanding the significant gains achieved in the latter 1970s, the lesbian and gay movement became less visible during the following decade, mainly due to the HIV/AIDS crisis, as well as the inability of the nascent movement to build a collective identity in the face of the economic and political crisis, which surfaced in 1982. The economic crisis led to the creation of social movements that confronted the problems of falling oil prices, rising inflation and devaluation, which mobilized the masses (Foweraker and Craig 1990). However, the lesbian and gay movement was unable to articulate a new collective identity that responded to the new economic situation of social discontent.

Mexico faced the arrival of HIV/AIDS in 1983. As in many other countries, homosexuality was blamed for its appearance and spread. In the midst of social panic and fear, people held homosexuals responsible and discrimination against homosexuals rose dramatically (Diez 2011, p. 701). The Catholic church was the most vocal; in 1985, the Papal Nuncio in Mexico declared that "AIDS is the punishment sent by God to those who ignore His laws [...] and homosexuality is one of the vices most condemned by the Church" (Figueroa 2003, p. 3). This hate speech and persecution of homosexuals led to the weakening and temporary retreat of the lesbian and gay movement from the public sphere. For almost a decade the movement turned inwards; groups organized meetings and workshops aimed at understanding the causes and consequences of HIV infections and its relation to homosexuality (Figueroa 2003; Díaz 1998).

A new start

The second half of the 1990s witnessed a "second wave" of lesbian and gay activism. Again, the convergence of a more open, democratic regime and the creation of a new collective identity within the movement made this possible. In 1994 the last president from the Institutional Revolutionary Party (PRI, which had ruled Mexico since 1929) took office in a context riddled by economic and political tensions; the country entered a new economic crisis, known as the December mistake or the Tequila effect, and opposition parties were gaining unprecedented political power. In 1997 the PRI lost its majority in Congress for the first time, and the government was forced to give concessions to other political parties. Patria Jiménez, the founder of the *Claustro de Sor Juana* lesbian movement and one of the most prominent lesbian activists in Mexico, took office as Federal Deputy under the proportional representation scheme (Figueroa 2003). The appointment of Jiménez as a Congresswoman was seen as another political victory for the lesbian and gay movement.

Also in 1997, homosexuals were able to articulate a new collective identity around the concept of "sexual diversity," favored by a more diverse social structure in Mexico and the broader discourse of multiculturalism in a world that promoted the adoption of multicultural policies in several countries (Kymlicka 2007). Furthermore, with the end of the Cold War, human rights became central in the international agenda. Social movements around the world began demanding more respect for their human rights, including rights for minority groups. The lesbian and gay movement in Mexico became one of those groups to claim respect for their rights.

In 1998, the sexual diversity concept was consolidated in the "Sexual Diversity Forum" organized by the Mexico City Legislative Assembly. For the first time, a government institution convened sexual minorities to debate about their demands and policy proposals (Diez 2011, p. 707). One year later, the new collective identity of the lesbian and gay movement was materialized in the Pride parade, which was called "Gay, Lesbian,

Bisexual and Transgender Pride Parade." Since then, Pride parades in Mexico City have taken place every year in late June on the *Paseo de la Reforma* with thousands of people marching together to demand more rights and more attention by the government to their claims. In the 2014 and 2015 Pride parades, between 500,000 and 600,000 people participated.

In the 2010s Mexico has witnessed (unexpected) initiatives by the government to acknowledge the rights of LGBT people. Already in 2009, inspired by Spain's progressive LGBT legislation, Mexico City's assembly legalized same-sex marriage (Encarnación 2016, p. 64). In June 2015, the Mexican Supreme Court ruled that all civil codes that outlawed same-sex marriages were unconstitutional. In other words, same-sex marriages became constitutional nationwide, and not only in the three states where it was already lawful (Mexico City, Coahuila and Quintana Roo) (El País 2015). This landmark ruling was followed, in February 2016, by a bill presented by President Enrique Peña Nieto to legalize same-sex marriages nationwide, in response to the decision of the Supreme Court. The bill seeks to modify Article 4 of the Mexican Constitution in order to recognize the human rights of men and women to marry and have a family, regardless of their sexual preferences. This initiative also proposes a number of measures to recognize the gender identity of all citizens, including in their birth certificates and passports (Excélsior 2016).

The constitutional and Civil Codes' amendments proposed by President Peña Nieto provoked political mobilization both in favor of and against same-sex marriage. On September 10th, 2016, the National Front for the Family (*Frente Nacional por la Familia*, FNF) organized marches in several cities to demonstrate against the initiatives of President Peña Nieto and support for the "traditional" or "natural" family model. This march caused an intense political reaction, particularly on social networks such as Facebook and Twitter – individuals, groups and organizations published posts and articles to support or reject this march. Subsequently, on September 24th, 2016, two simultaneous marches took place in the *Reforma* in Mexico City: one organized by the FNF to reject the initiatives of President Peña Nieto, and another convened by LGBT groups to show their support for the constitutionality of same-sex marriages and respect for their rights (SDP noticias 2016).

Pride parades have become an entrenched tradition in Mexico. Mexico City Pride is far and away the largest attracting since 2013 hundreds of thousands of participants. In 2003 the first Lesbian Pride March was staged in the country's capital. In Guadalajara, well-attended LGBT Pride Parades have also been held every June since 1996. LGBT Pride Parades have continuously occurred in Monterrey, Tijuana, Puebla, Veracruz, Xalapa, Cuernavaca, Tuxtla Gutiérrez, Acapulco, Chilpancingo and Mérida. Furthermore, more than 70 smaller events across the country are listed in the 2016/2017 PrideRadar report (InterPride 2016). The proliferation of Pride events in Mexico appears to be connected to the recent juridical rulings extending Mexico City's LGBT progressive legislation nationwide, in particular same-sex marriage.

The history of Pride parades in Italy

Early community building

While homosexuality was decriminalized as early as 1890 (Hildebrandt 2014), homophile groups were largely underground in the face of the Catholic Church's aggressive censorship of homosexual practices. However, during the 1970s small gay groups emerged above ground, together with lesbian separatist groups (Malici 2011). In 1971 "A Manifesto for the Moral Revolution: Revolutionary Homosexuality" was mimeographed in Amsterdam, but addressed to the Italian public, and the F.U.O.R.I! Association was established. In 1972 the first street demonstration for gay rights took place in Rome mobilized by the Organization for the Political Movement of Homosexuals (formerly Homosexual Revolt). The same year the Italian Association for the Recognition of Homophile Rights was formed (Nardi 1998, p. 578). The Italian gay movement early in its history split into a more pragmatic reformist wing (F.U.O.R.I.) and a militant wing, which aligned with the feminist movement and the class struggles of the far left. The budding gay liberation movement, while alienating lesbians, adopted the feminist slogan the "personal is political" and engaged in small group consciousness-raising (Malagreca 2007, pp. 100ff). This strategy in turn resulted in a degree of isolation from the outside world, as well as triggering strong personal bonds, "which represented the very foundation of the movement at that time" (Mudu 2002, p. 191). Given the political successes of the Italian feminist movement in the early 1970s, according to Nardi (1998),

> it was not accidental that the earliest gay movements echoed many of the practices of the feminist movement, took a trans-class approach while still critiquing economic oppression, drew upon a left intellectual culture, and sought coalitions with the women's movement.
> (p. 580; see also Malici 2011, p. 115)

National Organizations Emerge

Malagreca (2007) argues that 1980 marked a shift in the gay movement in Italy from a revolutionary culture of provocation and sexual liberation to a "pragmatic" culture of normalcy and later in the 1990s an application of Anglo-American identity politics frameworks (p.125 and p. 236). The fragmented gay and lesbian movement of the 1970s was locally orientated; organizing on a national basis came relatively late in Italy as did gay and lesbian mass demonstrations. *Cirolo Mario Mieli*, a Rome gay association was founded in 1983 and Arcigay,[12] Italy's largest national gay rights organization, was founded in 1985, with its headquarters in Bologna. Both of these new associations marked a more instrumental turn in the GLBT[13] movement (Mudu 2002, p. 192). In 1990 a group of lesbian women founded Women's Arcigay and the two parallel organizations consolidated in 1994 to become Arcigay Arcilesbica, the only organization in Italy that elected its executive on the basis of a 50 percent quota for women and men. At the same congress the organization decided to launch a national Gay and Lesbian Pride, which was held in Rome in collaboration with other associations; "the first mass gay rights demonstration ever held in Italy."[14] The second national Gay and Lesbian Pride took place in Bologna 1995 and the third in Naples 1996 under the banner: "The Sun's Coming Out." The same year the organization officially transformed into two distinct organizations and Arcilesbica became the first national non-separatist lesbian association. In 1997 Arcigay organized a Pride event in Venice. In June 1999 associations across the country re-united their efforts to hold a Gay and Lesbian Pride in Rome.[15]

The ambition of the organizers of Pride parades in Italy during the 1990s was to increase the visibility of lesbian and gay issues and to further the collective identity of the movement when at the time the movement was split into dozens of associations and groups. Despite successful and colorful parades, gathering around 10,000 participants on both occasions in Rome, the press ignored them altogether (Mudu 2002, p. 192). The parades had not attracted the media visibility organizers had hoped for. This would change in 2000 when Rome hosted the first WorldPride event overlapping with the "holy year of the Jubilee." Despite heavy opposition from the Vatican hierarchy and conservative parties demanding a stop to the event, more than two hundred thousand people marched through the center of Rome. "For the first time, gay politics was front page news in Rome" and part of the parade was covered on Italian public television (Mudu 2002, p. 193). The major European and US media attended a press conference at the headquarters of Mario Mieli, which provided details for the coming events, in addition to all major Italian media. This event emboldened the movement.

International events

Italian Gay Pride organizers had achieved the visibility they had sought. *Cirolo Mario Mieli* had made a bid with the European Pride Organizers Association (EPOA) and in 1997 EPOA named Rome the site for the 2000 EuroPride, an annual pan-European event. That is when the planning began and a new association arrived on the scene – InterPride, an international association of Pride organizers.[16] The WorldPride in Rome was the first staged and during 2000 no EuroPride was planned in order to avoid conflicts of interest.

According to Glen Freedman of InterPride, the event was called World Pride "because of the Jubilee [which] gave more credence to the event being in the city of Rome".

(cited in Luongo 2002, p. 169)

The then director of WorldPride, American Deborah Oakley-Melvin, claimed that the event had the specific purpose of altering public perceptions of gays and lesbians in Italy, and moreover the event was planned as a global manifestation and high on the WorldPride's political agenda was the participation of people from developing countries, supported by financial assistance given by the "First World" (Luongo 2002, p. 171). Given the power differences in the exchange of ideas, not surprisingly, detractors criticized the intervention as a Eurocentric model of liberation; but despite critique the WorldPride was a significant public and political success. The event attracted the involvement of other actors for which GLBT rights were important. Amnesty International held a rally; ILGA conducted its annual meeting in the city during the event; and the International Gay and Lesbian Human Rights Commission, an international NGO, sponsored a number of panel discussions with the panel on religion and homosexuality garnering intense media coverage. But as Luongo points out, the success of the event also depended on the tens of thousands of tourists who streamed to the city, "the vast majority of them from the United States and northern Europe" (p. 172).

According to the President of *Mario Mieli* during WorldPride, in the minds of the gay world, July 8th will be just as historic as late June[17] as a reminder of Italy's "conscious rebellion against religious oppression." According to Luongo (2002, p. 179),

> she is considering permanently rescheduling Rome's pride for that date to commemorate it forever as a significant event for the entire country. "They never believed that it would happen in Italy".

WorldPride was unquestionably an important event for the Italian GLBT movement, but much of its success, and the international media coverage it drew, can be attributed to the efforts and resources of the largely Anglo-American InterPride executive. On their website they could feature political letters of support, including a letter from then US Vice-President Al Gore; and they could recruit international celebrities to increase media attention. Furthermore, they could coordinate the travel of the tens of thousands of lesbian and gay tourists from the US visiting the event.

Rome's WorldPride ignited a fresh debate within the gay movement as to what strategies should be pursued to further its struggle for visibility and political and social rights. On the one side were those organizations, groups and activists who prioritized coalition building with anti-globalization movements and (left) political parties and on the other a "sector bent on capitalizing on the event in commercial terms" (Mudu 2002, p. 194). This tension remains today. A spokesperson for the Bologna Pride covered in our data sample compared the Pride in Rome with Bologna Pride. "There the Pride is much more commercial and dominated by gay men. Here we emphasize the political struggle for gay and lesbian rights" (interview, lesbian organizer).

Cirolo Mario Mieli again took on the local organizing responsibilities in 2011 when Rome was the site for a spectacular and spectacularized Euro-Pride. According to Colpani and Habed (2014), "the marketing-led and de-politicized spirit of the event made it possible for Lady Gaga to 'represent' European queers in Rome" (p. 86). Citing the event's manifesto, these authors claim that:

> Rome was not an accidental location for the European demonstration, for [the] absence of attention and rights on GLBTQI issues places Italy dramatically outside of Europe, making EuroPride in Rome particularly [significant].
>
> (ibid.)

EuroPride 2011, like WorldPride 2000 in Rome, was staged in the city, with the support of these international associations, to call attention, through a spectacular performance of visibility, to the lack of gay and lesbian rights in the country. Approximately 1,000,000 marched in the parade, which was culminated with a performance and speech by Lady Gaga at Circus Maximus. The European frame was mobilized in Rome to reflect the situation of LGBT people in Italy, currently at the peripheral sexual political boundaries of "Europeanness," yet struggling for inclusion in a "Rainbow Europe."

Bologna Pride – "The red one"

Pride events are not confined to Rome. The 2016/2017 PrideRadar reports over 18 Pride events across the country (InterPride 2016). While Rome Pride is the largest, Bologna Pride is the second largest. Since 1995 annual Pride parades have been held in "The red one" (*la rossa*) – Bologna, the capital of the region of Emilia-Romagna. While the nickname originally referred to the color of the roofs in the historic center, it also refers to the political situation in the city and the region. Since the end of World War II and until the election of a center-right mayor in 1999, center-left parties have governed the city. The center-left regained power again in the 2004 mayoral elections and have remained in power. Furthermore, the city was renowned as a bastion of the Italian Communist Party. The political situation has proven to be propitious for the LGBT community in the region and it also appears to have influenced the local LGBT movement as well as the Pride parades in the city. Eighty-three percent of the participants in the 2012 Bologna Pride in our sample report a left-wing position (0–3) on the left-right scale, far and away the most left-wing Pride parade in our sample (Chapter 4, this volume).

Poland's "Equality Marches"

The LGBT movement under communism

Poland became independent in 1918, and the country's first penal code in 1932 did not criminalize same-sex activities. Apart from during the Nazi occupation of the country in 1939–1945, homosexuality was legal both during the inter-war years and in Communist Poland (Kliszczyński 2001; Hildebrandt 2014). Open homosexuality was, however, very rare and in general socially disapproved, due to the influence of the Roman Catholic Church in the country, also during State Socialism. Amongst the officially sanctioned associations and printed media during Communist times, there were no registered LGBT organizations or press (Ayoub 2016, p. 168).

The gay and lesbian movement in Poland, however, emerged during the Communist regime during the mid-1980s. Despite the country's relatively liberal laws on same-sex activities, repression of gay men by the police was common. Especially during the years following the Martial Law period in 1981–1983 (when the trade union Solidarity was banned) surveillance and repression toward gay men increased, in particular during the so-called "Operation Hyacinth" in 1985–1987 when over 10,000 gay men were forced by the police to sign documents stating their sexual orientation. Partly in response to this, groups for gay men were created in some of the largest cities during the years 1987–1989. For instance, *Warszawski Ruch Homoseksualny*, WRH (the Warsaw Homosexual Movement) tried to make repression against gay men a public matter in the media as well as requested to be officially registered as an association (which they were denied). During this time the international gay and lesbian organization ILGA intensified its work to establish connections with Eastern European groups, and in 1988 WRH were the hosts for an ILGA meeting. It was however not until the fall of the Communist regime that the nation-wide umbrella organization *Stowarzyszenie Grup Lambda*, SGL (the Association of Lambda Groups) was created in 1990 on the basis of existing local groups (Kliszczyński 2001, pp. 161–164; Chetaille 2011, pp. 121–122).

Post-socialist Times and the European Union

Post-socialist Poland did in some ways improve the situation for gay men and lesbians (e.g. the abolishment of state censorship and the possibility to form state-independent associations), but the 1990s did not witness a flourishing gay and lesbian movement. Homosexuality was still in general regarded as a social taboo, and in the public debate gay rights did not have saliency as a political issue. During the 1990s the Roman Catholic Church also strengthened its influence over Polish society, for example, through the partial criminalization of abortion in 1993. The few gay and lesbian organizations that existed (in particular local *Lambda* groups) primarily focused on AIDS-prevention and strengthening the community in larger cities, albeit a few attempts were made to use political lobbying in issues regarding rights and discrimination (Chetaille 2011, pp. 122–123; O'Dwyer 2012, pp. 340–341; Szulc 2011).

Important for changing this situation was the start of Poland's negotiations with the EU for becoming a member state in 1998. Before becoming a member state, all candidate countries had to implement the laws of the EU, which since the 1997 Amsterdam Treaty also included laws against discrimination on the grounds of sexual orientation. The pressure from the EU on Poland to implement the Union's laws opened up new opportunities for the gay and lesbian movement in Poland (O'Dwyer 2012, pp. 341–344). Another factor contributing to the change in political opportunities for the gay and lesbian movement was the election of a left-wing government in 2001, after eight years of right-wing rule. During the electoral campaign, the winning Social Democratic party SLD promised the introduction of same-sex registered partnership and laws against discrimination of sexual minorities (Gruszczynska 2009, p. 315).

As a consequence of these changes, new organizations with a more outspoken political agenda were formed. One of these was *Kampania Przeciw Homofobii*, KPH (Campaign Against Homophobia), which was established in 2001. KPH was modeled as a professional NGO, engaged in lobbying on gay and lesbian issues, and worked closely with ILGA-Europe as well as cultivated links to EU institutions. In 2001 ILGCN-Polska, the Polish branch of the International Lesbian and Gay Cultural Network, was also founded. ILGCN was a loose network that had been created at the 1992 ILGA world conference. It had a secretariat in Sweden and was in particular active in the Baltic Sea region. In contrast to KPH, ILGCN-Polska was more oriented toward grassroots activism (Chetaille 2011, pp. 125–126; O'Dwyer 2012, pp. 343–344). The emergent flora of LGBT organizations, in a relatively short period of time, reflects the Eastern European situation. Instead of following the more or less standardized linear sequence we have seen in most of the countries covered in our study – moving from homophile, to gay liberation, AIDS activism, rights activism, to queer activism – in Poland all of these traditions or paths – homophile/LGBT and queer – were taken all at once (Kulpa and Mizielinska 2011).

Equality parades

ILGCN-Polska was the main force behind *Parada Równości*, the Warsaw Equality Parade, which was the first Pride parade organized in Poland. The first Equality Parade was organized on May 1st, 2001, and around 300 participants attended (Chetaille 2011, p. 125). During the following two years, 2002 and 2003, the number of participants in the Equality Parade was 2,000 and 3,500 respectively, drawing people from all over the country (Gruszczynska 2009, p. 315). During the years 2001–2004, individual members of ILGCN-Polska organized the Equality Parade. For the purpose of organizing the parade in 2005, the three largest Polish LGBT organizations at the time – ILGCN-Polska, KPH and Lambda Warszawa – formed the Equality Foundation, which until 2010 served as the main organizer of the parade. Since 2011, the Equality Parade has been organized by an informal group involving individuals and organizations (Parada Równości 2016).

According to the autobiography of Szymon Niemiec, the leading activist of ILGCN-Polska, the idea for a Pride parade came after gay and lesbian groups for the first time had been invited to participate in a Women's March on March 8th, 2001 (the so-called *Manifa* march). The experience of marching in the streets, and the fact that the group shortly thereafter watched a documentary about the Pride parade in Sydney, led to the decision that a parade was going to be organized in Warsaw (Niemiec 2006, pp. 129–130). In contrast to other gay and lesbian Pride parades, the organizers, however, did not want to use the names "pride" or "gay" and "lesbian":

> We didn't want to call our march a Parade of Gays and Lesbians, because we knew well, that the city wouldn't agree to allow for such a march. Besides, we didn't want our parade to gather solely homosexual persons, but everyone also, who met with injustice or social exclusion. [...] So, why couldn't we call that the Equality Parade? Equality for everyone. In this way, the name was born. It's been used by media, politicians and also ordinary people to define marches of sexual minorities in Poland. It's not a Gay Pride, but Equality Parade.
> (Niemiec 2006, pp. 130–131)

The media coverage of the first Equality Parade was very limited, and the first parade didn't seem to create that much public controversy (Niemiec 2006, p. 135). Robert Biedroń, one of the founders of KPH and between 2011 and 2014 a MP for the anti-clerical and social liberal party *Twój Ruch* (Your Movement), recalls his impressions from walking in the first Equality Parade.

> It was very peaceful, very small. It was maybe 300 people walking on the street. Nobody harassed us. There were a few police protecting us. Me and one other guy, we were the only public figures who appeared at this Gay Pride. Well, a happy day, very proud, at this time, when I was present there, I didn't feel that it was an exceptional moment. Today I see how exceptional and important it was, but at that time, when you were there, I didn't have that feeling. I was happy that we were able to march, I was happy that something was changing, that

this will be a beginning of something, but I didn't know what, but it was very important.

In a few years similar parades were organized in other Polish cities, for instance the March of Tolerance in Cracow and the March of Equality in Poznań, which were both first held in 2004 (Gruszczynska 2009, p. 315). During the years following 2001 the LGBT movement in Poland was also in other ways becoming more present in the public debate, for example, through a billboard campaign organized by KPH in 2002–2003, showing posters of same-sex couples holding hands (Chetaille 2011, p. 126). Despite the fact that Poland became a full member of the EU in May 2004, gay rights issues became a controversial issue in Polish politics. What was labeled "the homosexual lobby" increasingly became the target of campaigns by conservative and nationalist right-wing politicians during the years 2004–2007. After the EU entry, these issues once again became internal affairs for Poland, and the European Commission could not use the prospect of EU membership to demand the introduction of discrimination legislation. During the nationalist government between 2005 and 2007, attempts were instead made to ban "homosexual propaganda" and gay rights that had been planned to be implemented were instead revoked (O'Dwyer 2012, pp. 344–348).

The increasing polarization around LGBT issues also led conservative right-wing politicians and other actors from the nationalist-conservative right to target the parades. This took the form of counter-movement actions during the parades, such as physical attacks on marchers and efforts to block the parades. Behind these actions were members of the nationalist conservative party *Liga Polskich Rodzin*, LPR (League of Polish Families) and its youth organization *Młodzież Wszechpolska* (All-Polish Youth). Such attacks took place at the March of Tolerance in Cracow in 2004 and 2006 and at the March of Equality in Poznań in 2004. In cities with conservative right-wing mayors, the parade organizers were denied to carry through their marches. This happened in 2005 in both Cracow and Poznań, and in the latter city 68 activists were detained when attempting to carry through the parade. Even if the Equality Parade had been allowed in Warsaw in 2001–2003, the city's mayor Lech Kaczyński decided to ban the parade both in 2004 and 2005. Between 2001 and 2003, Kaczyński had been the party leader of the national-conservative party *Prawo i Sprawiedliwość*, PiS (Law and Justice), and used an anti-LGBT stance to profile his party and himself for upcoming elections (the 2005–2007 Polish government was based on PiS and LPR, and in 2005–2010 Kaczyński was the president of Poland). Furthermore, in 2005, Kaczyński allowed All-Polish Youth to organize a counter-demonstration called the "Parade of Normality" (Selinger 2008, p. 19; Gruszczynska 2009, p. 315; Binnie and Klesse 2012, p. 448; O'Dwyer 2012, p. 346).

In Warsaw the organizers of the Equality Parade nevertheless obeyed the mayor's ban. Instead in 2004 a rally outside the city hall was staged, however on June 11th, 2005 a march of 5,000 people defied the authorities with the support and participation of many prominent politicians from Poland as well as from other EU countries (for instance Poland's Vice Prime Minister and the Deputy Marshal of the parliament, and MPs from Germany) (Ayoub 2016, p. 53; Parada Równości 2016). The ban of the Warsaw Equality Parade apparently led to increased support for the LGBT activists amongst both domestic and EU-level political elites. In the interview with Robert, one of the organizers of the "illegal" 2005 parade, he stressed that this event was a decisive moment for the Polish LGBT movement:

> Before it was banned, it was regarded mainly as the business of LGBT people [...]. Others were not interested in that. When the mayor of Warsaw started to ban it, something changed. A lot of intellectuals, politicians who were only observing, not supporting the event, they now said: "This is a fundamental freedom, it does not only concern LGBT people anymore, it concerns all of us. Today the mayor of Warsaw bans the Equality Parade for LGBT people; tomorrow he might ban another event which concerns us." At this stage in 2004 and 2005 I could see the shift in perceiving LGBT rights in Poland. Many people who would never join the gay pride, the Equality Parade, they joined us in 2005 and they marched in the front, just to symbolize the importance of the freedom to assembly [...]. Many public figures, actors, film directors, and intellectuals who thought "this is not only LGBT rights, this is human rights, and we must be here," and they were there. So that was a big shift in 2005.

In the aftermath of these events, both domestic and supranational judicial bodies became involved in efforts to counteract the decisions to ban the parades. In September 2005 the regional administrative court in Warsaw claimed that the Mayor's decision was illegal (Selinger 2008, p. 20). Some of the organizers of the Warsaw parade also filed a lawsuit against Poland with the European Court of Human Rights, ECtHR, for denying them their democratic rights. In 2007, the ECtHR decided that the decision was in violation of central articles of the European Convention on Human Rights (Holzhacker 2013, p. 10; Ayoub 2016, pp. 84–85).

Despite the polarization around LGBT issues in Poland and the country's nationalist-conservative government in 2005–2007, the LGBT movement both broadened and intensified its activities. In particular KPH, with Robert Biedroń as president, conducted extensive lobbying both in Poland and toward the EU institutions. After 2007, when the PiS/LPR government collapsed due to a corruption scandal, the anti-gay rhetoric became less central for Polish right-wing parties, and anti-gay activism was weakened (O'Dwyer 2012, pp. 346–347).

The new alliances that were being forged and the political developments also led to the election of central LGBT activists in the Polish parliament.

Both Robert Biedroń and the transgender activist Anna Grodzka became candidates for the newly formed social liberal and anti-clerical party *Twój Ruch* (Your Movement), which had gay rights as one of its main political foci. In 2011 the party became the third largest in the parliament (with 11 percent of the vote), and both were elected as MPs. In the case of Biedroń, he was the first openly gay male to become a Polish MP, and in the case of Grodzka, she was one of the first openly transgender MPs in Europe. The increased focus on LGBT rights also pressed other parties to adopt policies that were supportive of some gay rights, even the large liberal-conservative party *Platforma Obywatelska*, PO (Civic Platform) (O'Dwyer and Vermeersch 2016, pp. 134–136).

In July 2010 Warsaw hosted EuroPride, and it was the first EuroPride to be held in a post-communist country. The event was organized by the Equality Foundation, which had been coordinating the Equality Parade since 2005. Thousands of activists came from across Europe and about 8,000 participated in the march (O'Dwyer 2012, p. 347; Holzhacker 2013, pp. 10–11).

Since 2011 an informal group called the "organizing committee" arranges the annual Equality Parade in Warsaw. Amongst those organizations that have supported or taken part in this committee, we find LGBT organizations, political parties – SDPL (the Social Democrats), *Partia Zieloni* (The Greens), and Your Movement – disability organizations, animal rights organizations, Amnesty, etc. Since 2014 the LGBT Business Forum Foundation has held a conference parallel with the Equality Parade, in order to promote equality and non-discrimination for LGBT people in the workplace. Economic support to the Equality Parade is, however, limited and only very few companies contribute. Even multinational corporations that usually brand themselves as LGBT friendly are hesitant to contribute economically to the parade, something the organizers see as reflecting that these companies believe that such sponsoring would harm their brand amongst Polish consumers (interviews with Yga and Andreas).

Still today, the parade in Warsaw is called the Equality Parade, and for the organizers this seems to be a very important way of how it is framed. According to Jej Perfekcyjność, one of the principle organizers of the parade in 2011–2016, to stress that the parade is about more than only LGBT issues is even more important today than it was in the beginning.

> We are still trying to underline as much as possible that this is about equality for all people that are excluded, and for opposing exclusion in a general sense [...] Of course the media usually stress the LGBT part in the parade and show the LGBT community since it's very colorful and happy and, well, gay. But I think each and every year we are managing to point out to the media that it is an equality parade, not a gay parade and I think that the message is now coming across and one can say that the media is starting to understand that. That this is not

the Polish version of Gay Pride, but this is a Polish way of enjoying equality and to fight for equality as well.

Even though the Equality Parade in Warsaw is the largest Pride event in Poland, parades are today also organized in Cracow, Poznań, Wrocław, Gdańsk, Łódź and Toruń (InterPride 2016, p. 66; interviews with Yga and Jej). Although mobilizing relatively small numbers of demonstrators, the Equality Parades are now an established annual event in Poland.

History of Pride in the Czech Republic

Homosexuality tolerated if held private

The Czech Republic provides an idiosyncratic Pride history. Czechoslovakia decriminalized homosexuality already in 1962 (Hildebrandt 2014), and by Central and Eastern European standards the attitudes to homosexuality have been comparatively tolerant (O'Dwyer 2013). Prague was nevertheless the last capital city in the region to organize a Pride parade.

Both academic texts on the history of homosexuality in the Czech Republic and our respondents' reflections support the impression that homosexuality is largely regarded as a private matter in the country, and although largely tolerated as such, expressing it in public has not been as accepted. The legalization of homosexuality in the 1960s was coupled with legislation stipulating the public display of homosexuality as a public offense. The late 1960s in Czechoslovakia witnessed a short period of liberalization and democratization of the socialist system, labeled the "Prague Spring" of 1968. This was followed by the Soviet crackdown and a period of repressive "normalization," i.e. the repression of anyone dissenting to Soviet Socialism. Sloboda (2010, p. 32) links this period to the entrenched strategy of keeping homosexuality private in Czech life.

> The period of Normalization taught Czech people to go with the flow, not to step out of line, on the outside pretend to be active (go to parades, or local party meetings) but live their private, true lives behind closed doors (or at their weekend houses).

This impression that homosexuality still is a private matter, tolerated when practiced behind closed doors, was expressed by several of our activist interviewees. Another defining characteristic of the Czech context, according to Sokolová (2004), is the strongly medicalized discourse about homosexuality, which was established in the 1990s. Long (1999) traces this medicalization further back to the flourishing of Czech sexology already in the mid-twentieth century. According to this view, homosexuality is an inborn trait, which is fixed and not affected by society or culture. This perspective was adopted in the rhetoric of the domestic LGBT movement.

While the advantage of the notion of innate homosexuality is that it safeguards against the conservative and religious perspective that homosexuality is an immoral choice, it excludes critical constructionist ideas about gender and sexuality, which, according to Sokolová (2004), has rendered it difficult to incorporate feminist perspectives in the movement.

O'Dwyer (2013) notes that the Czech LGBT movement has had a very strong NGO-orientation. In contrast to most other countries from the former Soviet bloc, Czechoslovakia had gay rights groups before 1989, already established in the 1970s, originally as therapeutic groups intended to help gay people come to terms with their sexual orientation. In 1988, a nationally based organization was formed – the Socio-Therapeutic Club of Homosexuals (later called Lambda). Through supportive medical professionals, these groups managed to gain early state support, and the organization received legal recognition in early 1990. Later the same year, lesbian and gay organizations from different parts of the country formed an umbrella organization – *Sdružení organizací homosexuálních občanů* (SOHO) (Association of Organizations of Homosexual Citizens) – which was to become the main promoter of political reforms on lesbian and gay issues during the following decade. While this umbrella group ensured some connections to a grassroots movement, the tactics of the movement were never based on broad grassroots mobilization. Instead the tactical focus was from the start political behind-the-scenes lobbying from a decidedly pragmatist starting point. Broader protest actions or Pride parades were judged to be too provocative. This approach arguably inhibited the growth of an identity-based movement and little effort was made to change broader values in society regarding LGBT issues. Long (1999) claims that the organization, although including lesbian groups, was strongly male dominated, and that a male president was more or less taken for granted among many activists.

The strategy of centralization, professionalization and backstage lobbying was reinforced in 2000, with the replacement of SOHO with the new organization *Gay Iniciativa* (Gay Initiative), which consolidated the leadership of the markedly pragmatic activist Jiří Hromada. This new organization, according to O'Dwyer (2013), deliberately marginalized the issue of adoption rights in their lobbying for same-sex partnerships. Dissatisfaction with the leadership of Hromada led to an organizational split and the formation of the Gay and Lesbian League, which had a stronger support for identity-based approaches. Curiously, both organizations disbanded after the passing of a same-sex partnership law in 2006, which left a vacuum that eventually opened up for a somewhat more grassroots-based movement.

Latecomers to Pride

The first Pride-like event organized in the Czech Republic was a rainbow festival organized in the small tourist resort Karlovy Vary in 1998. This was held on a very small scale until 2001 (Seidl 2012, pp. 391–392), and is said to have included a small Pride parade with not more than 100 participants.

In 2008 a "Queer parade" was organized in Brno, the second largest city of the Czech Republic. The parade attracted only a few hundred people and was harassed by right-wing counterdemonstrators, who managed to get past the police to attack the Pride participants. The small influx of participants was a significant disappointment for the organizers. Nevertheless, the next year a parade was organized in the city of Tabor. In 2010 the event was again held in Brno, this time with an exceptionally high level of police protection that, although prevented any attacks, also severely obstructed the visibility of the march. Several of the individuals organizing these events were members of feminist queer groups at the Masaryk University in Brno, and the events are described by our respondents as relatively politicized, with an explicit "queer" label.

The first Pride parade in Prague was organized in 2011. The initiative was taken by a group largely composed of expatriates from other parts of Europe who thought that Prague as a European capital city needed a Pride event. The organizing committee was later complemented by some native Czech activists with experiences from various NGOs. The parade was initially less politicized than its predecessors in Brno and Tabor, but the level of conflict around the first event escalated due to hostile statements by the president Vaclav Klaus (representing the conservative party *Občanská demokratická strana* [ODS]), who distanced himself from what he termed the "homosexualism" of Pride (Konviser 2011). He did this in support of his senior adviser Petr Hajek who had called homosexuals "deviants" and the upcoming Pride festival a "political demonstration of a world with deformed values" (Tabery 2011). Willem, a co-organizer of Dutch origin says:

> The funny thing is at first, when we started to organize it, mainly the Czech response from the local Czech gays was like "Do we really need it? Do we have to go out on the streets?" Because we have registered partnership here [...] and we have this gay-infrastructure, you can be happy as a gay guy in Prague, so "Why do you need to go on the streets and manifest yourself?" [...] But I think after the first Pride you could see that change in mentality within the Czech gay community – that they really saw that it was necessary especially because the first Prague Pride met loads of resistance from the government. The President at that time – it was Vaclav Klaus – he was publicly opposing Pride events, he called gays "deviants," he didn't say it himself, but his spokesman said like "Why should deviants go on the streets like that? We have nothing against homosexuality, but we are against homosexualism." so he tried to put it as some sort of political movement like communism, socialism, or liberalism, whatever.

These statements, and similar ones by Klaus' affiliates, appear to have resulted in a backlash against the conservative government in terms of increased media attention and support from non-LGBT Czechs who were provoked by the reactionary tone of the president, who had overstepped the boundaries of the politically acceptable (not unlike the critique against the mayor of Warsaw, described in the section on Poland). Also, the city Mayor in Prague, Bohuslav Svoboda (ODS), expressed his support for the event. Petr, one of the initial co-organizers, points to the enormous rise in media coverage following the comments about homosexuals as "deviants":

> Suddenly a storm happened you know [...] and all the media started to pay attention to the Prague Pride. [...] The first year we received more than a thousand hits in the Czech media, which is a lot. If you ... The second year was 350 just for comparison.

During subsequent years the Prague Pride parade has become an annual event that gathers LGBT people from across the country. Since it started, however, only one Pride parade has been hosted in a town outside Prague (at the time of writing): in Plzen in September 2017.[18] The activists in Brno (when interviewed in 2014) did not appear to seriously consider organizing smaller Pride parades. One of the Brno activists says:

> I think that many of the organizers are just burned out, they don't feel like organizing anything. We have something, which is called "Pride Parade Echoes" – when there are some discussions and movies during the time of the Parade or before and after, so the people could visit everything, all the events in Brno and then go to Prague. I think more or less people accept that the main thing is in Prague now, because there are more people who can cooperate, more organizations as well, they can do the lobbying in the parliament as well. The feeling is like "we started it, we were the first actually," but we sort of accept that Prague is the capital and I think that more people really come to Prague than to Brno.

Apart from pointing out that Prague is a more attractive tourist location, she also notes the importance of the attitudes expressed by local authorities in relation to Pride:

> In Prague there was better cooperation with the police as well. Also the Mayor of the city said that he's quite happy about this Parade, [...] not because he's a human rights activist, but because he saw it as kind of promotion for Prague and business and even his name was on some of the posters. In his political party [ODS] many people were against it, but he sort of defended his view. Although I don't approve of his politics, I think it was a big thing for him to do, because in Brno no

Mayor, no politicians – except the Greens, who were always in the opposition – stepped up and said "I'm here with you too."

The same year as the first Prague Pride parade, PROUD, a new LGBT organization was also established. This seems to mark a turning point toward a broader movement that encompasses a wider spectrum of positions within the LGBT movement as well as an intention to push legislation further, e.g. toward adoption rights, manifested in the Jsme Fér (We Are Fair) campaign launched in 2017. Still PROUD is not a mass-based organization but is composed of a small number of individual members (about 20) as well as a handful of organizations, including Prague Pride.

The imprints of local and national contexts

Our study is based on empirical materials collected between 2011 and 2017, hence we offer synchronic comparative analyses of Pride parades in seven European countries and Mexico. Nevertheless, we claim that a historical background, however brief, is vital for our understanding of Pride parades in these countries today. First of all, the length of the tradition and its degree of institutionalization is a potentially important factor that varies across the countries in our sample, with some Pride traditions, like the UK's, harking back to the early 1970s and others, like the Czech Republic's, which started around 2010. Second, traditions become institutionalized and self-perpetuating – the major parade cities, the route, and which actors typically organize the event. Already large events also raise expectations, and create incentives for attracting private sponsors in order to cover rising costs. Third, the history of the movement and its main political strategies and focal issues also has consequences for form and content of the parades. The national histories that we have accounted for also reveal that countries differ in terms of the degree of centralization of Pride. Capital cities are often the location of the main Pride events, but whereas some countries have few or no other events outside the capital (the Czech Republic and Netherlands), others have disseminated to numerous small cities and towns (Sweden and the UK).

In terms of international dissemination, we identified two rather distinct "waves" in the spread of the Pride tradition. The first can be dated to the 1970s in the aftermath of Stonewall and Gay Liberation and appears to have involved very little active promotion from any centralized actors. The second wave came in the 1990s with the establishment of international events like EuroPride in 1992 and WorldPride in 2000 and the concomitant promotion of the unifying label "Pride." However, the traditions of Pride parades in the cities and countries included in our study have taken very different trajectories. Some cases, like the Warsaw Equality parade, even raise the question as to whether the traditions we study are too heterogeneous to make international comparison of the events plausible. As we discuss in the next chapter, the parade format, the underlying cultural script of coming out, and the iconography of the rainbow flag, nevertheless, unite the events. So, for sure there are similarities, however, political and cultural contexts have had a strong influence on the historical trajectories of Pride performances. The preconditions for staging large and inclusive Pride parades vary among the countries included in our sample. In the following chapter we will discuss these mobilizing contexts for Pride parades today. As Adam, Duyvendak and Krouwel (1999, p. 9, emphasis in original) have pointed out, "gay and lesbian movements are both *a part of* and *apart from* the societies around them, both resisting and participating in – even reproducing – dominant public discourses." Pride performances are embedded in the societies where they are staged. National (and even city) political and cultural contexts play a crucial role in the development of Pride parades. These mobilizing contexts set the stage for the parades included in our study.

Notes

1 See Murray (1996).
2 http://www.interpride.org/?page=history, accessed August 30, 2016.
3 http://www.interpride.org/?page=WorldPride, accessed September 20, 2017.
4 For a brief history of Europride and EPOA, written by one of the initiators, see https://www.france.qrd.org/assocs/epoa/history.en.html, accessed September 21, 2017. For the constitution of EPOA, see http://epoa.eu/wp-content/uploads/2015/01/EPOA_Constitution_191011.pdf, accessed September 21, 2017.
5 http://www.pinknews.co.uk/2012/06/28/pride-london-funding-shortfall-sees-worldpride-heavily-scaled-back, accessed February 6, 2017.
6 www.reguliers.net/history-gaypride.php, accessed July 10, 2016.
7 Anita Bryant, a popular singer at the time, became known as an outspoken opponent of gay rights and for her 1977 "Save Our Children" campaign to repeal a local ordinance in Dade County, Florida, that prohibited discrimination on the basis of sexual orientation. The campaign was based on conservative Christian beliefs regarding the sinfulness of homosexuality and the perceived threat of homosexual recruitment of children and child molestation.
8 www.reguliers.net/history-gaypride.php, accessed July 10, 2016.
9 www.reguliers.net/history-gaypride.php, accessed July 10, 2016.
10 Diego Dominguez Cartona wrote most of the section on Mexico.
11 Okiabeth derives from the Mayan words *olling iskan katuntat bebeth thot*, which means "women warriors that open spaces by spreading flowers."
12 ARCI (Associazione Ricreativa e Culturale Italiana) is an independent association for the promotion of social and civil rights. With its 5,400 clubs and more than 1,100,000 members, it represents a broad structure for democratic participation. ARCI is committed to the promotion and development of associations as a factor for social cohesion, as places for civil and democratic commitment, for asserting peace and the rights of citizenship as well as to fight any form of exclusion and discrimination. https://www.linkedin.com/company/arci—associazione-ricreativa-e-culturale-italiana, accessed August 25, 2017.
13 In Italy the gay and lesbian movement has always been shortened to GLB and later GLBT.
14 www.arcigay.it, accessed November 11, 2015; Nardi (1998).

15 www.arcigay.it, accessed November 12, 2015.
16 National Association of Lesbian/Gay Pride Coordinators (NAL/GPC), before changing the name to International Association of Lesbian/Gay Pride Coordinators (IAL/GPC) in October 1985, the International Association of Lesbian, Gay, Bisexual and Transgender Pride Coordinators at the conference in West Hollywood, California, and eventually to InterPride in the late 1990s (www.interpride.org).
17 Since the first Gay Pride in 1994 the events had been organized in late June.
18 See, e.g., www.romea.cz/en/news/czech/czech-extremists-abuse-lgbt-pride-march-in-town-of-plzen-but-fail-to-block-it, accessed February 12, 2018.

References

Adam, B.D. (1995). *The rise of a gay and lesbian movement*. Boston, MA: Twayne Publishers.

Adam, B.D., Duyvendak, J.W., and Krouwel, A. (1999). Gay and lesbian movements beyond borders? In Adam, B.D., Duyvendak, J.W., and Krouwel, A. (Eds) *The global emergence of gay and lesbian politics* (pp. 344–371). Philadelphia, PA: Temple University Press.

Armstrong, E.A. (2002). *Forging gay identities: Organizing sexuality in San Francisco, 1950-1994*. Chicago, IL: University of Chicago Press.

Armstrong, E.A., and Crage, S.M. (2006). Movements and memory: The making of the Stonewall myth. *American Sociological Review*, 71(5), 724–751.

Ayoub, P. (2016). *When states come out: Europe's sexual minorities and the politics of visibility*. New York: Cambridge University Press.

Bernstein, M. (2002). Identities and politics. *Social Science History*, 26(3), 531–581.

Binnie, J., and Klesse, C. (2012). Solidarities and tensions: Feminism and transnational LGBTQ politics in Poland. *European Journal of Women's Studies*, 19(4), 444–459.

Browne, K., and Bakshi, M.L. (2013). *Ordinary in Brighton? LGBT, activisms and the city*. Farnham: Ashgate Publishing, Ltd.

Carter, D. (2004). *Stonewall: The riots that sparked the revolution*. New York: St. Martins Press.

Chetaille, A. (2011). Poland: Sovereignty and sexuality in post-socialist times. In Tremblay, M., Paternotte, D., and Johnson, C. (Eds) *The lesbian and gay movement and the state: Comparative insights into a transformed relationship* (pp. 119–133). Farnham: Ashgate.

Colpani, G., and Habed, A.J. (2014). "In Europe it's different": Homonationalism and peripheral desires for Europe. In Ayoub, P.M., and Paternotte, D. (Eds) *LGBT activism and the making of Europe. A rainbow Europe* (pp. 73–96). London and New York: Palgrave Macmillan.

Corrales, J. (2015). The politics of LGBT rights in Latin America and the Caribbean: Research Agenda. *European Review of Latin American and Caribbean Studies*, 100, 53–62.

d'Emilio, J. (1992). After Stonewall. In D'Emilio, J. (Ed.) *Making trouble: Essays on gay history, politics, and the university* (pp. 234–274). New York: Routledge.

d'Emilio, J. (1998 [1983]). *Sexual politics, sexual communities. The making of a homosexual minority in the United States, 1940–1970*. 2nd edition. Chicago and London: The University of Chicago Press.

Delessert, T., and Voegtli, M. (2012). *Homosexualités masculines en Suisse: De l'invisibilité aux mobilisations*. Lausanne: Presses polytechniques et universitaires romandes.
Diez, J. (2011). La trayectoria del movimiento Lésbico-Gay en México. *Estudios Sociológicos* 86 (May–August), 687–712.
Drissel, D. (2016). Rainbows of resistance: LGBTQ Pride parades contesting space in post-conflict Belfast. *Culture Unbound: Journal of Current Cultural Research*, 8(3), 240–262.
Duberman, M.B. (1993). *Stonewall*. New York: Dutton.
El País. (2015). El Supremo de México avala el matrimonio homosexual. *El País*. June 16. Available at: http://internacional.elpais.com/internacional/2015/06/15/a ctualidad/ 1434391282_348815.html [accessed February 15, 2016].
El Universal. (2016). La persecución gay en México, historia de odio. *El Universal*. September 25. Available at: www.eluniversal.com.mx/articulo/cultura/letras/ 201 6/09/24/la-persecucion-gay-en-mexico-historia-de-odio [accessed February 15, 2016].
Encarnación, O.G. (2016). *Out in the periphery: Latin America's gay rights revolution*. Oxford: Oxford University Press.
Engel, S.M. (2001). *The unfinished revolution: Social movement theory and the gay and lesbian movement*. Cambridge: Cambridge University Press.
Excélsior (2016). Peña Nieto anuncia reforma que reconocerá matrimonio gay en todo el país. *Excélsior*. May 18. Available at: www.excelsior.com.mx/nacional/20 16/05/17/1093190 [accessed February 15, 2016].
Figueroa, M. (2003). Chronology mínima: del clóset a la calle. *Letra S*. 5 June. Available at: www.jornada.unam.mx/2003/06/05/ls-cronologia.html [accessed February 15, 2016].
Foweraker, J., and Craig, A. (1990). *Popular movements and political change in Mexico*. Boulder, CO: Lynne Reinner.
Galván Díaz, F. (1998). *El sida en México: los efectos sociales*. México: UAM.
Ghaziani, A. (2008). *The dividends of dissent. How conflict and culture work in lesbian and gay marches on Washington*. Chicago, IL: University of Chicago Press.
González Pérez, M. de J. (2005). Marcha del orgullo por la diversidad sexual. Manifestación colectiva que desafía las políticas del cuerpo. *El Cotidiano*, 131 (May–June), 90–97.
Gruszczynska, A. (2009). Sowing the seeds of solidarity in public space: Case study of the Poznan March of Equality. *Sexualities*, 12(3), 312–333.
Hallgren, H. (2008). *När lesbiska blev kvinnor: Lesbiskfeministiska kvinnors diskursproduktion rörande kön, sexualitet, kropp och identitet under 1970- och 1980-talen i Sverige*. Göteborg: Kabusa böcker.
Hayton, R. (2010). Conservative Party modernisation and David Cameron's politics of the family. *The Political Quarterly*, 81(4), 492–500.
Hekma, G. (2000). Netherlands. *Encyclopedia of Gay Histories and Cultures*. New York and London: Garland Publishing, 639–640.
Hekma, G. (2014). A radical break with a Puritanical past: The Dutch case. In Hekma, G., and Giami, A. (Eds) *Sexual revolutions* (pp. 60–80). London: Palgrave Macmillan.
Hekma, G., and Duyvendak, J.W. (2007). Gay men and lesbians in the Netherlands. Seidman, S., Fischer, N., and Meeks, C. (Eds) *Handbook of the new sexuality studies* (pp. 411–415). New York: Routledge.

Hekma, G., and Duyvendak, J.W. (2011a). Queer Netherlands: A puzzling example. *Sexualities*, 14(6), 625–642.

Hekma, G., and Duyvendak, J.W. (2011b). The Netherlands: Depolitization of homosexuality and the homosexualization of politics. In Tremblay, M., Paternotte, D., and Johnson, C. (Eds) *The lesbian and gay movement and the state: Comparative insights into a transformed relationship* (pp. 103–118). Farnham: Ashgate.

Hernández, J.J., and Manrique, R. (1989). 10 años de movimiento gay en México: el brillo de la ausencia. *Boletín informativo para América Latina 3*. Guadalajara.

Hildebrandt, A. (2014). Routes to decriminalization: A comparative analysis of the legalization of same-sex sexual acts. *Sexualities*, 17(1–2), 230–253.

Holzhacker, R. (2013). State-sponsored homophobia and the denial of the right of assembly in Central and Eastern Europe: The "boomerang" and the "ricochet" between European organizations and civil society to uphold human rights. *Law & Policy* 35(1–2), 1–28.

Hughes, H.L. (2006). Gay and lesbian festivals: Tourism in the change from politics to party. In Picard, D., and Robinson, M. (Eds) *Festivals, tourism and social change. Remaking worlds* (pp. 238–254). Clevedon; Buffalo, and Toronto: Channel View Publications.

Humphreys, L. (1972). *Out of the closets: The sociology of homosexual liberation*. New York: Prentice Hall.

InterPride (2016). PrideRadar2016/2017. Available at: https://interpride.site-ym.com/resource/resmgr/docs/IP_Pride-Radar_2016-2017_Hig.pdf [accessed December 13, 2017].

Jackson, J. (2015). The homophile movement. In Paternotte, D., and Tremblay, M. (Eds) *The Ashgate research companion to lesbian and gay activism* (pp. 31–44). Farnham: Ashgate.

Johnston, J. (1994). Introduction. In McDarrah, F., and McDarrah, T. (Eds) *Gay Pride: Photographs from Stonewall to today* (pp. 1–9). Chicago, IL: a cappella books.

Kennedy, H. (1999). *The ideal gay man: The story of Der Kreis*. Binghamton, NY: The Haworth Press.

Kliszczyński, K. (2001). A child of a young democracy: The Polish gay movement, 1989–1999. In Flam, H. (Ed.) *Pink, purple, green: Women's, religious, environmental, and gay/lesbian movements in Central Europe today* (pp. 161–168). Boulder, CO: East European Monographs.

Knowles, J.J. (2009). *An investigation into the relationship between gay activism and the establishment of a gay community in Birmingham, 1967–1997*. Masters thesis, Department of Modern History, University of Birmingham, Birmingham.

Konviser, B. (2011). Czech leader is isolated in opposing gay parade. *New York Times*, August 15.

Kulpa, R., and Mizielinska, J. (Eds) (2011). *De-centring Western sexualities: Central and Eastern European perspectives*. Farnham and Burlington: Ashgate Publishing, Ltd.

Kymlicka, W. (2007). *Multicultural odysseys: Navigating the new international politics of diversity*. Oxford: Oxford University Press.

Laughland, O. (2012). Is Pride today about gay rights or just partying? *The Guardian* 07.06. Online at: www.theguardian.com/commentisfree/2012/jul/06/conversation-pride-gay-rights-party [accessed February 7, 2017].

Lent, A. (2001). *British social movements since 1945: Sex, colour, peace and power.* Basingstoke: Palgrave.

Long, S. (1999). Gay and lesbian movements in Eastern Europe: Romania, Hungary, and the Czech Republic. In Adam, B.D., Duyvendak, J.W., and Krouwel, A. (Eds) *The global emergence of gay and lesbian politics* (pp. 242–265). Philadelphia, PA: Temple University Press.

Lumsden, I. (1991). *Homosexualidad. Sociedad y Estado en México.* México: Sol Ediciones, Canadian Gay Archives.

Luongo, M. (2002). Rome's World Pride: Making the eternal city an international gay tourism destination. *GLA: A Journal of Lesbian and Gay Studies*, 8(1), 167–181.

Malagreca, M.A. (2007). *Queer Italy: Contexts, antecedents and representations.* New York: Peter Lang.

Malici, L. (2011). Queer in Italy: Italian televisibility and the "queerable" audience. In Downing, L., and Gillett, R. (Eds) *Queer in Europe: Contemporary case studies* (pp. 113–128). Farnham and Burlington: Ashgate.

Marti, M. (2000). Switzerland. In Zimmerman, B. (Ed.) *Encyclopedia of lesbian and gay histories and cultures. Vol. 1, Lesbian histories and cultures: An encyclopedia* (pp. 745–747). New York: Garland.

McFarland, K. (2012). *Cultural contestation and community building at LGBT Pride parades.* Unpublished doctoral dissertation; Chapel Hill, South Carolina.

McFarland Bruce, K. (2016). *Pride Parades: How a parade changed the world.* New York: NYU Press.

Mizielinska, J., and Kulpa, R. (2011). "Contemporary peripheries": Queer, studies, circulation of knowledge and East/West divide. In Kulpa, J., and Mizielinska, J. (Eds) *De-centring Western sexualities. Central and Eastern European perspectives* (pp. 11–26). Farnham and Burlington: Ashgate.

Mogrovejo, N. (1996). *Una propuesta de análisis histórico-metodológico del movimiento lésbico y sus amores con los movimientos homosexual y feminista en América Latina.* México: CDAHL.

Mudu, P. (2002). Repressive tolerance: The gay movement and the Vatican in Rome. *GeoJournal*, 58, 189–196.

Murray, S.O. (1996). *American gay.* Chicago, IL: University of Chicago Press.

Nagle, J. (2013). "Unity in diversity": Non-sectarian social movement challenges to the politics of ethnic antagonism in violently divided cities. *International Journal of Urban and Regional Research*, 37(1), 78–92.

Nardi, P.M. (1998). The globalization of the gay & lesbian socio-political movement: Some observations about Europe with a focus on Italy. *Sociological Perspectives*, 41(3), 567–586.

Niemiec, S. (2006). *Rainbow humming bird on the butt: Autobiography.* Warsaw: LGBT Press.

O'Dwyer, C. (2012). Does the EU help or hinder gay-rights movements in post-Communist Europe? The case of Poland. *East European Politics*, 28(4): 332–352.

O'Dwyer, C. (2013). From NGOs to naught: The rise and fall of the Czech gay-rights movement. In Jacobsson, K., and Saxonberg, S. (Eds) *Beyond NGO-ization: The development of social movements in Central and Eastern Europe* (pp. 117–138). Farnham: Ashgate Publishing.

O'Dwyer, C., and Vermeersch, P. (2016). From Pride to politics: Niche-party politics and LGBT rights in Poland. In Slootmaeckers, K., Touquet, H., and Vermeersch, P. (Eds) *The EU enlargement and gay politics: The impact of Eastern*

enlargement on rights, activism and prejudice (pp. 123–144). London: Palgrave Macmillan.
Parada Równości (2016). A brief history of Equality Parade. http://en.paradarownosci.eu/a-brief-history-of-equality-parade [accessed December 21, 2016].
Peralta, B. (2006). *Los nombres del arcoíris*. México: Nueva Imagen.
Peterson, A., Wahlström, M., and Wennerhag, M. (2017). "Normalized" Pride? Pride parade participants in six European countries. *Sexualities*. Article first published online August 3, 2017: https://doi.org/10.1177/1363460717715032.
Petersson, S-Å. (2000). En svensk homorörelse växer fram: RFSL 1950–2000. In Andreasson, M. (Ed.) *Homo i folkhemmet: Homo- och bisexuella i Sverige 1950–2000* (pp. 11–35). Göteborg: Anamma.
Plummer, K. (1999). The lesbian and gay movement in Britain: Schisms, solidarities, and social worlds. In Adam, B.D., Duyvendak, J.M., and Krouwel, A. (Eds) *The global emergence of gay and lesbian politics* (pp. 133–157). Philadelphia, PA: Temple University Press.
Rayside, D. (2001). The structuring of sexual minority activist opportunities in the political mainstream: Britain, Canada, and the United States. In Blasius, M. (Ed.) *Sexual identities, queer politics* (pp. 23–55). Princeton, NJ: Princeton University Press.
RFSL (2016). Pridekartan – din guide till landets Pridefestivaler. www.pridekartan.se [accessed October 22, 2016].
Rimmerman, C.A. (2015). *The lesbian and gay movements: Assimilation or liberation?* Boulder, CO: Westview Press.
Rydström, J. (2007a). Piska och morot: HBT mellan stat och folkrörelse 1944–2007. In Hedin, M. (Ed.) *Staten som vän eller fiende?: Individ och samhälle i svenskt 1900-tal* (pp. 157–192). Stockholm: Institutet för framtidsstudier.
Rydström, J. (2007b). Sweden 1864–1978: Beasts and beauties. In Rydström, J. (Ed.) *Sweden 1864–1978: Beasts and beauties* (pp. 183–213). Amsterdam: Aksant.
Schuyf, J., and Krouwel, A. (1999). The Dutch lesbian and gay movement: The politics of accommodation. In Adam, B.D., Duyvendak, J.M., and Krouwel, A. (Eds) *The global emergence of gay and lesbian politics* (pp. 158–183). Philadelphia, PA: Temple University Press.
Seidl, J., Wintr, J., and Nozar, L. (2012). *Od žaláře k oltáři. Emancipace homosexuality v českých zemích od roku 1867 do současnosti*. Prague: Host.
schwulengeschichte.ch. (2017). Epochen: Vom Scheiterhaufen zum Partnerschaftsgesetz. http://schwulengeschichte.ch/epochen/ [accessed March 14, 2017].
SDP noticias. (2016). Arriba marcha del Frente Nacional por la Familia al Ángel. *SDP Noticias*. September 24. Available at: www.sdpnoticias.com/local/ciudad-de-mexico/2016/09/24/arriba-marcha-del-frente-nacional-por-la-familia-al-angel [accessed February 15, 2016].
Selinger, M. (2008). Intolerance toward gays and lesbians in Poland. *Human Rights Review* 9(1), 15–27.
Shepard, B. (2005). Play, creativity, and the new community organizing. *Journal of Progressive Human Services*, 16(2), 47–69.
Shepard, B. (2010). *Queer political performance and protest*. New York: Routledge.
Sloboda, Z. (2010). Specifics of the contemporary Czech homosexual community: History, evolution and ambivalences. In Clarke, C. (Ed.) *Examining aspects of sexualities and the self* (pp. 3–19). Oxford: Inter Disciplinary Press.

Sokolová, V. (2004). Don't get pricked! Representation and the politics of sexuality in the Czech Republic. In Forrester, S., Zaborowksa, M.J., and Gapova, A. (Eds) *Over the Wall/After the fall: Postcommunist cultures through an East-West gaze* (pp. 251–267). Indianapolis IN: Indiana University Press.
Stockholm Pride (2016). Föreningen Stockholm Pride. www.stockholmpride.org/foreningen/om/ [accessed October 22, 2016].
Szulc, L. (2011). Queer in Poland: Under construction. In Downing, L., and Gillett, R. (Eds) *Queer in Europe: Contemporary case studies* (pp. 159–172). Farnham and Burlington: Ashgate.
Söderström, G. (1999). Bildandet av RFSL and Föreningsliv. In Silverstolpe, F., and Söderström, G. (Eds) *Sympatiens hemlighetsfulla makt: Stockholms homosexuella 1860–1960.* (pp. 630–677). Stockholm: Stockholmia.
Tabery, E. (2011). In Prague, a fight for gay rights goes international. *The Atlantic*, September 14, 2011. Online at: www.theatlantic.com/international/archive/2011/09/in-prague-a-fight-for-gay-rights-goes-international/245064/ [March 14, 2017].
Tamagne, F. (2006). *A history of homosexuality in Europe: Berlin, London, Paris, 1919–1939. Volume 1.* New York: Algora.
Tiemeyer, P. (2013). *Plane queer: Labor, sexuality, and AIDS in the history of male flight attendants.* Oakland, CA: University of California Press.
Tremblay, S. (2015). "And it is still not much different in Europe!" Understanding and translating anxiety: Homophile emotional ties across the Atlantic, 1950–1965. *Global Histories: A Student Journal*, 1(1), 61–78.
Weeks, J. ([1977] 1990). *Coming out: Homosexual politics in Britain from the nineteenth century to the present. Revised and updated version.* London: Quartet Books.
Wennerhag, M. (2017). Pride anländer till Sverige: En resa i två etapper. In Wijkström, F., Reuter, M., and Emami, A. (Eds) *Civilsamhället i det transnationella rummet* (pp. 33–61). Stockholm: European Civil Society Press.
Whisnant, C.J. (2012). *Male homosexuality in West Germany: Between persecution and freedom, 1945–69.* Basingstoke: Palgrave Macmillan.
Williams, J. (2016). What is the point of Manchester Pride? Thirty years of partying and politics... but the battle isn't over yet. *Manchester Evening News*, August 27, 2016. Online at: www.manchestereveningnews.co.uk/news/greater-manchester-news/whats-the-point-manchester-pride-11806275 [accessed March 13, 2017].
Zurich Pride (2016). Zurich Pride festival Geschichte. http://zurichpridefestival.ch/geschichte/ [accessed March 14, 2017].

3 Context Matters

We seek to understand how, and in what ways, an international phenomenon such as Pride parades, which undeniably bear similarities in their formats, choreographies, actors, scripts and props, are nonetheless impacted by their national and local mobilizing contexts. LGBT movements are strongly influenced by local, national and even regional political and cultural contexts; all movements show a clear local and national imprint, manifesting what Adam, Duyvendak and Krouwel (1999) have called a national "paradigm." In our analyses we uncover the dynamics producing *both* similarities *and* differences between LGBT Pride parades.

Diffusion and similarities

Ken Plummer (1992, p. 17) has observed that,

> same-sex experiences have become increasingly fashioned through the interconnectedness of the world. ... The gay and lesbian movements house identities, politics, cultures, markets, intellectual programmes which nowadays quite simply know no national boundaries. Homosexualities have become globalized.

The diffusion of the concept of a gay identity, the circulation on worldwide media (including the Internet) of expressive and symbolic gay culture throughout the world, and the appearance of organized national LGBT movements, as well as international LGBT organizations, to effect legal and social changes illustrate some aspects of this globalization (see McAdam and Rucht, 1993 for seminal work on the cross-national diffusion of movement ideas, strategies and tactics). We investigate cross-national *similarities* by analyzing how diffusion processes may provoke similarities among some of the features of Pride parades from one country to the other. To be sure, we found similar aspects of the Pride parades across countries included in our sample: (1) issues, themes and goals; (2) strategies, tactics and forms of action; and (3) cultural frames, ideas and discourses (taken from Guigni's [2002] list of six potential aspects of social movements that can potentially diffuse across countries). We found cross-national similarities, or more accurately, relative cross-national similarities, in the Pride events in all of these aspects; not least, the underlying cultural script – the "coming out" performance of individual and collective pride and, of course, the parade format and the iconography of rainbow flags.

In focus for Ayoub and Paternotte (2014), Adam (1995), Chabot and Duyvendak (2002) and Swiebel (2009) are processes of Europeanization and globalization in gay and lesbian politics that can occur when groups deliberately work together and coordinate activities across national borders, for example, with the formation in 1978 of the International Lesbian, Gay, Bisexual, Trans and Intersex Association (ILGA), ILGA-Europe, European Pride Organizers Association (EPOA) in 1991, and InterPride in 1982. In addition, in Europe we find the Network European Families Association, the European Forum of LGBT Christian Groups, and RainbowRose, the European network of Socialist Parties' LGBT caucuses, which further bear witness to the transnational ambitions of European LGBT movements for defining "Europe" (Ayoub and Paternotte 2014). These organizations have provided venues for Pride parade organizers in Europe and across the globe to exchange experiences and learn from one another. Scholars have also highlighted how these organizations have been important vehicles for the process of diffusion of ideas and action repertoires. They point out that the processes of Europeanization and globalization are highly linked and influence the strategies pursued by LGBT movements.

Arguing against Europeanization theory's expectations, O'Dwyer (2012) in a study of the gay rights movement in Poland finds that the EU has influenced movement development, but more through the unintended consequences of backlash than through the mechanisms of conditionality and social learning. While the EU made respect for minority rights, including those of sexual minorities, a requirement for membership, after entry these rights have been difficult to proactively defend. In the case of Poland, the extension of gay rights is hindered by a constellation of domestic factors: the post-communist legacy, with its twin impediments of a weak civil society and a history of state repression, as well as an influential and politically active Catholic church. Putnam (1988) has introduced the concept of the "two-level game" to analyze the link between international developments and domestic politics. While the political opportunity structures of European lesbian and gay movements have expanded into a two-level game with the gradual advancement of the EU into the area of public policy, the conflict-ridden contestation of these issues remains largely grounded at the member state level. Whereas processes of globalization in which both international and EU level organizations and other national groups are sources of inspiration, ideas, successful strategies, and resources, these are nonetheless domestically translated to adapt to national contexts. Pride organizers, as well as Pride participants, translate the opportunities opened by Pride events in relation to the local and national contexts within which they are embedded.

Pride parades, like labor movements' annual ritual of May Day, have travelled globally and carry with them shared elements that lend them, at least on the surface, manifest similarities. However, Pride parades, just as May Day rituals, are translated to adapt to national and even local political and cultural contexts (Peterson and Reiter 2016). So while at first blush we observed some similarities – a "thin coherence" – in the events we studied, a more careful examination revealed marked differences. The parade format, the underlying cultural script of coming out, and the iconography of the rainbow flag, we argue, are the "cultural anchors" that moor the performances, providing what Ghaziani and Baldassarri (2011) call a "thin coherence" to Pride performances across the mobilizing contexts we have studied. Pride organizers use these cultural anchors to secure their mobilization efforts

> around a political logic (e.g., we march to fight against discrimination and to demand equality), a cultural logic (e.g., we march to influence public opinion, to educate society about gay people, and to demand acceptance), and an organizational logic (e.g. ... we present ourselves as united).
>
> (p. 198)

"Cultural anchors" are polyvocal. The "thin coherence" we observed in all of the parades we studied, however, allowed the organizers and participants to translate and give new cultural meanings to their events. In the following pages we will look more closely at the factors which produce the differences in the choreographies, actors, scripts, costumes and props, that we have observed in different mobilizing contexts.

National and local imprints

While arguments can be made to make a case for the emergence of a more global gay identity and LGBT movement, there remain specific structural conditions that work to maintain local variations and to resist globalization (Encarnación 2016; Nardi 1998). We argue that LGBT politics are shaped only in part by globalization, they are also fundamentally shaped by their national and local contexts, which set the parameters for their specific translations of identities, political goals and strategies, and cultural practices. Herdt (1992, p. 64) reminds us that,

> all kinds of social practices can be borrowed, appropriated, recombined, rejected, and ultimately made over into an image that has the same appearance as another but is actually a different experiential and symbolic form.

In this study we have remained receptive to the dialectic between the global and the national/local in order to untangle and explain both similarities and differences in the Pride parades in our sample.

The impact of contextual variation on the dynamics of protest has been studied through a comparison of Pride demonstrations staged in different countries/cities. A first attempt, using data similar to our own, to study in depth the complex relationship between protest and context was a comparative study of the worldwide demonstrations on February 15, 2003 against the imminent war on Iraq (Walgrave and Rucht 2010). Their analysis revealed that the size and composition (the "who") of the anti-Iraq-war demonstrations as well as the motivation ("why") and mobilization ("how") of their participants varied strikingly between countries. Although the events were staged at the same time and around the same if not identical issues, there were remarkable differences from country to country. Mobilization campaigns, coalitions, use of allies among the political elites and the media, turnout and attitudes of the individual protesters varied in ways that could largely be traced back to differences in the national contexts. So whereas processes of globalization in which international organizations, EU level organizations and other national groups are sources of inspiration, ideas, successful strategies and resources, these are domestically translated to adapt to national and even local contexts.

Countries vary in terms of the conditions they create for political protest. In social movement literature the political opportunity structure, together with the temporal political configuration, are conventionally identified as influencing the incidence, type of protest, and who protests (McAdam 1996; Kriesi 2004; Tarrow 1998; Koopmans 1999). Social movement researchers have usually explained "cross-national differences in the structure, extent and success of comparable movements on the basis of differences in the political characteristics of the nation states in which they are embedded" (McAdam, McCarthy and Zald 1996, p. 3). Using the same CCC data set, we investigated the tension between what we call oppositional rituality and official rituality in May Day demonstrations in five European countries. We found significant differences in the motives of demonstration participants (Peterson et al. 2012). Yet, it was not possible to explain these differences in terms of the stable elements in the national "political opportunity structures" (Kitschelt 1986). Instead, the differences in the degree of oppositionality or officiality were explained by cultural traditions combining with volatile factors such as the political orientation of the sitting government and the level of grievances. The political context thus matters, but not necessarily the context *qua* the political opportunity structure as ordinarily defined. Like May Day demonstrations, Pride parades are annual ritual events, and, through an examination of them in different national contexts, we critically interrogate the dominant notion of political opportunity structures in comparative social movement research. We argue that LGBT movements are challenging both state *and* non-state targets across a myriad institutional settings. Power in late modern societies is best conceptualized as "multidimensional and as both symbolic and material," culture is also constitutive of domination (Wulff, Bernstein and Taylor 2015, p. 114; also Armstrong and Bernstein 2008). Inspired by Ronald Holzhacker, in our model we weigh together political factors with cultural factors.

Holzhacker (2007, 2012) has developed a useful categorization of the modes of interaction of LGBT movements based on movement organizations' layered interactions with their political environment. He identifies three modes of interaction and their accompanying typical LGBT organizational strategies. First, in countries where the public and elite attitudes regarding LGBT people remain internally polarized (as in, typically, countries or regions showing strong religious, in particular Catholic, influence), LGBT organizations are embroiled in *morality politics*. In these cases, Holzhacker argues, the organizations will most often pursue highly visible confrontational strategies, to be able to push their causes onto the political agenda. In places where at least the elite opinion is supportive, the organizations will seek *incremental change*, favoring small-scale events and working discreetly behind the scenes through lobbying, and cooperating with, government authorities. Where both the elite and public attitudes are supportive or even highly supportive, LGBT organizations will practice a *high-profile politics* mode of interaction vis-à-vis their political environment, staging large-scale celebratory public events, engaging in close cooperation with government authorities and exporting their ideas and resources. While we have found Holzhacker's model valuable for our analysis, the countries in our sample of cases cannot be unreservedly grouped within these three categories.

We have adapted Holzhacker's model to better fit the countries included in our study. In our model the degree of secularity in the country is an underlying factor, which influences *both* the cultural and the political context for LGBT Pride performances. First, in order to operationalize the cultural contexts we look at public opinion. Public opinion toward gay and lesbians measures the degree that inhabitants perceive gay rights as threatening important institutions such as the church and the institution of marriage, "the status of heterosexuality in the culture, the moral standards of the community, or their personal religious beliefs" (Mucciaroni 2008, p. 9). Gary Mucciaroni has found that gay rights issues related to sexual conduct and family life are more threatening to Americans than issues related to marketplace discrimination and hate crimes. The former issues are more directly challenging traditional cultural values and religious beliefs and institutions. In addition to public opinion, we also take into consideration the level of gay hate crimes in the country. According to Encarnación (2016, p. 202), violence against LGBT people in Latin America spiked between 2004 and 2008 when the Catholic Church rallied a venomous opposition to the proposed same-sex marriage legislation in many countries. However, the level of hate crimes has proven to be impossible to accurately gauge, as reliable and comparable data are not available. Hence, we must rely on rough estimations for this measure.

76 Abby Peterson

Figure 3.1 visualizes how public opinion toward LGBT people is distributed among the countries in our sample. On the one end we have Poland and Italy, where 53.4 percent respective 50.9 percent responded that they never find homosexuality justifiable and only 3.6 percent respective 6.2 percent always find homosexuality justifiable. On the other end we have Sweden and the Netherlands where 55.9 percent respective 46 percent always find homosexuality justifiable. The remaining four countries we locate between these two poles. We begin to see the contours of the analytical categories, which will emerge in our model.

This brings us, second, to the political context in our model. Angelia Wilson (2013, pp. 133–34) found empirical support for the connection between countries and US states with less religiosity (and economic security) and gay and lesbian "friendly" legislation. Wilson suggests that on the basis of her analysis of US states, faring well economically, together with experiencing security, leads to less religiosity, which in turn appears to lead to gay friendly legislation. Wilson's analysis reminds us that the degree of secularity also influences the political context. So second, in order to operationalize the political context in our model, we weigh together the degree of openness of the state to LGBT movement demands measured by LGBT friendly legislation, the support or non-support of political elite allies and third-party stakeholders, and the existence or non-existence of an organized countermovement. These factors capture the political contexts in our study.

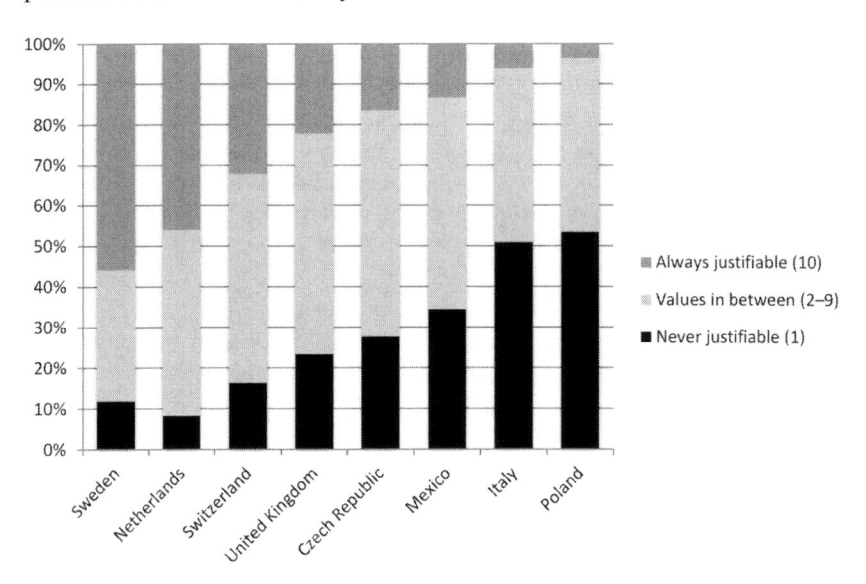

Figure 3.1 Homosexuality always or never justifiable, attitudes in eight countries
Data for Czech Republic, Netherlands, Sweden, Switzerland and United Kingdom from European Values Survey 2008–2009. Data for Italy and Mexico from World Values Survey 2005. Poststratification weights have been used in the analysis.

Third and last, we emphasize that political institutions, particularly the judiciary, can mitigate the role of public opinion on policy. For example, the Mexico City left-wing government, with the support of the judicial system, has proven to be among the world leaders in pushing through LGBT friendly policies despite the relative lack of public support and the opposition of the powerful Catholic Church (Encarnación 2016, pp. 62–64; Corrales 2015). Our model is thus sensitive to the impact of the dynamics between the political context and the cultural context upon Pride events in our study.

Borrowing from Wilson (2013), we depart from the notion of "gay and lesbian friendly" contexts to construct our categories. As she points out, the notion of "friendly is sufficiently fluid as to allow for comparisons and substantive difference" (p. 7). We have subsequently differentiated three categories: LGBT unfriendly, LGBT less friendly, and LGBT friendly contexts. However, we warn that these context categories do not form homogeneous groups. The sources and even intensity of unfriendliness/friendliness differ.

LGBT unfriendly contexts

Included in our study we have two countries with an LGBT unfriendly climate for LGBT movements – Poland and to a somewhat lesser degree, Italy. Poland has passed only one LGBT friendly law, legislation prohibiting discrimination in employment based on sexual orientation, enacted in 2003 prior to the country's entry in the EU (Carroll 2016). In 1997 the Polish Constitution was amended to protect opposite-sex marriage, hence the High Court has issued an opinion that the bills that would have introduced civil partnerships for both opposite-sex and same-sex couples were unconstitutional (Wilson 2013, pp. 74ff). Amnesty International in a report from 2015 warned that Poland's legal system falls dangerously short when it comes to protecting lesbian, gay, bisexual, transgender and intersex (LGBTI) people from hate crimes.[1] Efforts to reform the criminal code to protect LGBTI individuals from hate crimes have been met with "furious resistance from some parts of Polish society, with one MP in 2015 calling the proposal an attempt 'to introduce a sick ideology of gender which promotes sexual pathologies'" (ibid.). Since Poland's entry in the EU the now ruling Law and Justice Party has consistently opposed the LGBT movement and, relevant for our study, even banned Equality Parades 2004 and 2005 in defiance of EU directives. In 2007 the European Court of Human Rights declared the ban illegal.

Szulc (2011, p. 166) points out that Poland is one of three countries to opt out of the Charter of Fundamental Rights of the European Union out of fear that the Charter could force the legalization of same-sex marriage. "In the Polish context, sexual minorities are still associated, by conservatives, with a Western, European Union 'degeneration of moral values'." In 2006 the publication of *Compass*, the manual for human rights education of the Council of Europe, constituted the reason for the Polish government to dismiss the director of the government agency, which had financed and distributed the Polish version of the manual. In the view of the government the manual did not reflect Polish values since it did not depict homosexuality as a deviation. The Secretary General of the Council of Europe and the Commissioner for Human Rights spoke publicly against this point of view (Council of Europe 2011, p. 77).

The cultural context more or less mirrors the political. While there are no reliable official statistics, Campaign against Homophobia, a major Polish LGBT organization, recorded at least 120 homophobic or transphobic hate crimes in 2014 alone, though the true figure is believed to be much higher.[2]

Relevant for our study is that a majority of Poles oppose Pride parades; a poll from 2008 revealed that 68 percent of Poles believe that gay people should not have the right to organize public demonstrations.[3] A poll in Warsaw from 2010 revealed that 55 percent were against holding the EuroPride in the city.[4] The LGBT community in Poland faces widespread and ingrained discrimination across the country. Wilson (2013) argues that with the transition from socialism and the uncertainty connected with it, the levels of religiosity have risen dramatically, as has nationalism. These two trends she claims have underpinned anti-gay attitudes as the prevailing norms in the country. Homophobia pervades in the political and cultural rhetoric (p. 74). Among the countries included in our study, Poland has by far the most unfriendly political and cultural contexts for LGBT politics and public manifestations.

Since 1982 in Italy transgender people have been allowed to change their legal gender identity; in 2003 legislation was passed to prohibit discrimination in employment on the basis of sexual orientation (Carroll 2016). The Constitutional Court's (*Corte Constituzionale*) ruling in 2010 declared that same-sex couples were a "legitimate social formation, similar to and deserving homogeneous treatment as marriage" and the European Court of Human Rights ruled in 2015 that in not recognizing any form of civil union or same-sex marriage in Italy, the country was violating human rights. Subsequently, in 2016 a registered partnership bill was finally passed, which offers limited rights attached to marriage (Carroll 2016). While regions ruled by center-left governments have extended anti-discrimination protection, no other anti-discrimination laws regarding sexual orientation or gender identity and expression have been enacted. The principle of the fascist Rocco Code that homosexual conduct is an issue of morality and religion, and not criminal sanctions by the State, lives on in Italian politics, which makes it difficult to address LGBT demands in the parliamentary sphere (Gibson 2002). Support for LGBT demands are highly polarized among political elites, with support coming solely from left and center-left parties.

Data reveals that the percentage of Italians who have a positive attitude toward homosexuality and are in favor of legal recognition of gay and lesbian couples is nonetheless growing. According to data from the 2010 Italy Eurispes report, 82 percent of the respondents consider homosexuals equal to all others; 41 percent of citizens think that homosexual couples have the right to marry in a civil ceremony, and 20.4 percent agree with civil unions. In total, 61.4 percent are in favor of a form of legal recognition for gay and lesbian couples – an increase of 2.5 percent from 2009 (58.9 percent) and almost 10 percent in seven years (51.6 percent in 2003).[5] While public opinion appears to be becoming more favorable to LGBT demands, strong resistance continues from the Catholic Church (Garbagnoli 2016). The anti-gay counter-movement, supported by the Catholic Church, attracted tens of thousands for a 2016 "family day" rally, protesting the impending parliamentary vote on a civil union act.[6] However, this was a far cry from the reported 1,500,000 who in 2007 attended a *Più Familia* (more family) rally in anticipation of a civil union bill that would be introduced by the then center-left Prodi government.[7] The anti-gay countermovement is well organized, but appears to be waning in strength.

Less friendly LGBT contexts

Aside from the Czech Republic, which is the most secular country in our sample, these are the countries (with the UK) that are in the mid-range in the scale of secularity measured by the World Values Survey. Mexico is an anomaly in this category. Mexico City, a Federal State in Mexico, has a set of highly progressive LGBT legislation in place. Since 1871, in their Penal Code, Mexico has an equal age of consent for same and different sex sexual acts; since 2003 there is legislation prohibiting discrimination in employment based on sexual orientation, which created the National Council to Prevent Discrimination (CONAPRED); since 2011 there is a constitutional prohibition of discrimination based on sexual orientation (only 7 percent of UN States have this in place, and only Sweden and Switzerland in our sample); in Mexico City hate crimes based on sexual orientation are considered an aggravating circumstance; incitement to hatred based on sexual orientation is prohibited; marriage is open for same-sex couples, and since 2010 same-sex marriages and joint adoption by same-sex couples is allowed (Carroll 2016). Mexico City is one of a handful world-leaders in initiating LGBT friendly legislation. Furthermore, Pride parades in Mexico City enjoy strong support by the City government, which provides critical resources for their mobilization – security and cleanup, as well as setting up scenes in the main square of the City, *Zócalo* – the most symbolically important square in Mexico. One can say that LGBT activists in Mexico City, like those in Sweden and the Netherlands, work *with* and *within* the local state (Browne and Bakshi 2013, p. 5). Mexico City and São Paulo are the only two cities outside of Europe that are members of the Rainbow Cities Network – a network of municipal administrators committed to furthering LGBT rights by sharing "best practices." The LGBT movement's allies are solely among political parties on the left, together with the powerful judiciary. So far the picture is indeed a rosy one. The political context for Pride parades in Mexico City is propitious. However, the role of the state in instigating "modernizing" change is constrained by Mexico's deeply rooted homophobic and misogynist cultural context supported by the twin pillars of the Catholic Church and the Mexican machismo culture (Carrillo 2007).

Public opinion is relatively polarized. In 2016 sixty-five percent of Mexican people were in favor of same-sex marriages nationwide. Sixty-four percent of Mexicans believed that homosexuality should be an "accepted" way of life. Eighty-six percent of Mexicans surveyed were in favor of the establishment of measures to eradicate discrimination against homosexuals. Only 25 percent believed that same-sex marriage is an attack against the family (Beltrán and Cruz 2016). The results of the same survey in 2010 show that public opinion is becoming more LGBT friendly. In 2010, two years before our survey, 53 percent of Mexicans approved same-sex marriage and 56 percent believed that homosexuality should be an "accepted way of life." Despite increasing acceptance of homosexuality, only 21 percent of LGBT Mexicans are openly gay, bisexual or trans to their workmates. Thirty-five percent of Mexican workers who are LGBT have been victims of discrimination due to their sexual identity or orientation in their workplace (ADIL 2014).

But that is only one side of the picture. The level of violence against LGBT people is alarming, particularly vulnerable are gays and transsexuals. In 2015, a survey reported that between 1995 and 2015 1,310 people had been murdered in homophobic crimes, making Mexico, after Brazil, the country with the second-highest rate of homophobic crimes in the world (Becerra-Acosta 2016). So despite Mexico City's highly supportive political context, the deep-rootedness of homophobia and the level of homophobic violence motivate our placement of the Federal District in the category of less friendly LGBT climates.

Switzerland decriminalized same-sex relation activities at the federal level in 1942, and has recognized equal age of consent for same and different sex sexual acts since 1992; legislation has been in place since 2003 prohibiting discrimination in employment, as well as the provision of goods and services and housing; since 2007 Switzerland has legislation recognizing civil unions offering most of the rights attached to marriage; Switzerland lacks legislation allowing joint parent adoption and/or second parent adoption (Carroll 2016). Among the major political parties, the Social Democratic Party, the Green Party, the Green Liberal Party and the Conservative Democratic Party (BDP/PBD) are generally in favor of LGBT rights whereas the Christian Democratic People's Party and the Swiss People's Party are generally opposed. The Liberals (FDP/PLR) are mostly divided on the issue.[8] However, Switzerland, a federal state, is the only so-called direct Jacobin democracy in our sample. Hence citizens through a plebiscite can challenge any law passed by the National Assembly. Legislation to introduce same-sex marriage and adoption rights will be subject to a plebiscite (the civil union law became subject to this in 2005), which impacts on the country's Pride parades – where they are staged, their choreographies and scripts.

As we can see in Figure 3.1, positive public opinion is more or less on par with that of the UK, furthermore this positive LGBT opinion appears to be increasing. (Nonetheless, we will remind our readers that our surveys are from 2011 and 2012.) A 2016 poll commissioned by the gay rights organization Pink Cross found that 69 percent of the Swiss population voiced support for same-sex marriage, with 25 percent opposed and 6 percent undecided. Divided by political orientation, the poll found 94 percent among Green Party voters, 63 percent among Christian Democrat voters and 59 percent among Swiss People's Party voters were in support.[9] Furthermore, Switzerland is geographically and linguistically divided in its support for LGBT demands; people living in the German-speaking cantons are more positive to LGBT rights than those living in French- and Italian-speaking cantons, the latter more influenced by the Catholic Church.

The Czech Republic recognized equal age of consent for same and different sex sexual acts in 1990; passed legislation prohibiting discrimination in employment 1999 and, in addition, legislation prohibiting discrimination in goods and services, education and housing. Since 2006 there is some recognition of same-sex relationships in law, which is, however, far weaker than civil union bills in other EU countries (Carroll 2016). Nonetheless, the Czech Republic is perhaps the most liberal Central Eastern European country with regard to lesbian, gay, bisexual and transgender rights (ibid.). For example, the first sex reassignment surgery in the country took place in 1942, when a trans man subsequently changed his legal sex to male. Currently, 50–60 people undergo such surgeries annually in the country covered by health insurance.[10] While far-right and socially conservative parties, together with the Catholic Church, continue to be opponents to LGBT rights, other political parties, particularly neo-liberal parties and the Green Party, are political allies.

In 2006, the Eurobarometer showed that 52 percent of Czechs supported same-sex marriage (above the EU average of 44 percent) and 39 percent supported same-sex adoption. The 2015 Eurobarometer indicated a record high support of 57 percent for same-sex marriage, a five percent increase from 2006.[11] A Pew Research Center opinion survey from 2013 reported that 80 percent of Czechs believed homosexuality should be accepted by society, while 16 percent believed it should not. We can contrast the results from the Czech Republic with those from Poland, where 46 percent responded negatively and 42 percent positively.[12] The report concluded that the gay-friendliness they found among Czech respondents is probably helped by the low levels of religious belief in the country. In the World Values Survey, Wave Three (1995 in Czech Republic), 76.2 percent of the Czech respondents responded to the question "how important is religion to you?" with "not very/not at all important." The Czech Republic is the most secular country in our sample, closely followed by Sweden and the Netherlands. Nonetheless, cultural support for Pride parades is modified by an underlying perception in the country that homosexuality should be tolerated *if* kept private (see Chapter 2 this volume).

Friendly LGBT contexts

In this category we have placed three countries in our sample, all engaged in what Holzhacker (2007) calls "high profile politics," but again, the category is not homogeneous. England and Wales have recognized equal age of consent for same and different sex sexual acts since 2001 (first 2010 throughout the United Kingdom); legislation has been in place since 2000 prohibiting discrimination in employment, and the same year a constitutional prohibition of discrimination based on sexual orientation was enacted. In 2015 legislation was passed that prohibits incitement to hatred based on sexual orientation. Since 2014 England, Scotland and Wales recognize marriage for same-sex couples; and since 2005 England and Wales have legislation allowing joint parent adoption and second parent adoption (2014 for the rest of the UK). The Gender Recognition Act was passed in 2004, making it possible for transgender people to change their legal gender in the UK, allowing them to acquire a new birth certificate, and affording them full recognition of their acquired sex in law (Carroll 2016). The LGBT movement enjoys support by political elites from all three major parties. The UK currently holds the world record for having the most LGBT people in parliament with 45 "out" LGBT MPs elected at the 2017 election. The new Parliament now includes 19 Labour LGBT MPs, 19 Conservatives and seven from the Scottish National Party.[13]

A Pew Research Center opinion survey from 2013 reported that 76 percent of UK respondents believed homosexuality should be accepted by society, while 18 percent believed it should not.[14] A poll in 2009 found that 61 percent agreed that gay couples should have equal rights to get married, not just to have civil partnerships.[15] While not on the same levels as our two most LGBT friendly countries, the cultural context for LGBT politics and public manifestations are relatively supportive.

Both the Netherlands and Sweden recognize same-sex marriage, adoption rights, and robust anti-discrimination legislation is in place, as well as prohibitions and sanctions of hate crimes. In 2003 Sweden amended its Constitution to include a prohibition of discrimination based on sexual orientation (Carroll 2016). LGBT movements in these countries more or less enjoy the support of the political parties across the political spectrum, with some exceptions. In the Netherlands, as in Sweden, support for LGBT rights came originally from left-wing and liberal parties, this support has now been extended across the political spectrum. The Dutch nationalist and right wing populist Party for Freedom has appropriated LGBT rights as an element in their Islamophobic propaganda. This move on the part of the far right has been actively counteracted in Sweden. The Swedish radical populist right parliamentary party, the Sweden Democrats (which has its roots in the neo-Nazi movement), has been consistently criticized by LGBT spokespersons and their attempts to participate in Swedish Pride events have been banned. While traditionally support for LGBT rights has been weakest within the small Christian Democrat Party, their party leader participated in the 2016 Stockholm Pride Parade (however, not without considerable internal critique from her party). In both countries LGBT movement organizations and Pride parades are awarded substantial government and municipal funding.

As we can conclude from Figure 3.1, public opinion in both the Netherlands and Sweden is highly supportive of LGBT people. Netherlands and Sweden have the most supportive and accommodating political and cultural contexts for LGBT movements and their Pride events. Both countries are regarded as corporatist with interest organizations closely tied to centralized government bureaucracies, and both with a single dominant LGBT nongovernmental organization. Nonetheless, the contexts differ significantly. Sweden's interest organizations, such as the LGBT nongovernmental organization RFSL, retain their political independence. The Dutch brand of a "culture of consensus" traditionally sublimates political challenges in apolitical directions, whilst Sweden's deep-seated heritage of demonstrations, closely linked with the May Day tradition in the country (Peterson and Reiter 2016), reinforces the LGBT movement's political performances and ambitions.

We have summarized the contextual factors, which we argue impact upon the performances of Pride parades, in Table 3.1.

Table 3.1 Contextual factors that influence Pride parades

	Poland	Italy	Mexico	Czech Republic	Switzerland	UK	Netherlands	Sweden
Legislation	-	-/+	+	-/+	-/+	+	+	+
Political elite support	-	-/+	+/-	-/+	+/-	+	+	+
Counter movement	yes	yes	yes	no	no	no	no	no
Public opinion	-	-/+	-/+	+/-	+/-	+/-	+	+
Violence	yes	n.a.	yes	n.a.	n.a.	n.a.	n.a.	n.a.
Secular	no	no	no	yes	somewhat	somewhat	yes	yes

Note: - indicates unequivocally negative, + unequivocally positive, +/- and -/+ a more ambivalent position.

Global cultural anchors and contextual translations

We suggest that the idea of pride, the collective and individual performances of coming out, the format of a parade, and the iconography of the rainbow flag are the "cultural anchors" (Ghaziani and Baldassarri 2011, p. 179) that lend the Pride parades in our study their apparent similarities despite their very different mobilizing contexts. Even across national and local political and cultural contexts the cultural anchors "build a thinly coherent foundation" for Pride parades (ibid.). This small collection of ideas and cultural artefacts is the anchoring mechanism that facilitates the global attractiveness of Pride events, which overcomes significant differences in contexts. These integrative cultural anchors have been diffused across country boundaries through the media, the mobility of LGBT activists, and transnational LGBT organizations.

According to Ghaziani and Baldassarri (2011),

> Within and across marches, a small collection of ideas remains fixed in the national conversation, yet in a way that allows activists to address their internal diversity and respond to unfolding historical events. These results suggest that activists do not simply organize around their similarities but, through cultural anchors, they use their commonalities to build a thinly coherent foundation that can also support their differences.
>
> (p. 179)

The Pride parades' cultural anchors allow organizers to at least partially unite in their diversity, to "address their internal diversity and respond to unfolding historical events" (ibid.). The anchoring mechanism also allows organizers and activists to translate this global collection of ideas and symbols to resonate with their specific "national conversations." The underlying scripts and choreographies of the events are adapted to the political and cultural contexts where they are staged. We have observed significant differences in the performances of Pride parades in our study, which impacts upon who participates, how they participate, and why they participate. These contextual differences will be in focus in the analyses in the remaining chapters in our book.

Notes

1 https://www.amnesty.org/en/latest/news/2015/09/poland-abandoning-hundreds-of-victims-ofhatecrimes-1/, p. 1, accessed March 12, 2017.
2 https://www.amnesty.org/en/latest/news/2015/09/poland-abandoning-hundreds-of-victims-of-hate-crimes-1/, p. 1, accessed March 12, 2017.
3 http://wyborcza.pl/1,75398,20221638,dzis-w-warszawie-parada-rownosci-rodzicow-osob-lgbt.html?disableRedirects=true, accessed March 12, 2017.
4 *Gazeta Wyborcza*, January 9, 2010, "Europride – test dla warszawiaków," accessed March 12, 2017.
5 http://www.eurispes.eu/content/ rapporto-italia-2010, accessed March 13, 2017.

6 https://www.thelocal.it/20160131/poor-turnout-for-rome-anti-gay-protest, accessed March 13, 2017.
7 http://rorate-caeli.blogspot.com/2016/01/romes-family-day-defiant-catholic-laity.html, accessed March 13, 2017.
8 *Gazeta Wyborcza,* January 9, 2010.01.09, "Europride – test dla warszawiaków," accessed March 12, 2017.
9 http://360.ch/blog/magazine/2016/10/large-consensus-pour-les-droits-des-lgbt/, accessed March 13, 2017.
10 http://www.denik.cz/z_domova/operacni-zmenu-pohlavi-podstoupi-v-cr-rocne-50-az-60-lidi-20121129.html, accessed March 12, 2017.
11 http://www.equineteurope.org/IMG/pdf/ebs_437_en.pdf, accessed March 12, 2017.
12 http://www.pewglobal.org/2013/06/04/the-global-divide-on-homosexuality/, accessed March 12, 2017.
13 http://www.pinknews.co.uk/2017/06/09/the-uk-just-elected-a-record-number-of-lgbtq-people-to-parliament/, accessed December 14, 2017.
14 http://www.pewglobal.org/2013/06/04/the-global-divide-on-homosexuality/, accessed March 12, 2017.
15 http://www.thetimes.co.uk/article/church-out-of-touch-as-public-supports-equal-rights-for-homosexuals-p9wkvw7xk6w, accessed March 3, 2017.

References

Adam, B.D. (1995). *The rise of the gay and lesbian movement.* Boston, MA: Twayne Publishing.
Adam, B.D., Duyvendak, J.W., and Krouwel, A. (1999). Gay and lesbian movements beyond borders? In Adam, B.D., Duyvendak, J.W., and Krouwel, A. (Eds) *The global emergence of gay and lesbian Politics* (pp. 344–371). Philadelphia, PA: Temple University Press.
ADIL. (2014). *1° encuesta sobre homofobia y el mundo laboral en México.* Mexico City: ADIL.
Armstrong, E.A., and Bernstein, M. (2008). Culture, power, and institutions: A multi-institutional politics approach to social movements. *Sociological theory,* 26 (1), 74–99.
Ayoub, P.M., and Paternotte, D. (2014). Conclusion. In Ayoub, P.M., and Paternotte, D. (Eds) *LGBT activism and the making of Europe. A rainbow Europe* (pp. 233–240). London and New York: Palgrave Macmillan.
Becerra-Acosta, J.P. 2016. México, segundo lugar mundial en crímenes por homofobia. http://sipse.com/mexico/mexico-segundo-lugar-nivel-mundial-crimenes-homofobia-205750.html [accessed February 15, 2017].
Beltrán, U. and Cruz, J. (2016). Apoyan legalizar las uniones gay en el país; 25% cree que afecta los valores morales. *Excélsior* 23rd May. Online at: www.excelsior.com.mx/nacional/2016/05/23/1094344#imagen-2. [accessed February 15, 2017].
Browne, K., and Bakshi, M.L. (2013). *Ordinary in Brighton? LGBT, activisms and the city.* Farnham: Ashgate Publishing, Ltd.
Carrillo, H. (2007). Imagining modernity: Sexuality, policy, and social change in Mexico. *Sexuality Research & Social Policy,* 4(3), 74–91.
Carroll, A. (2016). *State-sponsored homophobia – A world survey of sexual orientation laws: Criminalisation, protection and recognition. 11th Edition.* Geneva: International Lesbian, Gay, Bisexual, Trans and Intersex Association (ILGA).

Chabot, S., and Duyvendak, J.W. (2002). Globalization and transnational diffusion between social movements: Reconceptualizing the dissemination of the Gandhian repertoire and the "coming out" routine. *Theory and Society*, 31, 697–740.

Corrales, J. (2015). The politics of LGBT rights in Latin America and the Caribbean: Research Agenda- *European Review of Latin American and Caribbean Studies*, 100, 53–62.

Council of Europe (2011) *Discrimination on grounds of sexual orientation and gender identity in Europe.* 2nd edition. Strasbourg: Council of Europe Publishing.

Del Collardo, F. (2007). *Homofobia: odio, crimen y justicia, 1995–2005.* Mexico City: Tusquets.

Duyvendak, J.W. (1996). The de-politicization of the Dutch gay identity, or why Dutch gays aren't queer. In Seidman, S. (Ed.) *Queer Theory/Sociology* (pp. 421–438). Cambridge, MA: Blackwell Press.

Encarnación, O.G. (2016). *Out in the periphery: Latin America's gay rights revolution.* Oxford: Oxford University Press.

Engel, S.M. (2001). *The unfinished revolution. Social movement theory and the gay and lesbian movement.* Cambridge: Cambridge University Press.

GarbaGnoli, S. (2016). Against the heresy of immanence: Vatican's "gender" as a new rhetorical device against the denaturalization of the sexual order. *Religion and Gender*, 6(2), 187–204.

Ghaziani, A., and Baldassarri, D. (2011). Cultural anchors and the organization of differences: a multi-method analysis of LGBT marches on Washington. *American Sociological Review*, 76(2), 179–206.

Gibson, M. (2002). *Born to crime: Cesare Lombroso and the origins of biological criminology.* Westport, CT: Praeger.

Giugni, M.G. (2002). Explaining cross-national similarities among social movements. In Ayres, J.M., Caniglia, B.S., Chabot, S., Giugni, M.G., Hanagan, M., Lewis, T.L., and Rothman, F.D. (Eds) *Globalization and resistance: Transnational dimensions of social movements* (pp. 13–29). Lanham, MD: Rowman and Littlefield Publishers.

Herdt, G.H. (1992). "Coming out" as a rite of passage: A Chicago study. In Herdt, G.H. (Ed.) *Gay culture in America: Essays from the field* (pp. 29–69). Boston, MA: Beacon Press.

Holzhacker, R. (2012). National and transnational strategies of LGBT civil society organizations in different political environments: Modes of interaction in Western and Eastern Europe for equality. *Comparative European Politics*, 10(1), 23–47.

Holzhacker, R. (2007). *The Europeanization and transnationalization of civil society organizations striving for equality: Goals and strategies of gay and lesbian groups in Italy and the Netherlands. EUI Working Papers RSCAS 2007/36.* Florence: Robert Schuman Centre for Advanced Studies.

Kitschelt, H.P. (1986). Political opportunity structures and political protest: Antinuclear movements in four democracies. *British Journal of Political Science*, 16(1), 57–85.

Koopmans, R. (1999). Political opportunity structure. Some splitting to balance the lumping. *Sociological Forum*, 14(1), 93–105.

Kriesi, H. (2004). Political context and opportunity. In Snow, D.A., Soule, S.A., and Kriesi, H. (Eds) *The Blackwell companion to social movements* (pp. 67–90). New York: John Wiley & Sons.

McAdam, D. (1996). In McAdam, D., McCarthy, J.D., and Zald, M.N. (Eds) *Comparative perspectives on social movements: Political opportunities, mobilizing structures, and cultural framings*. Cambridge: Cambridge University Press.

McAdam, D., and Rucht, D. (1993). The cross-national diffusion of movement ideas. *The Annals of the American Academy of Political and Social Science*, 528(1), 56–74.

McAdam, D., McCarthy, J.D., and Zald, M.N. (1996). *Comparative perspectives on social movements*. New York: Cambridge University Press.

Mucciaroni, G. (2008). *Same sex, different politics: Success and failure in the struggles over gay rights*. Chicago, IL: Chicago University Press.

Nardi, P.M. (1998). The globalization of the gay & lesbian socio-political movement: Some observations about Europe with a focus on Italy. *Sociological Perspectives*, 41(3), 567–586.

O'Dwyer, C. (2012). Does the EU help or hinder gay-rights movements in post-communist Europe? The case of Poland. *East European Politics*, 28(4), 332–352.

Peterson, A., and Reiter, H. (2016). *The ritual of May Day in Western Europe: Past, present and future*. Farnham and New York: Routledge.

Peterson, A., Wahlström, M., Wennerhag, M., Christancho, C., and Sabucedo, J.M. (2012). May Day demonstrations in five European countries. *Mobilization*, 17 (3), 281–300.

Plummer, K. (1992). Speaking its name. In Plumer, K. (Ed.) *Modern homosexualities: Fragments of lesbian and gay experiences* (pp. 3–28). London: Routledge.

Putnam, R. (1988). Diplomacy and domestic politics. The logic of two-level games. *International Organisation*, 42(2), 427–460.

Smith, M. (2008). *Political institutions and lesbian and gay rights in the United States and Canada*. New York: Routledge.

Swiebel, J. (2009). Lesbian, gay, bisexual and transgender human rights: the search for an international strategy. *Contemporary Politics*, 15(1), 19–35.

Szulc, L. (2011). Queer in Poland: Under construction. In Downing, L., and Gillett, R. (Eds) *Queer in Europe: Contemporary case studies* (pp. 159–172). Farnham and Burlington: Ashgate.

Tarrow, S. (1998). *Power in movement: Social movements, collective action, and politics*. Cambridge and New York: Cambridge.

Tremblay, M., Paternotte, D., and Johnson, C. (Eds) (2011). *The lesbian and gay movement and the state: Comparative insights into a transformed relationship*. Farnham: Ashgate Publishing, Ltd.

Walgrave, S., and Rucht, D. (Eds) (2010). *The world says no to war: Demonstrations against the war on Iraq*. Minneapolis, MN: University of Minnesota Press.

Wilson, A.R. (2013). *Why Europe is lesbian and gay friendly (and why America never will be)*. Albany, NY: Suny Press.

Wulff, S., Bernstein, M., and Taylor, V. (2015). Study of gender and sexuality movements. In della Porta, D., and Diani, M. (Eds) *The Oxford handbook of social movements* (pp. 108–132). Oxford: Oxford University Press.

4 Who Participates?

As discussed in the introduction of this book, Pride parades have been a way to display and celebrate both the diversity and unity of the LGBT community. Furthermore, an important strategy for the LGBT community has been to strategically display "identity for education" (Bernstein 1997; McFarland 2012) in the parades to show that apart from sexual orientation, gender identity, or gender expression, LGBT people are "just like everybody else." In this chapter, we will engage with the question regarding which groups actually participate in Pride parades. Which parts of the diverse LGBT community are mobilized? And to what degree do people outside of the LGBT community take part in the parades? Are Pride participants "just like everybody else," in the sense that they mirror the social and political composition of the general population? And when this is not the case, how can we explain why some groups are more present in the parades than others? To seek answers to these questions, we analyze protest survey data from 11 Pride parades in seven European countries and Mexico (for more information about the survey data, see the Appendix). The survey data also allow us to examine whether the national mobilizing context, which we discussed in Chapter 3, impacts the social and political composition of the parades.

Our study of Pride parade participants allows us to say something about the composition of the mobilized segments of the broader LGBT community, and not just about key activists or members of specific LGBT organizations. Pride parades have in many countries become the most visible manifestation of the LGBT movement. Pride parades include people from the broader LGBT community that are not active in the movement's activities, apart from their participation in the annual parade. This role of the parades is highlighted by Yves, a former member of the organizing team of Pride Romandy in Switzerland and formerly a member of ILGA's World Board:

> If you are an organization, you have maybe 100 or 200 members. In Gay Prides, you have people that you have never seen in any organization. So it's maybe the most representative body that you have. [...]

The vast majority of LGBTIQ people are not members of organizations. Otherwise you would have many tens of thousands of members of LGBTIQ organizations, which is not the case. So actually the people who go out for Pride parades are often a bit more representative of the overall LGBTIQ population [...] They are not visible the rest of the year because they don't talk about their homosexuality, bisexuality, transgenderness, etcetera, when they work, when they serve you in a restaurant, or when they are in the bank and give you your change. But when they are at the Gay Pride they go, even if they are dressed like you and me, and they say, "Yes, I am a gay, lesbian, bisexual, transgender – or we are here, we are queer."

The Pride participants' level of involvement in the LGBT movement and its organizations is of course in the end an empirical question. We analyze their organizational involvement and degree of political participation and whether this differs between national mobilizing contexts as well as between the different groups making up the LGBT movement.

In the introduction of the book, we discussed some of the tensions and differences within the LGBT movement regarding political goals and strategies – for example, between lesbian women and gay men, and between moderate groups focusing on equal rights and radical groups demanding more profound structural changes. In order to see whether these differences still play out as tensions between different groups within the LGBT movement, our analysis of who takes part in contemporary Pride parades examines both their general political attitudes and their ideas about which strategies best contribute to making society better for LGBT people.

In this chapter, we first focus on the socio-demographic composition of Pride parades, and we investigate whether different mobilizing contexts lead to differences in which groups are mobilized. We then look into what groups from the LGBT community – both in terms of sexual orientation and gender identity – primarily take part in Pride parades, and to what degree the friends of the LGBT community are involved in the parades. This is followed by an analysis of the Pride participants' degree of involvement in LGBT organizations and various forms of political participation. In conclusion, we look into the diversity of political positions and ideas about LGBT politics that characterize those taking part in Pride parades.

"Just like everybody else"?

The "normalization" of protests and the protester

What socio-demographic composition can be expected in Pride parades? Research on social movements and political participation has noted that citizens in liberal-democratic societies have become increasingly inclined to take part in demonstrations to express their grievances, opinions and political preferences. Since the 1960s, the staging of street protests has become a central repertoire of action for a wide variety of social movements, and authorities have come to regard demonstrations as a legitimate form of political action (see e.g. Marsh and Kaase 1979; Meyer and Tarrow 1998; Norris 2002; Norris, Walgrave and Van Aelst 2005; Tilly 1983; Van Aelst and Walgrave 2001). Subsequently, demonstrations have become an increasingly "normalized" form of political participation (Van Aelst and Walgrave 2001).

While the issues of demonstrations have become more diversified and the diversity in social groups that today stage street protests has increased, Walgrave and Verhulst (2009, pp. 1356–1358) argue that this increasing "external diversity" in street protests should not be conflated with whether one can see an increasing "internal diversity" within demonstration populations. The empirical research that first analyzed the social profiles of demonstrators concluded that protesters were largely young, male and highly educated (Marsh and Kaase 1979). Later surveys, however, showed that differences due to gender and age had decreased, while differences in the level of education persisted (Van Aelst and Walgrave 2001, pp. 466–473; see also Verba, Schlozman and Brady 1995). This overall development has been described as a "normalization of the protester" in the sense that demonstration participants today are *increasingly* from a cross-section of the general population, but still "the underrepresentation of those with less education and the less affluent prevents us from speaking about a genuine democratization of street protest" (Van Aelst and Walgrave 2001, p. 482; for an account of this discussion, see Peterson, Wahlström and Wennerhag 2017).

Much of the early research on the social profile of demonstrators was based on surveys answered by a random sample of the general population, thus only allowing knowledge about protestors in general. The increased use of protest surveys directly handed out during specific demonstrations has, however, provided more accurate knowledge about whether demonstrations with different themes and staged by different types of movements vary in their social composition. This research has shown that protests staged by "new social movements" and radical left movements tend to have a social composition that is younger, more well educated, and more likely to be middle class compared to trade union and labor movement demonstrations, which are more similar to the general population in these respects (e.g. Peterson, Wahlström and Wennerhag 2015; Wennerhag 2016).

What can we then expect of the social composition of Pride parades? Although not always in equal proportions across all socio-demographic categories, LGBT persons are found in all parts of society and among different classes, ethnicities/races, age cohorts and genders (Gates 2012). This suggests that Pride parades would potentially have a composition that is closer to the general population than many other types of demonstrations that represent interests that are more unevenly distributed among different segments in society. On the other hand, Pride parades were first established during the 1970s by gay and lesbian groups that were often well integrated into a political environment characterized by new social movements and the radical left. This suggests that the parades might instead have a socio-demographic composition closer to these types of movements.

The impact of national mobilizing context

As discussed in Chapter 3, the LGBT movements that stage Pride parades in the countries in our study operate in very different political and cultural contexts – some in less LGBT friendly, or even hostile, contexts and others in politically and culturally very LGBT friendly contexts. How do these differences affect the social and political composition of the parades?

In cross-national comparisons based on protest surveys of demonstrations targeting identical issues, both elite stances and public opinion have been found to affect the socio-demographic profiles of protests. For instance, Walgrave and Verhulst (2009) show that the internal diversity of the 2003 anti-Iraq war protests, which were staged simultaneously in many countries, was profoundly shaped by the government's and the opposition's positions on the war. In countries where both the government and the opposition were against the war, demonstrations were the most internally diverse. In countries whose governments and/or opposition supported the war, the demonstration populations were much less diverse. Walgrave and Verhulst conclude that rowing against mainstream politics results in a higher share of participants from socio-demographically stronger groups, especially when it comes to level of education. One might therefore expect that Pride parades staged in settings where LGBT movements row against mainstream politics – in LGBT unfriendly or less friendly contexts – should have a higher share of participants from socio-demographically stronger groups.

These expected differences might all be related to more general theories within social movement studies about why certain groups tend to be more inclined to take part in movements and protest activities. One concept often used to explain why the social composition of movements often differs from the general population is "biographical availability," which McAdam (1986, p. 70) defines as "the absence of personal constraints that may increase the costs and risks of movement participation." The main point here is that potential costs and risks differ between individuals in different social circumstances. The overrepresentation of young people in movements and demonstrations can thus be related to the fact that they have fewer obligations (e.g. family and work responsibilities) and more time available for activism. The overrepresentation of the well educated and people from higher classes can be related to the fact that these groups have a higher status and would expect their dissidence to be treated more fairly than if they lacked such status. Not only individual circumstances differ; the risks and costs of taking part in political activism also vary between movements and national contexts. To engage in a movement that is regarded as far from the political mainstream increases the potential costs and risks for the individual because such engagement might lead to negative social responses and jeopardize personal relationships, status and career (this is further discussed in Chapter 5 as "overcoming the barrier of stigma"). Such costs and risks are even higher when movements become subjects of state repression, which might imply physical violence and judicial consequences. But the threat of violence might also result from widespread contempt among the general public against specific social groups. Although the countries of our study are all liberal democracies that allow LGBT groups to organize and stage parades, we nonetheless expect that national and even local mobilizing contexts impact the socio-demographic composition of the parades.

The Pride parades' socio-demographic composition

Table 4.1 shows the socio-demographic composition of the Pride parades in this study with regards to some of the variables that have been discussed above as central in previous research on participation in demonstrations. In order to focus on national differences, we have taken the mean value for the two parades in the countries where more than one Pride parade was surveyed (for precise figures for each of the surveyed parades, see Peterson, Wahlström and Wennerhag 2017). The figures for Pride participants in each country are shown in bold in the table, while the figure for the difference vis-à-vis each country's national population is shown in italics.

Regarding age, the participants in the surveyed Pride parades are generally young. On average, two of five are younger than 30 years and four of five are younger than 50 years. In comparison to the general population, the percentage of young people up to 29 years is higher in all parades but one (the Dutch parade in Haarlem). Regarding cross-national differences, the age profiles of the Pride parades conform to our expectations. The parades staged in hostile or less LGBT friendly environments tend to have a higher percentage of young participants than in the population in general. The two Swedish parades (in Stockholm and Gothenburg), however, go against our expectations; the percentage of young people is very high despite Sweden being one of the most LGBT friendly countries in our study.

Among the participants in Pride parades, the percentage having a completed or on-going university education is also very high at almost 70 percent, which is on average more than 40 percent higher than in the national populations. The variation between countries regarding the percentage of highly educated participants conforms relatively well to our expectations. Poland and Italy display the highest difference between Pride participants and the general population, while the difference is smaller in Switzerland, the Netherlands and Sweden.

When it comes to social class, our analysis focuses on occupational class – i.e. the individual's position in the workplace and labor market – on the basis of the class scheme developed by Daniel Oesch (2008).[1] Here, the survey data show that 53 percent of the Pride participants are professionals and other employees with middle-class occupations, while only 14 percent have working class occupations. Compared to the general populations, this means an overrepresentation for middle class occupations by 22 percent and an underrepresentation of working class occupations by 31 percent. In Table 4.1, the occupational classes are only shown on an aggregated level. In a previous analysis of Pride parade participants based on the same data, we used a more detailed categorization of the different classes, which also divided the occupational classes according to their dominant "work logic" (Oesch 2008). Our analysis showed that among the middle-class occupations, it was primarily the highly educated "socio-cultural professionals and semi-professionals" – e.g. teachers, social workers and medical doctors – that were overrepresented in the parades (Peterson, Wahlström and Wennerhag 2017). This is also an occupational class that in earlier research on class voting has been shown to primarily support left-libertarian political parties, i.e. green, left socialist and left liberal parties (Oesch 2008). Such parties have often, together with social democratic parties, been at the forefront in supporting LGBT rights. However, in regards to the cross-national variation in the class composition of the Pride parades, it is difficult to find any distinct patterns that would confirm our expectations because the middle class overrepresentation is strong in the parades in both more and less LGBT friendly countries.

A further, and for many countries increasingly central, aspect of the socio-demographic composition of demonstrations that we have not yet discussed is ethnicity and race. Ethnic minorities are often underrepresented in forms of political participation like voting, but not necessarily in demonstrations (Gallego 2007; Just 2017). In Table 4.1 we show the proportion of the Pride participants living in the country of the parade but born abroad, a proxy for ethnic minority status that is often used in national statistics. On average, the percentage of foreign-born does not differ significantly from the corresponding figures for the national populations, and it is difficult to identify any distinct cross-national pattern for these differences. In the table, the proportion of individuals both born and living abroad is also shown. This heterogeneous group includes both tourists and other temporary foreign visitors, and it is probable that some of them only visited the country to take part in the parade. This group is overall quite small (on average 2 percent), with the exception of Switzerland at 8 percent. It is particularly the Pride parade in Geneva that contributes to this, with 13 percent of the participants in this category. Because more than nine in 10 in this group lived in France, this can be seen as a case of cross-border mobilization from a proximate country. Given that we surveyed the WorldPride in London 2012, it is perhaps surprising that only 4 percent of the London survey respondents were foreign participants.

Table 4.1 The socio-demographic composition of Pride parades in eight countries, compared to national populations

	Poland		Italy		Mexico		Czech Republic		Switzerland		United Kingdom		Netherlands		Sweden		Mean value	
Age																		
–29 years	47	+22	47	+26	66	+37	53	+32	29	+7	22	+3	12	-6	39	+17	39	+17
30–49 years	45	+14	42	+8	30	-13	40	+3	54	+21	52	+21	39	+5	40	+10	43	+9
50–64 years	7	-20	10	-14	4	-12	5	-21	14	-11	21	-5	44	+16	16	-8	15	-9
65– years	2	-16	1	-20	1	-11	2	-14	3	-18	5	-19	6	-15	5	-19	3	-16
Education																		
Completed or on-going university education	82	+62	75	+55	55	+42	58	+44	56	+25	77	+45	65	+34	72	+40	68	+43
Social class																		
Self-employed	21	+7	12	-9	12		18	+9	10	-2	17	+6	11	+/-0	8	-3	14	+1
Middle class occupations	33	+2	40	+24	43		44	+24	64	+26	69	+39	74	+30	58	+21	53	+22
Working class occupations	27	-16	15	-34	14		11	-47	14	-27	8	-44	13	-24	13	-28	14	-31
Students not working	20	+7	33	+19	31		28	+15	12	+3	7	-1	1	-5	21	+9	19	+8

	Poland	Italy	Mexico	Czech Republic	Switzerland	United Kingdom	Netherlands	Sweden	Mean value
Born abroad									
National inhabitant born abroad	**4** *+3*	**4** *-3*		**4** *+2*	**17** *-7*	**20** *+6*	**4** *-5*	**13** *+/-0*	**9** *-1*
Born abroad and live in another country	**3**	**1**		**1**	**8**	**4**	**0**	**1**	**2**

Comment: Figures in bold stand for Pride participants in each country, while figures in italics stand for the difference between Pride participants and each country's national population. For the national populations of the European countries, data from ESS round 6 (2012) were used, except for social class, where ESS round 5 (2010) was used (except for Italy, for which ESS round 2 (2004) was used). For Mexico, data for the national population were taken from ISSP 2012 for age and education (this source lacked data on social class). Because ESS only contains data for inhabitants, no comparable data were available for those born and living abroad. The Pride parade survey in Mexico City lacked a question about country of birth.

Judging from the figures in Table 4.1, it is evident that participants in Pride parades are much younger, more well educated, and more often have middle-class occupations than the general population. Given that earlier research has shown that such socio-demographic characteristics are more common among demonstrators in general, it would of course be interesting to see whether the composition of Pride parades differs from other types of demonstrations. In a previous study using protest survey data from the same dataset and focusing on demonstrations in four of the countries in our study, the composition of May Day marches was compared with Pride parades, trade union and environmental demonstrations (Wennerhag 2016). A comparison with that analysis shows that Pride parades, environmental demonstrations and May Day marches staged by radical left groups have a similar socio-demographic composition, with a relative overrepresentation of young and well-educated participants, whereas these groups are not overrepresented in trade union demonstrations. We can thus conclude that in terms of socio-demographic composition, the Pride parades are closer to the protests staged by "new social movements" and the radical left than, for example, trade union demonstrations.

In the interviews with the organizers of the Pride parades, many stress social diversity as an important feature of the parades, especially when discussing their ideas about what groups the Pride parades should primarily mobilize. Sandra, president of the Stockholm Pride Association in 2014–2016, explains:

> Our only way to define a target group is to say "LGBT people and our friends" [...] in general, we have nothing in common. We are from the city and from the countryside, we are old and young and we are rich and poor and we love Schlager music or we hate Schlager music. [...] LGBT persons are everywhere, in all social groups [...].

Our analysis of the survey data shows that this is only partly true. Some socio-demographic groups tend to be overrepresented in Pride parades, but on the other hand these are groups that tend to be overrepresented in most types of demonstrations and in almost all forms of political participation.

Apart from such overall patterns that are common to most forms of political participation, one could also argue that the socio-demographic composition of the Pride parades can result from the organizers' ideas about who to mobilize for the parades. When discussing the primary goals of the parades with David, the president of the Zurich Pride association, he stresses that the parades are very important for young people during their coming out processes: "If they see [the parade] at least in the newspaper or in the media, or if they participate in Zurich, [and see] that many people in the streets are gay, openly – that's always helpful for them." Victor, one of the organizers of Stockholm Pride, also emphasizes the function of the parade and the festival as a "safe space" for those who are "young and not always really self-confident." In societies where it is still often seen as shameful to be LGBT, young people becoming adults will be more vulnerable when trying to define their sexual or gender identities, which makes it important for organizers to mobilize the young for the parades (also see our discussion about youth and "social stigma" in Chapter 5).

In this chapter we have so far discussed the composition of Pride parades with respect to age, ethnicity/race, educational level and class, i.e. social characteristics that are not *per se* related to the LGBT community, but could be expected to vary within the LGBT population as they do within the general population. It is now time to turn to the question regarding which parts of the LGBT community are mobilized to the Pride parades in terms of sexual orientation and gender identity – the two social categories that are the principle basis for the movement and its self-identity.

The diversity of LGBT groups and identities in the Pride parades

As discussed in the introduction of this book, and uncovered in Chapter 2's historical accounts of the Pride traditions in the countries included in our study, the various groups organizing different parts of the movement have differed in strength, visibility, and influence over the broader LGBT community and its Pride parades. At times these differences have led to tensions and outright conflicts, often between lesbian women and gay men.

The question then is which genders primarily take part in contemporary Pride parades. With the LGBT movement's expansion of political focus over the years, more attention has been given to questions about gender identity and gender expression – in particular transgender, but also queer and non-binary/intergender identities. It is therefore important to not only see women and men, but also other genders that people might self-identify with. In the questionnaire handed out during the Pride parades, we therefore did not ask the traditional survey question limiting the possible answers to only two options, but instead posed an open question letting everybody write down their self-perceived gender identity (only the survey in Mexico City did not use an open question).

In Table 4.2 the composition of gender identities in the surveyed Pride parades is shown. On an overall level, the most common gender identities are men (50 percent) and women (47 percent), and only 3 percent self-identify as other genders. However, we find variation both regarding whether women or men are more numerous and regarding the percentage identifying with other genders. It is only in the parades in Sweden, the Netherlands and Switzerland that the percentage of women is higher than for men. The percentage of gender identities other than men and women are highest in Sweden (6 percent) and the UK (5 percent).

It is not obvious what these differences really tell us about possible variation in the local and national settings in which the parades were organized

Table 4.2 The composition of gender identities in Pride parades in eight countries

Gender identity	Poland	Italy	Mexico	Czech Republic	Switzerland	United Kingdom	Netherlands	Sweden	Mean value
Woman	48	45	34	40	50	38	61	61	47.0
Man	50	52	66	60	47	58	38	33	50.4
Transgender	0	1		1	1	1	1	1	0.8
Queer	2	1		0	1	2	0	1	0.9
Non-binary / Intergender	1	1		0	1	0	0	4	0.9
Other gender identity	0	0		0	0	2	0	1	0.4
Cases (N)	183	167	212	265	344	191	99	393	1,854
Missing cases (N)	1	49	0	1	3	3	1	7	65

Comment: The Pride parade survey in Mexico City only asked about two genders.

regarding the composition of the LGBT community as such and whether the organizers have specifically tried to mobilize specific parts of the community. The overall figures nevertheless tell us that the more common gender identities also dominate Pride parades and that those not conforming to conventional gender identities are still relatively small minorities among those in the LGBT community that take to the streets during Pride parades. It is worth noting, however, that our operationalization of gender does not differentiate between those men and women who have a gender that is consistent with the one assigned to them at birth and those who do not.

One way of casting more light on the variation in gender identities between Pride parades is to relate them to the sexual orientations of the participants. All women participating in the parades cannot be presumed to be lesbian, and all men cannot be presumed to be gay. One of the parade organizers quoted earlier in this chapter said that the primary target group to mobilize was "LGBT people and our friends." It is therefore interesting to see to what degree non-LGBT participants are mobilized to the Pride parades.

One problem with our data is, however, that a question regarding sexual orientation was only posed in four of the surveyed parades (in Haarlem, London, Stockholm and Warsaw). This was partly motivated by a suspicion that asking about people's sexual orientation might be too intimate of a question. However, in the surveys in which this was asked it turned out that this was a very minor problem because the number of missing cases or those indicating the alternative "Do not want to answer" was very low. These four surveys nevertheless offer possibilities to gain insights about possible differences in LGBT groups' Pride participation for around 40 percent of our survey data.

Table 4.3 shows the composition of sexual orientations at these four Pride parades. On average, the overall largest group are gays (34 percent), followed by heterosexuals (28 percent), lesbians (20 percent), bisexuals (13 percent), and other sexual orientations totaling only 4 percent. Table 4.4 summarizes which gender identities dominate within each sexual orientation. Although lesbians are fewer than gays, those reporting bisexual and heterosexual orientations predominantly self-identify as women. The table also shows figures for two of the socio-demographic factors earlier shown as being important – age and level of education. It is quite striking here that the percentage of young people is slightly lower than the average among both gays and lesbians, whereas it is much higher among bisexuals and those stating other sexual orientations. This seems to indicate that gender identities are more plural, and sometimes more fluid, within some parts of the LGBT community than in others; for example, almost all gays self-identified as men. The parts of the community that actively question binary gender roles are furthermore more dominated by young people. Perhaps this can be seen as an expression of the development of the LGBT

100 Magnus Wennerhag

Table 4.3 The composition of sexual orientations in Pride parades in four countries

	Poland	United Kingdom	Netherlands	Sweden	Mean value (between countries)
Sexual orientation					
Lesbian	14	18	33	15	20.3
Gay	38	53	27	18	34.0
Bisexual	17	8	10	18	13.1
Transgender	1	3	1	2	1.8
Pansexual	1	0	0	5	1.3
Asexual	0	3	0	0	0.8
Other sexuality	1	0	0	1	0.5
Heterosexual	28	15	29	41	28.1
Do not want to answer	0	0	0	0	0.1
Cases (N)	182	187	93	237	699
Missing cases (N)	2	7	7	1	17

Table 4.4 Socio-demographic characteristics in different LGBT groups in Pride parades in four countries.

	Lesbian	Gay	Bisexual	Other LGBT	Heterosexual	Total (%)
Gender identity						
Woman	98	0	69	37	70	51
Man	0	100	22	16	30	45
Transgender	0	0	0	22	0	1
Queer	0	0	4	10	0	1
Non-binary / Intergender	2	0	4	10	0	2
Age: – 29 years	33	29	51	50	33	34
University education (completed or ongoing)	67	67	62	66	72	68
Cases (N)	124–125	233–235	96–97	34–36	199–201	688–697

movement toward a broader focus beyond the earlier primary focus on homosexuality, which might also potentially lead to tensions within the movement. Such possible tensions are discussed by one of the organizers of Pride Stockholm:

> A lot of people are extremely happy that the laws have changed and want to get married to somebody of the same sex and have children and live in a terraced house, and want to emphasize during the Pride parade that "we are just like any family." Perhaps they might panic by the fact that in the same Pride parade, there are people dressing up totally awkward, or undressing, and wonder what they have in common with those people [...] I think the clashes will accentuate, between those wanting to be mainstream, who only want to live according to some norm of monogamy and family, and those wanting to go against the whole structure of two genders or monogamy [...] This is very obvious with the BDSMF community, where you find a mix of LGBT persons and hetero people. [...] They have much more in common with other norm breakers than with the terraced-house lesbians.

Such potential tensions notwithstanding, our survey data suggest that in sheer numbers those LGBT persons that in the words of the interviewee can be seen as "mainstream" still dominate on the streets – at least when it comes to their gender identities. We will later come back to whether one can find other differences regarding attitudes toward LGBT-related issues.

The relatively significant presence of "the friends" of the LGBT community, i.e. non-LGBT persons, is also an interesting result. Even though this varies between the four surveyed Pride parades, it shows that contemporary Pride parades do not just include LGBT people. Many of the interviewed organizers stress the importance of not only mobilizing LGBT people to the parades – but also mobilizing "the friends" of the community. "Friends" usually refers to personal friends and families of LGBT persons as well as individuals and groups that want to support the causes of the LGBT movement (for an extended discussion about the role of "friends" of the LGBT community, see Chapter 6).

In a previous analysis of non-LGBT Pride parade participants using the same survey data (Wahlström, Peterson and Wennerhag 2018), we found that non-LGBT participants in the Netherlands, Poland, Sweden and the UK often participated with friends, colleagues, co-members of an organization, and children, but also that more politically grounded motives were important for this group. Furthermore, we found that the experience of types of discrimination other than against sexuality was relatively common among the non-LGBT parade participants. A markedly high percentage of non-LGBT participants reported that they belonged to a discriminated group in society, considerably more than the general population in their country. Among the non-LGBT participants, gender was the main perceived basis for one's discrimination. As can be seen in Table 4.4, heterosexual Pride participants are predominantly women – almost three in four. This indicates that one's own personal experience of discrimination increases one's tendency to show solidarity with other discriminated groups (ibid.). This is presumably partly related to close links between directions within feminism and influential mobilizing frames within the LGBT movement.

In previous research on individuals supporting a movement despite not being part of the group that the movement claims to represent – what McCarthy and Zald (1977) call "conscience adherents" and "conscience constituents" – it has been claimed that these individuals are typically more resource-rich than the beneficiaries of the movement. This was, however, not the case in our study, and aside from gender the non-LGBT parade participants more or less mirrored the LGBT individuals who took part in the parades (Wahlström, Peterson and Wennerhag 2018).

Hitherto in this chapter, we have discussed the composition of the Pride parades in terms of the participating individuals' belonging to certain socio-demographic groups and groups within the LGBT community. We will now look into other aspects of what characterizes those taking part in Pride parades, in particular their involvement in LGBT activism and other types of political participation, but also their ideological orientation and attitudes to LGBT-relevant political issues.

Non-political party people or die-hard activists?

Political engagement among Pride participants

Earlier in this chapter we discussed whether those who take part in Pride parades mirror the general population in regards to socio-demographic characteristics. We then saw that despite mobilizing individuals from a diversity of socio-demographic groups, some specific groups still tend to be "overrepresented" in the Pride parades – in particular the young and the well-educated. We also saw that this was even more the case in parades that were staged in less LGBT friendly mobilizing contexts. This was also discussed in relation to the theories within social movement studies emphasizing the important role of "biographical availability" (McAdam 1986), according to which the costs and risks of engaging in political activism vary due to the individuals' different social circumstances and the context in which the activism takes place.

While admitting that "biographical availability" is important for explaining why some individuals become engaged in social movements or take part in demonstrations, Schussman and Soule (2005) also underscore the importance of what they call "political engagement" and "structural availability." Whereas the former stands for the individual's degree of political interest and political participation, the latter stands for the individual's connection to social networks where activism is more common, for example, through membership in political organizations and/or politically committed social networks.

In line with our earlier discussion about "the normalization of the protester", which focused on socio-demographic aspects, we can now turn to the question of whether Pride participants mirror the general population also in terms of political participation, political interest, and political orientation. If Pride participants are "just like everybody else," we would expect them to be as politically engaged as a cross-section of the general population are. However, if Pride parades share characteristics with other forms of political participation, we would expect participants to be both more politically engaged and more structurally available than the average citizen (Schussman and Soule 2005). In line with our previous discussion about the impact of the mobilizing context, we would then also expect this difference vis-à-vis the general population to be greater in unfriendly or less LGBT friendly contexts.

Table 4.5 summarizes the Pride participants' level of political engagement and membership in various types of political organizations for each of the countries in our sample. The table also shows to what degree this level of engagement differs from the general population for some of the variables. On average, the parade participants are more interested in politics than their national populations. Regarding membership in political parties and women's and environmental organizations, Pride participants are on average more often members in these than the general population. The differences vis-à-vis national populations are even greater when it comes to various forms of political participation. On average, 69 percent of the Pride participants have taken part in a demonstration during the last year.

In our survey we also asked about the use of more disruptive and/or illegal repertoires of action, such as taking part in direct action – e.g. blockades, occupations, or civil disobedience – or using violent forms of action against property or people (questions for which we do not have any comparable data for the general population). On average, a relatively low percentage of the Pride participants have taken part in direct actions, and almost none in violent activities, but it is worth noting that the highest figures for these forms of political participation are found in the mobilizing contexts that are LGBT unfriendly – Poland and Italy.

Table 4.5 also presents figures for political engagement that specifically concerns the LGBT movement. On average, 30 percent of the Pride participants are members of an LGBT organization, even though we find variation between mobilizing contexts. Nevertheless, this reveals that Pride parades manage to mobilize a high proportion of their participants beyond those that are members of LGBT organizations – in line with what one of the Pride organizers from Switzerland expressed in the quotation in the beginning of this chapter. In the questionnaires handed out during five of the surveyed parades, we also asked about the participants' attendance

Table 4.5 Participants' political engagement in Pride parades in eight countries

	Poland		Italy		Mexico		Czech Republic		Switzerland		United Kingdom		Netherlands		Sweden		Mean value (between countries)	
Political interest																		
Quite or very interested in politics	80	+41	73	+28	34	-13	59	+38	72	+11	75	+27	78	+14	84	+28	70	+22
Organization membership (during last 12 months)																		
Political party	8	+6	8	+3	8	+1	7	+5	11	+4	18	+16	24	+21	29	+25	14	+10
Women's organization	10	+9	13	+12	8		3	-1	8	+3	10	+6	7	+/-0	17	+15	9	+6
Environmental organization	10	+10	16	+13	14		8	+2	21	+9	13	+6	21	-18	17	+9	15	+4
Anti-racist/migrant organization	4		13		16		6		7		11		9		13		10	
Political participation (during last 12 months)																		
Contacted politician or official	35	+28	21	+7	13	+2	20	+7	15	+/-0	52	+37	21	+7	30	+14	26	+13
Signed a petition	79	+69	79	+58	19	+7	70	+52	73	+38	86	+54	51	+29	70	+26	66	+42
Took part in a demonstration	79	+76	87	+71	80	+73	43	+36	79	+75	75	+72	33	+30	73	+66	69	+62

	Poland	Italy	Mexico	Czech Republic	Switzerland	United Kingdom	Netherlands	Sweden	Mean value (between countries)
Took part in a direct action	14	25	5	8	8	8	4	10	10
Used violent forms of action	8	2	0	1	1	0	0	3	2
LGBT organization membership (during last 12 months)									
Both active and passive members	25	45	22	17	44	40	24	26	30
Active member	15	19	16	9	18	25	13	10	16
Passive member	10	26	7	8	26	15	11	16	15
Have previously taken part in Pride parades									
Never	20				12	18		33	21
One time or more	80				88	82		67	79
More than five times	26				57	50		23	39

Comment: For the national populations of the European countries, data from ESS round 6 (2012) were used for political interest, political party membership and political participation, while data from European Values Survey 2008 were used for membership in women's and environmental organizations. For the national population of Mexico, data from ISSP 2004 were used for political interest and political party membership, signing a petition, and contacting a politician or official, while data from ISSP 2014 were used for demonstration participation. The question about earlier participation in Pride parades was not asked in the surveys in Zurich, Prague, Bologna, Mexico City and Haarlem.

at previous Pride parades. The results show that, on average, 21 percent were newcomers in the parade. However, around four in 10 had previously participated in more than five parades, which tells us that the annual parades play an important role as a recurring ritual within the LGBT movement.

As discussed earlier, we asked in four of the surveyed parades about the sexual orientation of the participants. This allows us to see if there are differences in degrees and types of political engagement among lesbians, gays, bisexuals, other LGBT people and heterosexuals that take part in the Pride parades.

In the interviews with the organizers, different LGBT groups' level of political engagement was discussed. Some of the organizers primarily saw this as a more or less well-grounded part of the movement's self-understanding. For instance, Victor from Stockholm Pride says: "There are very stereotypical images that lesbians only want to have political seminars while the gays only want to drink champagne and party." Tasso, from West Pride in Gothenburg, confirms the stereotype:

> In Gothenburg, it is very easy to see that it is mostly women and lesbian activists that become engaged in the festival. And that's how it is in Stockholm as well. It is kind of a tradition, that the gays are more interested in partying and hanging at Bee Bar [a gay bar in Gothenburg]. They are the ones standing watching the parade. While the lesbian women arrange and take part in the seminars, and then walk in the parade. They are more political. And that has been the picture for a while, that lesbian women are more politically active than gay men.

If we look at Table 4.6, however, this view is not easily confirmed – at least if we focus on the part of the LGBT community that participates in Pride parades. Regarding political interest, there are no substantive differences between the LGBT groups. When it comes to membership in LGBT organizations, the figures are roughly the same for lesbians and gays. Around half consider themselves to be active members of such organizations, but this does not differ substantially between the LGBT groups. Lesbians, on the other hand, are more frequently members in women's, environmental and anti-racist organizations. More disruptive forms of political participation, however, are more common among bisexuals and other LGBT persons and less common among lesbians and gays. However, when it comes to participating in Pride parades, both lesbians and gays are those that have most often taken part in parades.

The Pride participants' political orientations

Another aspect of what Schussman and Soule (2005) call "political engagement" is the individual's political orientation. Despite the proposed

Table 4.6 Political engagement among LGBT groups in Pride parades in four countries

	Lesbian	Gay	Bisexual	Other LGBT	Hetero-sexual	Total (%)
Political interest						
Quite or very interested in politics	67	77	77	77	79	75
Organization membership (during last 12 months)						
Political party	10	16	19	16	19	16
Women's organization	16	2	18	15	10	10
Environmental organization	17	14	21	9	15	15
Anti-racist/migrant organization	10	8	11	9	9	9
Political participation (during last 12 months)						
Contacted politician or official	15	29	33	47	28	27
Signed a petition	69	70	75	83	71	70
Took part in a demonstration	68	67	74	75	62	67
Took part in a direct action	7	9	15	24	8	9
Used violent forms of action	2	1	4	4	2	2
LGBT organization membership (during last 12 months)						
Both active and passive members	44	44	28	43	9	35
Active member	17	24	17	28	5	17
Passive member	27	21	11	15	5	18
Have previously taken part in Pride parades						
Never	8	14	26	18	43	22
One time or more	92	86	74	82	57	78
More than five times	51	55	22	37	12	39
Cases (N)	96–128	210–236	88–97	34–36	173–202	602–699

"normalization of the protester" (Van Aelst and Walgrave 2001), research on protest participants has shown that people with left-wing views tend to be overrepresented in demonstrations in Western countries (see e.g. Schussman and Soule 2005; Schlozman, Verba and Brady, 2012; Corrigall-Brown 2012; Torcal, Rodon and Hierro 2016). From this perspective, it would be reasonable to expect that Pride parades are also dominated by left-wing people.

Taking into account the specificities of the group that Pride parades primarily seek to mobilize – LGBT people – one could also expect that the participants in the parades are predominantly left-oriented. Even though this group potentially criss-crosses ideological and party political barriers, previous research has shown that LGBT people less frequently vote for parties with illiberal stances on LGBT rights – parties that are more often found on the right wing of the political spectrum. For example, LGBT voters in the US show disproportionately weak support for the Republican Party (e.g. Herek et al. 2010; Gates, 2012).

In Western Europe, however, it has lately been discussed whether parts of the LGBT population – in particular gay men – have started showing more support for right-wing populist parties. This has furthermore been interpreted as a result of many right-wing populist parties' active efforts at re-branding themselves as gay-friendly, with reference to their framing of Muslim people as anti-Western, morally conservative, and anti-gay – despite the fact that many of these parties themselves are morally conservative and have a relatively recent history of homophobic stances. Particularly in the Netherlands, but also in France, the main right-wing populist parties have tried to attract LGBT voters with their anti-immigration and anti-Muslim message. Even though there is very little empirical research regarding this, one research report in France showed that the support for the right-wing populist party National Front was slightly higher among gay men than among straight men, while it was lower among lesbian women (Brouard 2016). Whether such tendencies within parts of the LGBT electorate can also be seen in other European countries is an open question because there is very little systematic research on this in most countries. Nevertheless, the fear of an increase in anti-immigrant attitudes also within the LGBT community has led to debates in many countries, warning of the risks of increasing "homonationalist" sentiments, in particular among gay men (see e.g. Drucker 2016; Rogers 2017).

When it comes to the political orientations of the surveyed Pride participants, however, it is hard to find much evidence of these developments. Overall, these figures are instead much in line with what previous research from the US has shown about LGBT people's political orientations. Furthermore, the figures resonate with the findings of previous research on protest participants' political orientations in terms of self-placement on the left–right spectrum. As can be seen in Table 4.7, those identifying themselves as "left" constitute the majority of Pride participants on average. In comparison to the national populations, the group of Pride participants defining themselves as left is larger in almost all surveyed countries. In line with our expectations about cross-national differences, the difference vis-à-vis the national population is largest in the countries that are less LGBT friendly – Poland and Italy.

The main exception to this overall tendency of Pride participants to be predominantly left oriented is found in the Czech Republic. While the Czech parade participants are more representative of the general population with regards to their left–right political orientation, they are nevertheless more orientated to the right and less center-orientated than the Czech electorate. One possible explanation for this is that the meanings of the left–right divide are different in some Eastern European post-communist countries than in Western European countries (e.g. Deegan-Krause 2006; Noël and Thérien 2008, pp. 47–54). A study of the saliency of the left–right scale measured by personally held core values within the electorates in 20 countries found that the Czech voters displayed a different attitude toward "left" and "right": "A right orientation was associated with the openness to change values and a left orientation with security and conformity values" (Piurko et al. 2011, pp. 551–552). It is thus not unanticipated that Czech Pride participants, who are challenging conformity to sexual norms and demanding strengthened rights for LGBT people, tend to orient themselves more toward the right of the left–right scale (Peterson, Wahlström and Wennerhag 2017).

When it comes to sympathies for specific political parties, Table 4.7 shows that Pride parade participants tend to support left-libertarian parties, such as green, left socialist, and left liberal parties, but also social democratic parties. As discussed earlier in this chapter, these types of political parties have in many countries also been the ones that first championed LGBT rights. In comparison to the national populations, it is the left-libertarian parties that are "overrepresented" amongst the participants of the parades. Conservative, Christian democrat, and right-wing liberal parties are, on the contrary, underrepresented on average. However, the Czech Pride participants are again the exception in this case, at least regarding support for conservative parties (34 percent), which they support almost to the same degree as the Czech electorate. However, the one morally conservative Christian democrat party (Christian and Democratic Union – Czechoslovak People's Party, KDU-ČSL) received only marginal support among the Czech pride participants (1 percent). They also deviate from the Czech electorate in their support (+37 percent) for the marginal Green Party, a typical "new social movement party" that champions LGBT communities having the same rights as everyone else. Similarly, we can observe the Swedish Pride participants' support for the recently formed party Feminist Initiative, which in the table is included under other political parties. In the survey carried out at Stockholm Pride, held a few weeks before Election Day in 2014, this was the party that most

Table 4.7 Participants' political orientation in Pride parades in eight countries

	Poland		Italy		Mexico		Czech Republic		Switzerland		United Kingdom		Netherlands		Sweden		Mean value	
Left-Right placement																		
Left (0–3)	70	+56	83	+54	31	+6	21	+1	56	+37	55	+41	52	+34	67	+46	54	+35
Center (4–6)	20	-22	11	-31	39	+/-0	28	-13	28	-23	23	-29	29	-17	17	-26	24	-20
Right (7–10)	4	-24	2	-18	24	-13	38	+10	12	-13	12	-5	15	-18	12	-20	15	-13
Don't know	6	-10	4	-5	7		13	+2	5	-1	10	-7	4	+1	5	+/-0	7	-3
Party sympathy																		
Right-wing populist or Extreme right	0	-36	0	-3	0	+/-0	1	+1	6	-19	1	+1	1	-6	0	-4	1	-8
Conservative or Christian Democrat	1	-12	3	-20	14	-29	34	-4	6	-11	12	-20	5	-14	5	-27	10	-17
Liberal	18	-16	0	-2	0	+/-0	3	+3	4	-11	0	+/-0	7	-17	9	+/-0	5	-5
Left Liberal	34	+31	13	+12	24	-14	1	+1	0	+/-0	23	+14	23	+14	0	+/-0	15	+7
Green	28	+28	1	+1	0	-1	37	+37	36	+20	17	+15	21	+13	24	+11	20	+16
Social Democrat / Socialist	18	+3	24	-19	58	+41	17	-21	42	+17	42	-9	15	-4	17	-15	29	-1
Left Socialist	1	+1	41	+32	0	+/-0	1	+1	5	+4	3	+3	24	+13	22	+16	12	+9
Communist	0	+/-0	9	+9	3	+2	4	-16	0	+/-0	1	+1	0	+/-0	0	+/-0	2	-1
Other political party	2	+1	9	-10	1	+1	4	+/-0	1	-1	0	-5	4	+2	22	+19	5	+1

	Poland	Italy	Mexico	Czech Republic	Switzerland	United Kingdom	Netherlands	Sweden	Mean value
General political values: Agree or Agree strongly with the following statements									
Government should redistribute income from the better off to those who are less well off.	65	74	80	33	57	65	46	63	60
People from other countries should be allowed to come to my country and live here permanently if they want to.	90	71	74	50	49	46	47	72	62

Comment: For the national populations of the European countries, data from ESS round 6 (2012) were used for left–right orientation and sympathies with political parties. For the national population of Mexico, data from LAPOP 2012 were used for left–right orientation and sympathies with political parties. The LAPOP survey had a slightly different scale (1–10 instead of 0–10), which was here interpreted the following way: Left = 1–4; Center = 5–6; Right = 7–10. It furthermore lacked the alternative "Don't know." For the two statements about redistribution and immigration, five different answers were possible (Strongly disagree, Disagree, Neither, Agree and Strongly Agree).

participants supported (28 percent). This shows that when a party has LGBT rights as one of its primary goals, as Feminist Initiative and the Czech Green Party do, it can manage to draw many votes from the LGBT community.

It is also quite evident in Table 4.7 that the support for right-wing populist parties is on average very low among the surveyed Pride parade participants, and much lower than in the general electorates. Only in Switzerland, with many right-wing populist parties, do the participants of the parades support these parties to a degree worth mentioning (6 percent), but the support for these parties is still much lower than in the general electorate. When it comes to the parts of the LGBT community that take to the streets during Pride parades, it is thus hard to find any evidence of any significant support for the radical right. When using the survey data from the four Pride parades where we asked about sexual orientation, it is furthermore not possible to see that gay men are more inclined to support such parties, as is shown in Table 4.8. It is, however, possible to see that gay men participating in Pride parades support conservative parties to a higher degree than other LGBT groups and that gays are the LGBT group in which the highest percentage of people identifying themselves as "right" can be found (albeit half of them consider themselves to be "left"). Here, one should also take into account that gender can play a decisive role, and it has been shown that women more often characterize themselves as "left" than "right," especially in advanced industrialized countries (Inglehart and Norris 2000).

One could, however, ask whether anti-migrant attitudes could be seen in other ways among the participants. Apart from focusing on the traditional left–right divide, which is often structured by attitudes on socio-economic issues (e.g. about the degree to which the state should regulate markets or engage in economic redistribution), researchers have increasingly started focusing on what has sometimes been called "a new cleavage based on values" (Kitschelt and Hellemans 1990; Bornschier 2010; Kriesi 2010). This "new" cleavage has been labelled in various ways, e.g. "green-alternative-libertarian vs. traditional-authoritarian-nationalist" (Hooghe et al. 2002) and "libertarian-universalistic/traditionalist-communitarian" (Bornschier 2010). The main idea has been that politics is increasingly structured by conflicts over socio-cultural values, and not just by the socio-economic values and interests traditionally associated with the left–right divide. These socio-cultural conflicts have more generally been seen as expressions of either "libertarian" or "authoritarian" values regarding conflicts around, for example, immigration levels or LGBT persons' rights. While libertarian values have been equated with more pluralist and tolerant views, authoritarian values have been seen as embracing social hierarchies, conformity, and nativist ideas about who belongs to the community.

In this context, it would of course be far-fetched to expect any anti-LGBT stances, but attitudes toward immigration could be seen as a good proxy for whether authoritarian values are found among the Pride

Table 4.8 Political orientations amongst LGBT groups in Pride parades in four countries

	Lesbian	Gay	Bisexual	Other LGBT	Hetero-sexual	Total (%)
Left-Right placement						
Left (0–3)	60	50	68	69	57	57
Center (4–6)	25	27	18	8	18	22
Right (7–10)	8	16	6	11	18	14
Don't know	7	6	8	12	7	7
Party sympathy						
Radical Right Populist or Extreme Right	1	1	1	0	2	1
Conservative or Christian Democrat	5	12	3	2	9	8
Liberal	3	7	3	6	12	7
Left Liberal	14	18	7	14	10	14
Green	26	20	27	30	21	23
Social Democrat / Socialist	27	30	23	18	22	26
Left Socialist	13	9	20	5	13	12
Communist	1	2	0	2	1	1
Other political party	10	3	17	12	7	7
General political values: Agree or Agree strongly with the following statements						
Government should redistribute income from the better off to those who are less well off.	59	56	67	68	52	57
People from other countries should be allowed to come to my country and live here permanently if they want to.	60	56	70	68	65	61
Cases (N)	107–125	205–235	82–96	26–36	171–200	591–692

114 *Magnus Wennerhag*

participants. As can be seen in Table 4.7, a large majority on average agrees with the statement: "People from other countries should be allowed to come to my country and live here permanently if they want to." In Table 4.8, it is shown that this attitude does not differ substantially between the different LGBT groups. When it comes to cross-national differences, the general tendency is that the Pride participants in less LGBT friendly countries have the most positive attitude toward immigration.

This question about socio-cultural attitudes, together with a question regarding socio-economic conflicts (about wealth redistribution), has been used in Figure 4.1 to construct a diagram illustrating differences between Pride participants regarding the countries of the parades, the gender identities of the participants, and their left–right orientation. This is a way to graphically map where parades and groups of participants on average are placed within a political space defined by their attitudes toward both socio-economic and socio-cultural issues (each point corresponds to the mean values for each parade or group and for the different types of issues). Overall, it can be seen that almost all parades are found in the upper left quadrant, which is in line with the tendency toward left-libertarian party support that has been shown earlier. Gender identity has little overall effect on individuals' political orientations according to the two political dimensions, even though the group "other gender identity" does display more libertarian-minded attitudes. The differences are larger between the

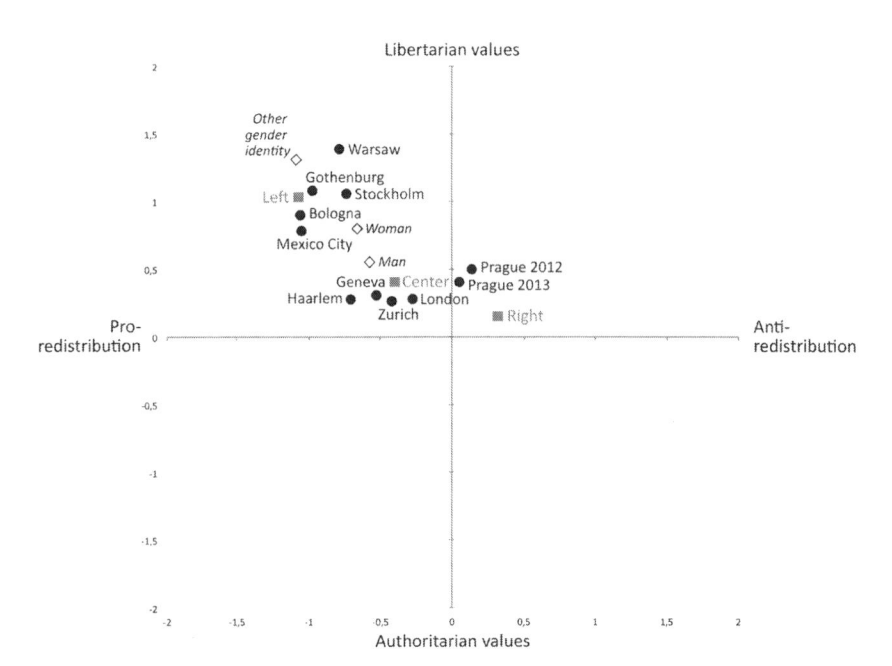

Figure 4.1 Political orientations amongst LGBT groups in Pride parades in four countries

parades. One can notice two clusters of parades: the Swedish, Polish, Italian and Mexican parades, which are both more libertarian and more pro-redistribution, whereas the Czech, British, Swiss and Dutch parades on average are closer to the political middle according to the two dimensions. That more radical stances, according to both political dimensions, are found in less LGBT friendly countries is in line with our expectations, but this does not explain why the participants of the Swedish parades also display more radical attitudes. However, the largest differences in individuals' attitudes is related to their left–right orientation, where the left-oriented are not only favorable to more redistribution, but also more libertarian.

The participants' ideas about LGBT movement strategies

Earlier in this chapter we briefly mentioned potential conflicts within the LGBT movement when discussing the sexual orientations and gender identities that predominate at the parades. For instance, one of the organizers of Stockholm Pride saw possible tensions between groups within the community arising from an alleged tendency within some groups (in particular gays and lesbians) to primarily use the parades to celebrate and normalize hard-won equal rights, while other groups want to bring forward a more radical critique of dominant social norms like monogamy or social structures like patriarchy and capitalism. Another type of critique has been raised by queer scholars, claiming that equal rights and wider social acceptance for LGBT people have been gained only at the cost of conforming to prevalent capitalist institutions and structures of stratification, and these scholars call for the LGBT movement to radicalize by increasingly addressing anti-capitalist demands (see e.g. Sears 2005; Drucker 2011).

In the four parades in which we asked about sexual orientation (in the Netherlands, Poland, Sweden and the UK), we also asked some more specific questions about what changes need to be made in order to make society better for LGBT persons. The different statements can be said to represent different approaches to how the LGBT movement should work strategically and whether it should primarily aim at achieving equal rights and promoting tolerance or should have a more radical approach targeting various institutions and structures. The different statements also represent different priorities within the movement regarding whether it should work to make the majority population accept LGBT persons or actively work against hetero-normativity, or if it should strive to abolish patriarchy or capitalism. All of these questions thus highlight tensions within the LGBT movement, both regarding its political focus and how far it should push its demands.

In Table 4.9, one can see that almost all parade participants see promoting tolerance and state laws against discrimination as very important for making society better for LGBT persons. A majority also wants to

Table 4.9 Attitudes regarding LGBT movement strategies in Pride parades in four countries

	Lesbian	Gay	Bisexual	Other LGBT	Heterosexual	Total
What do you think needs to be done of the following in order to make society better for LGBT persons? Agree or Agree strongly.						
Change people's attitudes	94	94	97	95	94	95
Promote tolerance	96	97	92	84	95	95
Make state legislation non-discriminatory	94	92	89	77	84	89
Tougher laws against hate crimes	84	75	69	67	71	74
Abolish hetero-normativity	78	70	80	94	60	72
Promote liberal values	64	77	62	62	65	68
Abolish patriarchy	64	53	74	68	53	59
Challenge the norm of monogamy	25	32	51	68	32	35
Abolish capitalism	26	16	30	36	22	22
Cases (N)	95–125	202–229	85–96	33–35	170–196	585–678

Comment: For each of the statements, five different answers were possible: Strongly disagree, Disagree, Neither, Agree and Strongly Agree.

abolish hetero-normativity and patriarchy. However, when it comes to monogamy and capitalism, this is only something that a minority of the participants see as central obstacles. Overall, this shows that while almost all Pride parade participants see legal and cultural changes as pivotal for obtaining the goals of the LGBT movement, only a few advocate structural changes such as abolishing capitalism as a central strategy for the movement.

One can also notice some differences in the attitudes to these approaches between LGBT groups. Overall, bisexuals and the category "other LGBT" (which includes persons that are transgender, pansexual, asexual, etc.) tend to a higher degree to advocate for structural changes and to see the norm of monogamy as a central target for the movement compared to what lesbians, gays and heterosexuals think in these matters. But one can also see some differences between lesbians' and gays' attitudes, where the former group tends to advocate for structural changes to a slightly higher degree regarding hetero-normativity, patriarchy and capitalism.

Attitudes toward these kinds of movement demands might of course be influenced by other factors than sexual orientation, such as individual characteristics or the national mobilization context. We therefore made a regression analysis regarding four of the statements shown in Table 4.9 in order to control for gender identity, political orientation, age and the country of the parade. The results are shown in Table 4.10. When controlling for these other factors, sexual orientation only has a statistically significant effect on the attitudes toward monogamy and capitalism, and in both cases bisexuals and other LGBT display more radical attitudes than gays. Both women and "other genders" (which includes individuals identifying as queer, transgender and intergender) are more critical toward patriarchy than men are, and "other genders" are furthermore more critical to monogamy. However, for the attitudes toward hetero-normativity, patriarchy and capitalism, the participants' political orientation in left–right terms matters even more. Age has only a marginal effect on the attitudes toward capitalism, and the young are slightly more inclined to want to abolish capitalism.

The regression analysis also shows that the national context affects the degree of support for most of the statements. In particular Sweden stands out. Both Swedish and Polish participants are more inclined to want to abolish patriarchy, which might be seen as an effect of the feminist movements' close connections with the LGBT movement in both countries. But the Swedes are also much more critical toward monogamy and hetero-normativity than parade participants in the other countries. Perhaps this could be interpreted in light of Sweden being a LGBT friendly country where many of the movement's demands for equal rights have been achieved, but where the movement seeks new mobilizing issues.

Conclusions

In this chapter we have engaged with the question regarding which groups actually participate in Pride parades, and we have looked at this in terms of general socio-demographic characteristics and political orientations, as well as regarding the parade participants' belonging to the various groups that make up the LGBT community. We have also investigated whether different mobilizing contexts lead to differences in which groups are mobilized to the parades.

In this chapter, we used the so-called "protest normalization thesis" to examine whether Pride participants – apart from their sexual orientation and gender identity – are "just like everybody else" in the sense that they mirror the social and political composition of the general population (see Peterson, Wahlström and Wennerhag 2017). In contrast to what researchers

Table 4.10 Regression for attitudes regarding LGBT movement strategies in Pride parades in four countries

	Challenge norm of monogamy		Abolish hetero-normativity		Abolish patriarchy		Abolish capitalism	
	B	SE	B	SE	B	SE	B	SE
(Constant)	3.364 ***	0.166	3.678 ***	0.144	2.853 ***	0.147	1.489 ***	0.174
Gender identity (ref. = Man)								
Woman	-0.113	0.152	0.206	0.135	0.492 ***	0.136	0.212	0.16
Other gender	0.58 *	0.266	0.397 †	0.228	0.809 ***	0.23	0.155	0.262
Sexual orientation (ref. = Gay)								
Lesbian	0.076	0.2	0.124	0.175	-0.083	0.178	0.181	0.212
Bisexual	0.505 **	0.193	0.173	0.168	0.075	0.174	0.468 *	0.202
Other LGBT	0.633 *	0.249	0.317	0.22	0.147	0.22	0.719 **	0.253
Heterosexual	0.03	0.162	-0.314 *	0.142	-0.213	0.144	0.057	0.171
Political orientation (ref. = Right)								
Left	0.142	0.147	0.606 ***	0.129	0.905 ***	0.131	1.109 ***	0.16
Centre	0.102	0.167	0.246 †	0.145	0.473 **	0.148	0.257	0.181
Do not know	0.185	0.229	0.143	0.198	0.424 *	0.201	0.635 **	0.237
Country (ref. = Sweden)								
Netherlands	-0.757 ***	0.152	-0.499 ***	0.133	-0.357 **	0.136		
Poland	-0.749 ***	0.121	-0.191 †	0.105	0.332 **	0.106	-0.155	0.12

	Challenge norm of monogamy		Abolish hetero-normativity		Abolish patriarchy		Abolish capitalism	
United Kingdom	-0.565 ***	0.123	-0.102	0.107	-0.053	0.109	0.031	0.123
Age (ref. = 30+ years)								
-29 years	0.047	0.104	-0.017	0.089	0.097	0.091	0.235 *	0.106
	Units 656		Units 663		Units 658		Units 576	
	R2 0.14		R2 0.129		R2 0.188		R2 0.18	

Levels of significance: † = 10%, * = 5%, ** = 1%, and *** = 0.1%.

have found regarding the social and political profiles of participants in other types of demonstrations, we had no reason to assume that LGBT individuals are only found in certain age groups or social classes. However, much like those taking part in other types of demonstrations, Pride participants were predominantly young, well educated, and had middle-class occupations. The socio-demographic composition of the Pride parades was closer to what is often found in demonstrations staged by "new social movements" or the radical left compared to, for example, trade union demonstrations, which often tend to better reflect the socio-demographic composition of the general population. Nor did we have any reason to assume that LGBT individuals are per definition left wing. However, Pride participants in none of the parades mirrored the general populations regarding their political orientation, and they primarily supported left-libertarian parties and self-identified as "left." The parade participants were furthermore much more politically engaged than the general populations regarding both organizational membership and taking part in grass-roots political activities.

We found that the differences vis-à-vis the general population tended to be larger in the Pride parades that were staged in the unfriendly or less LGBT friendly countries. This was in line with our expectations, and previous research about movement participation has shown that the potential risks and costs of movement activism explain both why certain groups (e.g. young people and the well-educated) tend to be overrepresented and why this is even more the case in national contexts where a movement is regarded as far from the political mainstream. This was most evident in the LGBT unfriendly countries of Poland and Italy, where parade participants on average were younger, more well educated, more left-leaning, and had much more experience with political activism than the general population in these countries.

Because we asked about the participants' sexual orientation in four of the surveyed parades, we were also able to investigate which groups from the diverse LGBT community are mobilized to the parades. Although we found variation between parades, gays were the overall largest group followed by lesbians and bisexuals. We also found that quite a large proportion of the participants (15–41 percent) were non-LGBT heterosexuals, which shows that Pride parades also mobilize substantially among the "friends" of the movement. However, even though gay men were on average the largest group, women were on average the most common gender because both bisexuals and heterosexuals were predominantly women. When it comes to these groups' level of involvement in LGBT organizations, it did not substantially differ between the different groups and it was overall relatively high (26–45 percent). But still, the majority was not affiliated with any LGBT organization, which shows that Pride parades manage to mobilize a wider circle of individuals from the LGBT community whose movement activity primarily consists of their participation in the annual parade. When it comes to the various LGBT groups' political orientation, the support for conservative parties was highest amongst gays; however, the majority of this group nonetheless self-identified as "left," supported left-libertarian parties, and were positive to unrestricted immigration. This shows that while right-wing populist parties might use "homonationalism" (Puar 2013) as a way to attract gay voters, this does not find resonance among the gay Pride participants. The overall most left-oriented groups were bisexuals and those belonging to the group of "other LGBT," i.e. persons that are transgender, pansexual and asexual. Finally, we looked at how these groups differed in their ideas about which strategies the LGBT movement should employ to make society better. Here, our analysis showed that almost all parade participants saw legal and cultural changes as central for achieving the goals of the movement, while only a few saw more structural changes as necessary.

Overall, this chapter has shown that Pride participants might not be "just like everybody else" in the sense that they mirror the social and political composition of the general population. For sure, some groups are overrepresented, but simultaneously these are groups that tend to also be overrepresented in other types of demonstrations and in almost all forms of political participation. There is still extensive social and political variation among the participants, and they thus display both diversity and mirror the fact that LGBT persons are found in all parts of society.

Note

1 Here we would especially like to thank Anders Hylmö for manually classifying the occupation of all cases in the CCC dataset, as well as managing all the coding of the data into Oesch's class categories for both CCC and ESS data.

References

Bernstein, M. (1997). Celebration and suppression: The strategic uses of identity by the lesbian and gay movement. *American Journal of Sociology*, 103(3), 531–565.

Bornschier, S. (2010). The New Cultural Divide and the Two-Dimensional Political Space in Western Europe. *West European Politics*, 33(3), 419–444.

Brouard, S. (2016). Orientation sexuelle et action publique: Les bénéficiaires du mariage pour tous votent-ils plus à gauche? Research report Note #9/vague 2/ février 2016, Cevipof, Sciences Po, Paris. Available at: http://ses.ens-lyon.fr/actua lites/rapports-etudes-et-4-pages/les-beneficiaires-du-mariage-pour-tous-votent-ils-plus-a-gauche-cevipof-fevrier-2016-297428 [accessed August 31, 2017].

Corrigall-Brown, C. (2012). *Patterns of Protest: Trajectories of Participation in Social Movements*. Palo Alto, CA: Stanford University Press.

Deegan-Krause, K. (2006). *Elected Affinities: Democracy and Party Competition in Slovakia and the Czech Republic*. Palo Alto, CA: Stanford University Press.

Drucker, P. (2011). The Fracturing of LGBT Identities under Neoliberal Capitalism. *Historical Materialism*, 19(4), 3–32.

Drucker, P. (2016). Homonationalism, Heteronationalism and LGBTI Rights in the EU. Published on *Public Seminar* August 31, 2016. Available at: www.publicseminar.org/2016/08/homonationalism-heteronationalism-and-lgbti-rights-in-the-eu/#.Wbu8ZBSXuCi [accessed September 15, 2017].

Gallego, A. (2007). Unequal Political Participation in Europe. *International Journal of Sociology*, 37(4), 10–25.

Gates G.J. (2012). LGBT Vote 2012. UCLA: The Williams Institute. Available at: https://williamsinstitute.law.ucla.edu/wp-content/uploads/Gate-LGBT-Vote-Nov-2012.pdf [accessed August 31, 2017].

Herek, G.M., Norton, A.T., Allen, T.J., and Sims, C.L. (2010). Demographic, Psychological, and Social Characteristics of Self-Identified Lesbian, Gay, and Bisexual Adults in a US Probability Sample. *Sexuality Research and Social Policy*, 7(3), 176–200.

Hooghe, L., Marks, G., and Wilson, C. (2002). Does Left/Right Structure Party Positions on European Integration? *Comparative Political Studies*, 35(8), 965–989.

Inglehart, R., and Norris, P. (2000). The Developmental Theory of the Gender Gap: Women's and Men's Voting Behavior in Global Perspective. *International Political Science Review*, 21(4), 441–463.

Just, A. (2017). Race, Ethnicity, and Political Behavior. In *Oxford Research Encyclopedia of Politics*. doi:10.1093/acrefore/9780190228637.013.238.

Kitschelt, H., and Hellemans, S. (1990). The Left-Right Semantics and the New Politics Cleavage. *Comparative Political Studies*, 23(2), 210–238.

Kriesi, H. (2010). Restructuration of Partisan Politics and the Emergence of a New Cleavage Based on Values. *West European Politics*, 33(3), 673–685.

Marsh, A., and Kaase, M. (1979). Background of Political Action. In Barnes, S.H., and Kaase, M. (Eds) *Political Action: Mass Participation in Five Western Democracies* (pp. 97–136). London: Sage.

Meyer D., and Tarrow, S. (Eds) (1998). *The Social Movement Society: Contentious Politics for a New Century*. Lanham; Boulder, New York and Oxford: Rowman & Littlefield Publishers.

McAdam, D. (1986). Recruitment to high-risk activism: The case of Freedom Summer. *American Journal of Sociology*, 92(1), 64–90.

McCarthy, J.D., and Zald, M.N. (1977). Resource Mobilization and Social Movements: A Partial Theory. *American Journal of Sociology*, 82(6), 1212–1241.

McFarland, K. (2012). *Cultural contestation and community building at LGBT Pride parades* (Unpublished doctoral dissertation): Chapel Hill, South Carolina.

Noël, A., and Thérien, J-P. (2008). *Left and Right in Global Politics*. Cambridge: Cambridge University Press.

Norris, P. (2002). *Democratic Phoenix: Reinventing Political Activism*. Cambridge: Cambridge University Press.

Norris, P., Walgrave, S., and Van Aelst, P. (2005). Who Demonstrates? Anti-state Rebels, Conventional Participants, or Everyone? *Comparative Politics*, 37(2), 189–205.

Oesch, D. (2008). The Changing Shape of Class Voting. *European Societies*, 10(3), 329–355.

Peterson, A., Wahlström, M., and Wennerhag, M. (2015). European Anti-Austerity Protests – Beyond "old" and "new" social movements? *Acta Sociologica*, 58(4), 293–310.

Peterson, A., Wahlström, M., and Wennerhag, M. (2017). "Normalized" Pride? Pride Parade Participants in Six European Countries. *Sexualities*. http://journals.sagepub.com/doi/10.1177/1363460717715032. Published first online.

Piurko, Y., Schwartz, S.H., and Davidov, E. (2011). Basic Personal Values and the Meaning of Left–Right Political Orientations in 20 Countries. *Political Psychology*, 32(4), 537–561.

Puar, J. (2013). Rethinking Homonationalism. *International Journal of Middle East Studies*, 45(2), 336–339.

Rogers, T. (2017). Gays Really Love Germany's Racist, Homophobic Far Right Party. Published on Vice 11 May 2017. Available at: www.vice.com/en_nz/article/53ndzd/gays-really-love-germanys-racist-homophobic-far-right-party (accessed September 15, 2017).

Schlozman, K.L., Verba, S. and Brady, H.E. (2012). *The unheavenly chorus: Unequal political voice and the broken promise of American democracy*. Princeton, NJ: Princeton University Press.

Schussman, A., and Soule, S.A. (2005). Process and Protest: Accounting for Individual Protest Participation. *Social Forces*, 84(2), 1083–1108.

Sears, A. (2005). Queer Anti-Capitalism: What's Left of Lesbian and Gay Liberation? *Science & Society*, 69(1), 92–112.

Tilly, C. (1983). Speaking Your Mind without Elections, Surveys, or Social Movements. *Public Opinion Quarterly*, 47(4), 461–478.

Torcal, M., Rodon, T., and Hierro, M.J. (2016). Word on the Street: The Persistence of Leftist-dominated Protest in Europe. *West European Politics*, 39(2), 326–350.

Van Aelst, P., and Walgrave, S. (2001). Who is that (Wo)man in the Street? From the Normalisation of Protest to the Normalisation of the Protester. *European Journal of Political Research*, 39(4), 461–486.

Verba, S., Schlozman, K.L., and Brady, H.E. (1995). *Voice and Equality: Civic Voluntarism in American Politics*. Cambridge, MA: Harvard University Press.

Wahlström, M., Peterson, A., and Wennerhag, M. (2018). "Conscience Adherents" Revisited: Heterosexual Pride Parade Participants. *Mobilization: An International Quarterly*, 23(1), 83–100.

Walgrave, S., and Verhulst, J. (2009). Government Stance and Internal Diversity of Protest: A Comparative Study of Protest against the War in Iraq in Eight Countries. *Social Forces*, 87(3), 1355–1387.

Wennerhag, M. (2016). Who Takes Part in May Day Marches? In Peterson, A., and Reiter, H. (Eds) *The Ritual of May Day in Western Europe – Past, Present and Future* (pp. 187–216). Abingdon: Routledge.

5 Pride Parade Mobilizing and the Barrier of Stigma

Of course Pride organizers want their parades to be big. Large events are conceivably more empowering for the participants, receive more media attention, and signify force behind any claims put forth. In the case of Pride parades, there is also a point in demonstrating to politicians and the public that there are many citizens from a broad range of spheres in society identifying as LGBT or supporting the rights of LGBT people. Regarded as forms of protest, Pride parades are an expression of what della Porta and Diani (2006, pp. 171–173) call a "logic of numbers," which is related to the core principle of representative democracy and majority rule. A movement mobilizing large numbers of people to the streets conveys a message that it is a player that should be listened to. With large numbers of participants in a Pride parade, it also becomes a reminder to onlookers that LGBT people comprise a sizeable proportion of the population and exist in all parts of the society, as observed by Yves, member of the organizing team in Geneva:

> When you have Pride events, when you have 7,000, 10,000, 15,000 people in the streets, even though they might not all be LGBTIQ people, […] you cannot say, for example, that homosexuality doesn't exist, that Switzerland has no homosexuals, that my city has no homosexuals. […] It's just plain numbers, figures that show that the issue is there and it can be anybody, it can be a waiter, your boulanger, your hairdresser, your, you know, tax employee of the state, it can be your mayor, it can be anybody and of course, the numbers actually make people think: "oh yeah well, 10,000 people in the street, it's one in twenty inhabitants, […] so maybe among the 20 people I know there is one gay, lesbian or bi, or trans and I just don't know it."

Conversely, a parade with very few participants can even have a demobilizing effect. Stig-Åke recalled the first attempt to mobilize a Christopher Street Liberation Day demonstration in Stockholm in 1971.

> There were so few people in the parade, only sixteen, so our enthusiasm dampened a little. To be sure we didn't think that thousands

would come, but a few more than sixteen. ... So we reasoned that the time was not ripe as it [homosexuality] was still taboo. Coming out in the open wasn't uncontroversial back then.

The times were perhaps not ripe for mobilizing large numbers of lesbians and gay men to come out in Sweden in 1971, but the times have changed. In many countries contemporary Pride parades have indeed been very successful in mobilizing large numbers of participants. That includes most parades in the sample used for our study. Stockholm Pride 2014 stands out with up to 60,000 participants, followed by World Pride in London 2012, with 20,000 participants. The parade in Mexico City drew around 15,000 participants,[1] and Prague around 10,000, whereas those in Gothenburg, Geneva, Warsaw and Zürich attracted around 3,000 participants. The comparatively small Pink Saturday Parade in Haarlem – 1,000 participants – is dwarfed by another Dutch Pride event, the typically enormous Amsterdam Canal Pride.[2]

An analysis of the mobilization process of Pride participants provides a key to understanding the relative success of the LGBT movement in bringing such large numbers to the streets. As we shall see below, there are several aspects for the mobilization process which will be in focus: information channels; being asked to participate and asking others; and formal membership in a social movement organization (SMO). The parades take place in different political and cultural contexts that influence the relative importance of various types of mobilization. Since Pride parades are annual rituals, a large share of the participants consists of returnees with prior experiences of Pride participation. The difference between these and the newcomers will also be discussed in this chapter.

Pathways to mobilization and recruitment

According to Bert Klandermans (1984), mobilization has two aspects: *consensus mobilization*, i.e. the attempts to mobilize support for the views of the movement; and, *action mobilization*, i.e. the attempts to bring those sympathizing with the movement to protest. Insofar as Pride parades themselves raise awareness and build support for LGBT issues, they can be regarded as one form of consensus mobilization for LGBT issues. Klandermans and Oegema (1987) describe action mobilization as a multistage process. First, participants become part of the *mobilization potential* of a social movement, i.e. part of the population that shares the general ideas and values of the movement. This can be partly the effect of active consensus mobilization. Second, they are *targeted* by the organizers' mobilization attempts, that is, they become aware of the opportunity to protest. Third, some of those "targeted" additionally become *motivated* to participate. Motivation can follow different pathways and various types of motivation are further discussed in Chapter 8. Typically, the process of becoming motivated to participate in a protest is thought of as taking place separately from the protest event itself. However, some people may only have decided to watch a protest event, then taking the decisive step from bystander to participant as a consequence of being drawn in by the atmosphere of the event. This is arguably particularly likely during festive and carnivalesque protest events such as Pride. Since most Prides are annual events, there is also the possibility of watching the event on one occasion and then deciding to join next year. Enrique, a key activist in Mexico City, told us how he had begun his involvement in Pride parades.

> Interviewer: When was the first Pride parade that you took part in?
>
> Enrique: The first time I didn't actually march. I just stood by the march. It was the first time that I ever saw one. I was living in New York on a summer internship. This was 2008, and that was my first time. I knew the parade was happening, so I got there early. I had just arrived in town so I didn't have a lot of friends yet, so I went by myself. I found a spot very close to where the parade started, and I just stood there the whole Sunday just watching. And then the next year, I was still in New York and I marched with a group for the first time. So my first time was there, and then I started going.
>
> Interviewer: How did you experience your first march?
>
> Enrique: I loved it. I thought it was ... I had a lot of fun. I was just so amazed by how diverse and how different all the groups and all the organizations were both in the march and looking at the march. I remember thinking like being very much aware ... like this is so much different from what I've read about marches and what I've seen on TV shows. I had just seen like a peak of it, and this is a picture that no one is showing, and this is much better, cooler.

Enrique's path from spectator/bystander to participant found resonance in many of the interviews we conducted. While we have no quantitative data regarding this path for motivation, the typically large crowds of spectators at contemporary Pride parades makes it likely that many Pride participants experienced their first parade as spectators/bystanders. Some might even have been carried away by the festive exuberance of the event and spontaneously joined the ranks of marchers. In any case, for many Pride parades the boundaries between spectators and participants are blurry. Observing a Pride parade on the sidelines can provide potent motivation for future participation.

Finally, after targeting for participation and becoming motivated to participate, according to Klandermans and Oegema (1987), potential participants must also *overcome "barriers"* for participation, that is, the various inconveniences (or even dangers) associated with protesting. Apart from typical inconveniences such as sacrificing one's spare time and travelling to the location of a protest, a very real barrier for participation in

LGBT mobilizations is the risk of stigmatization. Erving Goffman (1968) explained that a stigmatized person is, "a blemished person, ritually polluted, is to be avoided, especially in public places" (p. 11), what Kuhar (2011) terms a "pariah." Certainly historically, and even today, LGBT individuals are seen (by some) as dangerous and as threats to the heteronormative fabric of society. Indeed, attitudes toward LGBT people have become increasingly positive in most countries all over the world, and particularly so among young adults (Smith et al. 2014). At the same time, especially young LGBT people still experience high levels of harassment and are more seldom open about being LGBT compared to older age groups (European Union Agency for Fundamental Rights 2014) and researchers have found pervasive negative attitudes towards homosexuals especially among adolescents (e.g. Herek 2002; Hoover and Fishbein 1999; Horn 2006). The social stigma associated with homosexuality, as well as with deviation from socially prescribed gender roles, has been found to be a major stress factor for LGBT youth (Almeida et al. 2009; Russell 2002; Russell and Joyner 2001; Russell et al. 2001). This situation would imply that particularly LGBT youth would perceive the barrier of stigma as challenging to overcome. The barrier of stigma therefore poses a potential challenge for LGBT movements in their efforts to mobilize young people to participate in Pride parades. However, despite this potential obstacle, aside from the Pink Saturday event in Haarlem, young people dominated the Pride parades in our study (see Chapter 4, this volume).

According to Linden and Klandermans (2006, p. 214), "stigmatization implies that a characteristic of a person is taken as evidence that this person is flawed, devalued, and less human." But, for example, unlike race, a lesbian or gay identity is not marked on the body – their stigmatized characteristic is not necessarily visible and can be hidden. However, LGBT people *can* in their bodily presentations also choose to display their stigma, most markedly, as drag queens and kings, or Dykes on Bikes. That is what the coming out process is all about – leaving the closet and publically affirming their sexual identities. But then the individual runs the risk of stigmatization and exclusion. McFarland Bruce (2016) cites a spectator respondent in her study, who admitted that even in 2010, in a very friendly cultural climate for LGBT people, "you have to be pretty brave to be gay on Pride Day" (p. 97). Even in an LGBT friendly city like Burlington, Vermont, a gay identity continues to bear a cultural stigma.

How is the barrier of stigma – the risk of being reduced "from a whole and usual person to a tainted, discounted one" (Goffman 1968, p. 3) – overcome in the mobilizing processes of LGBT parades? Taylor and Rupp (1993) emphasize the importance of underground support groups, coffee houses, bookstores, restaurants, music festivals, etcetera for lesbians' coming out process. The same holds true for gay men. These subcultural arenas are vital for the stage in the coming out process whereby lesbians and gay men seek the recognition of their peers. But moving to the stage to come out in public takes the process one step further – "out of the bars and into the streets." How are LGBT people inspired to leave the safety of their subcultural arenas and networks to publically confront heterosexual normativity? We argue that personal contacts are important for most Pride participants in overcoming the barrier of stigmatization. The participative support of friends, family and acquaintances is crucial for overcoming this barrier.

Another path to overcoming the barrier of stigma, evident in our interview data, was participating in another city or country. Yves, from Geneva, first participated in a Pride parade in New York in 1994. Enrique again: "There's also a lot of people who are not from Mexico City who come. ... Like 'no one is going to know me there, or if I run into people who know me, this is a safe space so I know you're cool with this.'" And lastly, perhaps self-evident, we argue that the barrier of stigma is most readily transgressed in LGBT friendly contexts and more difficult to overcome in unfriendly and less LGBT friendly cultural and political contexts where the "risks" of participation are higher.

It is worth noting that the sometimes high proportion of non-LGBT participants in Pride parades (discussed in Chapter 4 and Chapter 7 in this volume) adds yet another dimension to the challenge of overcoming stigma. On the one hand, non-LGBT Pride participants also take the risk of sharing the stigma of their LGBT peers and are thus potentially confronted with similar considerations before participating. On the other hand, when extensive non-LGBT Pride participation becomes an institutionalized phenomenon, such as in Sweden, marching in Pride no longer itself equates to coming out as LGBT.

There is an additional category of factors that can motivate and bring people to the streets. External events can act as catalysts for mobilization, by creating "moral shocks" that precipitate protest (Jasper and Poulsen 1995). The June 12, 2016 terrorist attack inside Pulse – a gay disco in Orlando, Florida – left 49 dead and 58 wounded and led the Social Democratic Prime Minister of Sweden – Stefan Löfven – to announce the next day that he would participate in that summer's Pride parade as a show of solidarity with LGBT people worldwide. While this announcement was not unanticipated, the declaration the same day by the leader of the Swedish Christian Democrat Party – Ebba Busch Thor – that she would join the march was unexpected. While she did not have to overcome the barrier of stigma, she did have to overcome the critique she encountered within her party that has its base in Evangelical churches in Sweden. In a subsequent polemical article in the Swedish major evening newspaper *Aftonbladet*, she tried to deflect some of the internal criticism by pointing to the importance of standing up for human rights and freedoms in the face of violent threats. At the same time she reminded readers that participating in Pride did not entail signing up for any specific policy demands, while explicitly repudiating what she termed "the radical norm criticism and identity politics" of Sweden's major LGBT organization RFSL (Busch Thor 2016).

The tragic events in Orlando and the same week in Xalapa, Mexico where gunmen entered a gay club killing five and wounding fourteen were also a mobilizing factor for participants in the 2016 Mexico City Pride parade. Donohue (2016) cites a Mexican Pride participant stating that: "The violence [in Orlando and Xalapa] probably didn't change the Pride parade in and of itself. But at least for me, it had an empowering effect. In a way, it gave me the force I needed to go out to the streets and be who I am without fear." The moral shocks created by external events can galvanize LGBT people and non-LGBT allies alike to participate, providing the emotional or moral motivation to overcome barriers to protest.

In the following, we will focus on action mobilization and some of the factors that help potential Pride participants pass through being targeted, to being motivated, to overcoming the barrier of stigma – indirectly, the social networks that helped participants to overcome the barrier of stigma. We will take particular note of newcomers to Pride, since they presumably are the ones most challenged by the barrier of stigma, coming out at their first parade.

Information channels and mobilizing networks

There are multiple ways for potential participants in a protest to become targeted. Snow and colleagues (1980) categorized information channels used in recruitment to SMOs according to two dimensions: whether the information is face-to-face or mediated and whether it is public or private. Inspired by these dimensions, Walgrave and Klandermans (2010) in a more recent study of mobilization to peace protests distinguish between more or less open information channels based on who is targeted. They write that:

> open mobilization channels have no restriction regarding whom they target, while closed mobilization channels only target people with certain characteristics, for instance, members of an organization. The broader the target groups, the less specific personal characteristics, the more open the mobilization channel.
>
> (p. 172)

TV and radio, as well as major newspapers, can be regarded as open channels in most countries, while organizations informing their own members of a protest represent the more closed end of the spectrum. Walgrave and Klandermans (2010) regard more personal information channels, such as friends, family, colleagues and schoolmates as rather open, and locate these channels in the middle of their spectrum. These channels, although restricted to interpersonal networks, can reach beyond the core activists in the movement. They regard channels such as websites, ads, flyers and posters as belonging to the more closed end of the scale (although not as closed as organizations). This is arguably rather variable, and we therefore prefer not to rank the openness of these information channels in relation to interpersonal networks. A last type of information channel, quite distinct and increasingly significant but not separately dealt with by Walgrave and Klandermans, is online social media, such as Twitter and Facebook (Van Laer 2010; Theocharis et al. 2015). Whereas Van Laer (2010) shows that it was mainly the organizationally affiliated protest participants in his sample who received information about the protest event from the Internet, others have emphasized the potential for different categories of protesters mobilized through Internet communication (Fisher and Boekkooi 2010; Mercea 2012; Anduiza et al. 2014). Online social media may be a particularly important resource for mobilization in LGBT unfriendly contexts where formally organized movements face repression and where the movement has few possibilities to put forth their perspectives in the mainstream public media channels (e.g. Breuer et al. 2015). Social media platforms may furthermore become sites of online *free social spaces*, which may facilitate the diffusion of messages from movements that are "deviant" in the context of their society (Törnberg and Törnberg 2017).

While impersonal information has the function of targeting potential participants, it is often not sufficient as a motivating factor (for an exception, see Walgrave and Manssens 2000) or overcoming the inconvenience barriers for actually participating in protest, in our case most notably the barrier of stigma. Several authors have pointed to the importance of interpersonal networks in this regard. A person asking others to participate is a crucial mechanism for the decision-shaping function of social networks (e.g. Passy 2001; Schussman and Soule 2005). When asked by somebody to join a protest, people tend to feel a stronger commitment compared to those who are only informed and not directly asked. Sandra who was the president of the Stockholm Pride Association 2014–2015 participated in her first Pride parade in 2003 when she had been asked to be a "tire watch"[3] for a float carrying a group of her older sister's friends. Asked by friends to participate and with a function for the parade was a compelling motivation for Sandra to take part. Yga, a Polish lesbian activist told us how she came to participate in her first parade.

> The first time was in 2003, so two years after the beginning of the equality parades. In the beginning I wasn't so conscious about the idea of the parade and I thought "It is just crazy" and so on, but people were talking to me about it and they said that it is our day and it is mobilizing and that we should do something so I started to be in the parade.

Closely connected to the importance of being asked to participate is to have company at a protest event. Few people participate in protests without the company of someone they know. Wahlström and Wennerhag (2014) show that this category is particularly uncommon in Pride parades compared to other types of protests – only on average 4 percent of Pride participants attended alone (and had not been asked by anybody to join). Pride parades appear to share this feature with other protest events that are based on relatively consolidated identities (e.g. May Day marches and women's marches) as opposed to more open mobilizations like anti-austerity demonstrations (with on average 15 percent loners), which to a lesser extent draw on specific social identities. It is also quite possible that, again, the barrier of stigma, and the concomitant need for supportive friends, contributes to the low proportion of loners in Pride parades.

Asking is also a mechanism for further diffusion of mobilization since people who are asked by someone to join a protest often ask others in turn. Whereas Passy (2001) demonstrates the importance of strong ties, such as close friends and (to a lesser extent) family for the chance that the person asked will eventually participate, Walgrave and Wouters (2014) show that those asked by weaker ties appear to be more prone to ask others in turn. This might be connected to another finding by the same authors that people tend to ask persons of the same kind as those whom they were asked by; those who were asked by colleagues also tended to ask colleagues, etcetera.

Of course, most protest mobilizations do not rely solely on informal ties but also on members of formal organizations. The centrality of formal organizations is a core assumption of the classic resource mobilization theory of social movements (McCarthy and Zald 1977). Still, larger protest mobilizations seldom rely solely on organizational membership since few organizations are large enough to bring a substantial crowd to the streets, with the exception of larger trade unions and environmental organizations. Indeed, a large proportion of participants in demonstrations are unaffiliated to the organizers, on average roughly half of the participants in a large sample of demonstrations and ritual parades, analyzed by Klandermans and colleagues (2014). However, in the case of Pride parades affiliation to the organizer is not a good general measure for comparison, since many of the organizers are not organizations based on individual memberships, but umbrella-organizations with other organizations as members or affiliates. People who are members of organizations that are official partners to the organizer may still perceive that they are affiliated with the organizers. However, the organizational structure behind a Pride parade is not always clear to the participants, and varies across cities. Therefore membership in an LGBT organization is a better measure of organizational affiliation (as we will return to below).

The type of channels used for action mobilization are likely to vary across different political and cultural contexts. In their study of peace mobilizations, Walgrave and Klandermans (2010) show that among the demonstrations in their study, those located in countries with public opinion supporting the issue, the participants were more likely to have been mobilized through open information channels. They argue that a more supportive public opinion makes the media more positive, which in turn leads to a more "open" mobilization. More contentious movement activity (measured by national survey data and reported participation in demonstrations) also led to more open mobilization patterns in Walgrave and Klandermans' study, but they are not explicit in their theoretical interpretation of this. Presumably, a higher level of contentiousness in the population in general means that more people are prepared to take part in a demonstration or parade even when they are not members of the organization staging it. The authors also argue that high density of the movement sector in a country – that is, the totality of all formal social movement organizations (engaged in any type of contentious issue) – should make more closed forms of mobilization relatively more important, since there are basically more opportunities for mobilizing within organizational networks. However, in their sample of eight countries, the effect of movement sector density on mobilizing channels was limited. With reference to our discussion about precipitating events above, preexisting formal and informal mobilizing networks may become less important in the presence of an event that gives rise to a moral shock (Jasper and Poulsen 1995). However, no obvious cases of preceding moral shocks were present in our data.

In the case of Pride parades, one could assume that similar patterns would occur as in the cited study on peace mobilizations. A generally more dense movement sector in society could mean proportionally less open overall mobilization. On the other hand, public opinion, which is more positive toward LGBT people should lead to more open forms of mobilization. For some countries these expectations would point in different directions. For example, in Sweden, where both tolerance for LGBT people and the movement sector organizational density is high, there would arguably be mechanisms present that simultaneously favor mobilization through both open and closed channels. Use of online social networks as information sources should be dependent on the level of internet penetration nationally, but can also be expected to be higher where formal organizing is more uncommon and in LGBT unfriendly countries where open channels are more perilous or simply uncommon in that upcoming Pride events are not reported in mass media.

Information channels used in Pride parade mobilizations

The respondents in our study were asked: "How did you find out about the parade?" and then provided with a list of alternatives, any number of which could be picked (see the questionnaire in the Appendix). They were also asked to rank their most important source of information from the mentioned list. In the analysis the alternatives were clustered into five categories: (1) mass media (radio/TV or newspapers), (2) personal ties (family, friends, acquaintances, school- or workmates), (3) bounded communication (communication with a more limited scope than typical mass media, i.e.

alternative online media, ads, flyers, or posters), (4) organization (fellow members or internal impersonal communication), and (5) online social networks as a separate category. Both measures provide relevant complimentary information, but the ranking of the most important information source arguably represents the information source that was most decisive in the mobilizing process.

Table 5.1 demonstrates that mass media is a rather common source of information for Pride participants in some countries, but the figures for the most important information channel (in italics) show that only a few found it decisive. This information source seems to have been most prominent in Haarlem, where more than one in four regarded it as the most important type of information source. This case fits well with the expectation derived from Walgrave and Klandermans (2010) that supportive public opinion on the protest issue would render open information channels more important. With low levels of stigma attached to coming out (or being out) for presumably many Pride participants in the friendly context of the Netherlands, one can expect lower barriers for participating and that mass media information more often will be sufficient for participating. Interestingly, Haarlem also had the highest number of people participating alone (16 percent, about half of whom also were not asked by anybody to participate; also Wahlström and Wennerhag 2014). In Gothenburg, Stockholm and London, where one might also have expected to find this pattern due to the similarly friendly mobilizing contexts, mass media was rarely mentioned as the main information channel. One partial explanation for this would be the much younger age groups with different media consumption patterns (i.e. more online social media), and in the London case, the strikingly high numbers of participants claiming formal organizations to be their most important channels of information.

The use of online social networks in mobilization fits our expectations, at least regarding the most frequent recipients of information through this medium. In the Czech Republic and in Poland, online social networks were most frequently rated as the most important source of information, which tallies with our expectation about the importance of online social networks in less friendly or unfriendly contexts. However, the proportion of Bologna Pride participants mobilized this way was less remarkable; personal ties and formal organizations were more important sources there, indicating stronger pre-existing mobilizing structures in the city. Czech Pride organizer Kamila also pointed to a campaign the organizers had on the social media platform, Facebook, in 2013. Indeed, 45 percent of participants in Prague Pride 2013 indicated that online social networks were their most important source of information about Pride. This figure was second only to the corresponding 52 percent among participants in the Warsaw Equality parade. Kamila argues that Facebook is an efficient way to target potential supporters:

> [It is even] one of the ways to get heterosexuals to see and participate, because you can easily target them. Like based on similar stuff,

Table 5.1 Types of information channels about the parade (%)

	Warsaw	Bologna	Mexico City	Prague 2012	Prague 2013	Geneva	Zurich	London	Haarlem	Gothenburg	Stockholm	Total (%)
Mass media	26	24	11	40	34	25	21	17	28	32	34	26
	6	*8*	*7*	*10*	*8*	*6*	*6*	*3*	*22*	*9*	*10*	*8*
Personal ties	56	68	45	65	60	59	53	59	46	59	61	58
	23	*35*	*42*	*26*	*17*	*37*	*36*	*38*	*31*	*35*	*31*	*33*
Bounded communication	39	39	15	49	52	37	47	32	35	31	34	36
	9	*10*	*13*	*24*	*16*	*12*	*21*	*10*	*16*	*7*	*10*	*13*
Organizations	32	45	3	29	30	57	39	55	41	49	51	40
	11	*26*	*4*	*12*	*14*	*31*	*27*	*39*	*23*	*27*	*25*	*22*
Online social networks	69	50	37	55	63	27	17	29	19	46	55	43
	52	*21*	*33*	*28*	*45*	*14*	*10*	*10*	*7*	*23*	*25*	*25*

Comment: Figures in italics are the proportions for those who considered each information channel to be the most important for their participation.

similar culture events they are interested in. So it's kind of nice. You can also see how many gays and lesbians are interested in these topics. You can actually find nice numbers and target on people. No other medium will do that.

Personal ties were the most frequently cited, as well as the most important source of information in Italy, Mexico, the Netherlands, Sweden and Switzerland. Neither these proportions nor the varying importance of "bounded communication" in our sample of countries is readily interpretable in terms of the degree of unfriendliness or friendliness of the context. Likely explanations must be sought in different organizers' mobilizing strategies and the existing domestic mobilizing networks.

A central aspect of these domestic mobilizing structures is the degree of formal organizing in the LGBT community. The proportion of Pride participants formally organized in LGBT organizations – studied in Chapter 4 – is an illustration of the varying organizational infrastructure underlying mobilization to the Pride parades in our sample. We could see in Table 4.5 that the parades with the most organized groups of participants were to be found in Italy, Switzerland and the UK, with over 40 percent of Pride participants being members of LGBT organizations. At the other end of the scale we find the Prague Pride parades, with only 17 percent of the participants who were members of LGBT organizations. The latter is not so surprising considering the lack of mass-based LGBT organizations in the Czech Republic.

Overall, the degree of membership in LGBT organizations among Pride participants corresponds rather well to the importance of organizational information channels. Formal organizations were the least important in Mexico City, which also had a relatively low level of membership in LGBT organizations. A contributing factor in the Mexican case also seems to be the entrenched tradition of the Mexico City Pride parade. Enrique explained that the Pride parade in Mexico City was more or less out of the hands of organizers. Even if organizers had wanted to change the date of the parade in 2012, when the event collided with the Mexican general elections, it wouldn't have been possible.

> The march is alive on its own regardless of who's organizing it and regardless if there's anyone organizing it. I'm convinced that people would come to *Reforma* the last Saturday in June every year even if there were no posters on the street or no official information about the march. People know and they come, and that is a great thing. ... People are coming to the march regardless of who's organizing it, and they [the organizers] don't like that because that takes the power away from them. ... Most people who come to the march don't even know who organized it.

Overcoming barriers for participation – being asked and asking others to participate

Turning from information channels to the later stages in Klandermans and Oegema's (1987) model of the mobilization process, we turn to the question of overcoming the barriers for participation. As we have argued above, in the case of Pride parades a distinctive type of barrier is the fear of becoming stigmatized. As argued by Passy and Monsch (2014) social networks are particularly important for shaping the decisions of prospective participants in potentially costly protests. In the case of Pride parades, attending with the support of friends, relatives, acquaintances, and/or colleagues provides the emotional and social support to take the "risk" of participating and overcoming the barrier of stigma. One way of simplifying the complex social interactions that provide support and motivation to participate is to focus on the practice of being asked to participate. In addition, as noted by Walgrave and Wouters (2014), if being asked is crucial for participation, studying the practice of asking others is a key mechanism in networked mobilization processes. In order to estimate the role of these practices in mobilizing participants in Pride parades, we analyzed Pride participants' responses to the question: "Which of the following people specifically asked you to take part in the parade, and which people did you yourself ask to participate. (Check as many as apply)" (see Appendix). In order to simplify the analysis, "partner/family," "relatives," and "friends" were grouped into the broader category *strong ties*, while "acquaintances," "colleagues or fellow students," and "co-members of an organization" were classified as *weak ties*.

In Table 5.2, it is evident that the practice of asking and being asked vary depending on context. In Mexico City and Warsaw, more than half of the participants claimed not to have been asked by anyone to participate, and in Mexico City more than a third had not asked anyone either. As pointed out by Walgrave and Wouters (2014), asking others can be costly if there is a risk that those who are asked will judge one negatively because of one's engagement in a particular protest issue. One might therefore assume that people in more unfriendly contexts would be more hesitant to ask others about participating in a controversial protest, at least among their weak ties. However, it is difficult to empirically disentangle this possible tendency from the parallel likelihood that protest participants in more unfriendly contexts may have a greater need to be asked to overcome barriers to participate.

In our sample of Pride parades, the overall prevalence of being asked was high with the notable exceptions of Mexico City and Warsaw, where over half of the respondents claim not to have been asked by anyone to participate. In Mexico City only 3 percent claim to have been asked to join by a weak tie. Participants having been asked by a weak tie were most common in the British (51 percent) and Swedish (42 percent) Pride

Table 5.2 Proportions of participants asked to join and asking others to participate (%)

	Warsaw	Bologna	Mexico City	Prague 2012	Prague 2013	Geneva	Zurich	London	Haarlem	Gothenburg	Stockholm	Total (%)
Asked by no-one	59	19	53	13	16	21	39	18	39	11	14	28
Asked by strong tie	22	63	25	70	66	52	41	36	34	52	61	47
Asked by weak tie	14	36	3	35	34	29	21	51	14	42	42	30
Asked no-one	15	10	35	8	5	13	14	13	18	8	6	14
Asked strong tie	61	78	41	81	82	63	65	51	51	69	66	64
Asked weak tie	58	75	32	72	78	51	59	43	38	62	61	57

parades. The prevalence of participants having been asked by a strong social tie was highest in Prague (66–70 percent), but also common in Bologna, Gothenburg and Stockholm.

The practice of having asked others to join was also relatively high compared to the figures presented by Walgrave and Wouters (2014). The participants in Mexico City also appear to have been the least active in asking others, whereas the Swedish and Czech respondents appear to have been the most active recruiting others. Overall the participants seem to have been more active in recruiting strong ties compared to weak ties. This is perhaps not so surprising, considering that one reason for asking others is that one wants camaraderie at the parade. Few take part in Pride parades alone (Wahlström and Wennerhag 2014). The comparatively high proportions of participants having been asked by a weak tie in Sweden and the UK also correspond to the assumption that asking practices among weak ties would be more common in LGBT friendly environments.

The low figures for having been asked and for asking others in Mexico City and Warsaw emphasize the potential costs of asking others in less friendly and unfriendly LGBT environments. The apparently frequent asking practices in Bologna constitute a counter-example, possibly corresponding to the other mechanism, hypothetically prevalent in less friendly environments, of requiring direct support from others in order take the step to participate. As we will see in Chapter 8, the Bologna Pride parade participants were also distinctly protest-oriented, which may have meant a more intense and dedicated mobilizing process, thus involving more frequent asking. Conversely, although the Netherlands was a friendly context, asking and having been asked appeared not to be very common in Haarlem, perhaps reflecting a more relaxed and less protest-oriented mobilization.

Newcomers and returning participants

We have already argued that the fear of stigmatization when coming out in public space is a significant barrier for many Pride participants. This fear should be most acute for first-time participants since returnees have already taken this step at least once. Similar differences between first-time and returnee protest participants also exist in other types of demonstrations (Verhulst and Walgrave 2009; Saunders et al. 2012), although the personal significance of coming out is arguably distinctive to Pride parades. We therefore conclude the analysis in this chapter by examining this group of participants compared to others who have participated before.

Verhulst and Walgrave (2009) have argued that first-timers are distinct in terms of biographical availability (i.e. life conditions that to a lower degree compete with protest participation), which they substantiated by pointing to a younger age among first-timers. They also show that first-timers are more prone to use open information channels (mass media and friends/

acquaintances) rather than more closed ones, like sources linked to formal social movement organizations. Curiously, they also argue that first-timers are typically driven by stronger identification with other participants in the protest, compared to returners. Similar patterns were found by Saunders and colleagues (2012) who found first-time participants to be more biographically available, but less entrenched in the social networks and organizations of the movement, compared to other categories of participants.

We base our analysis on a question about prior participation in Pride, posed only in London, Gothenburg, Stockholm, Warsaw and Zurich. When comparing what the two different groups considered their most important

Table 5.3 Most important information channels, first-timers vs. returnees (%)

	First-timer	Returnee	Total
Most important information channel			
Mass media	11	5	7
Personal ties	46	29	32
Bounded communication	5	13	12
Organization	20	27	26
Online social networks	17	26	24
Asked by no-one	20	31	28
Asked no-one	14	11	11
Age groups			
<30 years	55	28	34
30–49 years	29	52	47
50–64 years	12	16	15
>64 years	4	4	4
Identification with other participants: quite or very much	55	76	71
Determined to participate: very much	33	56	51
Decision time			
On the day of the parade	20	7	10
A few days before	33	16	20
A few weeks before	17	12	13
Over a month ago	31	65	57

information channel, in Table 5.3 we can see that mass media and informal social networks (friends and acquaintances) were more important information channels for first-timers, while returnees more often relied on more closed channels. A higher proportion of first-timers had been asked by someone to participate, and the categories were not significantly different in terms of asking others. In line with our expectations, first-timers in Pride parades predominantly belonged to the youngest age group, which could arguably indicate both higher biographical availability as well as fewer opportunities for prior Pride participation. Not surprisingly, but contrary to Verhulst and Walgrave's (2009) findings, the first-timers had a lower degree of identification than other participants, and they also expressed a lower degree of determination to participate. Compared to returnees, first-timers also decided to participate rather late: 20 percent on the day of the parade.

Taken together, these data indicate that first-timers to Pride were indeed different from returnees in terms of their predominant mobilizing patterns. They were more heavily reliant on open information channels and the support from social networks through being asked. This support compensated for their generally lower determination to participate and lower identification with other Pride participants.

Conclusion

The pathways to coming out in Pride parades are many. Whereas our Pride data does not cover all aspects of this complex process, we can point to channels for targeting, and indirectly, channels for motivation and lastly, for overcoming barriers for stigmatization. We detected patterns in these channels for the countries included in our study, although the patterns were not unambiguous. The figures for Pride in the Netherlands and Sweden indicate that supportive public opinion in a country positively influences the importance of mass media as a source of information for mobilization. Prague Pride was the exception, however, where information through mass media and online social networks compensated for a limited organized social movement sector. The mobilization in Mexico City relied heavily on personal ties for information, but curiously a higher proportion considered social ties to be their most important source of information compared to the proportion who have been asked by someone to join. Presumably, being told about the parade did not necessarily mean that the individual was directly asked to participate with their informant. The comparatively high figures for online social networks in countries like the Czech Republic, Mexico and Poland indicate that these channels become more important in environments that are both rather hostile in terms of public opinion, *and* have weak mobilizing structures in terms of formal mass-based LGBT organizations.

A central theme in this chapter has been the challenge of publically coming out as a LGBT person in Pride. We termed this the *barrier of stigma*, which we argued is also potentially applicable to non-LGBT people participating in Pride. The group that we expected to be most sensitive about taking this step was the first-timers in Pride and we concluded the chapter by paying particular attention to this group. Indeed our data confirmed that support from informal personal networks appeared to have had a more important role for first-timers to help them cross the barrier of stigma, compared to the returnees who were both more determined, had stronger identification with other participants, and were more likely to be mobilized through more closed information channels.

Notes

1 The Pride parade in 2012 collided with the national elections, which is one explanation for the meagre turnout. Pride parades in Mexico City during the 2010s usually mobilize between 400,000 to 500,000 participants.
2 Canal Pride is limited in regards to the number of participants as these take part on boats, which are restricted in number. It is the number of spectators, which makes this parade massive.
3 A tire watch is a required safety functionary to assure that no one falls under the vehicle.

References

Almeida, J., Johnson, R.M., Corliss, H.L., Molnar, B.E., and Azrael, D. (2009). Emotional distress among LGBT youth: The influence of perceived discrimination based on sexual orientation. *Journal of Youth and Adolescence*, 38(7), 1001–1014.
Anduiza, E., Cristancho, C., and Sabucedo, J.M. (2014). Mobilization through online social networks: the political protest of the indignados in Spain. *Information, Communication & Society*, 17(6), 750–764.
Breuer, A., Landman, T., and Farquhar, D. (2015). Social media and protest mobilization: Evidence from the Tunisian Revolution. *Democratization*, 22(4), 764–792.
Busch Thor, E. (2016). Jag tvekar inte över att gå med i Prideparaden. *Aftonbladet*, July 29, 2016, p. 6.
della Porta, D., and Diani, M. (2006). *Social movements: an introduction*, 2nd Ed. Malden, MA: Blackwell.
Donohue, C. (2016). Photo: The 38th Mexico City Pride celebrations conquered fear of anti-LGBT violence. *Remezcla*, 2016-06-28. Available at URL: http://remezcla.com/lists/culture/mexico-city-pride-2016-photos/ (accessed July 27, 2017).
European Union Agency for Fundamental Rights. (2014). *European Union lesbian, gay, bisexual and transgender survey: Main results*. Luxembourg: Publications Office of the European Union.
Fisher, D.R., and Boekkooi, M. (2010). Mobilizing friends and strangers. *Information, Communication & Society*, 13(2), 193–208.
Goffman, E. (1968). *Stigma: Notes on the management of spoiled identity*. Harmondsworth: Penguin.
Herek G.M. (2002). Heterosexuals' attitudes toward bisexual men and women in the United States. *Journal of Sexualities Research*, 39(4), 264–274.

Hoover R., and Fishbein H.D. (1999). The development of prejudice and sex role stereotyping in white adolescents and white young adults. *Journal of Applied Developmental Psychology*, 20(3), 431–448.

Horn S.S. (2006). Heterosexual adolescents' and young adults' beliefs and attitudes about homosexuality and gay and lesbian peers. *Cognitive Development*, 21(4), 420–440.

Jasper, J.M., and Poulsen, J.D. (1995). Recruiting strangers and friends: Moral shocks and social networks in animal rights and anti-nuclear protests. *Social Problems*, 42(4), 493–512.

Klandermans, B. (1984). Mobilization and participation: Social-psychological expansions of resource mobilization theory. *American Sociological Review*, 583–600.

Klandermans, B. (2004). The demand and supply of participation: Social-psychological correlates of participation in social movements. In Snow, D.A., Soule, S.A., and Kriesi, H. (Eds). *The Blackwell Companion to Social Movements* (pp. 360–379). Oxford: Blackwell Publishing.

Klandermans, B., and Oegema, D. (1987). Potentials, networks, motivations, and barriers: Steps towards participation in social movements. *American Sociological Review*, 52(4), 519–531.

Klandermans, B., van Stekelenburg, J., Damen, M-L., van Troost, D., and van Leeuwen, A., (2014). Mobilization without organization: The case of unaffiliated demonstrators. *European Sociological Review*, 30(6), 702–716.

Kuhar, R. (2011). The heteronormative panopticon and the transparent closet of the public space in Slovenia. In Kulpa, R., and Mizielinska, R. (Eds). *De-centring western sexualities: Central and Eastern European perspectives* (pp. 149–165). London: Routledge.

Linden, A., and Klandermans, B. (2006). Stigmatization and repression of extreme-right activism in the Netherlands. *Mobilization: An International Quarterly*, 11(2), 213–228.

McCarthy, J.D., and Zald, M.N. (1977). Resource mobilization and social movements: A partial theory. *The American Journal of Sociology*, 82(6), 1212–1241.

McFarland, Bruce K. (2016). *Pride parades: How a parade changed the world.* New York: NYU Press.

Mercea, D. (2012). Digital prefigurative participation: The entwinement of online communication and offline participation in protest events. *New Media & Society*, 14(1), 153–169.

Passy, F. (2001). Socialization, connection, and the structure/agency gap: A specification of the impact of networks on participation in social movements. *Mobilization*, 6(2), 173–192.

Passy, F., and Monsch, G-A. (2014). Do social networks really matter in contentious politics? *Social Movement Studies*, 13(1), 22–47.

Peterson, A., Wahlström, M., and Wennerhag, M. (2014). Contextual factors that lead to the normalization of Pride parade participation in six European countries. ECPR General Conference. Glasgow, UK.

Peterson, A., Wahlström, M., Wennerhag, M., Christancho, C., and Sabucedo, J.M. (2012). May Day demonstrations in five European countries. *Mobilization*, 17(3), 281–300.

Russell S.T. (2002). Queer in America: Citizenship for sexual minority youth. *Applied Developmental Science*, 6(4), 258–263.

Russell S.T., Franz B.T., and Driscoll A.K. (2001). Same-sex romantic attraction and experiences of violence in adolescence. *American Journal of Public Health*, 91(6), 903–906.

Russell S.T., and Joyner K. (2001). Adolescent sexual orientation and suicide risk: evidence from a national study. *American Journal of Public Health*, 91(8), 1276–1281.

Taylor, V., and Rupp, L.J. (1993). Women's culture and lesbian feminist activism: A reconsideration of cultural feminism. *Signs: Journal of Women in Culture and Society*, 19(1), 32–61.

Saunders, C., Grasso, M., Olcese, C., Rainsford, E., and Rootes, C. (2012). Explaining differential protest participation: Novices, returners, repeaters, and stalwarts. *Mobilization: An International Quarterly*, 17(3), 263–280.

Schussman, A., and Soule, S.A. (2005). Process and protest: Accounting for individual protest participation. *Social Forces*, 84(2), 1083–1108.

Smith, T.W., Son, J., and Kim, J. (2014). Public Attitudes towards Homosexuality and Gay Rights across Time and Countries. Report published by the Williams Institute, University of Chicago. Available at URL: https://williamsinstitute.law.ucla.edu/wp-content/uploads/public-attitudes-nov-2014.pdf (accessed September 20, 2017).

Snow, D.A., Zurcher, L.A., and Ekland-Olson, S. (1980). Social networks and social movements: A microstructural approach to differential recruitment. *American Sociological Review*, 45(5), 787–801.

Theocharis, Y., Lowe, W., van Deth, J.W., and García-Albacete, G. (2015). Using Twitter to mobilize protest action: Online mobilization patterns and action repertoires in the Occupy Wall Street, Indignados, and Aganaktismenoi movements. *Information, Communication & Society*, 18(2), 202–220.

Törnberg, A., and Törnberg, P. (2017). Modelling free social spaces and the diffusion of social mobilization. *Social Movement Studies*, 16(2), 182–202.

Van Laer, J. (2010). Activists online and offline: The Internet as an information channel for protest demonstrations. *Mobilization: An International Quarterly*, 15(3), 347–366.

Wahlström, M., and Wennerhag, M. (2014). Alone in the crowd: Lone protesters in Western European demonstrations. *International Sociology*, 29(6), 565–583.

Walgrave, S., and Klandermans, B. (2010). Open and closed mobilization patterns: The role of channels and ties. In Walgrave, S., and Rucht, D. (Eds) *The world says no to war: Demonstrations against the war on Iraq* (pp. 169–193). Minneapolis, MN: University of Minnesota Press, 169–193.

Walgrave, S., and Manssens, J. (2000). The making of the white march: The mass media as a mobilizing alternative to movement organizations. *Mobilization: An International Quarterly*, 5(2), 217–239.

Walgrave, S., and Wouters, R. (2014). The missing link in the diffusion of protest: Asking others. *American Journal of Sociology*, 119(6), 1670–1709.

Verhulst, J., and Walgrave, S. (2009). The first time is the hardest? A cross-national and cross-issue comparison of first-time protest participants. *Political Behavior*, 31(3), 455–484.

6 Friends of Pride
Challenges, Conflicts and Dilemmas

Dieter Rucht (2008, p. 198) reminds us that, "seeking allies can become critical for a movement's survival, particularly when it is in an outsider position. Only by broadening their support can most movements hope to make an impact" (see also McFarland Bruce 2016, p. 115 on straight allies). However, as Adam, Duyvendak and Krouwel (1999, p. 349) explain:

- the gay and lesbian movement is not only dependent on the solidarity of other social movements and allies; it also has to "fit" into the emancipation model used by other groups in society and recognized by authorities as valid and justified.

In this chapter we focus on how and why Pride organizers mobilize what we call "friends of Pride," and the opportunities as well as challenges, conflicts and dilemmas associated with allies. For LGBT movements that seek allies – both individual and collective friends – there are two types of challenges. First, how are (potential) friends mobilized? Second, how do LGBT movements deal with the opportunities – and risks – that are associated with different friendships? Can friends be too friendly? Do the organizers perceive a risk that the participation of friends can potentially "de-gay" Pride events as many queer scholars warn?

Friends of Pride

In our analysis, we find two forms of friends of Pride. First, *individuals* who are not themselves LGBT, but who nevertheless appear to be a significant element in contemporary Pride parades (Wahlström, Peterson and Wennerhag 2018). In Chapter 4 we account for the varying proportions of non-LGBT individuals who participated in the demonstrations in Stockholm, Haarlem, Warsaw and London. Suffice it here to remind the reader that individual friends of pride are a significant category of Pride participants. Second, we find *groups/organizations* that do not have LGBT issues as their main focus, but who nonetheless participate in Pride parades. We conceptualize *organizational* friends of Pride as organizations that act (or wish to act) as supporters or allies of the movement, but which do not have LGBT issues as their primary goal. These can be private businesses, public employers, sports groups not primarily organizing LGBT people, most political parties (the Swedish Feminist Initiative is a possible exception), labor unions, as well as political, ethnic and other organizations that do not have LGBT issues as their main goals or core identity. However, in our analysis, in order to recognize an organization as an ally of the LGBT/Pride movement it has to be acknowledged as such by the LGBT movement, and most decisively by the Pride organizers. For example (which we will return to below), pedofile/pedosexual groups, which, after historically having had a (controversial) position within the broader sexual liberation movement, are today widely repudiated by LGBT movements.

Using our extended secondary empirical sample,[1] we found a wide range of organizational friends in the 11 surveyed parades. WorldPride in London, along with Zurich Pride and Stockholm Pride, appear to have been those most prominently featuring commercial sponsors, including prominent financial, insurance and media companies. Bologna, Geneva, Mexico City, Prague and Warsaw had few or no visible commercial sponsors.

Various public employers were especially visible in London, Haarlem and Stockholm, including police and military sections in uniforms. Political parties (or at least LGBT organizations of political parties) were present in most parades, albeit with varying prominence. Their presence was probably most notable in the Stockholm Pride parade 2014, which was organized only a few weeks prior to a parliamentary election. While most Pride parades featured sports clubs specifically for LGBT people, only in the Swedish parades (Gothenburg and Stockholm) did we document the visible presence of "ordinary" sports clubs and supporter organizations. Trade unions were especially visible in Bologna, London, Gothenburg and Stockholm. Church groups also had a minor presence in most parades, as well as interest groups such as handicap associations. Most of the organizational friends of Pride were closely related to human rights issues, e.g. Amnesty International, however, we will also discuss other organizational friends that brought in issues that many would consider disconnected from core LGBT concerns.

In order to understand both similarities and differences in these patterns, as well as challenges that the participation of various types of friends may give rise to, we will turn to the organizers' framing of Pride events and their mobilizing context.

Contextual factors and the participation of "friends of Pride"

The main factor that is important for the participation of allies in Pride parades, we argue, is the character of the specific Pride parades, i.e. how organizers framed the event (see also Chapter 7 this volume). Overall, this regards whether the parades were staged as events primarily intended for the LGBT community, or if the organizers aimed at attracting broader groups to attend the parades. Whereas it is important to identify factors in the external context of Pride mobilizations that precondition their character, we argue that these mobilizations must also be understood as the outcome of fundamentally strategic choices by organizers. We agree with James Jasper (2004) insofar that such choices should not be reductionistically treated as an outcome of external structures. Instead one must acknowledge the agency involved in strategic decisions made by organizers to deal with genuine dilemmas. Some, if not most, of these dilemmas are common to many other mobilizations, but their specificity must be understood in order to make sense of the varying character of Pride parades.

The diversity *within* LGBT movements enhances the abilities of the movements for coalition building with other social movements and political parties (Salokar 2001, pp. 261–262). Diversity within the movements is the political (and social) precondition for the bridges they forge with allies. During the early Pride years in the 1970s there arose conflicts within lesbian and gay liberation movements over the role of bisexuals and non-homosexuals. It was argued that individuals without experiences of homosexual oppression could never understand what it meant to be gay (McLean 2015, p. 151). First in 1993, in conjunction with the LGB march on Washington D.C., bisexuals joined in the "alphabet soup" to become recognized, albeit marginalized, members of the US movement (Ghaziani 2008). Trans persons, while not always welcomed with open arms, arrived later to the fray (van der Ros and Motmans 2015). The strategic mobilization of straight allies was even later to occur. We argue that the increasing mobilization of friends of Pride is a relatively recent phenomenon, which gained in strength first with the so-called normalization of homosexuality strategy, together with the shift from sexual liberation to an emphasis on the human rights discourse in LGBT politics more generally. In our empirical samples, *all* of the organizers, some more and some less, strategically sought to mobilize friends of Pride; decidedly less in Mexico City. Enrique explains that in Mexico City Pride is an "insider" event.

> Like everyone is invited to the party, but this is a gay party and this is undoubtedly a gay event. I have many straight friends who come to the march with my boyfriend and I, and they love it. We have a party afterwards and they join, but they know that this is an explicitly gay event and there's no intention of erasing that or watering it down.

The Pride parade organizers' approach to individual friends

In this section we will focus on the organizers' framings of Pride parades in London, Haarlem, Stockholm and Warsaw, since these are the only parades for which we can relate an actual outcome in terms of the proportions of individual friends of Pride in the parades (see Chapter 4, this volume). The president of the Stockholm Pride Association stressed that the Pride parade in the country's capital had deliberately chosen to be both "close to the establishment," thereby encouraging elite allies, and "oriented towards the broader masses," thereby encouraging mass allies. Victor explained the broad political platform of Stockholm Pride in the following words: "Regardlesss if you are a corporate director, a Conservative Party leader or a Social Democratic Party leader, Pride week should be on your agenda." According to Victor, the Stockholm Pride organization bears the responsibility that the events during the week and the parade itself are so politically relevant that political parties are eager to participate.[2]

Expressly deploying what Bernstein (1997) calls a "identity strategy for education," Tasso clarified that for Stockholm Pride and West Pride in Gothenburg the goal was to change the attitudes of the general populace and therefore he explained that they have to mobilize a broad cross-section of Sweden's organized civil society. "For my part I am not interested in a separatist movement."

When the Stockholm organizer compared their parade to other large Pride parades in other parts of Europe, she also underlined that what makes Stockholm different from, for example, London, Madrid and Barcelona, is the more prominent role gay clubs and other companies connected to the LGBT community play for organizing the Pride parades in those cities. When comparing the Stockholm event with these parades, the Stockholm organizer thus portrayed other parades as more oriented towards having parties in the streets and going to clubs, and emphasized that these clubs are "in general gay clubs." This seems to suggest that Stockholm Pride has deliberately tried to be inclusive and also attract participants that do not necessarily want to participate in the (gay men–dominated) club scene of the LGBT community.

The organizers of the Warsaw Equality Parade also stressed that they try to have a broader framing of their parade, but for other reasons, and in another situation, than the parade organizers in Stockholm. First, the name of the parade is the Equality Parade, and not a Pride parade, which reflected a general framing of protesting against inequalities in society in general. "The equality parade is not only about LGBT issues, but this is for all the minorities and communities that are, can be, or might be discriminated or excluded." The parade was organized in connection with the Warsaw Equality Parade festival, and the symbol of the parade since 2012 is a heart with rainbow colors, but the parade also brought up other inequality issues including animal rights and discrimination of disabled people. For the Equality Parade organizers, the choice to use the broader frame of equality has been both ideological and strategic; regarding the latter, the organizers believe that the equality framing has made it easier to get support from Polish politicians and state officials than if it had been only framed as concerning LGBT issues (since these issues are still highly controversial in Polish politics), and it has also made it easier to involve other types of organizations in the organizing committee (e.g. political parties – from the left and from anti-clerical liberals, feminist groups, and animal rights organizations) (interviews: Polish organizers, see also Chapter 2 this volume).

But it is not always so easy to get their message across to the media.

> Of course the media usually stress the LGBT part in the parade and show the LGBT community since it's very colorful and happy and, well, gay. But I think each and every year we are managing to point out to the media that it is an equality parade, not a gay parade and I think that the message is now coming across and one can say that the media is starting to understand that. *That this is not the Polish version of Gay Pride, but this is a Polish way of enjoying equality and to fight for equality as well.*
>
> (interview Jej, our emphasis)

The Warsaw organizer clearly articulated the localizing tendency for a contextually responsive and unique framing of the globally transmitted Pride ritual event. The Pride ritual has proved attractive across Europe (and the globe) – the rainbow imagery prevails across national and local contexts – but local organizers are setting their own agendas (Altman 2001).

The organizers of the Pride events in Haarlem (2012) and Groningen (2011) all compared their Pride events and Pink Saturday Parades with Canal Pride in Amsterdam, which they asserted is dominated by gay men and commercial interests. They pointed out that most important for the success of the Pride events, which since 1982 have ambulated between the provincial cities in the Netherlands, was the provision of adequate camping facilities for all of the lesbians and their children. "Unlike the gay men participating in Amsterdam our participants do not want expensive hotel rooms." They claimed that these events provided a social outing for lesbians and their children and friends and much of the dynamics of the Pride events could be found in the informal meetings and activities in the camping sites. The accounts of their mobilizing strategies dovetail with researchers' claims that historically, almost from the very start in 1978, in Pink Saturday events "community dominated over political interests" (Schuyf and Krouwel 1999, p. 165).

The organizers of London Pride emphasized that their ambition is to open the parade for everyone who self-identifies as part of the LGBT community in London and their friends. Patrick, the head organizer in London, says:

> Our job is to facilitate an event ... within which you can demonstrate, you can march, you can parade, you can teeter on your high heels ... in other words be yourself. And our job today is to put on an event which allows everyone to safely do that.

According to the organizers, prominent politicians, such as the Mayor of London, as well as business figures regularly attend the Pride events. The authorities, according to the organizer, want to show that London is a LGBT friendly city and a great place for major corporations, which are generally LGBT friendly if not led by LGBT people.

According to Patrick,

> the parade is almost exclusively LGBT people. Those who watch and also come along for the day are, of course, not just from the LGBT+ community ... So you know, it's a day for London. We are officially now London's biggest single, one-day event.

The organizers in London, while they pointed out that the event was not just for the LGBT community, emphasized that their responsibility was to secure a safe space for the LGBT community to party and "be themselves." London Pride stands out among the four parades as the one most dominated by gay men (53 percent; Chapter 4, this volume) and the organizers emphasized the vital role of the street parties in Trafalgar Square for the success of the event.

In sum, whereas the organizers of all four parades in our primary empirical sample strived to be inclusive, they did this in different ways. The Warsaw Equality parade distinguished itself by adapting to a LGBT unfriendly, even hostile, environment through a radical frame extension from a focus on LGBT rights to deploying identity for education within a broader equality framework, while still retaining central aspects of Pride symbolism. Stockholm Pride achieved an even higher proportion of non-LGBT participants apparently through a general openness to politicization within a very LGBT friendly environment. London (WorldPride) and Haarlem Prides appeared to have been more community-oriented, albeit towards different parts of the LGBT community (gays, lesbians respectively). We will now turn to the question of the impact of friends of Pride who participate to various degrees in Pride Parades more generally using our aggregated interview dataset – both our primary sample above, complemented with our secondary sample of Pride organizers and key LGBT activists in the Czech Republic, Italy, Mexico and Switzerland.

Individual friends – strengthening or de-gaying Pride?

While social movements often actively seek the participation of allies, both mass and elite, their participation is not always without drawbacks. In the case of LGBT movements based on stigmatized identities, there are, according to LGBT scholars, limits to elite involvement. Elite participation in an event such as a Pride parade will inevitably skew the movement's framing of the event away from the articulations of a lesbian, gay, bisexual, transgender or queer identity, asserting the claims to rights and dignity on the basis of *difference* from the heterosexual norm to less challenging frames. Meyer and Gamson (1995, p. 200) argue that elite participation, and the attention it brings with it, slants visible movement action toward broadly defined issues that emphasize heterosexual and homosexual *sameness*, rather than difference. These broadly defined issues are readily formulated within the paradigm of human rights, thus bypassing the content of LGBT identities (also Bernstein 2005, p. 62; Duggan 2003; Richardson 2005) and thereby constructing a space, we argue, for the participation of non-LGBT individuals.

Furthermore, scholars caution, the visible inclusion of elite allies, together with the inclusion of mass allies, can disrupt the political construction of the LGBT community as a political force – "de-gaying" the event (Browne and Bakshi 2013, p. 163; Casey 2004; Skeggs 1999). Discussing the increased presence of heterosexuals, and in particular heterosexual women, in the gay nightlife scene Chatterton and Hollands (2003, p. 169) suggest that gay venues can become "too straight as the heterosexual population rush to join the fun." While Browne and Bakshi (2013) admit that there are obvious advantages won in "de-gaying" Pride parades "in terms of the absence of transgression," thereby making them more easily and comfortably assessable to heterosexual participants, they argue that there are underlying risks in this strategy (see also Hughes 2006). More forcefully, Crimp (2002) contends that this development signifies the normalization and de-sexualization of a more radical queer past (see also Warner 1999, Shepard 2010). The pacification of queer politics is, according to Crimp, a matter of aligning the desires of gays and lesbians with those of a heterosexual middle class (also Chasin 2000; Ghaziani 2008).

So while many LGBT scholars warn about the potential effects of non-LGBT allies for "de-gaying" Pride parades, the organizers we interviewed were more ambivalent or felt that it was simply not an issue. A Polish organizer emphasized that "we need more friends. ... Our problem is that there are too few people." Steve, a former Director of London Pride and now organizing Plymouth Pride, complained about the lack of political engagement of young gay men:[3]

> They just want a big party. They forget that we still have hearts and minds to win over. ... By having all these allies and children and families coming along, well they are the allies we need to make discrimination completely go away.

Steve, while sceptical as to the motives of straight allies – friends of Pride – who he felt were naïve, nevertheless felt that their engagement filled a political gap left by the political non-engagement of gay men. In general, our informants expressed a willingness and desire to include non-LGBT allies. We asked a Polish lesbian informant who she thought should be mobilized for the Equality Parades.

> I think friends and families of LGBT people, mostly heterosexual people, because sometimes, you know, the person that sees a parade thinks it is strange but after a while when this person goes to the parade they change their mind ... so I think like that. Everyone that is a little bit open minded and wants to be in the parade and comes and says it's okay is welcome.

The queer organizer of the Warsaw Equality Parade told us about a unique strategy they experimented with to mobilize friends of Pride.

> Of course there are straight people walking with us but they are walking with us because of LGBT issues. Last year we did a short happening called the "straight equation", which is a little bit tricky and the English translation does not do justice to the Polish complexity of the slogan. We got a micro grant from the Council of Europe to do that. We put a wall up where straight people could take pictures of themselves showing that they support LGBT issues. And we got a lot of attention and I was very happy, but it wasn't that easy to round up all the people because we did it before and during the parade, but actually by the end of the parade, people were queuing to do that.

While encouraging support from straight friends of Pride, this photo wall arguably provided a "safe" way to express support, while simultaneously demonstrating that you in fact did not belong to the stigmatized collective of LGBT people.

Binnie and Klesse (2014) similarly identify a central dilemma for the organizer of the 2008 "Krakow for Tolerance Festival" in Poland. Since many Polish LGBT persons are afraid to come out, the organizer described how she perceived that non-LGBT people were more visible than the LGBT participants in the parade. The organizer regarded the support of non-LGBT participants as vital for the marches, but she expressed ambivalence as to the relative invisibility of LGBT participants; "the only day when we are visible in the whole year" (p. 207). In the politically and culturally LGBT unfriendly context of Poland, organizers of Pride events are fully aware that they must frame their events in ways that resonate with what they perceive as "European values" – human rights, equality and tolerance. Furthermore, in this way they seek to forge broad coalitions between the LGBT movement in Poland and "diverse political projects with roots in feminism, anarchism, anti-capitalism, age awareness, and fat activism" (Binnie and Klesse 2014, p. 208). In LGBT unfriendly contexts parade organizers are challenged to be skillful coalition-builders to attract the support of friends of Pride (also Bernstein 2003).

Regarding the question as to whether Pride parades can become too inclusive and mainstream, according to the queer person organizing the

Equality Parade in Warsaw, "we are still so far away from the mainstream that it is not an issue I think." Even in a LGBT friendly context, unlike in Warsaw, the Pink Saturday organizers in the Netherlands had a similar mobilizing strategy.

> And that was one of our goals to make a party for everybody, not only LBGT's but also other people, so we wanted to mix; so the festivities were also in the open squares for everybody. Mainstream, well that's a goal.

Two of the organizers of the Pride Parade in Prague outline their strategy to include "straight people." They thought that their weeklong program of cultural events, human rights debates, and concerts could attract a broader participant profile to the concluding parade.

> We should show the different aspects of the gay community and try to get the local community and Czech community in general involved as much as possible. ... Now since two years ago we have for example Pride Village, which many other Prides have as well – it's like a public space, in the city center, where every day there's events, performances, people go there to get information.

Petr, an organizer from Prague, explained their motives for their inclusive strategy – an "identity strategy for education" (Bernstein 1997) – in the following words:

> Well of course it's by definition more interesting for LGBT people but to me it's important also to reach out to the straight people. Because first of all, a lot of them have daughters and sons who are gays or lesbians. They have friends and relatives who are gays and lesbians. So maybe it's a chance to look into their world a bit. ... To me it's very important. And we know from our numbers that we have between 30 and 40 percent each year that are straight participants.

Willem, one of the organizers of the Prague events, told us about the political backlash for the LGBT movement in the Czech Republic under the presidency of Václav Klaus who had taken a public stand against LGBT rights. He thought that this resulted in a turnabout for Pride resulting in a very political parade. "You could see loads of straight people marching with us and supporting us, just because of that, just because they wanted to show that they didn't agree with those statements of the president." Prague organizers, like organizers in other less LGBT friendly contexts for Pride Parades, actively sought and welcomed the support of straight allies – friends of Pride – and were little concerned that they would de-gay the event.

Kamila, also on the Prague organizing team, expressed her utopian version of Pride's mobilizing capacity.

> Pride is supposed to be for everyone, but that's hard to explain to people. So, um, well, I would like to see first of all diversity based companies, like IKEA and H&M, those that already have LGBT groups inside. And that's also because I think their strong name could help others that are still thinking about it and are not sure. So basically using their brand to say to other people that it's cool. ... But also of course, non-LGBT people that's like my dream that in a company all your colleagues support you and go to Pride with you like as a team or something. Even with friends, the same thing. We were also thinking about some kind of campaign like that. Haven't done that yet, like "Support your gay" is funny, you know, something like that. Go with your friend, it's like don't be scared to join the parade. I go to Roma festivals and I'm not a gypsy. It's just a cultural event, so probably that's one of our next steps to show people that it's just a festival and that it doesn't mean that they change their sexuality on the street, and there is nothing to be like scared of.

In general, the organizers and activists we interviewed were positive to the participation of straight allies. Only one organizer, a Social Democratic member of the Board of Stockholm Pride, expressed an ambivalent attitude to the increasing numbers of non-LGBT marchers in the parade. While he was personally in favor of the process of integrating straight allies in the event, which in Stockholm has been very successful, he pointed out that "at the same time a part of our own community do not any longer feel the relevance [of the parade] in the same way." Browne and Bakshi (2013) found a relatively widespread nostalgia among their respondents who in general mourn a bygone era when Pride was protest and the political divides were clearly drawn. This was an era of LGBT politics when Pride parades were less attractive for non-LGBT allies.

The operative chief of Stockholm Pride also claimed that they have found it necessary to charge entrance fees to "Pride Park." After criticism from within the LGBT movement the Pride organization experimented one year with free entry to the stages in Pride Park. "But then a lot of people came in that didn't have any business there. ... Suddenly we didn't own our own festival ... I left damned angry after being called a fagot three times at my own festival." He explained that by charging for entry they had a mechanism for excluding a lot of unwanted friends. His story echoed with another Swedish informant who told us that he had heard a lot of people complain that they had felt uncomfortable "when a mass of people came and just stared. People felt that it was like sitting in a zoo." Anders, a Stockholm Pride organizer, felt that Pride Park should be a "protected space" for the LGBT community. Pride organizers in Sweden make a sharp distinction between the parade with both a political and a festive content and the "street parties" in Pride Park. While they implement an inclusive mobilizing strategy in the parade, the organizers attempt to make the parties more exclusive for LGBT communities in order to reinforce the strategies – "identity as goal" and "identity for empowerment" – aspect of the event (Bernstein 1997).

Hughes (2006, p. 251) ominously warns that large-scale LGBT festivals, dependent on commercial funding, inevitably "touristifies gay space" and encourages "the undesireable incursion of non-gays." Heterosexual "acceptance," according to Hughes, is bought at the price of undermining the empowerment and cultural strength of gay people, and their subsequent "ownership" of the event. How perilous is commercialization?

Buying friendship? Commercial friends

Chasin (2000) traced the increasing commercialization of Pride in the US and how this resulted in an increasing professionalization of organizers' staffs, with paid employees whose role was to secure further commercial funding (also Browne and Bakshi 2013). This is a development we find elsewhere. Steve, the President of the Gay Businessmen Association and the former director of London Pride, explained what he considered the inevitability of the commercialization of Pride. When a float in Pride London costs between £5,000 and £10,000:

> well what gay organization can afford that? They can't. Unless they get sponsored. And then the gay community complains that, "Oh it's commercialised". Well you can't have it both ways, you know, where's the money going to come from if it is not commercialized?

However, not all LGBT community activists share Steve's commitment to seek corporate sponsors. Dan thought that the event should be free and that control of Pride should be wrested from corporations and placed in the hands of the LGBT community. "For me the decision making, the control of an event like Pride needs to incorporate the people who are being directly affected. We need to be led by those on the ground who are making changes."

Willem explained the Prague organizers' position on the issue of the commercialization of Pride.

> From the Prague Pride perspective we would like to be more commercial. We would hope to have more large commercial partners, because we are mainly dependent on partnerships. It's getting better, you see an increase of commercial sponsors, but when you compare it to Western Prides, in the Czech Republic there are far more reservations about affiliating themselves with gay events. It's something new

> in the society, so basically they are afraid that they would be damaged if they were associated with gay Pride. Even like international companies, which all over the world sponsor Pride events, like Smirnoff is sponsoring this, or Heineken, or whatever – but here they say no, no, no. Even Czech companies like Škoda, a car company, or Pilsner-Urquell, a beer company, abroad they sponsor gay events, but here in the Czech Republic they don't dare to and I think it's gonna change, like I said it's getting better, during the first year it was difficult. I think the only problem, which could appear if Pride would be commercial, is if they would like to dictate the program, but I don't really think that this is an actual problem.

Key activists in the Mexico City Pride are ambivalent in regards to commercialization. A gay activist could not understand why commercial funding was not actively sought. A lesbian activist told us that more businesses are now involved.

> Some of them are pushing their own economic interests by trying to advertise themselves. But there's another big group of companies that are participating because they are supporting our struggle and giving protection to their workers. ... We now have more than twenty companies that are involved, though most of them are international corporations, some are Mexican and they are involved in the labor-rights process. ... But the march hasn't had sponsors. Some time ago there was a small group of gay men who organized the march and they began asking companies and bars to give money, but the march doesn't really need money. It was only lining their own pockets.

She cautioned that when companies and bars gave money for the march the LGBT community potentially relinquished control over the Pride Parade – "this is our Pride." Sponsoring with funding allowed them, according to Gloria, to, amongst other things, negotiate regarding their place in the parade preferring to be at the front of the march. Instead their strategy, which was successful, was to secure the support from the local government, who provided security and set up the stages for the event – "it is the government that has responsibility for that." There appears to be a clear division within the LGBT movement in Mexico City regarding the question of commercialization. Our male informants in Mexico were generally positive to acquiring funding from companies and bars, while female informants, although positive to their participation, were highly sceptical to accepting sponsor funding, which they claimed would make the event vulnerable to market interests.

Ulrika, the former President of the Swedish Federation for Lesbian, Gay, Bisexual, Transgender and Queer Rights (RFSL) and president of the Stockholm Pride Association 2005–2006, explained that:

everyone is welcome, but on the other hand we don't want to have too many commercial actors because it is important that we maintain our credibility and political relevance. ... that it is actually a parade of, with, and for the LGBT community. ... It would be strange if the parade was taken over by non-LGBT persons, for example companies that were interested in "pink washing" themselves and just wanted a free ride in the spotlight. If it develops like that it would be unfortunate, it would hollow out the very meaning of Pride in the long run. ... But if a lot of allies want go in a Pride parade to show their support, then I don't see how it is a problem.

Tasso told us that West Pride in Gothenburg was even more restrictive than Stockholm Pride in regards to company sponsors. Unlike Stockholm Pride they do not accept sponsoring from tobacco companies or liquor companies. Sharing the concern that Gloria from Mexico City expressed that commercial sponsoring might potentially change the character of Pride, Tasso was also sceptical about what he perceived as commercialized Pride events in other countries.

You can see some of the large clubs that are sponsored by liquor companies that throw up some big stages and it is just party and music ... And they do that only because they make money, selling their alcohol, their beer ... and that is a very, very long way from how we do things in Sweden and especially Gothenburg.

In general our Swedish informants strived to restrict and regulate commercial sponsoring of Pride events so as not to relinquish its control of the Parade to the market (also Chasin 2000). In the case of Stockholm Pride, half of the organizing association's income is derived from entrance fees to "Pride Park" and one-fourth is from fees for organizations taking part in the parade and exhibitors at "Pride House" (where seminars and debates take place), while only 13 percent come from sponsors. However, in the case of West Pride, while relying on volunteers, it enjoys a (at least partly) state-sponsored full-time paid staff. We find the same state-funding situation, although to a lesser degree, in the Netherlands Pink Saturday organizations. Among the *haves*, that is, Pride organizations in countries that are very politically and culturally LGBT friendly, such as, in our primary sample, Sweden and the Netherlands, state-employed organizational staffs have the leeway to restrict and regulate commercial funding; they can more or less pick and choose among the potential commercial sponsors queuing at their doors, requiring LGBT friendly personnel policies for companies applying to participate. The *have-some*, the UK in our primary sample, receive only limited government funding and thereby must rely largely on commercial funding for their parades and street parties making them more vulnerable to the market. In contrast to Mexico City where the municipality provides the stages, street cleaning and security, the London organizers must supply these services themselves. The *have-nots*, Warsaw in our primary sample, are at this point only dreaming of financial support – government or commercial.

It is furthermore significant to acknowledge the radically divergent meanings of commercial sponsorship depending on the cultural context. This was evident from our Czech and Polish organizers' statements about international companies' reluctance to support their parades, despite expressing official support for Pride parades in other countries. In LGBT unfriendly and less friendly country contexts sponsoring becomes a commercial risk for businesses since they jeopardize "staining" their brands with LGBT issues. The "barrier of stigmatization," which we discussed in Chapter 5 in conjunction with mobilizing individual participants, proves to be also a barrier for companies. Because of the barrier of stigmatization, those that might nevertheless support Pride in such contexts can also be trusted by organizers to have genuine motives for providing such support. In stark contrast, in countries with a largely LGBT friendly context, sponsorship of Pride becomes a secure investment. There, Pride organizers and activists are sometimes understandably more suspicious as to the authenticity of commercial support, exacerbating the impression of "selling out" to commercial interests.

In our empirical sample London Pride was the most highly commercialized and the controversy over selling out to commercial interests came to its head in the 2015 London Pride. In 2015 organizers wished to highlight the historical link between the London LGBT movement and labor unions by commemorating the campaign by the organization LGSM (Lesbians and Gays Support the Miners) to support the striking miners in 1984–1985 (narrated in the film Pride [2014], see also Chapter 2, this volume). In 2015 LGSM was asked by the London Pride organizers to lead the parade, but refused since the organizers would not allow the unions to march immediately behind them. Mike, a prominent member of LGSM, describes the situation:

> [i]nitially the Pride London committee invited us to lead the Pride march, because it was indeed the thirtieth anniversary of LGSM leading it. And we thought that was what was going to happen, but when we made it clear that we expected the trade unions to be marching with us, they said "no." So we were in this ridiculous position where we were going to be put at what is called "head of march," and then there would be section one, section two, and section three – that is where the trade unions would be – so we would become completely isolated by a huge number, thousands, of people between us and the trade union movement, and we just said, "no, we are not gonna do it." So in the end, we agreed that we would lead section C, and instead of LGSM leading the Gay Pride march, Barclays Bank led it […] and the next contingent was led by Starbucks.

Mike found this gesture particularly provocative given the history of Barclays as investors in South Africa during apartheid and Starbucks' reputation for tax avoidance. However, the story of how LGSM was pushed back by the organizers allegedly contributed to a huge mobilization of trade union participants who had become angered by it. Mike thinks the commercialization of Pride is:

> reflective of a lot of other things in society whereby the neoliberal political ideology and agenda is dominating everything: there it is in Pride, allowing these corporations to parade and market themselves in a gay liberation march [...] and they like to pretend that is not political, but it is *completely* political [...] it is part of the hegemony, and they extend that hegemony onto gay pride, and that is completely unacceptable.

Bologna Pride responded to internal criticism that the participation of commercial sponsors and businesses was only a matter of "pink washing." Since 2015 commercial "friends" have been banned from the parades. "Sure along the parade route businesses and shops celebrate with rainbow flags, but they do this independently" (personal correspondence with Anna Lavizzari, August 10, 2017; see also Chapter 7, this volume). Perhaps it is not surprising that in Bologna, the most politicized and "leftist" Pride event (Chapters 4 and 8, this volume), the controversy over commercialization led to a ban on businesses and companies participating.

Unwanted friends

Not all friends are wanted. Among the unwanted friends in some LGBT friendly political and cultural contexts are political xenophobic and anti-Muslim political actors. There are limits to Stockholm Pride's inclusiveness. Ulrika explained RFSL's position regarding the limits for inclusion in Pride.

> Last year RFSL motioned at Pride's annual meeting that the Sweden Democrats [a radical populist right party with roots in the neo-Nazi movement, now the third largest party in Sweden] would not be welcomed at Pride. ... There is an ongoing discussion primarily within Western European LGBT movements that there are a number of examples of parties and movements that are racist, which try to use the LGBT movement for their racist purposes.

She emphasized that it is important that the LGBT movement does not offer these parties a platform for their Islamophobic messages, "even when they come with a LGBT friendly action." Radical right-wing activists with close ties to the Sweden Democrats in both 2015 and 2016 staged a "Pride walk" in a multicultural borough of Stockholm during Stockholm Pride Week, which very few attended, while a far larger counter demonstration was on site. RFSL published a statement together with the Stockholm Pride Association clarifying why the organization did not support the event:

> The work that RFSL and Stockholm Pride does is based on feminist and anti-racist values, since the work for human rights can't be done at the expense of others and because many of us have experienced both homophobia, racism and Islamophobia. You can't work against discrimination with any form of credibility if you at the same time endorse or reproduce other kinds of discrimination. ... The LGBTQ movement is broad and is made up of a host of different individuals and groups. We come from all parts of the city, all parts of the world and dream all kinds of different dreams. We practice different beliefs and religions and our organisations will never join racist or Islamophobic environments.[4]

Steve, a UK Pride organizer, had a more inclusive attitude towards Islamophobic contingents.

> Well you are probably aware that in Pride London there was an argument about allowing UKIP to have a contingent in the parade and it goes back to my argument before about where do you draw the line on free speech? Why shouldn't gay members of UKIP, why shouldn't a gay person be a member of UKIP? Just because some other members of UKIP are anti-gay, that's only their ignorance. By having a gay UKIP group they are going to change the attitudes of other UKIP members, that's my reasoning. ... You've got to have a group of right wing gay people because we are just a cross section of society.

However, the LGBT community in London is perhaps not so broad-minded as some of the Pride organizers. Whether to allow a UKIP contingent to participate in the parade stirred up a heated conflict among the wider LGBT community and Board members of London Pride. Patrick, the director of London Pride, personally felt that the parade should include everyone, regardless of their political affiliation, but the Board in 2014, under pressure from other groups within the LGBT community, voted to withdraw the application of UKIP's LGBT group on the grounds of safety. They anticipated protests against the group that they would not have been able to control.

> We'd received a lot of threats that if the UKIP group was allowed to march that there would be demonstrations, that groups would turn up, that people would chuck things at them; one of the ones mentioned

was water guns, which are frequently used but with urine in them. We've got stewards and security walking alongside all the groups to maintain the safety of the parade and in the end with these threats we were not prepared to put our volunteers and our subcontracted staff and members of the public in danger.

In LGBT friendly contexts the participation of xenophobic contingents is a bone of contention for Pride organizers and a potential source of division within the movement. In 2015 UKIP, while not allowed, nevertheless did participate, which led Act Up activists to stage an unpermitted mock funeral procession through the parade. These queer activists felt that UKIP's participation, "an explicitly homophobic organization," was "the final nail in the coffin." They wanted "to show their genuine feelings that Pride has actually died" (interview with Dan Glass). Working their way from the front of the parade to its end they confronted LGBT UKIP and non-violently "chased them off."

In the LGBT friendly Netherlands the LGBT movement has attracted support across the party political spectrum, including the far-right xenophobic party. Edwino, the organizer of the Haarlem Pink Saturday, explained where their political support comes from: "mostly the support came from the left. But since this century, when being anti-Islam became popular among people, suddenly everybody is pro-gay." In the Netherlands, perhaps more than any other Western European country, gay rights have been entangled with Orientalist and anti-Muslim discourses (Mepschen, Duyvendak and Tonkens 2010; also, Chapter 9, this volume). Hekma and Duyvendak (2011; also Boston et al. 2015) claim that with the normalization of homosexuality and the depoliticization of the Dutch LGBT movement followed a "homosexualization of politics" or what Puar (2007) calls "homonationalism."

> This [normalization of homosexuality] facilitated the crucial positioning of (homo) sexuality in the debate on the social integration of new (Muslim) immigrants: "liberated" homosexuals became the embodiment of Dutch modernity and the opposite of "backward" Muslim migrants.
> (Hekma and Duyvendak 2011, p. 104)

However, as yet in the Netherlands organizers have not been confronted with the question of allowing an expressly Islamophobic contingent to participate in their LGBT events for political purposes. The organizing committees have, however, sought to include Muslims by endorsing and subsidizing Muslim LGBT groups to take part in Pink Saturday and Amsterdam Canal Pride events. The "threat" of Islamophobic organizations "high-jacking" Pride events to promote their anti-immigrant messages is limited to friendly LGBT contexts. In unfriendly contexts these organizations will more likely be found among the counterdemonstrators as we have seen in, for example, Poland. When it comes to the broad mass of actual Pride participants, those sympathizing with right wing anti-immigrant parties are, however, in general negligible in all of the national contexts included in our study (see Chapter 4). We return to the question of "homonationalism" in the concluding chapter of this book.

This raises the question: how do you choose your friends? At least in Stockholm the bottom line appears to be if the participants share the LGBT movement's equality values and human rights principles. Tasso, the chair of West Pride HBTQ Festival in Gothenburg, Sweden, related on what grounds the strip club Chat Noir was denied entry in the parade.

> The point of departure was that they did not have any HBTQ program and they did not conduct any norm critical work. And the board pointed out that their perspective on women did not comply with the normative principles of West Pride.

The Pride associations in both Stockholm and Gothenburg have a code of principles they apply when screening potential participating groups, organizations and companies, similar to the code that London Pride is negotiating.

There are problems for organizers with an inclusive mobilizing strategy. Willem, a Prague organizer, related an account of a pedosexual group which while they claim that they are not active pedosexualists, they are attracted to children and have a website explaining the issues they have and the problems they encounter in society. In 2014 the group marched in Prague Pride after having asked for permission and were informed that "sure everyone can join." Then they declared on their website that,

> they were an official part in the parade and they had some banner [...] like "not only homos," or "not only gays" and it said that not only gays and lesbians have a coming out, but pedosexuals like themselves as well. ... And of course we got loads of negative press over it. The press often calls us a "festival of sexual minorities" and we are not a festival of sexual minorities, we are a LGBT – or LGBTQ whatever – festival. We focus on this minority, but not on ... because if you focus on sexual minorities you have necrophilia, you have bestiality, you can include anything, just to show you the issue here.

The Prague organizers subsequently made it clear that although they had nothing against the pedosexualists participating in the parade as individuals, they would not tolerate that the organization promoted their message or portrayed itself as an official partner of the Pride parade.

In the Netherlands, the powerful LGBT organization CoC (*Cultuur en Ontspanningscentrum* – Center for Culture and Leisure) took an official stance in 1980 in support of pedophiles. The tide turned during the 1990s in the wake of the UN's sanctioning of ILGA, as the organization included country groups supporting pedophiles (Paternotte 2014, pp. 271–274). Now the single group that all of our informants in the Netherlands pointed out as unwanted "friends" were the pedophiles, who had demonstrated in the 1990s with their organization. This led to what they called "bad press" and these groups have been officially banned. As the Dutch LGBT movement had become more mainstream, pedophilia had become an embarrassing issue. When diversity and difference became more and more key factors in LGBT movements across the globe, the most controversial link was with pedofilia (Weeks 2015, p. 49; Rupp 2014). Here we find a bottom line for the inclusiveness of contemporary Pride parades and their subsequent attractiveness for friends of Pride.

Multi-issue friends

In high-profile Pride parades in LGBT friendly contexts such as in Stockholm the event opens a public platform for other groups to bring up their political issues. In these cases some friends of Pride have their own political agendas and "piggy back" the event (Peterson et al. 2012). According to the operational manager of the 2014 Stockholm Pride parade,

> almost every year some groups hop into the parade from the side so to say, they aren't registered and they just show up and take up space in the parade. They are struggling for their own political questions that are not at all related to LGBT issues. And we don't want them there. Last summer [2014] we had a pro-Palestine group that just joined in in order to raise the Palestine question and that is of course a deserving issue but not with us. ... If they had struggled for LGBT rights in Palestine that would have of course been another matter. They can struggle for their cause but they can do it elsewhere.

At least one of the pro-Palestine groups he talks about above consisted of a large number of participants holding placards stating that they were "Queers against the Israeli offensive in Palestine" (field notes, August 6, 2014). During summer 2014 this was a burning issue in Sweden and conceivably this was an important question for many LGBT persons, as well as for friends of Pride. Further, the "Queers for a Palestinian State" hark back to what Epstein (1999) calls the single/multi-issue split he traced in the history of the US lesbian and gay movement. Also in Sweden, early gay and lesbian liberation groups forged connections with the new left and the feminist movement during the early 1970s, but finding their efforts to build coalitions unwelcomed, later in the decade advocated separatism, especially Lesbian Front (Peterson, Thörn and Wahlström 2018). This single-issue/multi-issue split has reappeared during later years and is highly visible in Pride Parades in Sweden. But the political context has radically changed. The powerful LGBT movement is now a welcome coalition partner for left wing and anarchist groups and other movements. We find LGBT individuals, groups and networks, and their friends, marching for a number of causes beyond LGBT concerns bringing a variety of issues to the fore in the parades – the plight of the people of Palestine, anti-racism, animal rights, anti-capitalism, climate change, etcetera.

The situation in the Netherlands is different, despite the country's powerful and well-organized LGBT movement. Edwino, a co-organizer of the first Pink Saturday Parade in 1988 and organizer of the Haarlem events in 2012, thought that the movement should not "be too political" as the LGBT community covers the range of the political spectrum and the focus should remain on LGBT rights. Some time back in the history of the LGBT movement, according to Edwino, the movement had been "kidnapped by the lefties, and I didn't think that's a good thing to do." Edwino took a definite single-issue stand on the LGBT movement's political agenda and *de facto* on Pink Saturday events. And it appears as if the single-issue position is well entrenched in the Netherlands, but there are cracks appearing as a burgeoning queer politics has emerged in response to what young queer activists perceived as a middle-class gay dominance of Amsterdam Pride week and its single-issue, gay-only politics (Epstein 1999; Gamson 1995; Valocchi 2013; Warner 1999; Ghaziani 2008). In 2012 young queer activists joined forces with the older "lefties" who had campaigned for a "homo monument" in the city commemorating the loss of gay and lesbian lives under the German occupation during WWII. Since then they have organized a LGBTQ walk through Amsterdam from a Surinese-dominated neighborhood to the homo monument in the city center with the purpose of re-engaging the movement with a "political message" and with the freedom to express a broader range of issues (interview, lesbian Amsterdam Pride organizer; Paternotte and Tremblay 2015). The event takes place during Amsterdam Pride week and has been a strategy of the Pride organizing committee to defuse the conflict between the critics of Canal Pride's "commercialization and de-politicization" by recognizing their event as part of Pride week. The initiative by the organizers to incorporate the more politically radical queer activists has proved successful.

Carlos, a Mexico City Pride organizer, had a very different perspective of the potential political scope of the ritual event.

> This year [2015] something very important happened. The committee decided to include in this year's political statement our protest of the extrajudicial disappearance of the 43 students of Ayotzinapa. That meant that sexual diversity groups joined in demanding justice. This decision had a very positive impact within the committee and outside of it. I think it is time to include other social movements that may have specific claims that we can adopt. It is time to express more solidarity with other social groups.

For Carlos, broadening their political agenda was an ideological commitment to political solidarity more generally. He wished to seek out coalitions with other aggrieved groups to foster more progressive social change (Rimmerman 2015). The single issue/multi-issue split, which arose among some Pride organizers, reflected the tension between a queer politics agenda (deploying identity for critique) and a reformist political/legal agenda (deploying identity for education), which we found in high-profile LGBT movements in friendly political and cultural contexts, such as Sweden and the Netherlands. Organizers adapted to unfriendly contexts, such as in Poland, and strategically and ideologically sought to include multi-issues of inequality and human rights alongside LGBT rights to attract straight allies and broaden their support.

The single issue/multi-issue split will probably pervade in politicized and inclusive Pride parades regardless of the organizers' preferences. The divide has been a bone of contention throughout Pride history (Ghaziani 2008, p. 103).

Conclusions

The Pride parades in which the organizers most explicitly employed an inclusive (and reform oriented) political strategy had the highest percentage of individual non-LGBT allies, which was the case for Stockholm (41 percent) and Warsaw (28 percent). The exception was the Dutch Pink Saturday Parade, where while the event had a broad political platform the organizers expressly catered to attracting lesbians and their children and friends and stressed the social aspects of the event. In Haarlem there were 29 percent non-LGBT participants, 61 percent of whom were women and 62 percent lesbian and bisexual women in the parade. The participants, both LGBT and non-LGBT respondents, emphasized social meanings for their involvement. London Pride, although the organizers also underlined their ambition to be inclusive, primarily appeared to have perceived their role as facilitators for the safe participation of the LGBT community in London and LGBT tourists. This event attracted only 15 percent friends of Pride.

Our interviewed Pride organizers and key activists regarded non-LGBT participants in Pride events as a major asset for the movement and voiced no major concerns about "de-gaying" Pride, in contrast with the warnings of many LGBTQ scholars. On the contrary, most had developed specific strategies to mobilize friends of Pride and welcomed the support they lent the event.

All Pride parades in our sample, albeit to different proportions and in different configurations, included organizational friends of Pride. Whereas some, such as London WorldPride, were heavily dominated by commercial organizations, others, such as the Gothenburg, Stockholm and Warsaw Pride events had a more prominent presence of political parties and groups representing various issues more or less closely linked to core LGBT issues.

Some parades, largely depending on the size of their budgets, were highly dependent on commercial sponsors, sometimes to the point of clearly prioritizing these actors to non-commercial interest groups (evident in the 2015 London Pride's unwillingness to let the LGSM and the trade unions march ahead of the main sponsor of the march). Whereas several organizers for this reason were somewhat ambivalent towards their commercial sponsors, the most positive attitudes were found among Pride organizers in Warsaw and Prague, where recruiting commercial sponsorship was difficult or nearly impossible. In these countries, sponsors would have taken a risk of bad PR by participating, in contrast to more LGBT friendly countries where company sponsors were instead sometimes accused of hypocrisy and "pink washing."

In addition, apart from organizers' occasional doubts about commercialization, some friends were more explicitly unwanted, most prominently extreme right and xenophobic populist right parties and organizations, which in some country contexts have tried to appropriate the LGBT issue for their political purposes. The other notable "unwanted friends" were pedofiles/pedosexuals, who had tried to be visible parts of the parades in both the Netherlands and Czech Republic.

In the case of friends bringing in other political issues that are not directly linked to "core" LGBT issues, we can on the one hand see organizers struggling with the risk of fragmentation and a sense that some groups "piggy back" merely to promote their own interests. However, as the Mexican case illustrates, friends of Pride also have the potential to broaden the political struggle and to create links with other aggrieved and oppressed groups. An illustrative example of the potential contribution of friends of Pride is the LGSM, an initiative from the lesbian and gay community in London to support the 1984–1985 miners' strike, which contributed to a sense of mutual support and solidarity between the LGBT movement and the miners' unions. The LGSM and the National Union of Mineworkers not only led the 1985 Pride parade in London, at the Labour Party convention in 1985 the union block voted its support for a resolution committing the party to support lesbian and gay rights issues. The Mineworkers were the most outspoken allies of the lesbian and gay community's 1986 campaign against the controversial anti-gay law Section 28 (Kelliher 2014).

In sum, friends of Pride are politically, numerically, and symbolically significant for contemporary Pride parades. They too run the risk of stigmatization, but nonetheless participate with the LGBT community (Chapter 5, this volume). The support performances of friends of Pride broadcast to the wider public their cultural acceptance of the LGBT community and their backing for the political demands of the LGBT movement. Friends are primarily an invaluable asset for the movement, but may simultaneously contribute to fragmentization and the "de-gaying" of the parades. Even if these challenges were not major concerns for the Pride organizers in our study, it was still evident that mobilizing and managing friends of Pride confronted organizers with unavoidable strategic dilemmas.

Notes

1 Our primary empirical sample are the interviews with organizers and key activists in the four countries for which we can identify statistically the number of non-LGBT participants; our secondary sample extends to all of the interviews with Pride organizers and key LGBT activists in the remaining four countries.
2 All political parties were/are encouraged to participate aside from the radical populist right party, the Sweden Democrats, which had been banned by the organizers.
3 He was referring to the Pride events staged in Plymouth, which he felt were dominated by well-meaning straight allies (who did not necessarily have a clue about the issues) and lesbians. The parade, he contended, had a more or less invisible presence of gay men.
4 www.stockholmpride.org/en/, accessed July 27, 2016.

References

Adam, B.D., Duyvendak, J.W., and Krouwel, A. (1999). Gay and lesbian movements beyond borders? In Adam, B.D., Duyvendak J.W., and Krouwel, A. (Eds) *The global emergence of gay and lesbian politics* (pp. 344–371). Philadelphia PA: Temple University Press.

Altman, D. (2001). Global Gaze/Gay Politics. In Blasius, M. (Ed.) *Sexual identities, queer politics* (pp. 96–117). Princeton, NJ: Princeton University Press.

Armstrong, E.A., and Crage, S.M. (2006). Movements and memory: The making of the Stonewall myth. *American Sociological Review*, 71(5), 724–751.

Bernstein, M. (1997). Celebration and suppression: The strategic uses of identity by the lesbian and gay movement. *American Journal of Sociology*, 103(3), 531–565.

Bernstein, M. (2003). Nothing ventured nothing gained? Conceptualizing social movement 'success' in the lesbian and gay movement. *Sociological Perspectives*, 46(3), 353–379.

Bernstein, M. (2005). Identity politics. *Annual Review of Sociology*, 31, 47–74.

Binnie, J., and Klesse, C. (2012). Solidarities and tensions: Feminism and transnational LGBTQ politics in Poland. *European Journal of Women's Studies*, 19(4), 444–459.

Binnie, J., and Klesse, C. (2014). Transnational solidarities and LGBTQ politics in Poland. In Ayoub, P.M., and Paternotte, D. (Eds) *LGBT activism and the making of Europe. A rainbow Europe?* (pp. 193–2011). Basingstoke: Palgrave Macmillan.

Boston, N., Duyvendak, J.W., Paternotte, D., and Tremblay, M. (2015). People of color mobilization in LGBT movements in the Netherlands and the United States. In Paternotte, D., and Tremblay, M. (Eds) *The Ashgate research companion to lesbian and gay activism* (pp. 135–156). Farnham: Ashgate.

Browne, K. (2007). A party with politics? (Re)making LGBTQ Pride spaces in Dublin and Brighton. *Social and Cultural Geography*, 8(1), 63–87.

Browne, K., and Bakshi, M.L. (2013). *Ordinary in Brighton? LGBT, activisms and the city*. Farnham: Ashgate Publishing, Ltd.

Calvo, K., and Trujillo, G. (2011). Fighting for love rights: Claims and strategies of the LGBT movement in Spain. *Sexualities*, 14(5), 562–579.

Casey, M. (2004). De-dyking queer space (s): Heterosexual female visibility in gay and lesbian spaces. *Sexualities*, 7(4), 446–461.

Chasin, A. (2000). *Selling out: The gay and lesbian movement goes to market*. New York: Palgrave.

Chatterton, P., and Hollands, R. (2003). *Urban nightscapes. Youth cultures, pleasure spaces and corporate power*. New York: Routledge.

Crimp, D. (2002). Mario Montez, for shame. In Barber, S.M., and Clark, D.L. (Eds) *Regarding Sedgwick: Essays on queer culture and critical theory* (pp. 57–70). New York: Routledge.

Duggan, L. (2003). *The twilight of inequality? Neoliberalism, cultural politics, and the attack on democracy*. Boston, MA: Beacon Press.

Duggan, M. (2010). Politics of Pride: Representing relegated sexual identities in Northern Ireland, *The Northern Ireland Legal Quarterly*, 61, 163.

Enguix, B. (2009). Identities, sexualities and commemorations: Pride parades, public space and sexual dissidence. *Anthropological Notebooks*, 15(2), 15–33.

Enguix, B. (2013). Sexual politics, Pride, and media mediation in Spain. *Observatorio (OBS*)*, 7(2), 61–86.

Epstein, B. (1995). Political correctness. In Darnovsky, M., Epstein, B., and Flaks, R. (Eds) *Cultural politics and social movements* (pp. 3–19). Philadelphia, PA: Temple University Press.

Epstein, S. (1999). Gay and lesbian movements in the United States: Dilemmas of identity, diversity, and political strategy. In Adam, B.D., Duyvendak, J.W., and Krouwel, A. (Eds) *The global emergence of gay and lesbian politics* (pp. 30–90). Philadelphia, PA: Temple University Press.

Gamson, J. (1995). Must identity movements self-destruct? A queer dilemma. *Social Problems*, 42(3), 178–199.

Ghaziani, A. (2008). *The dividends of dissent. How conflict and culture work in lesbian and gay marches on Washington*. Chicago, IL: University of Chicago Press.

Hekma, G., and Duyvendak, J.W. (2011). The Netherlands: Depolitization of homosexuality and the homosexualization of politics. In Tremblay, M., Paternotte D., and Johnson, C. (Eds) *The lesbian and gay movement and the state: Comparative insights into a transformed relationship* (pp. 103–118). Farnham: Ashgate.

Hughes, H.L. (2006). Gay and lesbian festivals: Tourism in the change from politics to party. In Picard, D., and Robinson, M. (Eds) *Festivals, tourism and social change. Remaking worlds* (pp. 238–254). Clevedon: Buffalo and Toronto: Channel View Publications.

Gruszczynska, A. (2009). Sowing the seeds of solidarity in public space: Case study of the Poznan March of Equality. *Sexualities*, 12(3), 312–333.

Holzhacker, R. (2012). National and transnational strategies of LGBT civil society organizations in different political environments: Modes of interaction in Western and Eastern Europe for equality. *Comparative European Politics*, 10(1), 23–47.

Kelliher, D. (2014). Solidarity and sexuality: Lesbians and gays support the miners 1984–1985. *History Workshop Journal*, 77(1), 240–262.

Jasper, J. (2004). A strategic approach to collective action: Looking for agency in social-movement choices. *Mobilization: An International Quarterly*, 9(1), 1–16.

Johnston, L., and Waitt, G. (2015). The spatial politics of gay Pride parades and festivals: Emotional activism. In Paternotte, D., and Tremblay, M. (Eds) *The Ashgate research companion to lesbian and gay activism* (pp. 105–120). Farnham: Ashgate.

Markwell, K. (2002). Mardi Gras tourism and the construction of Sydney as an international gay and lesbian city. *GLQ: A Journal of Lesbian and Gay Studies*, 8(1), 81–99.

McCarthy, J.D., and Zald, M.N. (1977). Resource mobilization and social movements: A partial theory. *American Journal of Sociology*, 82(6), 1212–1241.

McFarland Bruce, K. (2013). LGBT Pride as a cultural protest tactic in a Southern City. *Journal of Contemporary Ethnography*, 42(5), 608–625.

McFarland Bruce, K. (2016). *Pride Parades: How a parade changed the world*. New York: NYU Press.

McLean, K. (2015). Inside or outside? Bisexual activism and the LGBTQI community. In Paternotte, D., and Tremblay, M. (Eds) *The Ashgate research companion to lesbian and gay activism* (pp. 121–138). Farnham: Ashgate.

Mepschen, P., Duyvendak, J.W., and Tonkens, E. (2010). Sexual politics, Orientalism and multicultural citizenship in the Netherlands. *Sociology*, 44(2), 962–979.

Meyer, D.S., and Gamson, J. (1995). The challenge of cultural elites: Celebrities and social movements. *Sociological inquiry*, 65(2), 181–206.

Mizielinska, J., and Kulpa, R. (2011). "Contemporary Peripheries": Queer studies, circulation of knowledge and East/West divide. In Kulpa, J., and Mizielinska, J. (Eds) *De-centring Western sexualities. Central and Eastern European perspectives* (pp. 11–26). Farnham and Burlington: Ashgate.

Paternotte, D. (2014). Pedophilia, homosexuality and gay and lesbian activism. In Hekma, G., and Giami, A. (Eds) *Sexual revolutions* (pp. 264–278). London: Palgrave Macmillan.

Paternotte, D., and Tremblay, M. (2015). Introduction: Investigating lesbian and gay activism. In Paternotte, D., and Tremblay, M. (Eds) *The Ashgate research companion to lesbian and gay activism*. Farnham: Ashgate.

Peterson, A., Thörn, H., and Wahlström, M. (2018). Contentious politics and social movements in post-war Sweden: Between confrontation and conditioned cooperation. In Mikkelsen, F., Kjeldstadli, K., and Nyzell, S. (Eds) *Popular struggle and democracy in Scandinavia, 1700–2015* (pp. 377–432). Basingstoke: Palgrave Macmillan.

Peterson, A., Wahlström, M., Wennerhag, M., Christancho, C., and Sabucedo, J.M. (2012). May Day demonstrations in five European countries. *Mobilization*, 17(3), 281–300.

Plummer, K. (1999). The lesbian and gay movement in Britain: Schisms, solidarities, and social worlds. In Adam, B.D., Duyvendak, J.W., and Krouwel, A. (Eds) *The global emergence of gay and lesbian politics* (pp. 133–157). Philadelphia, PA: Temple University Press.

Puar, J. (2007). *Terrorist assembleges: Homonationalism in queer times*. Durham, NC: Duke University Press.

Rayside, D. (2001). The structuring of sexual minority activist opportunities in the political mainstream: Britain, Canada and the United States. In Blasius, M. (Ed.) *Sexual identities, queer politics* (pp. 23–55). Princeton, NJ: Princeton University Press.

Richardson, D. (2005). Desiring sameness: The rise of a neoliberal politics of normalization. *Antipode*, 37(3), 515–553.

Rimmerman, C.A. (2015). *The lesbian and gay movements: Assimilation or liberation?* 2nd ed. Boulder, CO: Westview Press.

Ross, C. (2008). Visions of visibility: LGBT communities in Turin. *Modern Italy*, 13(3), 241–260.

Rucht, D. (2008). Movement allies, adversaries, third parties. In Snow, D.A., Soule, S.A., and Kriesi, H. (Eds) *The Blackwell companion to social movements* (pp. 197–216). New York: John Wiley & Sons.

Rupp, L.J. (2014). The European origins of transnational organizing: The International Committee for Sexual Equality. In Ayoub, P., and Paternotte, D. (Eds) *LGBT activism and the making of Europe* (pp. 29–49). London: Palgrave Macmillan.

Salokar, R.M. (2001). Beyond gay rights litigation: Using a systematic strategy to effect social change in the United States. In Blasius, M. (Ed.) *Sexual identities, queer politics* (pp. 256–283). Princeton, NJ: Princeton University Press.

Schuyf, J., and Krouwel, A. (1999). The Dutch lesbian and gay movement: The politics of accomodation. In Adam, B.D., Duyvendak, J.W., and Krouwel, A. (Eds) *The global emergence of gay and lesbian politics* (pp. 158–183). Philadelphia, PA: Temple University Press.

Shepard, B. (2010). *Queer political performance and protest*. New York: Routledge.

Skeggs, B. (1999). Matter out of place: Visibility and sexualities in leisure spaces. *Leisure Studies*, 18(3), 213–232.

Vaid, U. (1995). *Virtual equality: The mainstreaming of lesbian and gay liberation*. New York: Anchor Books.

Valocchi, S. (2013). Gay and lesbian movement. In Snow, D.A., della Porta, D., Klandermans, B., and McAdam, D. (Eds) *The Wiley-Blackwell encyclopedia of social and political movements*. Hoboken, NJ: Wiley-Blackwell.

van der Ros, J., and Motmans, J. (2015). Trans activism and LGB movements: Odd bedfellows? In Paternotte, D., and Tremblay, M. (Eds) *The Ashgate research companion to lesbian and gay activism* (pp. 163–180). Farnham: Ashgate.

Wahlström, M., Peterson, A., and Wennerhag, M. (2018). "Conscience adherents" revisited: Non-LGBT Pride participants. *Mobilization: An International Quarterly*, 23(1), 83–100.

Wahlström, M. (2015). Proud protest and parading party: The meanings that Pride parades in six European countries have to their participants. Paper presented at the American Sociological Association Annual Meeting, August 22–25, Chicago, IL.

Warner, M. (1999). *The trouble with normal: Sex, politics, and the ethics of queer life*. New York: The Free Press.

Weeks, J. (2015). Gay liberation and its legacies. In Paternotte, D., and Tremblay, M. (Eds) *The Ashgate research companion to lesbian and gay activism* (pp. 45–58). Farnham: Ashgate.

7 Performances of Party and Politics

In this chapter we will explore the collective performances of "coming out." The coming out performances of LGBT communities are declarations that they will no longer allow the state, the heterosexual majority, or their antagonists to cast them in the shadows. On the one hand, some Pride performances transgressively challenge the dominant sexual and gender norms in society, on the other hand, participants perform in ways that will communicate that they are worthy, committed, and determined to achieve acceptance and inclusion in the wider political and cultural community. In this chapter we will explore this ostensible paradox by analyzing the performances of Pride in the different political and cultural contexts included in our study.

Pride parades include both elements of politics and protest *and* of party, what Jack Santino (2011) called the "carnivalesque," in, at times, an uneasy mixture. Carnivalesque is the ludic play, the festivity, and the spirited challenges to the hetero-normativity that dominates societies. We investigate in this chapter the differences and tensions between the performances of politics and party, but, as Santino reminds us, politics and party are not necessarily mutually exclusive but can be complimentary, as was the case in the Pride Parades studied here. The presence of the carnivalesque does not "negate their intention to make something happen, to change things, or to bring a new social reality into being" (p. 62). Not least this latter aspect of Pride parades is important to understand. Pride Parades are events when many of the participants perform an ephemeral and ludic experiment in an alternative vision of the world (Pershing 1996, p. 234), and at their heart they are events intended to change or transform society itself.

According to Benjamin Shepard (2010),

> when protest integrates with the model of carnival, it merges the joyous spirit of exhilarating entertainment with a political agenda aimed toward progressive political change. Within this festive theater, progressive elements of political change are linked with notions of social renewal, moving spectators to join the fun, to become part of the concrete action of social change. Along the road, public spectacle

becomes intimately linked with practical shifts in social and material conditions missing in people's lives. Party as protest thus becomes an invitation to a possibility.

(p. 457)

In Pride parades party as protest or protest as party invites participants to emotionally, cognitively and corporeally experience that a different world is possible – even if only just for a day. Jej, a Polish respondent, explained how showing your sexual orientation in public can provoke, in a unfriendly LGBT climate, an aggressive response. For Jej, the parade is a liberating experience.

> Yes, of course you can get punched in the face if you do that [holding hands] or be stared at. And that is for sure. So people don't feel free to do that, … so the Pride is a very freeing and liberating occasion once a year, unfortunately only once a year.

Pride parades move

Pride parades are the performances of the LGBT movement's collective identities and their visions of the future. As Ron Eyerman (2006) has pointed out, we can understand the concept of social movement as both a noun and, most importantly, as a verb. A social movement is a relatively integrated and coordinated collective actor, which aspires to *move* – emotionally, cognitively, and politically – its participants, sympathizers, the general public, as well as (in most cases) the political authorities.

For a social movement's participants, demonstrations can, at best, produce a powerful collective energy, an emotional sense of "belonging to some force greater than oneself" (Eyerman 2006, p. 195; Peterson 2001). The experience of collective performances moves their participants emotionally and cognitively, instilling that important sense of "we." Pride performances thus create spaces for the personal politics of coming out and expressing otherwise hidden or repressed identities (Bell and Valentine 1995; Johnston 2002). Kates and Belk (2001, p. 422) maintain that an event such as Pride "fortifies character and provides a shot in the arm that participants hope will last them until the next Lesbian and Gay Pride Day." Women cited being "part" of the "gay/queer community" or simply being part of something as reasons for attending. According to Kates and Belk, these annual ritual events are not solely individual enactments since, in part, (re)forming "myself" takes place through (re)creating an imaginary collective. Similarly, Armstrong and Crage (2006) point out that Pride parades proved to be ideal for the affirmation of gay collective identity and for the production of feelings of pride central to the emotional culture of the movement. "The emotional impact granted the parade lasting cultural power" (p. 742; also Gruszczynska 2009). Pride parades, and the carnivalesque within the parades, are vital for the internal dynamics and community building of the LGBT movement (Browne and Bakshi 2013). Barbara Ehrenreich (2007), discussing the importance of the carnivalesque in social movements in general, claims that:

> the media often derides the carnival spirit of such protests, as if it were a self-indulgent distraction from the serious political point. But seasoned organizers know that gratification cannot be deferred until after the "revolution".
>
> (p. 259)

LGBT movements recognize the importance of strategically combining party with politics for community building. The carnivalesque within Pride parades is an important factor, which "moves" participants. Carlos, a Mexican gay activist, told us about his first Pride parade. He had reluctantly attended with a stylist from the beauty salon where he then worked as a receptionist.

> I was timorous at my first Pride parade. I was only twenty and unaware of all this, so I thought I was going to be mugged or beaten. I imagined Pride parades to be sordid. So I arrived with this stylist and my camera. It was amazing to see the ability of the sexual diversity to show its muscle and strength. This moment was defining for me. I saw people from all religions, social levels, races. I saw all kinds of costumes, nude people. Everyone knew that it was our day and that was a milestone event for me. The following day I decided to come out, because I couldn't stand to continue as I was while there was all this diversity out there. I had to be part of this [LGBT] movement.

In short, the experience of his first Pride parade moved Carlos to come out as a gay man; for Carlos, Pride was a milestone event in his life. The meaning of Pride participation for individual participants is clearly dependent on their personal biographies, particularly from a life-course perspective in relation to beginning to self-identify as LGBT, as well as "coming out" to others (Herdt 1992). In our interviews with organizers and key activists, we largely focused on their general and strategic views of Pride. However, in most interviews our respondents also shared their personal experiences as participants in particular events. In one of our introductory questions we asked about their experiences from the first Pride parade they took part in, and the accounts that they developed confirmed that the first time participating in Pride was often very special.

> Oh, it was amazing! It was very empowering and that is the thing we can never forget because that's what the parades are for, they are super empowering and joyful, cheerful, happy, colorful, it was in a way a

little bit different from what the media showed when it came to Prides. At that time they didn't really show images from the Warsaw Pride, but they showed images from other events that took place in Europe. So it was a little bit unexpected for me. It was much more peaceful and much more, I didn't know the word yet, but it was more heteronormative then I would have expected. And that was surprising, not in a bad way or a good way, but I just didn't expect it. And I didn't know the words then but I thought it would be more gay. You know when you have seen it on TV, but it was amazing and since then I realized that parades are addictive, because I have been participating in the parade ever since.

(Jej, Polish activist and organizer)

In these narratives, Pride has an existential meaning as a turning point in the lives of LGBT individuals. Watching or participating in these powerful celebrations of non-normative sexualities and gender identities has probably led many people to make decisive steps in their lives as was the case for Carlos. This emotional response can be linked to what Breines (1980) termed "prefigurative politics," the promotion of a political vision through living it and showing that it is possible. As was evident from the account of the Polish activist, it is not necessarily the grand or extreme performances that have the greatest impact on individuals' lives. The performative display of ordinariness in Pride can also have a strong impact on bystanders and new parade participants. A crucial aspect of this lies in the production by Pride parades of temporary spaces where the sheer number of people breaking a dominant social norm achieves a localized suspension of that norm. In the process of collectively coming out shame is turned into pride.

When you find out that you're gay, you feel like daunted, you don't know any other gays around you and you have to make your coming out, you have to go the gay-scene to meet other gays, so it's like all those burdens you have to go through and then suddenly you have friends, where it seems that there are many people like you and suddenly you're not a minority for this one day, but you're part of the majority.

(Willem, Prague Pride organizer of Dutch origin)

In our interviews, it also became evident that Pride parades not only have the capacity to open up new routes in individuals' personal lives. As a form of political struggle Pride parades may also open up new possibilities. Julie Bindel, in a discussion with Peter Tatchell, described her first experience participating in a Pride parade.[1]

I attended my first when I was 16, in 1978. I was brought by a friend who was quite a bit older than me. I was overwhelmed to see people displaying their joy with other lesbians and gay men together in a way that, even when onlookers were shouting with rage, we felt completely safe. It was the first sense of how good it was to not have a label of "normal" attached to you. *I didn't understand at the time how political it was.* That the people on that march weren't just saying: "We can't help it, we were born this way – feel sorry for us." ... I remember a brilliant slogan carried by a lesbian that said: "Don't shout at me fella, your wife's in here!" – so irreverent and unapologetic. It wasn't: "Please accept us" – it was radical and it was in your face.

(our emphasis)

An Italian activist elaborates on the eye-opening experience of Pride in relation to other forms of political protest that she had hitherto experienced.

What I liked and remembered about it was that it was like a nice mixture of the kind of claims and feelings of being part of a common struggle that I knew from my rather scattered and random experiences in other social movements, but then without all that, I don't know ... gravity that has [plagued] other social movements. That atmosphere of darkness and rage and ... yeah and ... threat, that permeates those experiences. It was still a very powerful struggle and claim but done with such a positive, fun and ironic attitude that I liked it.

(Elisa, Italian activist)

Elisa's first experience of a Pride parade, as in the case of Julie, made her aware of the political force of the carnivalesque.

Pride parades' cultural challenge

While Pride parades are important annual rituals for LGBT movements in that they move their participants, the performances also interact with others and strive to move the general public, their opponents, as well as (in most cases) political authorities. Apart from the *in-group-oriented* aspects of Pride performances discussed above, in the following we will focus on the primarily *out-group-oriented* aspects of Pride performances (see also Chapter 8); how Pride parades engage with others and perform their collective identities and their political messages, together with their visions for the future. The element of the carnivalesque (at best) articulates LGBT movements' visions for the future. The carnivalesque, or ludic play of Pride performances, encourages participants and spectators alike to enjoy, have fun, and to imagine other possible worlds. McFarland (2012) takes a strong cultural position in her analysis of US Pride parades and argues that in contrast to traditional demonstrations, which aim to show political power for or against specific policies, Pride parades *imagine* a cultural alternative. But as she points out, "if Pride were not contentious, it would just be another parade" (p. 178). She explains:

> Pride parades engage in conflict by flipping a cultural code on its head. Pride parades use a cultural symbol of affirmation – a public parade – to make visible, support, and celebrate a community that is alternately invisible, misunderstood, and condemned through the macro-level cultural construction of queerness. Whereas traditional political marches follow a script in which they communicate political power, Pride parades enact a creative display to directly challenge cultural codes. [...] Pride parades are prefigurative: they attempt to change culture by actually doing what they want the wider culture to do. Participants do not simply say that LGBT people should be visible, supported, and celebrated, they do these things by staging a grand parade.
>
> (p. 179)

Pride parades bring together the visual, embodied and spatial aspects of the LGBT movements' public performances. Through visually playful and embodied "deconstructive spatial tactics" Pride performances resist hegemonic normative heterosexuality (Kates and Belk 2001; Johnston 2002, p. 77). McFarland Bruce (2016) argues that Pride parades are more than the provision of a safe space for party and commerce, rather they communicate a broad cultural message that "queer identity is a thing to be celebrated rather than condemned" (p. 15).

Mexican activist Carlos responded to our question as to whether Pride parades could become too "mainstream" in the following words:

> Even if Pride parades are increasingly seen as pure party, they will continue to be a movement that fights for more rights. Pride parades will continue to stand against "traditional" perspectives, and that will prevent them from becoming too mainstream. The march will continue to transgress the conservative positions of many groups.

Carlos, like McFarland Bruce, emphasizes the inherently cultural transgression posed by Pride performances. With the collective overcoming of the barrier of stigma (Chapter 5, this volume), cultural norms and discrimination based on the stigma are challenged – "either by asserting 'We are not like that' or by proclaiming 'The ways we are different are fine, or even valuable'" (Murray 1996, p. 192).

The political performances of Pride parades

While we acknowledge the centrality of the underlying cultural meaning of Pride performances, we will investigate how the carnivalesque intertwines with the political. The carnivalesque is vital for articulating visionary futures, but ludic play is combined with performances communicating the LGBT movement's political demands. However, as Santino (2011, pp. 66–67) points out, analysts often overlook the seriousness of purpose. Underlying the carnivalesque dimension in Pride Parades is an earnestness of purpose, what Charles Tilly (2004, pp. 53ff) defined as commitment, to accomplish a change or transformation in society.

Traditionally demonstrations are public performances of what Tilly called a movement's "worthiness, unity, numbers and commitment" (WUNC). For early May Day marches it was important for organizers that march stewards held order among the ranks of demonstrators – sobriety was paramount for the performance of worthiness. For the highly choreographed ritual May Day events demonstrators performed their unity and indirectly their commitment, their earnestness of purpose, with their coordinated and disciplined march formations bearing the red banners showing their membership in unions and/or support for a socialist/social democratic party; and of course their numbers, which signalled to society that organized labor was a political actor to be reckoned with (Peterson and Reiter 2016).

So while it is important for demonstration organizers to mobilize numbers, Tilly (2004) argues that for those who seek acceptance and inclusion in the larger social and/or political community, it is also important to perform worthiness and political determination, and, at least ephemerally, unity. However, the classical WUNC model of political performances has varying traction in contemporary contentious politics, given the type of social movement and the political and cultural context of the performance. For the LGBT movements' Pride performances, WUNC coexists with the carnivalesque – politics with party. Hence the WUNC model has only partial saliency for the Pride parades in our study; it is just one underlying tactical model for political, social and cultural change. Pride parades are more or less inclusive umbrella events for a wide range of actors to perform their political messages and cultural challenges. Like all ritual events, Pride is polyvocal and gives voice to different "moral economies" (Thompson 1991) appealing to abstract notions of, for example, human rights, social justice, freedom or morality. The format of the parade allows for those participating to stake out different, even conflicting, political positions, identities and tactics (Armstrong and Crage 2006).

As we stressed in the introduction to this book, the LGBT movement is intrinsically a tentative coalition of diverse interests, tactics and identities. For Pride organizers, a parade is an annual occasion to bring together the LGBT movement's diversity for a temporary, provisional, and often contested display of unity. Pride parades, we argue, rather than performances of unity in message, tactics and identity, are performances of *diversity unified* through their creative coordination and collaboration of simply coming together (Moon 2012). This is indeed one of the strengths of Pride parades. Pride parades highlight a new meaning to what unity in contemporary political protest more generally is – acknowledging diversity and emphasizing the spirit of cooperation (Moore and Wood 2002; Bogad 2006). McFarland (2012, p. 158) suggests that the political challenge posed by Pride parades is not their explicit statements, but the subtle communication of bringing so many diverse groups together. Pride parades communicate an indirect political message of unity in diversity showing broad cultural support rather than more narrow political advocacy, which, however, McFarland warns, may or may not be effective.

Despite these generalizing statements, performances are not the same everywhere. In the following pages we will focus on Pride performances staged in different political and cultural contexts investigating how the mobilizing context impacts upon the choreographies, actors, scripts, costumes and props engaged in the parades. Overall, the degree of friendliness, or of hostility, of the local and national context of Prides appears to have a considerable impact on Pride performances as well as organizers' strategic considerations.

Performing political worthiness on less friendly scenes

If we turn our attention from Tilly's notion of unity to worthiness and commitment, we have different choreographers, scripts, props, costumes, and not least, scenes in our comparative analysis. Pride organizers in LGBT friendly contexts appear to have a wider range of dramaturgical tools at their disposal than those staging parades on scenes that are less friendly or even hostile. Organizers in these latter unfriendly scenes are (somewhat) more committed to the traditional WUNC formulae, while the former are more inclined to encourage a more carnivalesque choreography, which leaves the performances of individuals and collectives to their own creativity. On less friendly scenes Pride organizers and participants alike are more concerned with performances of representation that emphasize the movement's worthiness, and subsequently, indirectly, the "normality" of the demonstrators. On these scenes Pride performances most often mobilize an identity strategy of education, emphasizing *similarities to* the straight majority (Bernstein 2002, p. 532). A Polish lesbian activist and Warsaw Equality Parade organizer we interviewed expressed her disappointment with what she felt was biased media coverage of the Warsaw event focusing on the more festive contingents and ignoring that "most of the participants are just regular, normal people." Carnivalesque transgressions of hetero-normativity in Pride performances, according to Cappellato and Mangarella (2014), define the identities of those engaging in them, rendering them, at least in unfriendly environments, perceived as unsuitable to enter the political arena. The idea of being respectable, particularly on the more constricted stages in LGBT unfriendly or less friendly contexts, is linked to the way people represent themselves in public and their ability to conform to the dominant hetero-normative models. In their study of the experiences of parents to lesbians and gays in Pride Parades in Italy, which like in Poland, offers less hospitable scenes for staging Pride events, they found that parents were highly critical of what they described as the "antics" and "exhibitionism" of gay men on the floats, which they felt distracted from their political demands.

> I didn't like it because they were almost clowning around for people ... if they want to do something ... it has to be something serious ... not making a show of their diversity ... but getting their problems out there and getting their voice heard ... not all that fooling around on floats and all the things they get up to ... at least that's how I see it. (Mother)
> (Cappellato and Mangarella 2014, p. 222)

Particularly in unfriendly contexts the negotiations for Pride organizers between politics and the carnivalesque, protest and party, are often conflict ridden. Sexual displays are, according to McFarland Bruce (2016, p. 103), "a flashpoint for debate over how Pride parades represent LGBT people to the broader world." Mexican activist Enrique explained that there is a deep conflict between those that support the parades and those that think that Pride parades detract from the respect that the LGBT movement deserves. The latter say: "you want respect and rights, but you go out and march down the streets in only shorts and glitter. ... How much skin you show is definitely a debate." A Czech gay Pride organizer related for us the difficulties they were confronted with in Prague regarding the exhibitionism of some members of the LGBT community.

> But now for the past two years it has been taken a bit to extremes, which is hurting our reputation, for example the leather community – they are well ... there are some people there who are kind of exhibitionists and they ... they have this guy naked like right in the city center, on the main shopping street, totally naked being spanked by some other guys with leather whips and [...] on the personal level I think people should express themselves, whatever, and it's the whole concept of any Gay Pride, but also we don't want to shock anyone. ... We have to think about our reputation and maybe in Berlin people wouldn't be shocked, but here in the Czech Republic it's a bit more conservative, so we have said "Really we can't cooperate with you anymore" and they like said "Well next year we won't march."

Organizers play an active role in negotiating and renegotiating what it means to be lesbian and gay, who can be part of the parade, and what the appropriate goals of the event are. It appears that in less LGBT friendly cultural and political contexts organizers assume a more vigilant gatekeeper role defining the parameters for appropriate behavior; context impacts on the perceived parameters for the performances.

Yves, active in organizing Pride parades in Swiss Romandy, related how the Pride parade organizers in Sion, the capital of the most conservative canton Valais, encouraged normalizing performances. Context impacts on the choice of costumes and presentations of self. In general he felt that:

> people who are totally disguised and you know wear very camp costumes etcetera have been slightly less present and visible than in the past. ... At the first Pride in Sion everybody was dressed as you and me right now because it is a very conservative canton so people paid attention to not be too provocative.

In Sion it appears as if the participants themselves censored their representations to more closely adhere to the culturally conservative hetero-normative context in the canton. Enrique again: "it is LGBT people who say 'no we have to' ... Like the bar for social behavior is higher for us, because we have to be extra polite and extra well behaved and extra, well, normal." Also, in Mexico City, at least some of the participants censor themselves and would readily censor others.

Gloria, former co-chair of ILGA and long-time Mexican lesbian activist, explained that in Mexico, in comparison with other Latin American countries, the culture of machismo is very deep-seated. According to Gloria, machismo forms a:

> big barrier within the movement and especially with trans women. They don't want the trans women to be at the front of the parade; they don't want the trans women to show very much, ... because of machismo. It's a small group of gay men in the organizing committee who are always talking about that. ... A few years ago there was a group of gay men who made a call for a "decent march", and they were very masculine gay men, dressed like cowboys. The first year they got about 50 people together, the second time around 300. And we were like "what's happening here". Now that Patria (Jiménez) is back as the head of the organizing committee trans women have been at the front because of the assassination of trans women. Last year they were at the front because they were negotiating with the government to change the law about gender reassignment.

The underlying culture of machismo constricts (at least to a degree) performances that most directly challenge hetero-normativity and appears to encourage performances of hyper-masculinity among gay men. And we could observe from images of Mexico City Pride parades that muscular bare breasted men with cowboy hats was a recurrent theme.

The choreography of Pride performances can be unexpectedly disrupted on less friendly LGBT stages. One co-organizer of the first Pride parade in

Brno in the Czech Republic describes the chaos that broke out when the parade was surprise-attacked by a group of Nazis:

> [The Nazis attacked] when nobody was expecting, because the police were standing there and everybody was having fun and it was a really nice atmosphere, everyone was cheering. They hit at that moment. They gathered and they ran into the crowd and the police were standing and shouting at people "hide behind cars!", "don't go there!". It was quite bizarre actually, because we noticed that this was happening and the police were trying to push us, like "stand behind the cars, don't go anywhere, don't do anything", but it took them about a minute before they actually pushed those Nazis away, because they were like standing there and watching what was happening.

On the less friendly LGBT scene in Brno the performances of Pride were violently disrupted with the entry of a new, unwelcome actor – a Nazi counter movement – and the arrival of the police with their apparently reluctant intervention to protect the marchers. The threat of unwelcome violent performances on the part of counter movements are not confined to less friendly LGBT contexts; even on very friendly LGBT scenes Pride performances are vulnerable to attacks from right-wing extremist groups. During Stockholm Pride in August 2017 a group from the neo-Nazi movement calling themselves Nordic Youth entered the parade with their banner and tumult ensued. The police, anticipating such an attack (it was not the first of its kind over the years), quickly rounded up the 15 young men and brought them into detention (*Svenska Dagbladet*, August 5, 2017). This was only a minor interruption in an otherwise joyous mass performance of pride in Stockholm. Very few among the reported 45,000 participants or estimated 500,000 bystanders were aware of the incident.

Performances on LGBT friendly scenes

In stark contrast with the parades in our study staged in politically and culturally less friendly contexts was the 2014 Stockholm Pride organized in a country with a high degree of tolerance for LBGT individuals and a LGBT movement practicing what Holzhacker (2012) calls "high profile politics." The celebratory performances of pride in Stockholm 2014 were highly colorful and very, very loud. Rainbow flags were everywhere and unit after unit marched and celebrated in colorful dress to a wide range of amplified music. A roaring rainbow decorated marine amphibian carrying a lesbian hard rock band rolled down the streets leading the Swedish gay military contingent, in turn led by the Commander and Chief of the Swedish Armed Forces and the Secretary of Defence – an archetypal performance of "high profile politics."

An LGBT movement with a strong and diversified organizational structure, robust access to the polity, and Pride organizers dedicated to promoting inclusivity, will at the same time deploy both an identity strategy of critique, emphasizing difference to the straight majority, *and* an identity strategy of education, accentuating similarities with the majority (Bernstein 1997, p. 532) – merging radicals with moderates. In these contexts Pride parades bring together the performances of politics and the carnivalesque more or less seamlessly. The ludic play of music, dance, costumes and symbolic props amalgamate with the politics of both transgression and moderate reformism referring and appealing to widely different moral economies (Santino 2011). Stockholm Pride provided an attractive political stage for a vast array of causes and political organizations/parties. Major institutional actors – government, political parties, the military, churches, unions, the judiciary, the police authority, etcetera – chose to march *with* LGBT people in addition to showing their support *for* LGBT people (McFarland Bruce 2016, p. 155). The political elite – political party leaders, government ministers, and in 2014 the Conservative Prime Minister[2] – performed their highly touted values of tolerance nested within the abstract concept of the neo-liberal "moral economy of human rights" (Richardson 2005).

Alongside the ludic carnivalesque with its performance of a radical vision of a different future (Shepard 2010, the Pride event *both* ritually consolidated those in authority *and* provided a space to challenge those in authority. So while the Pride parade in Stockholm provided the political elite a set stage to perform their adherence to human rights, a stage was *also* set for the performance of radical challenges on the part of Queer activists, and for activists for a Palestinian State and against the Israeli offensive in Gaza, for Socialist Revolutionaries, animal rights activists, feminist activists, etcetera. The Pride parade in Stockholm was a decidedly inclusive umbrella event for a wide range of groups to perform their political messages – disparate as they were. Directors of the performances – the Pride organizers – provide the stage and can suggest, but cannot dictate, the messages sent by the marchers. While they can forbid certain contingents in their bid to participate on grounds of not sharing Pride's values (even if they can hop in on the side, as one Stockholm organizer explained), the parade units are left to more or less direct their own performances – how they choose to represent themselves. Pride organizers generally, but not always, take a relatively hands-off approach to participant performances. The challenge for the directors of the performances is in these cases how to line up their very diverse cast of actors. Obviously you do not place the gay police contingent adjacent to a group of queer activists, nor do you place the Conservative Party delegation with the prime minister and government ministers in front of the Socialist Revolutionaries. Very large parades such as Stockholm Pride 2014 allow for the organizers to prudently choreograph the event, providing relatively autonomous spaces on the stage for the diversity of political performances by the cast of actors involved.

The carnivalesque Pride performances staged on LGBT friendly scenes are not only radical and playful visions of a different future. In the beginning of this chapter we quoted the Italian activist Elisa who expressed her appreciation regarding the absence in Pride parades of the "darkness and rage" present in many other protest performances; but not all participants agree with her. We can also observe performances of hatred – a strategy, which requires a certain position of privilege with the capital on hand to endure the risks of the resistance strategy. Cathrin Wasshede (2017) analyzes queer activists' participation, their "riot," in the 2010 Pride parade in Gothenburg as a case of the queer use of hate and dirt from an abject position.

> In the film, we follow a pink and black car pumping out music and bearing banners such as "Intersectional solidarity – the unity of the queer collective" and "Revolutionaries never walk in straight lines". From the car, people are chanting "We are angry, not nice, we are intersectional". When the riot reaches the halfway mark, it is met by a counter-demonstration; some members of the religious sect "The Word of Life" (Livets ord) are standing with big signs with slogans such as: "God loves you" and "Do not delude yourself". In the film we can see how the queer activists are booing, dancing, getting close to the religious demonstrators and screaming: "Fags hate God" and "We are here, we are queer, we're gonna fuck your children". Satisfied by their victory, we see the queer activists move on, having silenced the members of the religious sect.
>
> (Wasshede 2017, p. 47)

Later in the film the Queer Institute's participation shows them dancing to a song with the following lyrics:

> Before, when I was alone, it was hard to carry, all my hatred, and it was only mine, a pure private thing. But now, we are so many standing here, and with an organized anger, the hate carries us instead.
>
> (p. 48)

The collective performance of a rhetoric of hatred "carries" the activists – in our terms, their actions moves them. However, it is difficult to interpret if and how their speech acts, provocatively drawing on, instead of resenting, the discursive links that have existed between homosexuality and pedophilia, moved their religious counterdemonstrators. But, as Wasshede (2017) points out, the activists are not concerned with the impact of the words on their spectators. By embracing the "dirty" of implied pedophilia and perversion they are making the words their own – "a linguistic resistance and queer strategy" in the words of an activist quoted by Wasshede (p. 47).

This type of performance where activists deliberately seek out hateful and excessively provocative expressions appears to be closely linked to friendly contexts for Pride parades. In more unfriendly circumstances, the mere public presence of openly LGBT people is itself largely regarded as provocative and few activists see a need for further conflict escalation. This queer strategy of meeting hatred with hatred is a far cry from how the Gay Liberation Front responded to angry spectators in the less accommodating climate of London in the 1970s. Peter Tatchell related how he and his fellow demonstrators responded to an aggressive spectator at the first London Pride in 1972. "One belligerent man shouted: 'Aren't you ashamed?' To which everyone shouted back in chorus: 'No!' and half of us just blew him a kiss. He was gobsmacked."[3]

The spatial importance of the stage for Pride

London Pride was far and away the parade in our study with the greatest participation of company-sponsored contingents. Major multi-national companies, banks, insurance companies, chain stores and coffee shop chains were heavily visible. London Pride was also the most spectacularly carnivalesque parade included in our study, dominated by gay men and lifestyle performances, and in contrast with, for example, Stockholm Pride, the Warsaw Equality March or Bologna Pride, a more subdued political performance. Steve, chair of the London Pride 2003–2006, remembers a discussion he had with a young volunteer in 2006 about the parade route, which passes the Houses of Parliament.

> She said, "well what is the point, there's no members of parliament there, it's a Saturday? There's nobody there." She didn't understand that the whole point of the parade was political. ... Now whether the MPs were there or not, it doesn't matter, you wanted the photograph of the parade in front of Big Ben and the Houses of Parliament. That was the political statement and it might have just been a photo opportunity but that was the point.

Gloria talked about the importance of the symbolic stage for a Pride parade. In Mexico City the breakthrough was in 1999, she explained, when the authorities issued permits for the parade to march down the *Paseo de la Reforma*, the major avenue in central Mexico City, and conclude in the huge central square, the *Zócalo*. The symbolic significance of the parade route, the centrality of the route in the life of the city, underscores the degree of political recognition of the LGBT movement; conversely, if the authorities deny organizers a permit for a march in the center of the city this is an indication of the lack of recognition of the movement, which was the case in Warsaw. Geneva is a very compact metropolis and Richard, an organizer of the Geneva Pride, emphasized how important it was to obtain the authorization to close Mont Blanc Bridge. The bridge, connecting with the very center of the city, when closed effectively shuts down the city for cars and public transport so:

> everybody in Geneva knows it is closed and everybody asks why it is closed and it is because of Gay Pride. ... Pride for us is to be visible in the place where we live and the city where we live to say we are here. ... For me Pride is really to get in contact with the people in the streets.

Richard emphasizes the importance of visibility, what Bernstein (1997) calls deploying the strategy of identity. Also for Pink Saturday organizers in the Netherlands it was important to come into close contact with the general population.

> I was in The Hague for a Pink Saturday a few years ago and there it was held outside the city center. It was like a separate festival terrain for gays. ... That was a big difference from the Pink Saturday here in Groningen where we occupied the center of the city. So if you [in The Hague] had been out shopping you wouldn't even have noticed that there was a gay Pride going on.

The place for the performances of Pride is meaningful. Like other protest performances, Pride parades are shaped by their spatial location and simultaneously contribute to producing public space (Mitchell 2003; Wahlström 2010). Temporarily queering central and politically symbolic city streets and squares lends the parade an intrinsic political force. Markwell (2002, p. 90) argues that these parades and parties provide "gay times," "a temporal context in which spaces and places that might have been out of bounds to gays and lesbians can be appropriated by them." Pride parades, in other words, are read as rendering heterosexual spaces as fluid and constructed; artifacts that only give the illusion of stability (also Bell and Valentine 1995; Johnston 2002). Pride parades marching down *Paseo de la Reforma* in Mexico City, past Houses of Parliament in London, past the Royal Castle in central Stockholm, across the Mont Blanc Bridge in Geneva, convey a message of power – symbolically queering politically significant spaces. In contrast, in the LGBT unfriendly climate in Warsaw the parade was directed to a less politically significant part of the city.

Pride performances are not only impacted by the spatial context, they are performed in "times/spaces" (Czarniawska and Sevón 1996). The time of the planned event can impact on how organizers choreograph the performances. The Italian Pride parade included in our sample, Bologna Pride in June 2012, was staged in the recent aftermath of the earthquake tragedy that struck the region just weeks earlier when 27 lost their lives and more than 400 were injured. Sensitive to the timing of the event, a lesbian organizer explained that it was important for the parade that year to show respect for the victims and their families. Hence, the organizers decided to ban motorized floats with disco music, choosing to orchestrate a more restrained and sombre march that year. The organizers' efforts to perform their political (and cultural) worthiness in the wake of this tragedy downplayed the carnivalesque as a gesture of respect and solidarity with the victims and their families.

The cost of spectacular Pride performances

Jan-Willem, a staff member at CoC, told us about the organization's boat for the 2014 Canal Pride in Amsterdam.

> I think our boat had a budget of €30,000, because ... we had a DJ, you need electricity on the boat and if you want inflatables and all. There's a designer involved and artists and it makes it quite expensive. You can also have a small boat but for an organization like CoC we have to go professionally otherwise people will comment on it ... Last year we wanted to try to recreate the iconic image from Iwo Jima with American marines planting the flag and on the internet you see photos of the gay version of it with four gay men planting the rainbow flag. We had a lift on the boat, so after every bridge the lift went up again and we had four dancers on the lift with a huge rainbow flag, which was made from some sort of parachute fabric. ... That was really iconic.

Jan-Willem said that if people want to be on their boat, we ask them to pay as "it is a sort of floating party." A party on a designer boat is an expensive investment and Amsterdam's Canal Pride is a spectacular event, which draws an estimated one million spectators/consumers. The event is limited to 80 boats and participants must annually bid for a boat. While some of the boats are subsidized in order to include groups with fewer resources, the majority of the boats are acquired by groups, institutions, and businesses that have these economic resources.

Putting on a spectacular performance is costly and is usually dependent on LGBT movements that are rich in resources with access to commercial and/or state funding. And the stages for these resource-rich performances are most often LGBT friendly contexts. But this is not the only resource available for spectacular performances. People are also a resource – perhaps the most important. By mobilizing in sheer numbers, even in less friendly LGBT cultural contexts, but with, as in the case of Mexico City, a friendly political context, a spectacular performance of Pride can be staged. While corporate funded floats are few, and gay businesses, bars and clubs sponsor some floats with amplified music, it is the numbers of participants and above all their imaginative performances, costumes and props that makes the Mexico City Pride parades spectacular. Large flags are popular in

Mexico as witnessed by the enormous size of the national flag flying in *Zócalo*. In 2010 Mexico City officials presented Pride organizers with what a lesbian organizer/activist claimed was the largest rainbow flag in the world. The parade enters *Zócalo* after the long march down *Paseo de Reforma* with the flag carried at its front. Tens of thousands of participants, some imaginatively costumed, some not, perform a playful, prefigurative (ephemeral) joyous image of the world in which they wish to live (Shepard 2010, p. 1; Shepard, Bogad and Duncombe 2008). The imaginative acts of march units and individual participants – some using creativity to achieve policy change, some to primarily build community – come together *en masse* for a spectacular celebratory performance of pride.

Conclusions

We would like to conclude by emphasizing that Pride performances dynamically evolve. How parades combine performances of politics and party are not static. In the secondary literature, as in most of our interviews, scholars and respondents have reported the increasing importance of the carnivalesque. Interestingly, in the most politicized event in our sample – Bologna Pride (Chapter 8 this volume) – Pride performances have taken another turn. Lesbian activist Anna Lavizzari relates how she has experienced changes in Bologna Pride.

> I have seen the Bologna Pride changing quite a lot in the last 10 years, when I first participated. Particularly in the last two, maybe three years, there are less and less *"carri"* (wagons) pumping up music and staging performances; on the contrary, now the organizations take part in the parade walking one after the other, with their flags, signals, and symbols, with people moving between them. Some of them still play amplified music yet without trucks, others have small "orchestras", with drums, whistles and dancers. You can spot some drag queens and performers here and there but again, I have seen this less and less common. Overall the atmosphere seems less hardliner than years ago, more relaxed, non-violent, very respectful. The number of families and children (being rainbow families or not) has increased dramatically as has the number of non-LGBTQ participants and youth. ... I am not sure if this is the right way to say it but I would say that it has become less of a carnivalesque kind of atmosphere (still is, but less) and more of a "regular" march where you can really participate in an "individual mode".
>
> (personal correspondence August 9, 2017)

Bologna Pride is organized under the lead of Arcigay Il Cassero, the major LGBT organization in Bologna, with other organizations taking part in a committee. Under central direction by the major mass-based LGBT organization, it appears that Arcigay Il Cassero has greater control over the performances than what is more often assumed by organizing committees in the other countries in our study. In 2015 the organizers banned company sponsors and participation on the part of businesses (Chapter 6 this volume). The organizing committee has encouraged an environmental friendly, "sustainable Pride," hence the parade now features imaginative mini-floats drawn by bicycles, electric carts, and so on; motorized vehicles are not allowed. But that does not seem to have diminished the colorfulness or playfulness of the parade. The 2017 Bologna Pride Committee chose as a slogan "Space Pride" that they explained "intends to revive in the public debate the explorative dimension of social movements." Their official program declaration was in part an 11-page list of political demands and concerns of the LGBT movement and in part a visionary statement of the potential for the contribution of the LGBT movement and the Pride parade for the city of Bologna.

> Space for pride means, therefore, to have the courage to re-think pre-established logics. ... Space for pride means expanding the horizon, scrutinizing longitudes and latitudes. It gives oxygen to debates by reversing prospects, enhancing all points of view, moving in search of what has not yet been considered, measuring the real commitment of the institutions in making our cities more inclusive, livable and more just. Having spaces in which to be able to experiment freely on the political, cultural, social and sexual level is an indispensable necessity for individual and collective well-being.[4]

Prefigurative politics, or in the words of the 2017 Bologna Pride committee, "the explorative dimension of social movements," are at the heart of Pride performances. "Coming out" collectively, LGBT movements in all of their diversity (temporarily) manifest another possible world. Boundaries for the possible are explored, extended and challenged, and in doing so, participants and spectators alike are moved emotionally, cognitively and politically. Pride performances are experiments in the imaginable.

Notes

1 www.theguardian.com/commentisfree/2012/jul/06/conversation-pride-gay-rights-party, accessed August 29, 2017.
2 Conservative party leader Fredrik Reinfeldt was the first sitting Prime Minister in the world to march in a Pride parade. www.reuters.com/article/us-sweden-gay/swedish-pm-urges-tolerance-at-gay-festival-idUSL03804544220070803, accessed December 15, 2017.
3 www.theguardian.com/commentisfree/2012/jul/06/conversation-pride-gay-rights-party, accessed August 29, 2017.
4 www.bolognapride.it/bp12/wp-content/uploads/2017/06/DOCUMENTO-POLITICO-BOLOGNA-PRIDE-2017.pdf, accessed August 17, 2017.

References

Armstrong, E.A., and Crage, S.M. (2006). Movements and memory: The making of the Stonewall myth. *American Sociological Review*, 71(5), 724–751.

Bell, D., and Valentine, G. (1995). Queer country: rural lesbian and gay lives. *Journal of Rural Studies*, 11(2), 113–122.

Bernstein, M. (1997). Celebration and suppression: The strategic uses of identity by the lesbian and gay movement. *American Journal of Sociology*, 103(3), 531–565.

Bernstein, M. (2002). Identities and politics. *Social Science History*, 26(3), 531–581.

Binnie, J., and Klesse, C. (2011). 'Because it was a bit like going to an adventure park': The politics of hospitality in transnational lesbian, gay, bisexual, transgender and queer activist networks. *Tourist Studies*, 11(2), 157–174.

Binnie, J., and Klesse, C. (2012). Solidarities and tensions: Feminism and transnational LGBTQ politics in Poland. *European Journal of Women's Studies*, 19(4), 444–459.

Bogad, L.M. (2006). Tactical carnival: social movements, demonstrations, and dialogical performance. In Cohen-Cruz, J., and Schutzman M. (Eds) *A Boal companion: Dialogues on theatre and cultural politics* (pp. 46–58). New York: Routledge.

Breines, W. (1980). Community and organization: The New Left and Michels "Iron Law." *Social Problems*, 27(4), 419–429.

Browne, K. (2007). A party with politics? (Re)making LGBTQ Pride spaces in Dublin and Brighton. *Social and Cultural Geography*, 8(1), 63–87.

Browne, K., and Bakshi, M.L. (2013). *Ordinary in Brighton? LGBT, activisms and the city*. Farnham: Ashgate Publishing, Ltd.

Calvo, K., and Trujillo, G. (2011). Fighting for love rights: Claims and strategies of the LGBT movement in Spain. *Sexualities*, 14(5), 562–579.

Cappellato, V., and Mangarella, T. (2014). Sexual citizenship in private and public space: Parents of gay men and lesbians discuss their experiences of Pride parades, *Journal of GLBT Family Studies*, 10(1–2), 211–230.

Casey, M. (2004). De-dyking queer space (s): Heterosexual female visibility in gay and lesbian spaces. *Sexualities*, 7(4), 446–461.

Czarniawska, B., and Sevón, G. (Eds). (1996). *Translating organizational change*. 56. Berlin: Walter de Gruyter.

Duggan, M. (2010). Politics of Pride: Representing relegated sexual identities in Northern Ireland, *The Northern Ireland Legal Quarterly*, 61, 163.

Ehrenreich, B. (2007). *Dancing in the streets: A history of collective joy*. New York: Metropolitan books.

Enguix, B. (2009). Identities, sexualities and commemorations: Pride parades, public space and sexual dissidence. *Anthropological Notebooks*, 15(2), 15–33.

Enguix, B. (2013). Sexual politics, pride, and media mediation in Spain. *Observatorio (OBS*)*, 7(2).

Eyerman, R. (2006). Performing opposition or, how social movements move. In Alexander, J.C., Giesen, B., and Mast, J.L. (Eds) *Social performance: Symbolic action, cultural pragmatics, and ritual* (pp. 193–217). Cambridge: Cambridge University Press.

Gruszczynska, A. (2009). Sowing the seeds of solidarity in public space: Case study of the Poznan March of Equality. *Sexualities*, 12(3), 312–333.

Herdt, G.H. (1992). "Coming Out" as a rite of passage: A Chicago study. In Herdt, G.H. (Ed.) *Gay culture in America: Essays from the field* (pp. 29–69). Boston, MA: Beacon Press.

Holzhacker, R. (2012). National and transnational strategies of LGBT civil society organizations in different political environments: Modes of interaction in Western and Eastern Europe for equality. *Comparative European Politics*, 10(1), 23–47.

Kates, S.M., and Belk, R.W. (2001). The meanings of lesbian and gay pride day resistance through consumption and resistance to consumption. *Journal of Contemporary Ethnography*, 30(4), 392–429.

Johnston, L. (2002). Borderline bodies. In Bondi, L. et al. *Subjectivities, knowledges, and feminist geographies: The subjects and ethics of social research* (pp. 75–89). Lanham, MD: Rowman and Littlefield.

Johnston, L. (2007). *Queering tourism: Paradoxical performances of gay pride parades*. New York: Routledge.

Markwell, K. (2002). Mardi Gras tourism and the construction of Sydney as an international gay and lesbian city. *GLQ: A Journal of Lesbian and Gay Studies*, 8(1), 81–99.

McFarland, K. (2012). *Cultural contestation and community building at LGBT Pride parades*. (Unpublished doctoral dissertation): Chapel Hill, South Carolina.

McFarland Bruce, K. (2016). *Pride parades: How a parade changed the world*. New York: NYU Press.

Mitchell, D. (2003). *The right to the city: Social justice and the fight for public space*. New York: Guilford Press.

Moon, D. (2012). Who am I and who are we? Conflicting narratives of collective selfhood in stigmatized groups. *American Journal of Sociology*, 117(5), 1336–1379.

Moore, K., and Wood, L. (2002). Target practice: Community action in a global era. In Hayduk, R., & Shepard, B. (Eds) *From ACT UP to the WTO*. London: Verso.

Murray, S.O. (1996). *American gay*. Chicago, IL: University of Chicago Press.

Pershing, L. (1996). *The ribbon around the Pentagon: Peace by piecemakers*. Knoxville, TN: University of Tennessee Press.

Peterson, A. (2001). *Contemporary political protest: Essays on political militancy*. Aldershot: Ashgate.

Peterson, A., and Reiter, H. (2016). *The ritual of May Day in Western Europe: Past, present and future*. Farnham and New York: Routledge.

Richardson, D. (2005). Desiring sameness? The rise of a neoliberal politics of normalisation. *Antipode* 37(3), 515–535.

Robinson, B. A. (2012). Is this what equality looks like? *Sexuality Research and Social Policy*, 9(4), 327–336.

Santino, J. (2011). The carnivalesque and the ritualesque. *Journal of American Folklore*, 124(491), 61–73.

Shepard, B. (2010). *Queer political performance and protest*. New York: Routledge.

Shepard, B., Bogad, L.M., and Duncombe, S. (2008). Performing vs. the insurmountable: Theatrics, activism, and social movements. *Liminalities: A Journal of Performance Studies*, 4(3), 1–30.

Thompson, E.P. (1991). Rough music. In Thompson, E.P. (Ed.) *Customs in common* (pp. 467–538). New York: The New Press.

Tilly, C. (2004). *Social movements, 1768–2004*. Boulder, CO: Paradigm Publishers.

Wahlström, M. (2010). Producing spaces for representation: Racist marches, counterdemonstrations, and public-order policing. *Environment and Planning D: Society and Space*, 28(5), 811–827.

Wasshede, C. (2017). Queer hate and dirt rhetoric: An ambivalent resistance strategy. *Journal of Resistance Studies*, 3(1), 29–62.

8 The Meanings of Pride Parades for their Participants

What are the meanings of Pride parades today? Are they primarily social events for the LGBT community? Are Pride parades chiefly spectacular tourist attractions? Are there remnants of political protest left in the parades? These are provocative questions, but warranted given the critical attention that Pride events have garnered on the part of many LGBT scholars. In order to approach these questions in relation to our sample of countries, an important first step – taken in Chapter 7 – was to analyze the strategic performances intended by Pride organizers and participating organizations, as well as the ways in which Pride parades move their participants and onlookers on a personal, as well as political, level.

The analysis of performances focused on what might be described as holistic aspects of the meaning of collective events like Pride parades; the messages and impressions that an event as a whole conveys or is intended to convey. However, as we saw in Chapter 7, performances vary not only between Pride events in different contexts, but are also heterogeneous and fragmented within the parades. Furthermore, the meaning of collective activities cannot be reduced to the messages that organizers wish to convey or the interpretations of external observers. A complementary approach to the meanings of collective events is to regard them as aggregates of the meanings that their participants ascribe to the events and their participation in them. In line with Roth's (1995) proposition that ritual events should be studied through the action orientations of their individual participants, we need to return to the Pride participants and the meanings that they confer to Pride parades and to their own participation.

The meanings that collective events (in this case Pride parades) have for participants can be analyzed in terms of the meanings that the participants expect them to have for them, and unexpected meanings that, as it were, come to participants during or after the events. This distinction is methodologically important since expected meanings presumably constitute central aspects of the reason someone has to participate, and can hence be operationalized in terms of *participant motives* (Wahlström 2016). Unexpected – emergent – meanings are not likely to be evident from motives to participate but instead materialize in narrated memories of events. Examples of the latter are the descriptions of Pride parades as personal turning-points found in the narratives discussed in Chapter 7 on how first-time participants were "moved" in their first encounters with Pride parades.

However, based on the assumption that Pride parades largely turn out more or less as their participants expect them to, we direct attention in this chapter to participant motives as a key for understanding the multiple and varying meanings of Pride parades. This approach makes it possible to systematically compare the salience of different meanings in different Pride parades and between different categories of participants. First, on the basis of an analysis of responses to open survey questions in the CCC questionnaire, we identify the different types of meanings that the participants expressed for their participation; in short, why they participated. Second, a coding of the survey responses based on this typology provides a basis for a quantitative comparison of the different categories of participants, but also of the motive patterns found in the different parades. We argue that the latter indicates a varying degree of politicization of Pride parades depending on their context. However, we will begin with situating our discussion in relation to the broader literature on protest motivation.

Motives for protest

Previous research on the types of motives that propel participants to take part in protest actions has largely focused on participatory logics, summarized by Klandermans (2004) as instrumental, ideological and identity logics. Protesting for instrumental reasons means regarding the protest as a means to achieve a specific end, such as pushing for policy changes or influencing public opinion. This roughly equates to Weber's (1978) classic notion of "goal-rational" actions, and implies that participants in protests (and those who organize them) are motivated by a sense that the protest could actually affect one's chances to achieve a certain (political) goal. This assumption is what underlies much theorizing within the resource mobilization and political process traditions within social movement research: protest occurs when (given current political opportunities and a movement's mobilizing capacity) it has a chance to achieve something.

In contrast, the ideological motivational logic does not concern itself with the capacity of a protest action to achieve some ulterior political goal, but concerns honoring specific values and following ideological or moral principles and expressing these to others. In Weber's (1978) terms, this corresponds to "value-rational" action logic. As noted by Wahlström (2016), there are actually two related but distinct motive types conflated in this category: (1) protesting in order to adhere to a value, because it is "the right thing to do," and (2) protesting in order to express and communicate this value to others. In general, people protest for ideological reasons when they perceive a discrepancy between the state of things and how they think that the world should be, even when they see no obvious way for the protest to actually change the state of things.

The identity logic concerns itself with the social identity of the individual and the collective identity of a movement. According to this logic, people protest in order to express their identity and tend to be mobilized when they identify with others involved in a protest campaign. Snow and McAdam (2000) use the term "identity convergence" to conceptualize the latter fit between individual and collective identities that enables mobilization. Participating in a protest following an identity logic means protesting because of who you are and to be part of a group where you sense that you belong. Following Bernstein (1997), it is worth noting in this context that the identity logic behind participation does not exhaust the uses of identity in social movement mobilizing. Movement organizers do not only use *identity for empowerment* to mobilize participants, but also deploy identity *strategically*, either for criticizing dominant norms or for educating the public about the non-threatening character of one's mobilization by playing on similarities rather than differences. On the individual level, participating in a protest in order to use identity strategically would primarily imply instrumental motivation rather than following an identity logic in Klandermans' (2004) terms.

Research on protest motivation has also pointed to the crucial role of emotions in driving political participation (Van Stekelenburg et al. 2011). While some regard emotions primarily as amplifiers of the above mentioned motivational logics, others point to emotions' standalone role in protest activities. While anger is perhaps the emotion that comes first to mind when thinking about emotions driving protest, some researchers have also emphasized the role of positive emotional states, such as fun in protest activities (Wettergren 2009) and Lundberg (2007) specifically points to the subversive role of laughter in Pride parades. In addition, it is not far-fetched to assume that Pride parades should have something to do with the participants' sense of pride. Breaking societal norms is associated with shame, triggered by a negative evaluation of oneself in the actual or imagined gaze of others (Scheff 1988), something many LGBT persons struggle with in their daily lives. Britt and Heise (2000) elaborate on the central task for identity movements in general to turn shame, and concomitant emotions of fear and anger, into pride through collective actions. From this perspective, one can expect that many LGBT individuals participate in Pride from an urge to feel more pride in themselves in combination with a wish to help others feel the same. Britt and Heise also point to the positive emotional contagion occurring at Pride events, which may lead participants into a deepened involvement in the LGBT movement (see also Chapter 7).

Meanings of Pride

In line with the above motivational logics, a Pride parade can be regarded by its participants as a vehicle for achieving political or social change, as a way of upholding a set of values, and/or an expression of their social identity. From an emotional perspective, a parade can be regarded as a means to seek or to express the experience of specific emotions – paradigmatically the emotion of pride. However, as pointed out by Wahlström (2015), there are some problems associated with confining the analysis to the predominant conceptualization of motives for political participation when the task is to understand the meaning of Pride parades from the participants' points of view. First, there are other aspects of the meaning of participation beyond the action logics involved, and there are potentially important distinctions that are not captured with these concepts. For example, in their study of May Day march participants' perspectives on the events, Peterson et al. (2012) apply the distinction between *official and oppositional rituality*, hereby capturing the distinction between marching primarily to oppose the incumbent power structure, or to celebrate prior victories for changing past conditions. Wahlström (2016) also distinguishes between the *external and internal orientation* of May Day marchers – *external influence* versus *movement coherence* – to capture the difference between marching to impact on an external audience or to strengthen one's own group. Second, everyone does not agree that Pride parades today are political protests, and even if they are, they are arguably a relatively specific kind of protest. Hence, one needs to pay attention to the specifics of Pride parades in order to not miss central aspects of their meaning. Since the current degree of politicization of Pride parades (or lack of it) is heatedly debated, it is important to distinguish between explicitly political motives and other more socially orientated motives.

Measuring how politicized Pride parades are in terms of the action orientation of their participants must not be confused with assessing their political impact. As discussed elsewhere in this volume, and highlighted by McFarland Bruce (2016), Pride parades are not only political in the sense of pushing for political reforms, but they also – and perhaps first and foremost – pose cultural challenges to dominant norms. The mere act of LGBT persons becoming visible – *qua* LGBT persons – in large numbers is itself a cultural challenge, at least in environments that are predominantly hostile to the sexualities, gender expressions and relationships that are made visible. To the extent that Pride parades are regarded as political in the sense that they challenge cultural norms, it is not surprising that they are accused of becoming less politicized when dominant norms in some countries and locations converge with those expressed by the majority of Pride participants. In terms of the distinction made by Peterson et al. (2012) between official and oppositional rituality, the visibility of LGBT persons becomes more official than oppositional when it no longer challenges widely shared norms and ceases to push the boundaries for the socially acceptable. A paradigmatic example of a Pride event which is largely depoliticized in this sense would be the 2016 Amsterdam Canal Pride, observed by the authors, where participants present themselves partying on boats (mainly representing large and influential private businesses) that float past a highly supportive and equally festive crowd of spectators. In sum, comparing the level of cultural challenge through public LGBT visibility is difficult to do in a systematic way since the same displays carry different meanings depending on the context. Focusing on participants' action orientations implies a more narrow definition of politicization, which has the advantage of providing a stronger test if Pride parades are adequately described as political protests.

In previous research on Pride parades, both Browne (2007) and McFarland Bruce (2016, McFarland 2012) have taken an interest in the meanings that Pride events have for participants. Browne (2007), studying women participants in Pride events in Dublin and Brighton (and not specifically parades), distinguishes between several types of motives for taking part: having fun, celebration, political reasons, community, meeting friends, being in a safe space, and finding a (sexual) partner. McFarland Bruce (2016, McFarland 2012) interviewed participants in Pride parades in different US cities and identified three main themes in their accounts: celebration, support and visibility.

In the CCC survey, Pride respondents were posed the open question: "Please tell us why you participated in this Pride parade." In this analysis we have used the responses to this question in combination with the above studies on Pride participants and Wahlström's (2016) study of May Day march participants to develop a typology of Pride participants' motives. When the concepts from previous studies were found insufficient to capture patterns in the data, the existing terms were either redefined or new ones introduced. This stage in the analysis resulted in distinguishing 13 types of motives. As a group, they mirror the heterogeneous and multifaceted meanings that Pride parades hold for their participants. An overview of the typology and a comparison with previous typologies is presented in Table 8.1. In it, closely related concepts are horizontally close to each other. Each respondent in our data was assigned one or more of these codes depending on their responses to the open question. It is important to keep in mind when interpreting the figures below that the codes are not mutually exclusive, and that it was perfectly possible for respondents to state that they were participating, for example, both for fun and in order to protest against injustices. More details about the procedure and reliability tests can be found in the Appendix.

Protest (fight for rights, promote tolerance)

This category was used to code all cases where respondents motivated their participation with their wish to protest, stand up for LGBT rights,

Table 8.1 Motive types compared with previous studies

	Motive name in present study	In McFarland (2012)	In Browne (2007)	In Wahlström (2016)
1.	Protest/fight for rights/tolerance		Political	Protest government/Politics
				Accomplish change
2.	Conviction/duty			Conviction/duty
3.	Visibility/display identity/pride	Visibility		Display numbers
4.	Minority identity			Loyalty/identity
5.	Tradition/convenience			Tradition
6.	Show support	Support	Community	Support own movement
7.	Represent organization or group			
8.	Meet friends or co-members of organization		Friends/meet people	Meet friends/co-members
			Sex/"pulling"	
9.	Celebrate	Celebration	Celebrate/pride	Celebrate political accomplishments
10.	Commemoration			Celebrate workers' day
11.	Entertainment/fun		Fun/party	
12.	Feeling of community		Safe/gay/accepting space	
13.	Curiosity			Curiosity/interest

Comment: Location within the same area marked by dotted lines indicates approximate correspondence, but not necessarily identity, of codes.

publicly advocate tolerance, or otherwise communicate their dissatisfaction with the current state of affairs in their home country or in other parts of the world. This could also mean protesting against highly specific political incidents or occurrences, such as when the 2012 Pride participants in the Czech Republic directed their main message against the country's President Václav Klaus and his then recent homophobic pronouncements. Nevertheless, most often the statements coded with this category directly framed Pride as something forming part of a broader struggle to advance the interests of the LGBT movement.

Conviction/duty

This category was used to code motives arising from principles and values such as moral obligation, civic duty, or moral-political conviction. Participation in Pride was, for individuals expressing such motives, seen as something "one ought to do" according to the held precept or principle. Also included in this category were, however, statements of the type "I participate because I believe in …" or "because I value … .". In addition, some marchers also stated that they participated in order to that way pass on important values to their children or be able to teach them about tolerance. Such statements were then also included in this category since they, too, were centered on the importance of values and convictions.

Show support

In line with the findings of McFarland (2012), an expression that the Pride participants in the CCC dataset in this study frequently used when describing what they sought through their participation in the events was "to support," along with related terms such as "solidarity." Some respondents simply stated their motivation to have been to "show support" for the event in general, while others elaborated more in detail what exactly it was that they wanted to support. Some wanted to express support for some specific individual in one's life (e.g., parent, child), while most often respondents wanted to express support for the entire LGBT community or a specific subgroup or organization within this community. Particularly in the Swedish Pride parades, expressions of international solidarity were frequently cited as a motivation.

Follow tradition

As noted, for example, by Wahlström (2016), tradition and habit often shape motives for participation in certain forms of contentious collective action. Nevertheless, the two have remained largely neglected in research. Some of the actions studied, such as the Pride parades in Prague, were still too recent as annual events to allow their participants to detect any influence of tradition or personal habit in their decisions to join in, while in other cases the two could have conceivably played a role, as surmised also by a number of those taking part in the events.

Meet friends or co-members of an organization

This category was used to code all cases where the reported Pride participation motives centered on the possibility that the event was seen to offer for meeting friends, acquaintances, relatives, or co-members of one's organization. Also, statements to the effect that one's participation was due to having been asked by a friend or friends to do so were included in this category. In an earlier study, Browne (2007) included a separate code for those Pride participants who, according to themselves, took part in the hope of finding a romantic or sexual partner, but since there were only very few such cases among the respondents in this study, this particular motive was also included in the meet friends category.

Represent an organization or a group

This category was made up of statements to the effect that the respondent participated in the Pride event with the intent of representing an organization or a particular group in it. The organization or group in question could be an interest group promoting LGBT rights, *albeit* frequently one not directly linked to the LGBT movement itself; for example, a business company wanting to demonstrate its welcoming attitude toward LGBT employees and jobseekers, a church or a religious organization wishing to promote inclusion of LGBT persons, or a union or a political party/group wanting to proclaim its support for the LGBT movement goals. All statements about one's belonging to the category of LGBT persons and the like were excluded from this code, being assigned to the minority identity category instead.

Celebrate

Some Pride participants reported themselves as participating in the parade merely because it offered them an occasion to celebrate something. The object of the celebration here varied, although it was not always possible for the participants to identify it precisely or in concrete terms. When specified, it was often "the right to be different" or one's sexual identity. Also included in this category were descriptions such as "[I'm here] because it's our festival" (an Italian respondent). In any case, what is important to note here, as pointed out also by McFarland (2012, pp. 158–159), celebration is often not apolitical; it can be regarded as a way of countering repression and engaging in cultural contestation.

Entertainment/fun

Many participants reported fun, joy, or entertainment to be one of their motives, sometimes even their only motive, for participating in the Pride event. Under this category, statements of a less affirmative character, such as "I had nothing else to do," were also included when they were strong enough to imply that the enjoyment one looked to derive from one's parade participation was at least sufficient to counteract boredom. Taken on their own, these kinds of statements might be interpreted as indicating an individualistic and apolitical relation to the project of Pride, but in this study, at least, they were frequently articulated in conjunction with expressions of other, occasionally clearly political, motives.

Get visibility, display identity or pride

As also noted by McFarland (2012), a desire to contribute to the greater visibility of the LGBT community forms one of the more common motives Pride marchers report when describing their reasons for participating. Many want to help make LGBT people more visible in the context of the overall society, by showing that they are not an exception and that they can take pride in their sexual orientation or gender identity in public. As McFarland explains, there are two distinct logics in operation here: (1) LGBT visibility challenges dominant heterosexual norms (defiant visibility) and (2) LGBT visibility helps demonstrate that LGBT people are no different from others (educational visibility). This directly corresponds to Bernstein's (1997) distinction, mentioned above, between strategically deploying identity for critique or for education. As noted earlier in this chapter, LGBT visibility can also be more or less official or oppositional (Peterson et al. 2012) depending on how far the LGBT movement already has changed the dominant norms in society. In this study, this code was also used to mark out responses speaking of the personal challenge of overcoming previous fears and finally displaying one's sexual identity in public. As one respondent in the Prague parade explained, Pride offered a way to "come out." "I was tired of hiding my sexual orientation, so I wanted to show it [in public] somehow." To participate in Pride in order to become visible thus contains a spectrum of connotations from the personal level to a collective – and more obviously political – level.

Minority identity

Many respondents stated that they participated because they identified as gay, lesbian, bisexual, or transgender. Frequently, this was merely stated without any further elaboration of how that affected one's decision to participate in Pride, implying that the motivational logic linking the two was taken to be self-evident. In other cases, the respondents explicitly connected their self-identity to a need for greater visibility of one's kind or for defending one's rights, as a member of a minority group in society. In a couple of cases, other minority identities were also evoked in this way. As one participant with disability who took part in the Stockholm Pride parade described it, she joined the march "because I also belong to a group that's discriminated against."[1]

Commemoration

Some respondents explained their Pride participation as a way for them to "commemorate" or "remember" something of importance. In a couple of cases, a reference to the Stonewall riots was explicitly made in this connection, while in other cases the connection was only implicit. Occasionally, commemoration was of a more personal nature; for example, one respondent joined the march "to remember all the earlier times when I didn't dare to do so" (a Haarlem parade participant), another did so "in memory of my dead gay brother" (a London marcher).

Feeling of community

While many Pride participants motivated their participation by their desire to meet and socialize with friends or acquaintances, there were others who were more drawn by the idea of participating and being in the group as a whole. They had looked forward to "experiencing the atmosphere" and to being able to feel themselves as part of a community. This category of a feeling of community was employed to accommodate descriptions of such emotions, feelings, or a sense of security and belonging that motivated these individuals' decision to join the march.

Curiosity

There were also some participants who described their participation to have been motivated by sheer curiosity. Participating in Pride action or events was in these cases something one never had done before, and thus one wanted to satisfy one's curiosity about them and about being part of them. As one Italian respondent put it, "I've never participated before so I just wanted to experience it first-hand."

Broader categorizations

These categories are not straightforwardly reducible to any of the broader theoretical typologies discussed in the previous section. In terms of the motivational categories summarized by Klandermans (2004), only the "protest" category is compatible with what would be normally regarded as instrumental motives. However, some aspects of "protest" may be closer to the expressive motive type, along with the categories "visibility," "show support," "represent organization," and "conviction/duty." Social identity motives would in many cases overlap with the categories "minority identity," "tradition," "celebrate," "commemoration" and "feeling of community." "Meeting friends," "entertainment/fun" and "curiosity" display even more vague correspondence with the traditional tripartite typology of motivation. While these connections are important for interpreting the implications of research on contextual effects on participant motives, the analysis below will primarily depart from other analytical categories – in-group *vis-à-vis* out-group motives and explicitly politicized motives.

Closer to our analytical interests is the distinction between internally and externally oriented motives, whether the parade is primarily oriented toward the other participants and members of the LGBT community, or toward an external audience (Wahlström 2016). Arguably, whereas more internally oriented *movement coherence motives* capture the celebratory and mutually empowering aspect of participating in Pride parades, the *external influence* type of motives roughly capture the dual challenge Pride parades potentially pose against political power and cultural norms. In terms of this distinction the motive types "protest," "visibility" and "represent organization" imply a primarily out-group orientation, whereas motives in the categories "celebrate," "commemoration," "feeling of community," "meeting friends," "entertainment/fun," "show support," and "tradition," suggest an in-group orientation. In order to deal with the issue of an alleged de-politicization of Pride parades, we constructed a combined variable for "political motives." Whereas several of the motive categories have a potentially political dimension, we chose a rather restrictive operationalization to create more variation in the data, and to be able to make a stronger case that today also, many Pride participants still have a political action-orientation. Therefore, as political motives we chose to count those responses that were either coded as "protest" (the attempt to promote a political goal) or as "conviction/duty" (the adherence to a moral or political principle).

Our coding allows us to identify overall patterns in the data, both within and between Pride parades. In the next section we will provide an overview of the variation relating to individual participant characteristics, while in the following section we will turn to variation of motives across different Pride parades, and the possible effect of the national context.

How individual characteristics affect participant motives

Temporarily disregarding dissimilarities between parades in different countries in terms of their overall motive patterns, figures presented below represent overall percentages for the respondents in our data. However, we have made sure that the patterns discussed below are generally persistent also within each parade. Some of the more rare motive types, however, were difficult to control this way since numerically very few respondents expressed them in each parade. Since this section reaches over a large number of combinations of motive types and other variables, no table is provided to capture them all; for an overview of the motive distribution in the various parades, see Table 8.2 in the next section.

In terms of gender, women overall somewhat more often tended to emphasize protest motives (39 percent compared to 34 percent among men) and conviction/duty (12 percent compared to 8 percent among men). Those respondents who had non-normative gender identities to a higher degree expressed the visibility motive (41 percent vs. 22 percent for both women and men), but apart from this, gender differences were generally rather small. Age seemed to have some effect; younger age groups to a somewhat higher degree expressed protest motives compared to older respondents, with age groups over 50 years less often expressing this motive type. Protest motives are also typically more common among those with university education (40 percent overall), compared to those without (33 percent overall). Political left/right self-identification also had an effect on protest motives, with those further to the left typically more often stating protest or conviction/duty as motives for participating (i.e. political motives), while a higher proportion of those who identified more toward the right end of the political spectrum expressed fun and entertainment as motives. In terms of mobilization, discussed in Chapter 5, those who had decided to participate long before the event more often expressed protest motives, whereas those who decided on the day of the parade more often said they were there to show support. Motive types differed little depending on company at the event (but not surprisingly, those who were there with their children more often stated support motives).

In Chapter 6 we discussed the role of individual allies of Pride, that is, non-LGBT participants. Interestingly, in the four parades where this variable was measured this group did not differ overall from LGBT participants in terms of the frequency with which they regarded the Pride parade as a protest. However, non-LGBT participants to a greater degree referred to support as well as conviction/duty as their motives for participating, while LGBT participants to a higher degree emphasized visibility and sense of community.

In previous chapters, we have also discussed the category of first-timers in Pride, which several organizers mention as an important target group. In those cities where survey participants were asked about prior participation in Pride (London, Gothenburg, Stockholm, Warsaw and Zurich) there were indeed some significant differences between the meanings that newcomers and returnees attached to the Pride parade in which they participated. While the newcomers were significantly more often than the returnees participating out of curiosity (7 percent vs. 2 percent), to meet friends (16 percent vs. 10 percent) or to represent an organization (17 percent vs. 11 percent), they less often stated that they were there to protest (30 percent vs. 42 percent), to be visible (12 percent vs. 28 percent) or to feel a sense of community with other participants (5 percent vs. 10 percent). This indicates that first-timers more often need the social context of family or friends, or an organization or group, to take the decisive step to overcome the barrier of stigma to take part (Chapter 5), whereas returnees to a larger extent have developed protest oriented motives and from prior experience know the feeling of community that they can expect at a Pride parade.

Contextual variations in participant motives

Apart from variation in participant motives within parades, it is reasonable to expect that Pride parades do not mean quite the same thing to their participants everywhere, but that this is partly shaped in interaction with the context of the event. Previous research provides only limited guidance on what to expect in terms of the contextual impact on (protest) participants' meanings and motives. However, there are a few studies that provide some clues.

First, one must distinguish between the immediate context of the mobilization and broader local and national conditions. In terms of the former, van Stekelenburg and colleagues (2009) have argued that the type of overall orientation of a protest campaign affects the motives of protest participants. They use a distinction introduced by Turner and Killian (1972) and elaborated by Klandermans (1993) between campaigns with a (1) power orientation, (2) value orientation and (3) participation orientation. Van Stekelenburg and her associates (2009) find that power oriented campaigns, which are focused on exerting influence, attract participants for instrumental reasons. Value oriented campaigns, which focus on expressing a movement's values and goals, tend to a greater extent to lead people to participate for ideological reasons. No participation oriented campaigns were included in their study, i.e. campaigns that highlight the benefits of participation itself, but one might assume that such campaigns to a higher degree would involve participants motivated by an identity logic. These links between campaign orientations and individual motives appear rather commonsensical, but the bottom line of this research is that there is typically a correspondence between the overall framing of the campaign and the reasons for participants joining in. Of course, these are ideal types and real campaigns often express a mix of these orientations.

Wahlström (2016), in his comparison of motives among May Day participants, similarly finds that the type of organizer of May Day marches appears to have an effect on the motivational composition among the participants. May Day marchers organized by radical left parties and unions and by mixed coalitions were more often motivated by a will to protest, while those organized by dominant trade unions and social democratic parties more frequently were there to support their movement. Wahlström also found that May Day marches in different locations varied considerably in terms of the prevalence of motives related to external influence and internally oriented movement coherence, suggesting that broad coalitions of different actors would lead to stronger externally oriented motives and lesser focus on "internal celebration of a more tightly knit community" (p. 241).

Especially in relation to Pride there is the issue regarding the degree to which an organizer has the capacity to control the message and overall orientation of an event. As pointed out by McFarland Bruce (2016), Pride parade organizers set a general framework within which various actors can develop their own agenda. This most likely limits Pride organizers' impact on participants' motives, compared to other, less internally heterogeneous, demonstrations. Nevertheless, as previous chapters have revealed, the parades in our sample, while largely subscribing to the wider "Pride" script, appeared to differ (more or less) in terms of how they were staged by their organizers. All parades seemed to have at least an element of value orientation, as well as a clear participation orientation in terms of the sense of empowerment that Pride parades are expected to give their participants. Still they seemed to vary somewhat in terms of the types of value claims put forth as well as the general centrality of these values. A distinct case is the Warsaw parade that avoided the explicit Pride label and aimed for a much broader mobilization for equality among different groups in society under the slogan "A shared case for equal rights". In terms of the organizers' rhetoric, the Pride parade in Bologna, Italy, was the most markedly political and, following Klandermans (1993), power oriented. They demanded several political reforms and aimed to challenge the power of the Catholic Church. On the other end of the spectrum, the parade organizers in Haarlem and London, most clearly emphasized partying and celebrating (even if this was far from their sole aim).

As argued by Peterson et al. (2012) in relation to May Day parades, past local and national traditions are also likely to shape current events and the meanings that participants see in them. The impact of the broader national and political context could also have an effect on the motives people have for participating in demonstrations or, in our case, Pride parades. Walgrave et al. (2011) found that US anti-war protesters in 2003 were more often motivated by an instrumental belief that they could influence politics through their protest. Linking to the findings from several studies within the political process tradition that open political opportunity structures facilitate protest, Ketelaars (2014) argues that favorable attitudes among political elites toward the protest demands can lead to a higher proportion of instrumental motives among protest participants. However, in the case of Pride parades, where one persistent ambiguity concerns the degree to which they are political or primarily a party or celebration, it is not *prima facie* clear how the political opportunity structure plays out. Favorable opportunities could also mean less reason to protest and more reason to celebrate, and *vice versa*. Since LGBT movements not only target the political sphere directly but also try to affect the public opinion on LGBT issues, a plausible assumption is that public opinion also affects the balance between protest and celebration in Pride parades. Following Holzhacker (2012) (see Chapter 3, this volume) we therefore in our model propose that the context for LGBT mobilization should be understood as the intersection between the political context and the cultural context.

In a similar vein, McFarland Bruce (2016) compared the meanings that participants confer to Pride parades in different US cities, varying in size and state-level political conditions. While the celebration theme indeed seemed to be stronger in states and cities with more favorable conditions for LGBT people, the visibility and support themes were similarly strong everywhere. However, striving for visibility had slightly different connotations in different locations, meaning for example that Pride participants in more unfavorable contexts pursued visibility in more modest ways (but nevertheless rather provocative relative to the local context, see Chapter 7, this volume).

In sum, one would expect country contexts (political and public opinion) that we in Chapter 3 identified as less LGBT friendly at the time of the studied Pride parades, to lead to stronger protest orientations and stronger "political motives." Conversely, one might expect Pride parade participants in LGBT friendly countries to more frequently express celebratory or entertainment motives. The differences in what it means to become visible in different contexts makes it difficult to formulate clear expectations about how this motive would vary from one location to another, as noted earlier in this chapter and confirmed by McFarland Bruce (2016). Similarly, whereas one might expect that "showing support" might be more common in less friendly contexts (because LGBT people experience stronger grievances there) there are also so many nuances to this term, and so many possible objects for support, that one might as well expect many participants in more friendly contexts to parade in order to support those in need elsewhere.

As shown in Table 8.2, these expectations were at least partly confirmed in our data. The most protest-oriented and politicized Pride participants were found in Bologna, Italy (72 percent political motives), and Warsaw, Poland (70 percent political motives). Also in Sweden and Switzerland around half of the respondents in our survey expressed what we would, in our presently rather narrow sense, classify as political motives. Especially in the case of Sweden, one might have expected a less explicitly politicized profile. However, this might be explained partly by the prominent presence, described earlier in this volume, of political parties and various interest groups, together with the perspicuous political ambitions of the organizers. In Chapter 4 we also demonstrated that Swedish Pride participants to a comparatively high degree favor radical movement strategies/goals like abolishing patriarchy, heteronormativity and challenging the norm of monogamy. This indicates that Swedish LGBT activists to a large extent have reacted to movement victories by radicalizing their struggle instead of lapsing into complacency. On the other end of the spectrum, the Pride participants in Haarlem, Netherlands, displayed the lowest explicitly politicized orientation – only 20 percent – while more often than other Pride participants mentioning "entertainment/fun" as a reason for taking part. This and the rather low explicitly politicized orientation in the UK – 26 percent – also correspond with the fact that these parades took place in what we have classified as LGBT friendly contexts.

Table 8.2 Prevalence of different motive types in the demonstrations studied (percent)

Motive type	Poland	Italy	Mexico	Czech Republic	Switzerland	UK	Netherlands	Sweden	Mean value
Protest	56	67	29	25	45	24	15	36	37
Show support	20	14	20	44	22	37	16	31	26
Tradition/Convenience	5	2	2	2	3	6	11	3	4
Meet friends/co-members	8	5	6	22	20	11	13	10	12
Celebrate	0	1	2	2	2	10	5	2	3
Entertainment/fun	8	7	14	22	17	9	28	16	15
Visibility/display identity	22	17	10	20	32	27	32	19	22
Minority identity*	10	9	15	14	13	9	10	9	11
Commemoration*	0	0	1	0	1	2	2	0	1
Represent organization	2	2	2	5	4	28	7	14	8
Feeling of community	12	2	3	8	7	6	12	8	7
Conviction/duty	24	15	4	7	7	3	6	17	10
Curiosity	4	6	9	5	5	1	4	2	5
Political motives	70	72	32	30	49	26	20	48	43
External influence	67	77	38	46	67	69	49	60	59
Movement coherence	43	29	46	71	55	63	62	58	53
Total (N)	172	207	203	259	325	187	82	379	1814

Comment: The highest proportion for each motive type category is indicated by gray shading. The categories marked with an asterisk (*) did not display significantly different proportions between the countries. All other categories displayed an association with the country of at least 95 percent significance.

As expected, other frequently mentioned motives like "visibility" and "showing support" did not distribute themselves in ways that easily fit with the broad contextual dimension of more or less LGBT friendly contexts. The proportions were far from equal, but it is not clear how to explain their distribution. One might speculate from cases to case; for instance, the combination of strong "show support" and "meet friends" motives, and weak political motives in the Prague parade might be the product of a still less friendly political and cultural context, combined with a recent history where political advances have been achieved by backstage lobbying rather than large-scale collective mobilization.

The fact that the London Pride participants to a greater extent than other Pride participants attended in order to represent an organization, is most likely linked to the dominance of private businesses of which the London Pride has been accused by many. Since the Mexican respondents received all their survey questions in face-to-face interviews during the parade (see Appendix, this volume), they expressed fewer motives in general than the respondents in other cities. This means that all their percentages may have been higher if they had had time to formulate more reasons for their participation in a written survey.

When applying the distinction between external influence and movement coherence, made by Wahlström (2016) for interpreting participant motives in May Day marches, Italy again stands out with a strikingly externally oriented parade in Bologna (77 percent) and a comparatively low in-group orientation (29 percent). The Equality parade in Warsaw displays roughly the same pattern, although not as extreme. The Pride participants in the Czech Republic and the Netherlands, on the other hand, express weaker external influence motives and stronger movement coherence motives. Sweden and the UK display a balance between in-group and out-group oriented motives. Even though there is no complete correspondence between politicized motives and external orientation among the Pride parades in our sample, the results point roughly in the same direction, with participants in less friendly contexts tending toward externally oriented motives. An in-group orientation among participants on the other hand seems to be common in both friendly and less friendly contexts, although possibly for different reasons.

Pride and the meanings of collective events

This chapter has combined an interpretive and an explanatory approach to the meaning of collective actions. Instead of focusing on the meanings that are conferred to an event in media discourse, or by various interpreters, the approach in this chapter has been to regard the meaning of a collective event as an aggregation of the individual significance it has for its participants. In studying these individual significances through the motives that people have for participating in Pride, we have disregarded the unexpected significances that Pride events may have especially for newcomers, paradigmatically the life-changing turning-point that a first Pride participation might become in the biography of an individual. The meanings ascribed to Pride in this chapter should thus be read as a complement to the ways Pride parades constitute performances that "move" their participants or challenge their spectators, which we discussed in Chapter 7. In short, the meanings extracted from the motives of participants in collective events are not necessarily more "true" than the intended or externally perceived performances produced by these events, but they constitute an important dimension of collective action that is often overlooked.

In exploring the broad spectrum of meanings that Pride events have for their participants, we maintained a partly inductive approach sensitive to the specificities of Pride parades. The meanings of these events were studied through constructing a typology of reasons for participating based on previous studies and a qualitative analysis of responses to open survey questions. This analysis revealed a significant variation among Pride participants, illustrated by a distinction between 13 different motive types. In order to systematize this multitude of meanings, all survey responses were coded using this typology to determine the relative frequency of different motive types. Our focal interest was in the degree of protest orientation among participants, and more broadly their degree of political motives. These turned out to be more common among women as well as younger participants and those identifying with political leftist positions. LGBT and non-LGBT participants were roughly equally protest oriented, but while LGBT participants more often cited visibility as a motive, non-LGBT participants more often cited support motives.

The overall distribution of motives across Pride parades turned out to be rather complex, and the parades in our sample displayed a significant variation in motives expressed by their participants. Still some patterns could be discerned. In the LGBT unfriendly contexts of Italy and Poland, the parades had the strongest political protest orientation. Also, in the less friendly context of Switzerland participants had a relatively high protest orientation. In more LGBT friendly contexts, such as the UK and the Netherlands, participants displayed a significantly weaker protest orientation. However, Pride participants in Sweden on the other hand displayed a relatively strong political orientation despite the similarly LGBT friendly political and cultural climate. Conversely, one might have expected Pride participants in the less LGBT friendly contexts in Prague and Mexico City to have had a stronger protest orientation. Possibly the LGBT friendly legislation, and its favorable political context, contributed to a less protest oriented attitude in Mexico City. The weaker protest orientation of the Prague Pride participants can possibly be explained by the Czech LGBT movement's traditional preference to lobby behind the scenes to advance their claims. However, in Mexico City and Prague, as in the Netherlands, Sweden, Switzerland and the UK, the most common aggregated motives were to show support, show visibility and simply state one's identity as an LGBT person as a reason for participating. We have argued that these motives are analytically ambiguous in terms of their political or more personal connotations. Whereas the collective public visibility of LGBT persons in itself poses a cultural challenge to the (remaining) hetero-normative and patriarchal structures in society, the individual act of coming out or to display oneself in public as an already out LGBT person is not *necessarily* political from the individual's point of view. We therefore maintained a restrictive definition of politicized motives in this chapter, only counting the more explicitly protest oriented motives and references to one's moral or political convictions.

Even with this rather restrictive definition of politicization, Pride participants more or less across the board appear to have a rather high propensity to attach explicitly political or protest-oriented meanings to their participation. Only in Haarlem, Netherlands, and in London, less than 30 percent of the participants expressed this type of motive. Given that other motives also can be interpreted in a more or less political fashion, it would be misleading to characterize Pride participants in general as depoliticized and only seeking entertainment and pleasure. Even though this appears to be true for some, and some Pride performances may have become less provocative and contentious over time, most remain political events in the eyes of many of their participants.

It is interesting to draw a parallel to participant motives in another type of ritual political event. Pride parades, like May Day demonstrations, are annual ritual events for LGBT movements, respective labor movements. Overall, participants in Pride parades appeared to be equally, or even more, externally oriented than May Day participants and generally somewhat less focused on movement coherence (Wahlström 2016). More specifically, motives that were commonly expressed by May Day marchers – commemoration, celebration and tradition – did not find resonance among the Pride participants in our study. These motives were evoked to a degree in Haarlem and London, which can be related to their longstanding traditions of Pride events. Pink Saturday in the Netherlands has since its inception in 1979 evolved as an annual social outing for lesbians and their children and friends with the camping sites as the focal space for their activities (Chapter 6). This might explain the comparably high numbers that expressed the motive tradition/habit – 11 percent.

To sum up the apparent links between different contexts for Pride parades and participants' action orientations, less friendly contexts arguably provided more grievances to protest against, and thus more explicitly politicized motives, as we saw in Italy and Poland. To the extent that a friendly context for Pride can be regarded as an indicator of past successes of the LGBT movement, it is also not surprising that the participants in the Netherlands and in the UK appear less politicized and more focused on celebration, tradition and (in the case of the UK) parading to proudly represent an organization. Given the similarly friendly context in Sweden one would not have expected the comparatively strong politicized protest orientation among Pride participants in Gothenburg and Stockholm. This may be an indication that the LGBT movement in Sweden to a higher degree has used past successes as a springboard toward further challenging sexual, gender and relationship norms.

Note

1 Non-LGBT Pride participants' own personal experiences of discrimination often work as a catalyst for their engagement in LGBT politics; see, e.g., Wahlström, Peterson and Wennerhag (2018).

References

Bernstein, M. (1997). Celebration and suppression: The strategic uses of identity by the lesbian and gay movement. *American Journal of Sociology*, 103(3), 531–565.

Britt, L., and Heise, D. (2000). From shame to pride in identity politics. In Stryker, S., Owens, T.J., and White, R.W. (Eds) *Self, identity, and social movements* (pp. 252–268). Minneapolis, MN: University of Minnesota Press.

Browne, K. (2007). A party with politics? (Re)making LGBTQ Pride spaces in Dublin and Brighton. *Social & Cultural Geography*, 8(1), 63–87.

Holzhacker, R. (2012). National and transnational strategies of LGBT civil society organizations in different political environments: Modes of interaction in Western and Eastern Europe for equality. *Comparative European Politics*, 10(1), 23–47.

Ketelaars, P. (2014). *Bridging the protest macro-micro gap: Investigating the link between motivations, political efficacy and political context*. M2P working papers. Universiteit Antwerpen.

Klandermans, B. (1993). A theoretical framework for comparisons of social movement participation. *Sociological Forum*, 8(3), 383–402.

Klandermans, B. (2004). The demand and supply of participation: Social-psychological correlates of participation in social movements. In Snow, D.A., Soule, S. A., and Kriesi, H. (Eds) *The Blackwell Companion to Social Movements* (pp. 360–379). Oxford: Blackwell Publishing.

Lundberg, A. (2007). Queering laughter in the Stockholm Pride parade. *International Review of Social History*, 52(15), 169–187.

McFarland Bruce, K. (2016). *Pride parades: How a parade changed the world*. New York: NYU Press.

McFarland, K. (2012). *Cultural contestation and community building at LGBT Pride parades*. Chapel Hill: The University of North Carolina at Chapel Hill.

Peterson, A., Wahlström, M., Wennerhag, M., Christancho, C., and Sabucedo, J.M. (2012). May Day demonstrations in five European countries. *Mobilization*, 17(3), 281–300.

Roth, A.L. (1995). 'Men wearing masks': Issues of description in the analysis of ritual. *Sociological Theory*, 13(3), 301–327.

Scheff, T.J. (1988). Shame and conformity: The deference-emotion system. *American Sociological Review*, 53(3), 395–406.

Snow, D.A., and McAdam, D. (2000). Identity work processes in the context of social movements: Clarifying the identity/movement nexus. In Stryker, S. (Ed.) *Self, identity, and social movements* (pp. 41–67). Minneapolis, MN: University of Minnesota Press.

Turner, R.H., and Killian, L.M. (1972). *Collective behavior, 2nd edition*. Englewood Cliffs: Prentice-Hall.

Wahlström, M. (2015). Proud protest and parading party: The meanings that Pride parades in six European countries have to their participants. Annual conference of the American Sociological Association, August 22–25. Chicago, IL.

Wahlström, M. (2016). Why do people demonstrate on May Day? In Peterson, A., and Reiter, H. (Eds) *The ritual of May Day in Western Europe: Past, present and future* (pp. 217–244). London: Routledge.

Wahlström, M., Peterson, A., and Wennerhag, M. (2018). "Conscience adherents" revisited: Non-LGBT Pride participants. *Mobilization: An International Quarterly*, 23(1), 83–100.

Walgrave, S., Van Laer, J., Verhulst, J., and Wouters, R. (2011). Why do people protest? Comparing demonstrators' motives across issues and nations. M2P, Universiteit Antwerpen.

Van Stekelenburg, J., Klandermans, B., and van Dijk, W. (2009). Context matters: Explaining how and why mobilizing context influences motivational dynamics. *Journal of Social Issues*, 65(4), 815–838.

Van Stekelenburg, J., Klandermans, B., and van Dijk, W. (2011). Combining motivations and emotion: The motivational dynamics of protest participation. *Revista de Psicología Social*, 26(1), 91–104.

Weber, M. (1978). *Economy and society: An outline of interpretive sociology. Vol. 1.* Berkeley, CA: University of California Press.

Wettergren, Å. (2009). Fun and laughter: Culture jamming and the emotional regime of late capitalism. *Social Movement Studies*, 8(1), 1–15.

9 Between Politics and Party

> Our events broadcast to the world that: We are here, we are Queer, and we will no longer continue to be invisible and accept second-class citizenship. The determination of the global LGBTI population to not simply go away or be legislated out of existence is growing.
>
> (InterPride 2017, p. 10)

These are bold words from Frank van Delen, Vice-President of InterPride. Pride parades are indeed broadcasting to the world, but from the vantage point of different worlds. In the chapters of this volume, we have argued that the national contexts of Pride parades impact upon who participates, why they participate, and how they participate. Our analyses indicate that differences between parades are linked to the broad dimension of more or less friendly/unfriendly cultural and political contexts, outlined in Chapter 3. However our strategic selection of cases also displayed variation within comparable contexts that highlighted the importance of different strategic trajectories among domestic LGBT movements. The origins of these trajectories were traced in Chapter 2. The cases included in our unique comparative analysis were drawn from Europe and Mexico, but we expect that similar broad mechanisms behind variation can also be found in other countries and in other parts of the world. To be sure, even more extreme cases of, for example, unfriendly contexts – highly repressive and even violently hostile – are likely to produce dynamics that were not present in our study.

In the countries included in our sample, also in the most LGBT friendly contexts, Pride participants stood out as predominantly young, well-educated and middle-class. We had hypothesized that in the most LGBT friendly contexts the barrier of stigmatization would be easier to surmount and could attract a wider cross-section of the potential LGBT community, more representative of the general population. However, in the words of Walgrave and Verhulst (2009), the "usual suspects" one finds in demonstrations staged by so-called new social movements also dominated in these contexts (Peterson, Wahlström and Wennerhag 2017; Chapter 4, this volume). We found a varied level of participation among sexual orientations, with gay men the single largest category, followed by heterosexuals, bisexuals, lesbians and various other sexual orientations. Furthermore, a majority of the Pride participants, with the exception of the Czech participants, positioned themselves on the left of the political spectrum and supported left-libertarian and Social Democratic political parties. In the two LGBT unfriendly countries of our sample, Poland and Italy, we found the youngest and most left wing participants.

Contemporary Pride parades in major cities, in Europe as in Latin America, are typically much larger than those originally organized by the pioneers in the 1970s, and the growth has gone hand in hand with increased rights and acceptance for LGBT lifestyles. Pride parades are both the vehicle for political and cultural change and are also products of these changes. However, as discussed in Chapter 5, behind these numbers are mobilizing processes that vary depending on the cultural context as well as the resources and strategies of the organizers. In the absence of mass-based LGBT organizations or friendly mass media, organizers in some of the less friendly and unfriendly contexts have turned to online social networks as the main source of spreading information about Pride. Still, being informed about a parade is not enough. Even today, many prospective participants in Pride face the barrier of stigma before coming out as LGBT in public. For them, the support from interpersonal networks is particularly important for deciding to participate.

In the creation of broad and inclusive Pride parades, Pride organizers not only seek to mobilize people and organizations from within the LGBT community. In Chapter 6 we discuss organizers' views on the mobilization of friends, both individual friends in the form of non-LGBT persons, and organizational friends in the form of NGOs, private businesses and even public authorities. These different types of allies have raised concerns among some commentators about commercialization, mainstreaming and "de-gaying." However, even though the organizers and key activists interviewed for this research saw challenges in balancing different interests, the spatially dispersed heterogeneity, so characteristic of Pride parades, appears to facilitate the accommodation of disparate categories of friends under the same rainbow-colored umbrella. The national differences were particularly striking in relation to commercial allies, on whom organizers in friendly contexts were more often dependent for staging their large-scale events, giving rise to ongoing critical debates about companies buying goodwill through Pride. In unfriendly contexts such as Poland and where Pride is a newly established tradition such as the Czech Republic, organizers are more wholeheartedly positive to commercial sponsors. However, there few businesses are prepared to take the concomitant risks of stigmatization.

We have emphasized that Pride parades are political events. Contrary to many scholars' interpretations of contemporary Pride parades, Pride parades are highly political, both as challenges to cultural norms and political conditions. As shown in Chapter 7, Pride performances continue to pose cultural challenges to dominant gender, sexual and relationship norms, although differently depending on the degree of friendliness of the context. Under more unfriendly national conditions, Pride parades become controversial by their mere existence, and performances are often strategically made somewhat less contentious by stressing similarities with heterosexual majorities rather than differences. In more friendly contexts Pride parades are either relatively non-political celebratory performances, e.g. UK and the Netherlands, and/or contain performances that further challenge dominant norms, beyond prior victories, e.g. Sweden. In Chapter 8, we further demonstrated that – aside from the parades in Haarlem, Netherlands and in London, both LGBT friendly contexts – the participants often expressed explicitly political or protest-orientated motives for their participation. The high degree of "out-group" motives reported by respondents in our study, that is, motives for participation that are directed toward challenging or educating the general public, also witness the essentially political content of contemporary Pride parades. Pride parades today are not only fun and a source of entertainment, even though this may be the impression some of the major events superficially convey. However, at least for their participants – LGBT or not – the meaning of Pride cannot be reduced to mere entertainment as implied by, for example, Mason and Lo (2009) in their study of the Sydney "Mardi Gras" parade. For most participants in our study Pride is, in one sense or another, political.

On the whole, we contribute to the study of Pride events a mixed-methods comparative approach for taking both holistic and individual features into account when exploring the impact of contextual differences. Since qualitative methods have previously dominated the field, it is worth emphasizing the merits of the protest survey method, which takes the often neglected ordinary individual participants into account in the study of this type of event. We have shown how listening to the aggregate of a large number of individuals taking part in Pride parades nuances and problematizes the pictures painted in analyses purely based on observations and/or accounts of a smaller number of vocal spokespersons.

Of course, whereas the protest survey method enables systematic contextual comparison it is also costly and challenging to organize. Similar to other ambitious systematic comparisons of a single type of political event across contexts – including anti-war protests (Walgrave and Rucht 2010), May Day parades (Peterson and Reiter 2016), and anti-austerity protests (Giugni and Grasso 2016) – the number of country cases represented in this study has been too small for successful statistical isolation of different contextual factors on various levels. Doing more surveys in the studied countries as well as in other parts of the world, complemented with in-depth qualitative analyses, would further improve possibilities to more accurately trace the effect of contextual differences across locations and over time.

We will close this book by outlining a few broader themes that position our study in relation to contemporary challenges for Pride and LGBT movements. With this we would also like to indicate potential areas for future research.

Internal tensions

As shown in this book, the tensions between politics and party, commercialization and politicization, normalization and transgression, appeared to be at least temporarily defused and smoothed over in the Pride parades. Differences in messages and performances could often be solved by locating divergent groups and categories of participants in different sections of the parade, while the parades as a whole performed an image of unity in their diversity. Is the fit "perfect" between the format of the parade and the message of a unity in diversity as Armstrong (2002) suggests? Enrique claimed that in Mexico City the Pride parade is:

> one of the moments or one of the spaces within the LGBT movement in Mexico where you see men and women working more together, which you don't see as much for the rest of the year. ... My perception is that the march is one of those beacons of hope where you see men and women working together, or where you see the issue of difference between lesbians, gays or trans becomes less of an issue. It's like they take this pause on this constant tension to work together.

For Enrique, during Pride the tensions caused by the diversity of the LGBT movement are on pause. Pride parades for Enrique are a "beacon of hope." But are the tensions between lesbians and gay men on hold during Pride parades? And can Pride parades at least temporarily resolve the tensions, analyzed by Joshua Gamson (1995), between those whose activism is based on firm identities and those members of the movement who wish to deconstruct (aspects of) these identities? Do some fractions within the LGBT population even boycott the parades?

A shortcoming of our study is that we cannot capture LGBT people who feel excluded or choose not to participate. Our data does not cover LGBT people who in a sense boycott the event as a protest to the development toward normalization and commercialization that many Pride parades have had, particularly in friendly LGBT contexts. In our sample Stockholm Pride attracts the greatest number of non-LGBT participants including a significant involvement of political and cultural elites. In informal discussions with LGBT people in Sweden, particularly among those active in the 1970s and 1980s, we could observe a general dismay over the development of Pride from what they interpret as a departure from radical protest. A Stockholm organizer acknowledged that the increased participation of what we call friends of Pride has discouraged the participation of some former activists – "at the same time parts of our own community do not any longer feel the relevance [of the parade] in the same way." However, it might not only be the participation of certain types of "friends of Pride" that alienates some LGBT activists and some lesbians from participating in Pride. Many of the organizers indicated that there remained tensions between lesbians and gay men regarding the performances of pride. This is reflected in the 2016/2017 PrideRadar (InterPride 2017), in which the surveyed Pride organizers indicated that lesbians and trans people were less satisfied with the events than gay men who were largely or very satisfied (p. 25).

Julie Bindel in a discussion with Peter Tatchell related why she no longer takes part in London Pride.[1]

> Until the early 1980s I had always been delighted to be there. But many lesbians grew rightly critical of some of the lifestyle choices and political views of gay men. We felt that it didn't represent our own oppression. It became about sexual hedonism, and we wanted to march around liberation, rather than just saying "this is just one great party all about sexual access to as many other men we can secure." We felt that issues some gay men were supporting under the rainbow alliance were in opposition to us. We started to march separately. It wasn't a march any more, it was a parade, and it was taken over by the roller-skating nuns and the men with their backsides hanging out. All great street-party stuff, but it had stopped being a political event.

Many of our interviewees indicated a tension between lesbians and gays regarding the issue of politics and party, reflected in the interview with Julie Bindel above. For example, David, a gay Zurich Pride organizer, revealed an uneasy tension between lesbians emphasizing the political and gay men the importance of party.

> In Switzerland lesbians always say that you have to be political, which is also our approach of course. But I always say that the whole thing started in Stonewall Bar so that the coming out process, awareness of the LGBT community, started in a bar, which is also connected to party. So what I am also saying is that there must be political statements, but party is part of our culture, which can't be left aside.

However, among those who participated in the Pride parades where we have data on the sexual orientation of participants (Haarlem, London, Stockholm and Warsaw), there are few differences between lesbians and gay men that would unambiguously support this picture. Indeed, while women somewhat more often than men have explicitly politicized motives for participating in Pride (as shown in Chapter 8), gay and lesbian respondents did not significantly differ in their expression of such motives, nor in terms of expressing celebration, fun and entertainment as motives. The analysis of political values and preferences for movement strategies (as discussed in Chapter 4) also do not support the image of a significant gap between lesbian and gay Pride participants. Of course, there might be a selection effect if the most politicized fractions within the LGBT population largely abstain from participating in Pride at all.

The proportions of lesbians, gays, bisexuals and trans persons in different Pride parades might provide some information about possible non-participation of some groups. However, there is no clear baseline from which to judge whether any one group is underrepresented, since we have neither reliable figures from Pride parades in the past nor fully reliable population survey results regarding the size of the LGBT population in the sampled countries.[2] As we saw in Chapter 4, gay men were numerically overrepresented compared to lesbians in Pride London and the Warsaw Equality parade. However, lesbian women were more numerous than gay men in Haarlem and while there was a slightly higher proportion of gays (18 percent) compared to lesbians (15 percent) in Stockholm, the high proportion of bisexual women meant that LGBT men were proportionally fewer than LGBT women also in Stockholm.

Further research will need to investigate the extent to which lesbians or other categories of LGBT persons turn away from Pride for expressly political reasons. Some groups and individuals are obviously negative to perceived trends toward party, commercialization, and normalization of Pride. Dan, a queer activist in London, organized RIP Pride in 2015 – an Act Up contingent that jumped in the front of the Pride parade protesting UKIP's planned participation and what they perceived as the "sell-out" of the event to corporations. Dressed in black jackets and rainbow boas they staged a mock "funeral" procession carrying a coffin through the parade to mourn the "death of Pride." Dan explained why until the action in 2015 he had not been involved in Pride London.

> I've never found it that nourishing. Partly because you know I've grown up in London, I've seen it and for me it was just so corporatized, it was soulless and I found it quite superficial. So I found it depoliticized, you know the fact that you've just got Barclays and Starbucks, the Army, the Police, Tesco all trying to co-opt the LGBT struggle for their corporate profits. And for their ego and their branding.

Perhaps a common source of disenchantment with Pride parades today reflects a nostalgia for a bygone era of radical "in your face" LGBT politics as Browne and Bakshi (2013) suggest. We could also observe in Chapter 4 that aside from the Pink Saturday event in the Netherlands, few participants were 50 years or older. Pride parades today, in our sample, are increasingly being shaped by the concerns and priorities of a new generation of activists, bringing in claims and issues that go beyond previous struggles for rights and recognition.

The future of Pride?

As we pointed out in Chapter 7, Pride parades are not static, but rather dynamic and changing. The parades are not only constricted or new opportunities opened by the changing parameters set by the cultural and political contexts, organizers also strategically adapt to changing mobilizing contexts over time. We concluded our interviews by asking organizers to reflect on the future of Pride events in their country. Enrique was optimistic when he speculated as to how Pride parades in Mexico City would develop in the next five to 10 years.

> I think it's inevitably going to become more. ... visually, it's going to start looking more like the parades I've seen in larger cities in the US or in Brazil or in Argentina, where you see more presence of government or public agency groups, like firemen or police, which we haven't seen a lot. The presence of those groups is going to grow. Same thing with companies. What we saw this year was a very clear example that it's happening regardless of what the organizing committee wants or not, and they cannot ban them from marching. They can set the limits of like, "we won't take your money" or "we won't use your logo," but they are going to be coming. And that was one of the main stories in the media in the following days, and it's a story that appeared in business magazines, because, of course, they wanted people to know and they made sure that the people knew they were marching. So I think the presence of those groups is going to grow. Same thing with religious groups. I've seen LGBT religious organizations marching more and more. ... So, to sum up, I think that the march is going to continue to become more diverse and bigger with more people coming.

Willem, a Prague Pride organizer, was also hopeful; if only they would receive more financial support from the city, he envisioned that Pride could become a major tourist attraction.

> I would like to see it develop into a major European Pride, even though Prague might be a small city compared to Berlin, or other cities, but I think it has potential to develop further, to become bigger and I'm not saying that bigger is better, but when I think about what I said before about being an example, I would like Prague to be like sort of example for the East. In this sense I see some perspective there. Also like I said before I would like the Parade to be a bit more colorful and extravagant, and that people would come to the city just to

watch the Parade. That would be nice, because that is what I really like about Amsterdam, that it's really like it's one of the biggest events in Amsterdam, because people like to see it. I know I would like to see a bit more support from the city as such, because we've been calculating how many tourists we get and even Czechs from the countryside, how much money they spend and I think we bring like loads of money to the city and we don't get anything.

Both Enrique and Willem were expectant that their less friendly cultural and political contexts would improve in the future, which in turn would allow for larger and more extravagant events; in Willem's case he aspired to transforming Prague Pride to becoming a "spectacular spectacle," which would draw tourist hordes to the city. InterPride sent out questionnaires to Pride organizers around the world. They were asked to rank and choose the six main objectives of a Pride event. Economic impact, i.e. tourism, was perceived by far as the most important objective and empowering the community as the least important (InterPride 2017, p. 25). Willem's vision, while unique in our sample, does resound with that of many of the Pride organizers who responded to InterPride's questionnaire.

However, activists from LGBT less friendly contexts did not necessarily see the future in more extravagant Parades as unreservedly positive. We posed the same question to Carlos, a key gay activist in Mexico City, who did not share Enrique's optimism.

I would like to see a march where people are more aware of its meaning. However, I think the trend goes towards the projection of political discourses that claim the absolute freedom of the body and sexuality.

Carlos expressed a concern that Pride parades would in the future assume a hedonistic direction that he did not approve of, reminding us of the inherent tensions between politics and party.

Robert, a gay former organizer of the Warsaw Equality Parade and MP for the social liberal party *Twój Ruch*, soberly pointed out that how the Parade develops "depends on the political situation." And in the culturally and politically LGBT unfriendly context in Poland, he was far less hopeful than organizers in the Czech Republic and Mexico.

If we [his party] will be in power there will be some progress in the legislation, and I think it will go into the direction of the party. If we would lose it will be a very political manifestation. And I'm afraid that for a long time we will be asking for the rights, for civic partnerships. And support for leftist parties is still very low. So people will … I hope that the parades will be peaceful and I hope that they will not be harassed by counter-demonstrators as they were in previous years.

Context matters even for how organizers envision how Pride events will develop in the future. In unfriendly and less friendly contexts it is often clear how things can improve by letting the Pride parade grow and become more inclusive. However, even activists from LGBT friendly cultural and political contexts express concern over the future of Pride. Peter Tatchell (2017), in an open letter to the Pride in London committee, explained his concerns with the direction that the Pride event had taken.

> What began in 1972 as a protest for LGBT rights has now become an overly commercialised, bureaucratic and rule-bound event; which too often reflects the wishes of the city authorities, not the LGBT community.
>
> The admirable organisers, Pride in London, are being forced to operate with onerous controls and draconian costs. These have been imposed by the Mayor of London, Westminster Council and the Metropolitan Police, who have dictated conditions that mean a mere 26,500 people will be permitted to march on Saturday. This is a fraction of the numbers who'd march if it was a free and open event.
>
> Nowadays, LGBT organisations have to apply three months in advance, pay a fee and get wristbands for all their participants. The parade feels increasingly regimented, commodified and straight-jacketed.
>
> The city authorities are also enforcing punitive costs for road closures, pavement barriers, policing and security. They cite safety concerns and the disruptive impact on West End businesses if the parade was allowed to be bigger. Commerce comes first, it seems. Pride must not interfere with making money.

Tatchell argues that large demonstrations, and even the Notting Hill Carnival, are not subject to the same costs and restrictions as Pride, implying possibly homophobic motives on the part of Westminster Council. If Tatchell's analysis is correct, it appears that even in the ostensibly LGBT friendly context of the UK the future of Pride, at least as a mass event, is at risk. In the case of London Pride it seems that the political context has changed for the worse. Tatchell's solution to the bind that London authorities have placed the London Pride organizers in is a return to the event's roots.

> 1972 was a carnival march for LGBT human rights. It was political and fun; without all the restrictions, costs and red tape that are strangling Pride today. Let's put liberation back at the heart of Pride; reclaim it as a political march with a party atmosphere. No limits on numbers and no motorised floats. This would dramatically cut costs and bureaucracy; and return Pride to its roots. We can still have a fabulous carnival atmosphere. It worked in 1972. Why not now?

Bologna Pride organizers banned motorized floats in 2015 for political reasons, motivated by their desire to stage an environmental friendly and "sustainable" Pride event. London Pride organizers might be forced along the same route, perhaps not for political reasons or concerns for the environment, but to escape the restrictions placed on them by London authorities. London organizers might find themselves forced to adapt to what appears to be an increasingly unfriendly political context in the City of London as indicated by restrictions and costs placed on the organizers. In short, Pride parades and their organizers' strategic adaptions are impacted by changing cultural and political contexts lending the events their dynamic character.

Pride parades as a geopolitical battleground

Beyond the dilemmas and conflicts concerning commercialization and normalization, we expect that the future of Pride will be highly conditioned by the significances that are conferred to Pride by powerful actors on the geopolitical arena. As we have discussed, particularly in Chapters 7 and 8, collective events like Pride parades have multiple (sometimes even contradictory) meanings for their participants, organizers and bystanders. So while Pride participants collaborate – and struggle – among themselves regarding the meanings Pride parades have, or should have, Pride has become a symbolic marker for liberal democracy among players on the transnational arena. According to Kelly Kollman and Matthew Waites (2009), "the global politics of lesbian, gay, bisexual and transgender (LGBT) rights have emerged as the heart of global political struggles over culture and identities" (p. 1).

European LGBT movements have been long dedicated to transnationalism. Already in 1951, at a congress convened in Amsterdam, representatives from homophile organizations in Denmark, Germany, Italy, the Netherlands, Switzerland and the UK formed a new organization – the International Committee for Sexual Equality, which was the precursor to ILGA (Rupp 2014, p. 29). Europe took the lead in homophile transnationalism and later with ILGA-Europe, LGBT transnationalism. According to Phillip Ayoub and David Paternotte (2014, p. 233),

> over the years, an "idea of Europe" has shaped LGBT activism, just as LGBT activism has come to shape what "Europe" means. This relationship has transformed Europe into a privileged space for LGBT rights and a club whose members must, at the very least, address the fundamental rights of LGBT people.

This "club" is not exclusively European, other countries are clambering at the doors for membership. In 2008 the Organization of American States adopted a Brazilian resolution, "Human Rights, Sexual Orientation and

Gender Identity," criticizing human rights violations (Kollman and Waites 2009, p. 6), further positioning Latin America as LGBT friendly in the growing geopolitical divide around LGBT rights. Furthermore on the international scene, the International Commission of Jurists, the International Service for Human Rights, and a group of human rights experts developed the Yogyakarta Principles on the Application of International Human Rights Law in relation to Sexual Orientation and Gender Identity, in a meeting in 2006. Sponsored by Argentina, Brazil and Uruguay, the highly controversial Yogyakarta Principles were presented at the UN General Assembly in November 2007, but they have never been adopted by the United Nations. Nonetheless, we argue, the Principles are the landmark for the internationalization of LGBT human rights. The Principles promote the implementation of already existing obligations under international human rights law in relation to LGBT persons; as such, they propose baseline standards for the protection and promotion of the full enjoyment of all human rights irrespective of sexual orientation and gender identity, including the right to assembly. The Council of Europe has endorsed the Principles, which has informed EU policy regarding LGBT issues. Included in our study, the Czech Republic, Sweden and Switzerland have endorsed the Principles and/or referred to them in their statements at the United Nations Human Rights Council and Mexico, the Netherlands and the UK have sanctioned the principles at the executive and/or legislative levels (Council of Europe 2011, pp. 40–41; Swiebel 2009; Park 2014). Only Poland and Italy in our sample of cases have not endorsed the Yogyakarta Principles.

During the last decade, the internationalization of LGBT rights, defined as human rights, has entered the geopolitical arena to divide the world between those "civilized, progressive" countries, which are pro-gay, and those "backward, illiberal" countries, which are anti-gay. These latter countries, in turn, see LGBT rights and Pride parades as signs of the West's "moral deterioration," or as expressions of Western "cultural imperialism." This schism, spurred on by the Obama administration in the US and the European Union, was cemented with Russia's passing its "Anti-Homosexual Propaganda Law" in 2012. Sexual politics arose as a new symbolical divide in the cultural arena of geopolitics and Pride parades its litmus test.

"Homonationalism" (Puar 2007) on the European scale has become central in the making of "European-ness." Who has arrived to modernity and who has not? According to Judith Butler (2008, p. 2):

> It's my view that sexual politics, rather than operating to the side of this contestation, is in the middle of it, and that very often claims to new or radical sexual freedoms are appropriated precisely by that point of view – usually enunciated from within state power – that would try to define Europe and the sphere of modernity as the privileged site where sexual radicalism can and does take place. Often, but

not always, the further claim is made that such a privileged site of radical freedom must be protected against the putative orthodoxies associated with new immigrant communities.

The political debate involving certain ideas of the progress of "freedom" facilitates a political division between progressive sexual politics and the struggle against racism and the discrimination against religious minorities. One of the issues that follows from such a reconstellation is that a certain version and deployment of "freedom" can be used as an instrument of bigotry and coercion. According to Butler, this happens most inexcusably when women's sexual freedom or the freedom of expression and association for lesbian and gay people is invoked instrumentally to wage cultural assaults on Islam that reaffirm US sovereign violence (p.3). This is undeniably one side of the coin. The other side of the coin is equally disturbing. Russian-American LGBT activist, journalist and author, Masha Gessen (2017) claims that LGBT rights have become *"the* frontier in the global turn toward autocracy" (emphasis in original). According to Gessen, autocrats across the globe are spreading the nostalgic, almost evangelical message of a mythical "traditional" past – from Trump in the US, to Putin in Russia, Orban in Hungary, Erdogan in Turkey, Modi in India – "to 'take back' a sense of safety and 'bring back' a simpler time." The very sight of LGBT people, for example in a Pride parade, can conjure a sense of fear among those people who feel threatened by the uncertainty, freedom of choice and unpredictability that has followed in the wake of modernization's liberalization. Queers, Gessen argues, are the embodiment of all that is feared. Hence, the autocrats brandish their venom against LGBT people, banning Pride parades and LGBT "propaganda," re-criminalizing homosexuality, etcetera. LGBT people "serve as a convenient shorthand" for what people need to be protected against: "the strange, the unknown, the unpredictable" (ibid.; also Moran and Skeggs 2004). This has proved to be a potent populist autocratic message, which has spread across Europe and the globe. Among the countries studied in this book, Poland most clearly shows such tendencies, with its ruling party Law and Justice, which since its foundation in 2001 has kindled homophobic sentiments to increase its support.

In the EU the idea of modernity as possibility is challenged at its borders to the east and to the south by nationalist conservative discourses and politics – constructing a border between Europe "proper" and its wayward "peripheries." "Sexual politics proves to be central to the making and negotiations of European boundaries" (Colpani and Habed 2014, p. 87). In the context of Pride this perspective could arguably be traced in the main slogan of Amsterdam EuroPride in 2016 – "Join our freedom" – implying a Europe "proper" representing freedoms that outsiders (non-Europeans and Europe's "peripheries") should join (Chapter 2).

Pride parades have become a symbol for the Western liberal values cherished in (parts of) the European Union and their peaceful existence a pre-condition for membership. Serbia and Montenegro were negotiating with the European Union in 2012 to begin the process of joining the Union. Following the news that Serbian authorities would ban the scheduled Pride parade in Belgrade in 2012, then Swedish Minister for EU Affairs from the Liberal Party, Birgitta Ohlsson, who was to give the keynote speech at the event, provided the following comment:

> It is deeply troubling that authorities have banned Belgrade Pride this year too. Pride parades serve as a litmus test for freedom and human rights adherence in Europe. Today, in 2012, the rights of minorities, freedom of speech, and freedom of assembly should be guaranteed in countries that are members of the European Union or applying to join. I will still be making an official visit to Belgrade on Friday and Saturday where I will meet directly with LGBT activists but also the Serbian government.
> (Government Offices of Sweden: Press release, October 3, 2012, Prime Minister's Office)[3]

Baltic Pride is organized annually in one of the three Baltic States. When Baltic Pride was held in Vilnius in the spring of 2010, the parade was greeted by thousands of counter-demonstrators, including right-wing extremists, which prompted Ohlsson to announce that she would be attending the Pride Parade in Lithuania's capital in late July 2013. Also in this context she stressed, "Pride Parades are a litmus test for freedom and democracy. Pride parades serve as a litmus test for whether a country lives up to Human Rights obligations" (Government Offices of Sweden: Press release, July 24, 2013, Prime Minister's Office).[4]

Taking their cues from the LGBT friendly politics of Spain and Portugal, Pride parades are flourishing across most of Latin America (the Pride Radar 2016/2017 counted altogether 152 events in the Caribbean, Central America and South America [InterPride 2017]). Today, the Pride parades in São Paolo and Rio de Janeiro are typically larger than those staged in New York or San Francisco. Pride parades have become a symbol of modernity, of belonging to the exclusive club of wealthy liberal democracies that live up to Human Rights obligations, which has been a powerful incitement for Latin America's "Pink tide" of social liberal and left governments to partner with LGBT movements to see gay rights enacted in law (Encarnación 2016, pp. 7–8). But as Encarnación points out, the dramatic gay rights advances, for example, in Brazil and Mexico, have also led to a violent backlash with increasing levels of violence, "both symbolic and real, against LGBT people" (p. 13).

Pride parades epitomize both the power of popular mobilizations for social change, as well as the challenges facing originally highly contentious political rituals when many of their political goals have been achieved and the events become highly appreciated instead of reviled by societal elites.

The success of LGBT movements and the concomitant growth and spread of Pride in many European countries is indeed something that citizens and politicians in these states can and should be proud of. However, Pride parades are placed in an awkward position when used as both stick and scapegoat in geopolitical conflicts. Pride parades in Europe have become a symbol for liberal values; a litmus test that the country hosting them shares the European Union's highly touted values of human rights, tolerance and freedom. However, not all of the member countries, or those in line seeking membership, share those values. Domestic politics are in many cases at odds with EU's LGBT geopolitical agenda, which places Pride parades in some countries in the line of fire in the clash between conservative right-wing nationalists and liberal internationalists, for example, in Poland and Hungary. Domestic battle lines have been drawn on the issue of LGBT rights. According to Gessen (2017), "in Budapest, the Pride march has become an annual opposition parade: many, if not most, participants are straight people who use the day to come out against the Orbán government." The historical trajectory of Pride parades has taken a momentous leap from their inauspicious beginnings to the front stage of national and even world politics.

Dennis Altman and Jonathan Symons (2016, p. 77) maintain that:

> fifty years ago, as the early gay liberation movement called for radical social transformations, few would have guessed that marriage equality would one day become a central gay demand, that sexual freedom would come to be framed as a "human rights" issue, or that sexuality would be debated by state leaders and would come to polarize international human rights debates.

However, as these scholars point out, it is equally impossible to predict future developments. We believe that it will remain a challenge for participants and organizers of Pride events across the world to maintain the integrity of Pride in the tug-of-war between different political (as well as commercial) interests. LGBT rights understood as "human rights" has not won traction across the globe, far from it. The underlying political tensions produce vastly diverse challenges depending on the context. These geopolitical tensions reverberate differently in domestic settings, which must sensitize analyses of Pride events. While organizers in friendly contexts struggle with how to deal with unwanted support from various political and commercial actors, organizers in unfriendly contexts face outright violence and repression. In light of this, research must continue to follow – and compare – the development of Pride as manifestations of LGBT movements in different countries, especially research that acknowledges and further investigates its political dimensions. We hope that this book has improved the tools for such an endeavor.

Notes

1 www.theguardian.com/commentisfree/2012/jul/06/conversation-pride-gay-rights-party, accessed August 29, 2017.
2 In a recent comparison of estimations of the US LGBT population (Gates 2015), the proportions of men and women are consistently relatively even, whereas a majority of men in this group identify as gay, only a minority of women identify as lesbian. If Pride parades were to reflect the national populations – which they do not (see Chapter 4) – a somewhat higher proportion of gays compared to lesbians may actually be accurate.
3 www.swedenabroad.com/RSS/News/News-8166-en-GB.xml, accessed August 29, 2017.
4 www.swedenabroad.com/Pages/StandardPage.aspx?id=59619&epslanguage=en-GB, accessed August 29, 2017.

References

Altman, D., and Symons, J. (2016). *Queer wars*. Cambridge: Polity Press.
Armstrong, E.A. (2002). *Forging gay identities: Organizing sexuality in San Francisco, 1950-1994*. Chicago, IL: University of Chicago Press.
Ayoub, P.M., and Paternotte, D. (2014). Conclusion. In Ayoub, P.M., and Paternotte, D. (Eds) *LGBT activism and the making of Europe. A rainbow Europe* (pp. 233–240). London and New York: Palgrave Macmillan.
Browne, K., and Bakshi, M.L. (2013). *Ordinary in Brighton? LGBT, activisms and the city*. Farnham: Ashgate Publishing, Ltd.
Butler, J. (2008). Sexual politics, torture and secular time. *British Journal of Sociology*, 59(1), 1–23.
Colpani, G., and Habed, A.J. (2014). 'In Europe it's different': Homonationalism and peripheral desires for Europe. In Ayoub, P.M., and Paternotte, D. (Eds) *LGBT activism and the making of Europe. A rainbow Europe* (pp. 73–96). London and New York: Palgrave Macmillan.
Council of Europe (2011). *Discrimination on grounds of sexual orientation and gender identity in Europe*. 2nd edition. Strasbourg: Council of Europe Publishing.
Encarnación, O.G. (2016). *Out in the periphery: Latin America's gay rights revolution*. Oxford: Oxford University Press.
Gamson, J. (1995). Must identity movements self-destruct? A queer dilemma. *Social Problems*, 42(3), 390–407.
Gates, G. (2015). Lesbian, gay, bisexual, and transgender demographics. In Swan, W. (ed.) *Gay, lesbian, bisexual, and transgender civil rights: A public policy agenda for uniting a divided America* (pp. 1–19). Boca Raton, FL: CRC Press.
Gessen, M. (2017). Why Americans fear LGBT rights. *The New York Review of Books*. July 27, 2017.
Giugni, M., and Grasso, M., eds. (2016). *Austerity and protest: Popular contention in times of economic crisis*. London: Routledge.
InterPride (2017). *InterPride PrideRadar 2016/2017*. www.interpride.org [accessed July 22, 2017].
Kollman, K., and Waites, M. (2009). The global politics of lesbian, gay, bisexual and transgender human rights: an introduction. *Contemporary Politics*. 15(1), 1–17.

Mason, G., and Lo, G. (2009). Sexual tourism and the excitement of the strange: Heterosexuality and the Sydney Mardi Gras Parade. *Sexualities*, 12(1), 97–121.

Moran, L., and Skeggs, B. (2004). *Sexuality and the politics of violence and safety.* London: Routledge.

Park, A. (2014). Implementation of the Yogyakarta Principles: Key factors for implementation in Montenegro and achievements in implementation in other parts of the world. Presentation at "Promotion and Importance of Yogyakarta Principles" Roundtable, Ministry of Foreign Affairs and European Integration Podgorica, Montenegro, July 17.

Peterson, A., Wahlström, M., and Wennerhag, M. (2017). 'Normalized' Pride? Pride parade participants in six European countries. *Sexualities*. Published first online.

Peterson, A., and Reiter, H., eds. (2016). *The ritual of May Day in Western Europe: Past, present and future.* London: Routledge.

Puar, J. (2007). *Terrorist assembleges: Homonationalism in queer times.* Durham, NC: Duke University Press.

Rupp, L.J. (2014). The European origins of transnational organizing: The nternational Committee for Sexual Equality. In Ayoub, P.M. and Paternotte, D. (Eds) *LGBT activism and the making of Europe. A rainbow Europe* (pp. 29–49). London and New York: Palgrave Macmillan.

Swiebel, J. (2009). Lesbian, gay, bisexual and transgender human rights: the search for an international strategy. *Comparative Politics.* 15(1), 19–35.

Tatchell, P. (2017). *Has LGBT Pride lost its way?* Available at URL: www.petertatchellfoundation.org/has-lgbt-pride-lost-its-way/ (accessed August 31, 2017).

Walgrave, S., and Rucht, D. (Eds) (2010). *The world says no to war: Demonstrations against the war on Iraq.* Minneapolis, MN: University of Minnesota Press.

Walgrave, S., and Verhulst, J. (2009). Government stance and internal diversity of protest: A comparative study of protest against the war in Iraq in eight countries. *Social Forces* 87(3), 1355–1387.

List of Interviews

Mexico

Enrique Torre Molina, key LGBT activist and blogger, November 24, 2015.
Gloria Careaga, key lesbian activist and former co-chair of ILGA, November 22, 2015.
Carlos López López, key gay activist, December 1, 2015.

UK

Dan Glass, activist and member of the LGBTQI campaign Friends of the Joiners Arms and Act Up, March 3 2016.
Steve Coote, gay London Pride organizer and president of the Gay Business Association, July 22, 2015.
Patrick Lyster-Todd, gay London Pride organizer, July 27, 2015.
Peter Tatchell, gay Pride pioneer and co-organizer of the first Pride parade in London, July 23, 2015.
Mike Jackson, one of the founders of LGSM, March 2, 2016.

Netherlands

Group interview with Ferdi, Ron and Jan, Pink Saturday organizers in Groningen, March 7, 2014.
Erwino, gay Pink Saturday organizer in Haarlem, March 1, 2014.
Anja, lesbian Pride organizer in Amsterdam and Pink Saturday organizer in Amersfoort, March 6, 2014.
Irene, lesbian Pride organizer in Amsterdam, March 4, 2014.
Jan-Willem, CoC International Coordinator, March 3, 2014.

Italy

Daniela, lesbian Pride organizer, November 22, 2014.
Rosa, coordinator for Parents, Family and Friends of Gay and Lesbians Bologna, November 22, 2014.
Elisa, lesbian activist, February 16, 2016.

Sweden

Stig-Åke Petersson, president of RFSL 1972–1973 and 1984–1988, June 16, 2016.
Ulrika Westerlund, president of the Stockholm Pride Association 2005–2006 and president of RFSL 2010–2016, March 16, 2015.
Sandra Ehne, president of the Stockholm Pride Association 2014–2016, February 27, 2015.
Victor Harju, board member of the Stockholm Pride Association, June 21, 2016.
Anders Dillman, operational manager for the Stockholm Pride parade 2014–2016, March 4, 2015.
Tasso Stafilidis, main responsible for West Pride ("*Verksamhetschef*") 2007–2011 and president of the association West Pride since 2016, December 9, 2015.
Agneta, co-founder of the event West Pride, November 30, 2015.
Jan-Eric B. Norman, board member of the organization Örebro Pride, December 7, 2016.

Czech Republic

Petr Tomas, co-organizer of the first Prague Pride parade, October 19, 2014.
Andrea, LGBT activist and participant in the Pride parades organized in Brno, October 22, 2014.
Blanka, LGBT activist and co-organizer of Brno Pride parades, October 22, 2014.
Willem van der Bas, co-organizer of Prague Pride since its beginning with responsibility for international PR, October 23, 2014.
Kamila Fröhlichová, co-organizer of Prague Pride since its beginning, October 24, 2014.
Zdeněk Sloboda, researcher in the sociology of gender and sexuality, and board member of PROUD (Platforma pro Rovnoprávnost Uznáni a Diverzitu [Platform for Equality, Recognition and Diversity]), November 15, 2014.

Poland

Robert Biedroń, president of KPH (*Kampania Przeciw Homofobii*), 2001–2009, MP for Twój Ruch 2011–2014 and since 2014 Mayor of the city of Słupsk, July 4, 2014.
Jej Perfekcyjność, principle organizer of the Equality Parade in Warsaw, 2011–2016, June 12, 2014.
Yga Kostrzewa, organizer of the Equality Parade in Warsaw, 2004–2010 and president of Lambda Warszawa, 2005–2007, June 13, 2014.
Andreas, organizer of the Equality Parade in Warsaw, June 13, 2014.

Switzerland

Yves de Matteis, former organizer of Pride Romandy and formerly part of ILGA's World Board, November 25, 2015.
Richard Bonjour, organizer of Geneva Pride in 2004 and 2011, November 24, 2015.
David Reichlin, president of the association Zurich Pride since 2014, February 14, 2017.

Appendix

Data and Methods[1]

Our study combines quantitative survey data from our research collaboration *Caught in the Act of Protest: Contextualizing Contestation* (CCC, see www.protestsurvey.eu) with qualitative data in part collected in the CCC collaboration and in part collected specifically for this book. In regards to the quantitative basis for the study, the methodological foundation for the construction of the CCC database was the argument that previous methods used to study protest participation were unsatisfactory. Researchers tended to either study reported demonstration participation in the past (e.g. World Values Survey) or intentions to participate in the future. Both methods, we argued, were flawed. The former because survey questions usually relate to participation in protest in general rather than in specific protest events and the latter because intentions to participate are weak predictors of actual participation (see Klandermans and Oegema 1987). Subsequently we maintained that in order to improve our understanding of protest participation we *must compare protesters in the act of protesting.* By using the CCC database we capture participation in specific Pride demonstrations in the study's seven European countries and Mexico, and rather than measuring intentions we have comprehensive data on the individuals who actually participated in these Pride demonstrations. The CCC database contains unique data, which provide answers to the following questions: *Who* are the Pride demonstrators, what are their socio-demographic characteristics, what are their political orientations? *Why* do they demonstrate? What are the attitudes, motives, and beliefs driving them? *How* were they mobilized, through what channels, by which techniques? These are among the focal questions in our book.

The quantitative data and methods

The Pride parades

We have used survey data collected from participants in altogether 11 Pride parades, which took place between 2011 and 2014. Nine of these

Table A.1 Surveyed demonstrations, distributed questionnaires and response rates

	Poland	Italy	Mexico	Czech Republic		Switzerland		United Kingdom	Netherlands	Sweden		Total
	Warsaw	Bologna	Mexico City	Prague	Prague	Geneva	Zurich	London	Haarlem	Gothenburg	Stockholm	
Date	14 June 2014	9 June 2012	2 June 2012	18 August 2012	17 August 2013	2 July 2011	16 June 2012	7 July 2012	7 July 2012	3 June 2012	2 August 2014	
No. of participants in parade (according to CCC research teams)	2 500	15 000	15 000	9 000	10 000	3 000	3 000	20 000	1 000	3 300	40 000	121 800
No. of face-to-face surveys made	61	188	–	126	128	159	94	140	74	80	158	1 208
No. of distributed postal surveys	779	1 000	212*	646	835	792	478	1 000	368	445	810	7 153
No. of returned postal surveys	185	216	212*	135	131	197	150	194	100	162	238	1 708
Response rate (%)	24	22	100	21	16	25	31	19	27	36	29	24

Comment: * This figure for Mexico designates surveys conducted face-to-face, but with the equivalent of the standard postal CCC questionnaire.

parades were surveyed between 2011 and 2012 in the Czech Republic, Italy, Mexico, Netherlands, Sweden, Switzerland and the UK by the respective national teams of the CCC research program. This sample of countries was dictated by the selection of countries that were part of the CCC research program and the priorities of the respective country teams. However, as discussed in Chapter 3, the sample nicely captured some important contextual differences, from an LGBT perspective. Nevertheless, in 2014 we added Poland to ensure that the sample had enough countries where the cultural and political contexts were LGBT unfriendly, together with a survey of Stockholm Pride to capture the "main" national Pride event in a LGBT friendly context (see Table A.1 for an overview of the parades).

We regard the parades as more or less representative of the countries in our sample. For countries where the CCC research teams have sampled two Pride demonstrations in different cities – Sweden and Switzerland, they, however, capture some of the diversity of Pride events in these countries. In the Czech Republic, two surveys were made in two subsequent years, 2012 and 2013, which have allowed us to estimate differences between years at the same parade location. Along several of the analytical dimensions dealt with in the chapters of this volume, parades from the same countries were strikingly similar and were in these cases merged in the analysis.

Sampling of survey respondents

The sampling method of the CCC program has been described in detail by, for example, van Stekelenburg and colleagues (2012). Nevertheless, we will recapitulate the central aspects of the method here. These aspects are intended to address two challenges when surveying participants in a demonstration: to ensure that each person participating in the demonstration has an (in principle) equal chance of being sampled, and that potential response bias can be estimated.

To address the first challenge, the CCC teams used what might be characterized as a systematic random sampling method (since a fully random sample of participants in a demonstration would be practically impossible). During each demonstration, two or more teams of researchers distributed questionnaires to one person in every Nth row, according to an algorithm that was calculated on the basis of the estimated size of the demonstration. For example, if the demonstration was estimated to consist of approximately 10,000 people, and was estimated to be roughly 10 persons broad, the teams would use a rule that would make sure that one person in each row would receive a questionnaire (i.e., in practice every tenth person). The teams, distributing questionnaires from each side, would make sure that questionnaires were handed out to alternately the person on the edge of the march, the second person from the edge, the third person, etcetera. See the illustration below.

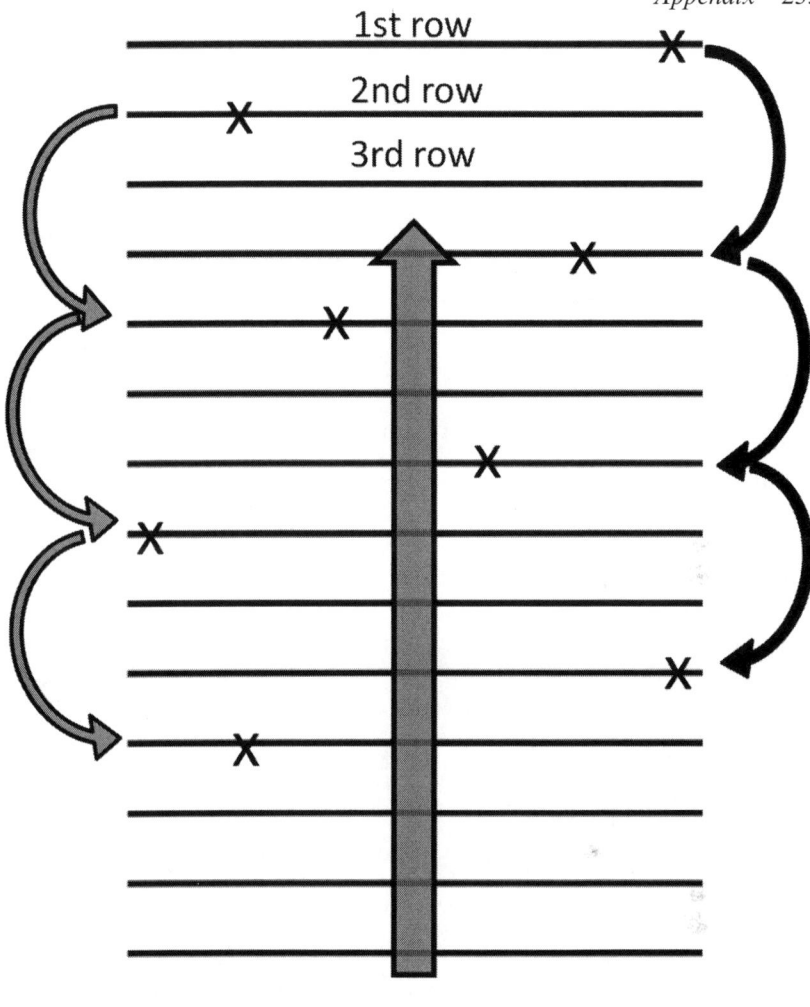

Figure A.1 Example of how an ideal-typical demonstration can be sampled

If interviewers were allowed to hand out questionnaires on their own, there would nevertheless be a risk that they would not stick strictly to the rules set at the beginning of the march. It seems that interviewers are generally disinclined to approach respondents that do not seem likely to accept a questionnaire, and more prone to approach people that look friendly and are roughly the same age as the interviewer (Walgrave and Verhulst, 2011). Therefore the interviewers were coordinated in teams by "pointers" who counted the rows and persons and assigned interviewees to the interviewers. Since the pointers did not have to approach the presumptive respondents themselves, they were presumably less biased than the interviewers in terms of sampling.

In order to assure a reasonable response rate, the interviewers were instructed to provide the respondents with information about the project and the importance of filling in the survey. The questionnaires included a prepaid postal envelope, whereby the participants could fill in the survey at home. Nevertheless, since we had no possibility to remind people, the response rates were low compared to many other population-based surveys. The response rates to the postal survey varied between a low of 16 percent (Prague 2013) and high of 36 percent (Gothenburg) (see Table A.1). There is therefore a risk of response bias. In order to address this second challenge of protest surveying, approximately every fifth participant also received a number of oral questions, which could be used as a reference point for the returned surveys.

The exception to this latter procedure was the survey of the Mexico City Pride parade. The Mexican research team assessed that the Mexican postal service would be too unreliable, hence the survey was only conducted orally on the spot; however, strictly following the structured sampling method described above. This meant that the Mexican survey team used a somewhat simplified questionnaire. The particular conditions for responding to the Mexican survey also meant that answers to open survey questions were almost invariably very concise. This was particularly noticeable in our analysis of motives for participating, where Mexican respondents on average mentioned fewer and less elaborate motives compared to the European respondents.

Estimating non-response bias

The method of posing face-to-face questions to every fifth respondent allows us to estimate possible non-response biases. This is based on the assumption that, with a response rate normally over 90 percent (Walgrave et al. 2016), those who respond to the face-to-face questions better approximate the demonstrator population, compared to those who return their questionnaires.

There is no necessary connection between high non-response to a survey and non-response bias in the results. Those who respond to a mail-back questionnaire do not necessarily differ in any significant respects from those who choose not to respond (Leslie 1972). However, previous research has shown that specific socio-demographic and other individual characteristics can influence response rates (e.g. Rogelberg et al. 2003), subsequently these characteristics may be sources of non-response bias. For example, according to the leverage-salience theory of survey participation (Groves et al. 2000) the saliency of a survey topic in combination with the respondent's general interest in this topic affects the respondent's general propensity to respond to a survey. This could mean that in a protest survey the least politically interested are also the least likely to respond. In an analysis of non-response bias in a survey of anti-Iraq war protesters in

Glasgow 2003, Rüdig (2010) found that women are more likely to answer questionnaires than men, the middle-aged more likely than young people, and the well-educated more likely than those having a lower level of education. However, he found no significant correlations in relation to political opinions or interest in politics. Walgrave and Verhulst (2011) compared selection and non-response bias in a number of demonstrations on different issues, and when using the same sampling methodology used here they found no significant non-response biases except for age and position on the issue at stake in the protest. A set of questions measuring these basic socio-demographic and political characteristics was also included in the CCC standard face-to-face questionnaire. Based on these questions Walgrave and colleagues (2016) made a systematic overview of 51 of the protest surveys in the CCC program. They note that respondents in 31 percent of the demonstrations were significantly biased in terms of higher age, and in 22 percent of the responses were biased toward higher levels of education. In somewhat fewer demonstrations respondents also appeared to be significantly biased toward high levels of motivation (16 percent) and high political interest (14 percent). In an analysis of the sample of May Day demonstrations in the CCC dataset, Wahlström and Wennerhag (2016) found similar patterns, but again only pertaining to a minority of the demonstrations for each variable.

The availability of data for both face-to-face interviews and returned postal questionnaires therefore allowed us to compare the group of individuals that did receive a postal questionnaire but did *not* return it (but still answered the face-to-face questions) with the respondents that sent in the postal questionnaire via mail. Our tests were conducted both on a general level, for all the parades except the survey in Mexico City (which was only conducted orally and did not use a postal questionnaire), and for each parade separately. The tests focused the characteristics that previously have been shown to influence response: young age, and no higher education. We also included measures of political interest and prior participation in demonstrations. We also controlled for gender, but since in most face-to-face surveys the values for this question were generated by the visual assessment by the interviewer of the respondent's gender, we regarded this measure as less reliable, especially considering the particular context of a Pride parade.

On the general level, the test shows statistically significant differences between the groups that sent in questionnaires and those that did not, regarding young age, university education level, high political interest and past participation in more than six demonstrations (see Table A.2). Gender did not turn out to be a significant source of bias. In Table A.2 we only present those individual demonstrations where statistically significant differences were found. There is a significant overall tendency that non-respondents are more often young (52 percent younger than 30 years vs. 43 percent among all respondents) and less often have ongoing or

Table A.2 Cases of significant non-response bias in the dataset

		Respondents sending in the questionnaire	Respondents not sending in the questionnaire	All respondents (excl. Mexico)	Total (N)	Cramer's V	
Age: – 29 years (%)							
All parades	Total	37	52	43	2613	.14	***
Parades with significant differences	Stockholm	35	60	43	345	.24	***
	London	22	44	30	310	.24	***
	Gothenburg	43	64	48	218	.18	**
	Zurich	23	39	28	218	.17	*
	Geneva	35	50	41	313	.15	**
	Prague 2012	53	68	59	234	.14	*
	Prague 2013	52	66	58	243	.13	*
	Warsaw	47	63	50	233	.13	*
Education: Ongoing or completed university education (%)							
All parades	Total	68	49	61	2602	.19	***
Parades with significant differences	Prague 2013	60	34	48	244	.26	***
	Bologna	75	50	65	363	.26	***
	Stockholm	74	47	66	348	.26	***
	Prague 2012	56	33	46	236	.23	***
	Gothenburg	70	44	65	197	.22	**

	Respondents sending in the questionnaire	Respondents not sending in the questionnaire	All respondents (excl. Mexico)	Total (N)	Cramer's V	
Interested in politics: quite or very much (%)						
All parades	Total	75	67	72	2617	.08	***
Parades with significant differences	Prague 2012	62	46	55	242	.16	*
Protest participation: Participated in 6 demonstrations or more, ever (%)						
All parades	Total	55	38	49	2571	.16	***
Parades with significant differences	London	64	35	52	302	.28	***
	Warsaw	55	33	50	225	.18	**
	Prague 2012	21	11	17	229	.13	*
	Bologna	75	62	69	353	.13	*
	Stockholm	59	46	55	342	.12	*
	Geneva	66	44	58	310	.10	***

completed university educations (49 percent vs. 61 percent among all respondents). Still, on the demonstration level, only the age difference is significant in a majority of demonstrations in our sample. Those who had taken part in more than six protests were also underrepresented among non-respondents. Differences among respondents regarding political interest were small overall and only significant in one demonstration.

The results of these non-response bias tests show that the descriptive data regarding particular age and educational level must be interpreted with some caution. The descriptive data presented regarding the percentage of young people should be regarded as possibly slightly underestimated, while the percentage of university educated may be slightly overestimated. It is however important to note that non-response biases have also been found in the surveys that we use to compare our CCC data. This is, for example, the case with the European Social Survey (ESS, which is made face-to-face and uses show cards), where non-response bias, in particular related to level of education, has been found, but also smaller differences regarding gender and age (Vehovar 2007). In conclusion, since the surveys with which we compare our data also display similar types of non-response biases as our own CCC surveys, the comparative analyses should still be considered as sufficiently accurate.

Some researchers suggest various methods for weighting data to compensate for estimated response bias (e.g. Cobben and Bethlehem 2005). However, apart from the inherent problems of these methods, the fact that not all parades display significant response biases for each variable creates difficult dilemmas. Should weights only be applied to those parades where non-response biases are significant, or should overall weights be applied? In either case, there is an imminent risk that the sample is only further distorted. We therefore chose not to weigh the data for these reasons.

Data aggregation

In the chapters of this book we often wish to say something not only about mean scores and correlations on the demonstration level, but also on the country level and among the entire group of Pride participants in our sample. To compensate for differences in sample sizes from different Pride parades, the mean values on the country level in countries where two Pride parades were surveyed, were calculated from the individual means of the two parades in that country. These country means were then used as a basis, together with the figures from countries where only one survey was conducted, to calculate common mean values for all countries in our sample. Correspondingly, in bivariate analyses comprising the whole sample the data was weighted to give equal weight to all countries in each analysis (and equal weight to the respective parades in each country), in order not to let higher response rates or different numbers of surveyed parades in a country impact on the figures. As discussed by Wahlström and Wennerhag (2016), there is no

Appendix 239

straightforward way of aggregating data with this structure, but we considered this procedure as the most appropriate for our purposes.

Comparative data

The participant profiles in Pride parades taking place in the diverse country contexts of our study is compared to the national populations, as measured by various established cross-national social surveys. One possible weakness of this approach is that the national populations from which the samples in these national social surveys are drawn are not necessarily equivalent to the populations that form the mobilizing potential of the demonstrations. First, the primary mobilizing potential of a demonstration in a particular city is the population of that particular city and its vicinity, and characteristics such as level of education and political opinion may differ in that city from the country as a whole. Second, the Pride parades in our sample also mobilized small proportions of participants from other countries, so in another sense the mobilizing potential extends beyond the borders of the nation state.[2] Nevertheless, considering the potentially national reach of most of our Pride events, we chose to regard the national populations as a reasonable approximation of the mobilizing potential, and therefore use national social survey data.

In order to make it possible to compare Pride participants with the national populations in Chapter 4, regarding socio-demographic characteristics, political participation, ideological orientation and party sympathies we used data from ESS round 6 (2012) for the national populations in the European countries. For social class, we used data from ESS round 5 (2010) for all countries but Italy, where ESS round 2 (2004) was used. Data from European Values Survey (EVS) 2008 were used for membership in women's and environmental organizations.

For Mexico, data for the national population were taken from ISSP (International Social Survey Programme) 2012 for age and university education (this source lacked data on social class), from ISSP 2004 for political interest, political party membership, signing a petition, and contacting a politician or official, from ISSP 2014 for demonstration participation, while data from LAPOP (Latin America Public Opinion Project) 2012 were used for left–right orientation and sympathies with political parties. ESS, EVS, ISSP and LAPOP data allow for a comparison between the Pride participants with the general population of each country, and thus provide indications as to whether the composition of the Pride parades mirror the general population.

Variables and survey questions

The survey questions used to measure the variables used in Chapter 4, Chapter 5 and Chapter 8 in this volume are listed below in Table A.3. As

Table A.3 Survey question wordings and response alternatives.

Variable	Survey question	Response alternatives
Protest motives	Please tell us why you participated in this protest event?	–
Organizational affiliation	If you have been involved in any of the following types of organizations in the past 12 months, please indicate whether you are a passive member or an active member? If you are a member of several organizations of the same type, tick the box for the organization of that type in which you are most "active." [Political party; Women's organization; Environmental organization; LGBT organization; Anti-racist/migrant organization]	Passive member / financial supporter; Active member
Political participation	There are many things people can do to prevent or promote change. Have you, in the past 12 months…? [Contacted a politician, government, or local government official; Signed a petition/public letter; Taken part in direct action (such as: blockade, occupation, civil disobedience; Used violent forms of action (against property or people)]	Yes; No
Demonstration participation	How many times have you in the past taken part in a demonstration? [Ever; Past 12 months]	Never; 1 to 5; 6 to 10; 11 to 20; 20+
General political values	To what extent do you agree or disagree with the following statements? [Government should redistribute income from the better off to those who are less well off; People from other countries should be allowed to come to my country and live here permanently if they want to.]	Strongly disagree; Disagree; Neither; Agree; Strongly agree
Political interest	How interested are you in politics?	Not at all; Not very; Quite; Very

Variable	Survey question	Response alternatives
Party sympathy	With which party do you most closely identify right now?	—
Political left-right identification	In politics people sometimes talk of "left" and "right." Where would you place yourself on this scale, where 0 *means* the left and 10 means the right?	Left=0; 1; 2; [...]; 8; 9; Right=10
LGBT movement strategies	What do you think needs to be done of the following, in order to make society better for LGBT persons? [Make state legislation non-discriminatory; Change people's attitudes; Challenge the norm of monogamy; Promote liberal values; Abolish patriarchy; Abolish hetero-normativity; Promote tolerance; Abolish capitalism; Tougher laws against hate crimes]	Strongly disagree; Disagree; Neither; Agree; Strongly agree
Pride parade participation	How many times have you in the past taken part in a pride parade, prior to this?	Never; 1 to 5; 6 to 10; 11 to 20; 20+
Gender identity	Which is your gender identity:	—
Sexual orientation	Do you consider yourself to be...? (check as many as apply):	Lesbian; Gay; Bisexual; Transgender; Heterosexual; Other...; Do not want to answer
Age	In which year were you born? [Answer subtracted from year of the demonstration]	—
Country of birth	In which country were you born?	—
Country of residence	In which country do you live?	—

(*Continued*)

Variable	Survey question	Response alternatives
Education	What is the highest level of education that you completed? If you are a student, at what level are you studying?	None, did not complete primary school; Primary School; Lower Secondary School; Higher Secondary School; Post-secondary, non-university; Bachelor's degree; Master's degree; PhD [Specific options adjusted to each national school system]
Employment situation	What is your employment situation? (Check as many as apply)	I work fulltime (including maternity leave or other temporary absence); I work part-time (including maternity leave or other temporary absence); I am freelance/self-employed (without employed staff); I am self-employed with employed staff; I study fulltime; I am unemployed/between jobs; I am (early) retired; I am a housewife / househusband; Other: …
Occupation	What is your occupation, or what was your last occupation?	—
Supervisory position at work	In your main job, do/did you have any responsibility for supervising the work of other (or your own) employees?	No; Yes, for 1 to 9 persons; Yes, for 10 persons or more

we have previously noted (Wahlström and Wennerhag 2014), because the questionnaire is filled in after protest participation (aside from Mexico City Pride) some variables need to be interpreted with some caution since they may be affected by participation. This should especially apply to variables such as sense of efficacy, trust, emotions and identification with other participants. Nevertheless, since the participants of a parade are arguably affected by their participation in a similar fashion, these variables can still be used in regressions as proxies for characteristics of the protesters prior to participation.

A few questions in the CCC questionnaire were constructed or reconstructed in order to cover participant characteristics that are highly relevant for particularly Pride parades. First, in almost all Pride surveys we changed the question regarding gender from a two-choice alternative (between man and woman), to an open question regarding gender identity. Second, in four of the parades we added a question regarding the sexual orientation of the participants.

When it comes to the question about gender identity, we wanted to focus on what gender the participants self-identified with, regardless of their sex at birth or what gender was registered as in official records. Since both trans and intergender people are central groups within the LGBT community, and the issue of gender identity and expression is a central concern for the movement, it seemed highly relevant to focus on gender identity. We expected that most trans people would write down the gender they self-identified with, but in a few cases (N=13) some of the respondents to the questionnaire only answered "transgender," and these are therefore shown as a separate row in the tables for gender identity. The answers to the open question were furthermore coded manually, into what seemed to be the major gender identities that were mentioned by the respondents. Apart from women, men and transgender, this made us create the categories "queer," "non-binary/intergender" (which also included answers such as "neither woman or man"), and "other gender identity" (N=7, which included answers such as "human"). The open question for gender identity was used in all parades but two (Prague 2013 and Mexico City).

The survey item about sexual orientation was only used in questionnaires at four of the surveyed parades (in Haarlem, London, Stockholm and Warsaw), partly because the CCC research teams originally suspected that asking about people's sexual orientation might be too intimate of a question. In more general population surveys, this is a type of question that has often been regarded as too sensitive (e.g. Alm and Westerståhl 2012). However, in the surveys in which this was asked it turned out that this was a very minor problem. Of the 716 returned surveys from these parades, only one person indicated the alternative "Do not want to answer" and there were only 17 missing cases for this question. We concluded that our original suspicion was unfounded, and in hindsight it should have been no surprise that this question should have been less controversial amongst Pride parade participants, a group that is partly brought together for taking pride in one's sexual orientation. In contrast to the question about gender identity, we chose to have a question with specified alternatives (Lesbian, Gay, Bisexual, Transgender, Heterosexual and Do not want to answer) plus an open "other" alternative. From the answers to the open "other" question the specific codes "pansexual" (N=12), "asexual" (N=6) and "other sexuality" (N=4) were then created. The question did not explicitly ask for sexual orientation – since we also included the alternative "transgender" – but instead asked: "Do you consider yourself to be...?", and it was furthermore possible to indicate more than one answer to this question.

Coding class

In Chapter 4, the class scheme constructed by Oesch (e.g. 2006a; 2006b) is used to analyze the class composition of Pride participants, and to compare these with ESS survey data for the general population. In order to conduct this analysis, the data available in the CCC and ESS databases were recoded according to the Oesch class scheme.[3]

In the Oesch class scheme class is coded based on information on individuals' (rather than households') employment status (employer, self-employed or employee), occupation, and supervision status, in case of supervisory functions. In the CCC dataset, the Oesch class position was therefore derived from the variables "employment situation," "supervisory status," "education level," and "occupation" (for details about these variables and their alternatives, see Table A.3). The relevant data for the variable "occupation" was maintained through a manual coding procedure, on the basis of the open-ended question in the CCC questionnaire about the respondent's current or former occupation. This manual coding was carried out according to the ISCO-88 standard.[4]

Since labor market position determines class position in the Oesch class scheme, a central concern was how to treat individuals not currently in employment. For instance, Oesch (2006a, p. 75) proposes a target population that covers only persons between the ages 20 and 65 currently working at least 20 hours per week, in order to only derive class positions for persons properly involved in the labor market. Full-time students, the retired and the unemployed are thus altogether left out of the original Oesch class scheme. In our analysis, we however wished to extend the population coverage and make it possible to identify the class position for those temporarily unemployed or retired. Everyone, disregarding his or her age or current employment status, was therefore included in the analysis. In order to make Oesch data comparable, this procedure was undertaken for all types of data that were analyzed (CCC and ESS). The unemployed were coded according to their last paid employment.

Furthermore, in order to analyze the relatively large group of full time students, an extra "class" consisting of students was added to the Oesch scheme. The small share of respondents who are both full-time students and in paid employment were class coded according to their occupation, and thus do not appear as students in the tables presenting Oesch data.

Coding the open question on motive for participation

In order to create a valid, and at the same time reliable, measure for Pride participants' motives analyzed in Chapter 8, we used the following method: In the CCC survey form handed out to Pride participants, the first item was the open-ended question "Please tell us why you participated in this Pride parade," and three blank lines were provided for the answer. Some responses were very brief, consisting only of one or two words, whereas others were more verbose and used more space than the lines assigned to the response in the questionnaire form. All responses were coded by the author of Chapter 8 using a coding scheme, which was developed according to the combined inductive and deductive procedures outlined in Chapter 8. The codes used were not exclusive, and since most respondents listed several reasons for their participation, more than one code was often ascribed to each response.

Since all responses were coded by the same individual, this alone should ensure a high degree of internal consistency. However, the reliability of the assigned codes needed to be further corroborated. After a first version of the coding scheme had been established, the researcher and an assistant coded 400 random data entries independently. Subsequently, all discrepancies between the two sets of codes were identified and analyzed, and the coding scheme was revised to avoid ambiguities that were deemed to have caused the differences. Then all responses in the full dataset were coded by the chapter author and a new sample of 400 random entries was drawn from the dataset and double-coded by the assistant. This second double-coding was used to test intercoder reliability. An intuitive way of checking the degree of correspondence between two coders is to calculate the percentage agreement between the coders for each code. However, this method is widely criticized since it does not take into account random agreement between the coders. Therefore, our main measure of intercoder reliability was Krippendorff's alpha (Hayes and Krippendorff 2007). This is a conservative measure that takes chance agreement into account. In contrast to some alternative measures, it remains applicable to a broad range of coding contexts and is therefore well suited as a standard measure. We calculated the Krippendorff's alpha intercoder reliability scores for each code. For descriptive analyses, a Krippendorff's alpha score of 0.70 or higher is regarded as an acceptable level of agreement (especially considering that the index is widely regarded as conservative). Only the codes Feeling of Community and Conviction/Duty failed to reach this level of reliability. However, when the Protest and Conviction/Duty codes were merged, the resulting Political Motives code reached a 0.81 Krippendorff's alpha score.

The qualitative data and methods

Interviews

To gather information on the organizers' strategic considerations regarding their Pride demonstrations, informant interviews were conducted with Pride organizers and key actors in the included countries' respective LGBT organizations. The identification of these actors was made with the assistance of our international CCC collaborators. We have collected between three to eight interviews for each of the eight countries in the study (see the List of Interviews on pp. 227–229 in this volume).

The informants were queried as to their reasons behind their "framing" of the Pride events they helped organize; how they had related to perceived tensions within the LGBT movement; how they had cooperated with state and/or local authorities in staging the event; if they had staged the event differently the following year, that is, what had they "learned" from their organizing efforts; and finally, what were their goals for the manifestations. On the basis of our interviews we could better reconstruct the histories of the Pride traditions in our sample; reconstruct how the organizers dealt with the potential dilemmas that "friends of Pride" posed, as well as tensions within the LGBT movement; discuss how the organizers "framed their events"; how they attempted to steer the "performances of pride"; and lastly, what they envisioned as the future of Pride in their countries.

The interviews ranged in general from one to two hours. Transcripts were made of the recorded interviews. We have only used the full names of the respondents when they had been expressly asked if we could refer to them and they thereafter granted permission.

Demonstration-level data

In regards to demonstration-level data identical data was collected by the CCC research teams on the countries included: the mobilizing contexts, the demonstration slogans and focused issues, media reports, etcetera, using specifically designed fact sheets and questionnaires. All data were checked, cleaned and then coded and entered into a central database in Antwerp. Media reports were drawn upon, as were organizer statements and demonstration records regarding slogans and participating organizations/Parade units. Most CCC teams also provided photographic evidence of the demonstrations, which we complemented with additional photographic documentation of the demonstrations systematically sampled from the Internet. However, in many cases the data in the fact sheets of the

CCC database proved insufficient for our purposes, and had to be complemented with data gathered from interviews, news media and organizers' web pages.

Notes

1 This chapter includes reworked excerpts from a previous publication by the authors: Wahlström, M. and Wennerhag, M. (2016). Methods for Studying May Day Demonstrators: Sampling, Estimating Non-Response Bias and Pooling Data with General Population Surveys. In Peterson A. and Reiter H. (Eds). *The Ritual of May Day in Western Europe: Past, Present and Future* (pp. 262–78). London: Routledge. Copyright © 2016.
2 The largest proportion of survey respondents born and resident in another country – 13 percent – was found in the Geneva Pride parade (which is not surprising considering the proximity to the French border). In London World Pride the corresponding figure was 4 percent and in the other events it was even smaller. Since the absolute numbers of foreign respondents are small, these figures should be interpreted with care, but they are nevertheless lower than expected considering the strong transnational dimension of LGBT mobilizations, noted by, e.g. Ayoub (2013).
3 We here especially wish to thank Anders Hylmö for manually classifying the occupation of all cases in the CCC dataset, as well as constructing SPSS syntaxes and managing all the coding of CCC data into Oesch's class categories. We also wish to thank Daniel Oesch for providing us corresponding SPSS syntaxes for ESS data.
4 For a detailed description of the coding process and the variables used, see Appendix C in Hylmö and Wennerhag (2012).

References

Ayoub, P.M. (2013). Cooperative transnationalism in contemporary Europe: Europeanization and political opportunities for LGBT mobilization in the European Union. *European Political Science Review* 5(2), 279–310.
Alm, E., and Westerståhl, A. (2012). Sexuell orientering. In Weibull, L., Oscarsson, H., and Bergström, A. (Eds) *I framtidens skugga: 42 kapitel om politik, medier och samhälle* (pp. 557–571). Göteborg: SOM-institutet.
Cobben, F., and Bethlehem, J. (2005). *Adjusting undercoverage and nonresponse bias in telephone surveys*. Voorburg/Heerlen: CBS Statistics Netherlands.
Goldstein, H. (2011). *Multilevel statistical models*. 4th ed. Chichester: Wiley.
Groves, R.M., Singer, E., and Corning, A. (2000). Leverage-saliency theory of survey participation: Description and an illustration. *Public Opinion Quarterly*, 64(3), 299–308.
Hayes, A.F., and Krippendorff, K. (2007). Answering the call for a standard reliability measure for coding data. *Communication Methods and Measures*, 1(1), 77–89.
Hylmö, A., and Wennerhag, M. (2012). Does class matter in protests? Social class, attitudes towards inequality, and political trust in European demonstrations in a time of economic crisis. *Working Paper*. Available at URL: www.protestsurvey.eu/index.php?page=publications&id=22 (accessed September 28, 2017).

Klandermans, B., and Oegema, D. (1987). Potentials, networks, motivations, and barriers: Steps toward participation in social movements. *American Sociological Review*, 52, 519–531.

Klandermans, B., Van Stekelenburg, J., Van Troost, D., Van Leeuwen, A., Walgrave, S., Verhulst, J., Van Laer, J., and Wouters, R. (2011). *Manual for data collection on protest demonstrations. Caught in the act of protest: Contextualizing Contestation (CCC-project). Version 3.0.* Amsterdam and Antwerp: VU University Amsterdam and University of Antwerp.

Leslie, L.L. (1972). Are high response rates essential to valid surveys? *Social Science Research*, 1(3), 323–334.

Manski, C.F., and McFadden, D. (1981). *Structural analysis of discrete data with econometric applications.* Cambridge, MA: MIT Press.

Oesch, D. (2006a). *Redrawing the class map: Stratification and institutions in Britain, Germany, Sweden, and Switzerland.* New York: Palgrave Macmillan.

Oesch, D. (2006b). Coming to grips with a changing class structure: An analysis of employment stratification in Britain, Germany, Sweden and Switzerland. *International Sociology*, 21(2), 263–288.

Rogelberg, S.G., Conway, J.M., Sederburg, M.E., Spitzmüller, C., Aziz, S., and Knight, W.E. (2003). Profiling active and passive nonrespondents to an organizational survey. *Journal of Applied Psychology*, 88(6), 1104–1114.

Rüdig, W. (2010). Assessing nonresponse bias in activist surveys. *Quality & Quantity* 44(1), 173–180.

Van Stekelenburg, J., Walgrave, S., Klandermans, B., and Verhulst, J. (2012). Contextualizing contention: Framework, design, and data. *Mobilization*, 17(3), 249–262.

Vehovar, V. (2007). Non-response bias in the European social survey. In Loosveldt, G., Swyngedouw, M., and Cambré, B. (Eds) *Measuring meaningful data in social research* (pp. 335–356). Leuven: Acco.

Wahlström, M., and Wennerhag, M. (2014). Alone in the crowd: Lone protesters in West European demonstrations. *International Sociology*, 29(6), 565–583.

Wahlström, M., and Wennerhag, M. (2016). Methods for studying May Day demonstrators: Sampling, estimating non-response bias and pooling data with general population surveys. In Peterson, A., and Reiter, H. (Eds) *The ritual of May Day in Western Europe: Past, present and future* (pp. 262–278). London: Routledge.

Walgrave, S., and Verhulst, J. (2011). Selection and response bias in protest surveys. *Mobilization: An International Quarterly*, 16(2), 203–222.

Walgrave, S., Wouters, R., and Ketelaars, P. (2016). Response problems in the protest survey design: Evidence from fifty-one protest events in seven countries. *Mobilization: An International Journal*, 21(1), 83–104.

Index

Act Up activists 160
Adam, B.D. 4, 72; et al. 3, 4, 64, 71, 144
adoption rights for same-sex couples 10, 11; in Czech Republic 60, 63; in Mexico 79; in Netherlands 82; in Sweden 82; in Switzerland 80; in UK 81
Advocate, The (newspaper) 18, 20
Aftonbladet (newspaper) 128
age of consent 79, 80, 81
AIDS 29, 41, 46–7, 54; *see also* HIV
Altman, Dennis, and Symons, Jonathan 224
Amersfoort, Netherlands 37
Amnesty International 51, 77, 145
Amsterdam, Netherlands: congress (1951) 220; Europride (1994) 38; EuroPride (2016) 38, 222; Gay Business Amsterdam 38; Gay Pride Amsterdam 38; homo monument 163; homosexual march (1970) 36; International Day of Liberation and Solidarity 36–7; Pink Saturday (2016) 38; *see also* Canal Pride
Amsterdam Leather Pride 38
Amsterdam Pride week 163
Amsterdam Treaty (1997) 54
AnarchoPride (Sweden) 35
Ann Arbor, Michigan, US 21
anti-austerity protests 213
anti-immigrant attitudes 108, 112, 160, 161
anti-Iraq-war demonstrations 74, 91, 203–4
ARCI *see Associazione Ricreativa e Culturale Italiana*
Arcigay Arcilesbica (Italy) 50
Arcigay Il Cassero (Italy) 186, 187

Arcigay (Italy) 50
Argentina 217, 221
Armstrong, Elizabeth A. 9, 14, 21, 214; and Crage, S.M. 19, 21, 171
asexual **100**, 116, 121
Associazione Ricreativa e Culturale Italiana (ARCI) 64n11
Atlanta, Georgia, US 4, 21
authoritarian values 112, 114, *114*
autocracy 222
Ayoub, Philip M., and Paternotte, David 72, 220

Baker, Gilbert 24
Baltic Pride 223
Barclays Bank 157, 158, 216
Basel, Switzerland 41
BDSMF 7, 101
"Bears" 7, 9
Belfast Pride 29
Belgrade Pride 223
Berlin, Germany, EuroPride 24
Bern, Switzerland 41, 42
Bernstein, Mary 8, 147, 184, 192, 198
Biedron, Robert 55–6, 57, 58
binary gender roles 99
Bindel, Julie 173–4, 215
Binnie, J., and Klesse, C. 151
biographical availability 91, 102, 138, 140; first-time Pride participants 138–9, 140; social movements and 102
Birmingham, Alabama, US 21
Birmingham, UK 29
bisexuals 22, 99, 146; LGBT strategies and **116**; political engagement and 106, **107**; political orientations **113**, 121; Pride parades and **100**, 106, 120
Black Pride, London 29

Bologna, Italy 1; Arcigay 50; Communist Party 52; Gay and Lesbian Pride (1995) 50; LGBT movement 52–3; politics 52
Bologna Pride 52–3, 145, 186, 220; aftermath of earthquake (2012) 184–5; Arcigay Il Cassero and 186, 187; Catholic Church and 203; changes in 186–7; commercialization and 158; contextual factors **83**; information channels 133, **134**; orientation of 203, 206; participants 92, **94–5**; participants asked/asking **137**, 138; participants' motives **205**, 207; "pink washing" 158; political orientations, participants and *114*; political reforms and 203; politicized participants 204; protest-oriented participants 138, 204; space for Pride (2017) 187; trade unions and 145
Boston, Massachusetts, US 21, 23
Boston, N., et al. 160
Brazil 80, 217, 220–1, 223
Breines, W. 173
Brighton, UK 29, 194
Britt, L., and Heise, D. 192
Brno, Czech Republic 61, 62, 180
Brooklyn, Gay Pride parade (1998) 23
Browne, K. 194, **195**, 197; and Bakshi, M.L. 150, 153, 216
Bryant, Anita 37, 64n7
Budapest, Hungary, Pride parade 224
Buffalo, New York State, US 21
Burlington, Vermont, US 4, 127
Butler, Judith 221–2

Cameron, David 28
camp performances 7
Campaign for Homosexual Equality (CHE) 26
Canada 5, 24
Canal Pride (Amsterdam) 12, 38, 39, 125, 148; boat cost, CoC and 185; commercialization 163, 194; depoliticization 163, 194; Muslims and 160; spectators and 141n2 185
capitalism 11, 115, 116, **116**, 117, **118–19**
Cappelliato, V., and Mangarella, T. 177, 178
carnivalesque, the: LGBT friendly contexts and 177, 182; LGBT unfriendly contexts and 178; London Pride and 183; perception of 178; political force of 174; politics and 181; Pride parades and 6, 7, 12, 170–1, 174, 175–6, 177, 181; social movements and 172
Carter, D. 19
Catholic Church: AIDS, views on 47; Bologna Pride and 203; in Czech Republic 81; homosexuality and 47, 49, 53; influence of 75, 76; in Italy 49, 78; LGBT rights and 81; in Mexico 79; *Più Familia* rally 78; in Poland 53, 54, 72; same-sex marriage and 75, 78; Swiss cantons and 80
Caught in the Art of Protest: Contextualizing Contestation (CCC) 3, 74, 121, 191, 194, 196
CCC *see* Caught in the Art of Protest: Contextualizing Contestation
Center for Recreation and Culture (CoC) (Netherlands) 36–7, 38, 161, 185
Central Eastern Europe 81
CGH *see* Coordinadora de Grupos Homosexuales (Coordinator of Homosexual Groups)
Chabot, S., Duyvendak, J.W. and 4, 72
Charter of Fundamental Rights of the European Union 77
Chasin, Alexandra 9, 12, 154
CHE *see* Campaign for Homosexual Equality
Chicago, Illinois, US 2, 14, 20–1
Christopher Street Days (CSD) (Switzerland) 40–2
Christopher Street Freedom march (Los Angeles) 20–1
Christopher Street Liberation Day (Stockholm) 30–1, 124–5
Christopher Street Liberation parade (New York) 20, 21
Christopher Street West: A Freedom Revival in Lavender 20–1
Cirolo Mario Mieli (Italy) 49–50, 51, 52
Civil Rights movement 19
Club68 40
CoC *see* Center for Recreation and Culture
collective events, meanings of 206–9
collective performances 171, 182; of coming out 170; of pride 5–8
Colpani, G., and Habed, A.J. 52

Index 251

coming out 127; barrier of stigma 140–1; becoming 7; gay liberation and 6; meaning of 6; performances 7, 84, 170; personal significance of 138; as a political act 6; Pride parades and 6, 171, 172, 173, 198; process of 127–8; visibility and 6, 198
commercialization 154–8; Bologna Pride and 158; effects of 155, 156; Gay Pride events and 23; Gay Shame and 23; London Pride and 28, 154, 157–8; Mexico City Pride and 155; Prague Pride and 154–5; Pride events and 12; Pride parades and 2, 165, 212; Stockholm Pride and 155–6; US Pride events 12, 154; West Pride and 156
Compass 77
CONAPRED *see Consejo Nacional para Prevenir La Discriminación* (National Council to Prevent Discrimination)
conscience adherents 102
conscience constituents 102
Consejo Nacional para Prevenir La Discriminación (National Council to Prevent Discrimination) (CONAPRED) (Mexico) 79
Coordinadora de Grupos Homosexuales (Coordinator of Homosexual Groups) (CGH) 45–6
corporate sponsorship 22; *see also* commercialization
Corrales, Javier 6
Council of Europe 77, 151, 221
Cracow, Poland 56, 59, 151
Crimp, D. 150
CSD Zürich 41, 42
cultural anchors 73, 84
cultural imperialism 221
Czech Pride 109, 115; motivation 195; political orientations, participants and 109, **110–11**; social media campaign 133
Czech Republic 1, 4, 59–64, 78; age of consent, sexual acts and 80; Brno parade 61, 62; Catholic Church 81; discrimination, legislation prohibiting 80; *Gay Iniciativa* (Gay Initiative) 60; Gay and Lesbian League 60; homosexuality, legalization of 59; homosexuality, medicalization of 59, 60; homosexuality, public opinion and *82*; homosexuality, tolerance of 59–60; information channels 133; Jsme Fér (We Are Fair) campaign 63; LGBT less friendly context 13, 59–62, 80–1, 157, 178, 180, 207; LGBT movement 59–60, 152, 207; LGBT organizations 135; LGBT rights 81, 152; ODS party 61, 62; online social media 133, 140; parade in Tabor 61; political reforms 60; Pride events 61–3; Pride history 59–63; PROUD 63; rainbow festival in Karlovy Vary 60–1; same-sex marriage, support for 81; same-sex relationships, recognition in law 80–1; secularity 81; Socio-Therapeutic Club of Homosexuals 60; SOHO 60; World Values Survey 81; Yogyakarta Principles and 221; *see also* Brno; Prague; Prague Pride
Czechoslovakia 1–2

Dade County, Florida, US 37, 64n7
Dallas, Texas, US 21
de-gaying of Pride parades 13, 144, 150, 152, 164, 166, 212
Delémont, Switzerland 42, 43
della Porta, D., and Diani, M. 124
d'Emilio, John 18, 19
demonstrations: anti-Iraq-war 74, 91, 203–4; biographical availability and 102; contextual variations 74; ethnic minorities and 93; mobilization and 74; motivation and 74; national/political context and 203; normalization of 90; social composition of 90, 96; social movements and 120; trade union 96, 120; US anti-war protesters (2003) 203; WUNC and 176; *see also* May Day marches
Denmark 36, 220; *Forbunder af 1948* (Federation of 1948) 30
Der Kreis (journal) 36, 39, 40
Detroit, Michigan, US 21
discrimination: constitutional prohibition of 79, 82; legislation and 80, 81, 82, 115; non-LGBT Pride participants and 101–2, 209n1; religious minorities and 222; women and 102
diversity: dissent and 9; of identities 97–102; identities and 9; infighting

252 *Index*

and 9–12; LGBT communities and 7, 8; LGBT groups and 97–102; LGBT movement and 146, 214; Pride parades and 176–7; sexual diversity 47–8
Donohue, C. 129
drag kings/queens 7, 127
Drissel, D. 29
Dublin, Ireland 194
Dutch Society for Homophiles 36
Dutch Society for the Integration of Homosexuals 36
Dyke Marches 23
Dykes on Bikes 127

Eastern Bloc 1–2
Eastern Europe 53, 54, 59, 109
Eastern Regional Conference of Homophile Organizations (ERCHO) 19
ECtHR *see* European Court of Human Rights
Egan, P.J., and Sherrill, K. 10
Ehrenreich, Barbara 172
Encarnación, Omar G. 5–6, 75, 223
Engel, S.M. 4–5
England 25, 81
EPOA *see* European Pride Organisers Association
Epstein, B. 162
equality/equal rights 10, 11, 115; demands for 11; liberty and 10; *see also* human rights; LGBT rights
ERCHO *see* Eastern Regional Conference of Homophile Organizations
Erdogan, Recep Tayyip 222
Eskilstuna, Sweden 34
ethnic minorities 93
EU *see* European Union
Eurobarometer 81
Europe: Central Eastern European countries 81; Eastern Europe 53, 54, 59, 109; LGBT movements, transnational ambitions of 72, 220; LGBT transnationalism 220; Pride parades, diffusion/standardization 24; Pride parades in 14; Western Europe 23, 109
European Court of Human Rights (ECtHR) 57, 77, 78
European Forum of LGBT Christian Groups 72
European Network of Socialist Parties' LGBT caucuses 72

European Pride Organisers Association (EPOA) 24, 32, 72; *Cirolo Mario Mieli* and 50
European Region of the International Lesbian, Gay, Trans and Intersex Association (ILGA-Europe) 4, 24, 51, 72, 220; KPH and 54
European Union (EU): Amsterdam Treaty (1997) 54; Charter of Fundamental Rights of the European Union 77; LGBT policy and 221, 224; liberal values 222–3; Poland and 54, 56, 72, 77; Yogyakarta Principles and 221
European-ness 221
Europeanization 4, 72
EuroPride 24; Amsterdam (1994) 38; Amsterdam (2016) 38, 222; establishment of (1992) 63; Gothenburg and Stockholm (2018) 34; Manchester (2003) 29; Rome (2000) 50; Rome (2011) 52; Stockholm (1998) 32–3; Warsaw (2010) 58, 77; Zurich (2009) 41
exhibitionism, Pride parades and 178
Eyerman, Ron 171

Facebook 130, 133–4
FAHR *see Frente Homosexual de Liberación Revolucionaria* (Homosexual Front of Revolutionary Action)
Fargo, North Dakota, US 4
feminist movement 19, 102; Italian 49; Polish 117; Swedish 31, 117, 162; *see also* lesbian feminism
first-time Pride participants 138–9, **139**, 141, 172–3, 174, 201
FNF *seeFrente Nacional por la Familia* (National Front for the Family)
Forbunder af 1948 (Federation of 1948) 30
France 36, 41, 93, 108
Freedman, Glen 51
Frente Homosexual de Liberación Revolucionaria (Homosexual Front of Revolutionary Action) (FAHR) 45
Frente Nacional por la Familia (National Front for the Family) (FNF) 48
friends of Pride 13, 144–66, 212, 214–15; commercial friends 154–8; commercial sponsors 145; contextual factors, participation and 145–6;

de-gaying Pride parades 13, 144, 150, 152, 164, 212; individual friends 144–5, 149–54, 212; individual friends, organizers' approach to 146–9; mobilization of 146; multi-issue friends 162–4; organizational 144–5, 164, 212; participation, contextual factors and 145–6; political parties 145; stigmatization, risk of 165; unwanted friends 158–62, 165
fun/entertainment 5, **195**, 197–8, 200, 204
F.U.O.R.I! Association (Italy) 49

Gamson, Joshua 214
Gay Business Amsterdam 38
Gay Businessmen Association 154
gay clubs/venues 147; heterosexual population and 150
gay hate crimes 75; in Mexico 80; in Mexico City 79; in Poland 77; Polish criminal code and 77
Gay Iniciativa (Gay Initiative) (Czech Republic) 60
Gay and Lesbian League (Czech Republic) 60
gay liberation, Stonewall myth and 18–24
Gay Liberation Front (GLF) 25–6, 29, 183
Gay Liberation Movement(s): birth of 2; political discourse in 1970s 11
gay men: coming out process 127–8; homonationalism 108, 121; lesbians, discord and 10, 14, 89, 214, 215–16; LGBT organizations, membership of 106; LGBT strategies and **116**, 117; political engagement and 106, **107**, 150; political orientation 112, **113**; Pride parades and **100**, 120; right-wing populism parties and 108; white gay men, dominance of 23
Gay Power Club 30
gay pride: adoption of name 22; British march (1972) 25–6; British marches 26–7; commercialization of events 23; demonstrations 11; London Gay Pride march (1985) 27
Gay Pride Amsterdam 38
Gay Pride Week (UK) 26
gay resistance events 18
gay rights issues, attitudes to 75
Gay Shame 23

Gaymoderaterna (Gay Conservatives) (Sweden) 32
gays of color 9, 22
gender identities: LGBT community 99; political engagement and 106; political orientations and 114; Pride parade participants 97, **98**, 99
Gender Recognition Act (2004) (UK) 81–2
Geneva Pride 43, 93, *114*, 124, 145; contextual factors **83**; gender identities **98**; gender of participants 97; information channels **134**, 135; participants 92, **94–5**; participants asked/asking **137**; participants' motives **205**; participants, number of 125; political engagement, participants and **104–5**, 204; political orientations, participants and **110–11**, 112, 115; route, symbolic significance of 184
Geneva, Switzerland 1, 42–3
geopolitics, Pride parades and 220–4
Germany 39, 40
Gessen, Masha 222
Ghaziani, Amin 9, 22; and Baldassarri, D. 73, 84
Glasgow, Scotland 23–4
Glass, Dan 160
GLBT (Italian acronym) 14n2, 64n12
GLF *see* Gay Liberation Front
global cultural anchors 84
globalization 71, 74; LGBT politics and 72, 73; Pride parades and 73
Goffman, Erving 127
Gore, Al 51
Gothenburg Rainbow Parade 34, 182
Gothenburg, Sweden 1, 10, 34; *HBT-festivalen* (LGBT Festival) 34; *see also* West Pride
Grodzka, Anna 58
Grøningen, Netherlands 148, 184
Grupo Lambda de Liberación Homosexual (Lambda Group of Homosexual Liberation) 45
Guadalajara, Mexico 48

Haarlem, Netherlands 1, 99
Haarlem Pink Saturday Parade 38, 39, 127, 146, 148, 163; community-oriented 149; contextual factors **83**; gender identities **98**; gender of participants 97; information channels **134**; lesbians, Pride parades and

216; mass media as information source 133; non-LGBT participants 101, 164; organizational friends of Pride 145; orientation of parade 203; participants 92, **94–5**; participants, age of 92; participants asked/asking **137**, 138; participants' motives 14, 204, **205**, 206, 207, 208, 213; participants, number of 125; political engagement, participants and **104–5**; political orientations, participants and **110–11**, *114*; political support for 160; sexual orientations **100**
HACH *see Homosexuellen Arbeitsgruppen Schweiz*
Hague, The, Netherlands 184
Hajek, Petr 61
HBT-festivalen (LGBT Festival) (Sweden) 34
HBTQ (Swedish acronym) 14n2
Hekma, Gert 36; and Duyvendak, J.W. 39, 160
Herdt, G.H. 73
hetero-normativity 5, 117, **118–19**; abolition of 116, **116**; carnivalesque transgressions of 177; challenging 5, 9; struggle against 11
heterosexuals: gay clubs/venues and 150; LGBT strategies and **116**; political engagement and 106, **107**; political orientations **113**; Pride parades and **100**, 106, 150, 154
HFG *see Homosexuelle Frauengruppe Zürich*
HIV 26, 46–7; *see also* AIDS
HLRS *see* Homosexual Law Reform Society
Holzhacker, Ronald 5, 75, 81, 180, 203
homonationalism 108, 121, 160, 161, 221
homophile organizations: congress (1951) 220; ERCHO and 19; Gay Liberation movement, birth of 2; legislation, lobbying for 1, 2; post-war period 1–2
homophobia 29, 45, 108, 159, 222; Mexico and 79, 80; Poland and 78, 222; *see also Kampania Przeciw Homofobii* (Campaign Against Homophobia)
homosexual acts: decriminalization of 29, 39, 49, 80; Netherlands and 35–6
homosexual emancipation, Netherlands and 35–6

Homosexual Law Reform Society (HLRS) 25
Homosexual Liberation Day/Week (Sweden) 31–2, 33
homosexuality: Americanization of 4; Catholic Church and 47, 49; Czech Republic, public opinion and 81, *82*; Italy, public opinion and 76, 78, 81, *82*; legalization in Czech Republic 59; Mexico, public opinion and 79, *82*; Netherlands, public opinion and 76, *82*; normalization of 146, 160; Poland, public opinion and 76, 77, 81, *82*; public opinion survey *82*; social stigma of 127; Sweden, public opinion and 76, *82*; Switzerland, public opinion and *82*; UK, public opinion and 82
homosexuals, attitudes towards 127
Homosexuella frigörelsedagen (Homosexual Liberation Day) 31
Homosexuella liberaler (Homosexual Liberals) 32
Homosexuella Socialister (Homosexual Socialists) (Sweden) 31, 32
Homosexuellen Arbeitsgruppen (Homosexual Working Groups) (Switzerland) 40, 42
Hromada, Jiří 60
Hughes, H.L. 154
human rights 11, 14, 47; Application of International Human Rights Law in relation to Sexual Orientation and Gender Identity 221; Brazilian resolution and 220–1; *Compass* 77; European Court of Human Rights 57; homosexuals and 36; International Gay and Lesbian Human Rights Commission 51; LGBT politics and 146; Mexico and 47; Netherlands and 36; organizational friends of Pride and 145; Universal Declaration of Human Rights (1949) 36; Yogyakarta Principles 221
Hungary 222, 224
Hylmö, Anders 121n1

IAL/GPC *see* International Association of Lesbian and Gay Pride Coordinators
ICSE *see* International Committee for Sexual Equality

identity: analytical dimensions of 8; stigmatized 8; strategy of 8–9, 184, 192
identity for empowerment 8, 154, 192
identity as goal 8, 154
identity politics 8, 49, 117, 128
ILGA *see* International Lesbian, Gay, Trans and Intersex Association
ILGA-Europe *see* European Region of the International Lesbian, Gay, Trans and Intersex Association
ILGCN *see* International Lesbian and Gay Cultural Network (ILGCN)
ILGCN-Polska *see* International Lesbian and Gay Cultural Network Poland
immigration, attitudes towards 108, 112, 114, 121, 160, 161
incongruity 7
infighting: diversity and 9–12; the role of 9
information channels: bounded communication 132–3, **134**, **139**; closed channels 129, 132; first-time Pride participants and 138–9, **139**; first-timers vs returnees **139**; Internet communication 130, 132; interpersonal networks 129, 130–1; mass media 132, 133, **134**, 138, **139**, 140, 212; mobilizing networks and 129–32, 212; online social media 130, 132, 133–4, **134**, 140, 212; open channels 129, 132, 133; organizational 133, **134**, 135, **139**; personal ties 132, **134**, 135, **139**, 140; Pride parade mobilizations and 132–5, **134**
intergender 97, **98**, **100**, 117
International Association of Lesbian and Gay Pride Coordinators (IAL/GPC) 23–4, 65n15
International Committee for Sexual Equality (ICSE) 36, 40, 220
International Day of Liberation and Solidarity (Amsterdam) 36–7
International Gay and Lesbian Human Rights Commission 51
international human rights law, LGBT persons and 221
International Lesbian and Gay Cultural Network (ILGCN) 54
International Lesbian and Gay Cultural Network Poland (ILGCN-Polska) 54–5

International Lesbian, Gay, Trans and Intersex Association (ILGA) 51, 72, 88; Eastern European groups and 53; WRH and 53; *see also* European Region of the International Lesbian, Gay, Trans and Intersex Association (ILGA-Europe)
International Liberation and Solidarity march (1978) 37
international solidarity 37, 196; LGBT friendly countries and 37; Pride parades and 37, 196
interpersonal networks 129, 130–1
InterPride 23, 24, 29, 35, 50–1, 72, 211; survey/questionnaire 218; WorldPride and 51
intersex 7, 22, 43, 77
Iraq 74
Islam: cultural assaults on 222; *see also* Muslims
Islamophobia 158, 159, 160
Italy 1, 49–53; Arcigay 50; Arcigay Arcilesbica 50; Association for the Recognition of Homophile Rights 49; Catholic Church 49, 78; *Circolo Mario Mieli* 49–50, 51, 52; Eurispes report 78; feminist movement 49; F.U.O.R.I! Association 49; Gay and Lesbian Pride 50; gay righs demonstration 50; GLBT 14n2, 50; homosexuality, public opinion and 76, 78, *82*; LGBT movement in 5, 50; LGBT unfriendly context 13, 14, 76–7, 78, 120, 178; "Manifesto for the Moral Revolution: Revolutionary Homosexuality" 49; national organizations, emergence of 49–50; Organization for the Political Movement of Homosexuals 49; post-war period, homophile organizations 1; Pride parade participants 92, **94–5**; Pride parades 49–53; Rocco Code 78; same-sex marriage 78; transgender people in 78; Women's Arcigay 50; WorldPride (2000) 24; Yogyakarta Principles and 221

Jackson, Mike 27
Jasper, James 146
Jerusalem, WorldPride (2006) 24
Jiménez, Patria 47, 179
Johnston, Jill 18
Johnston, Lynda 12; and Waitt, G. 3

256 *Index*

Jsme Fér (We Are Fair) campaign (Czech Republic) 63
Jura, Switzerland 43

Kaczyński, Lech 56
Kampania Przeciw Homofobii (Campaign Against Homophobia) (KPH) (Poland) 54, 55, 56, 57, 77
Karlovy Vary, Czech Republic 60–1
Karlstad, Sweden 34
Kates, S.M., and Belk, R.W. 171
Ketelaars, P. 203
Klandermans, Bert 125, 191, 192, 199, 202; et al. 131; and Oegema, D. 125, 126, 136
Klaus, Václav 61, 62, 152, 195
Kollman, Kelly, and Waites, Matthew 220
KPH *see Kampania Przeciw Homofobii* (Campaign Against Homophobia)
Krakow for Tolerance Festival 151; *see also* Cracow, Poland
Kreuzlinger, Switzerland, bi-annual CSD parade 41
Kuhar, R. 127

Lady Gaga 52
Lambda Group *see Grupo Lambda de Liberación Homosexual*
Las Cruces, New Mexico 21
Latin America 5; Catholic Church, same-sex marriage and 75; first gay Pride parade 46; gay hate crimes in 75; gay rights, attitudes to 75; LGBT rights and 221; Pride parades 5–6, 14, 46, 223
Lausanne, Switzerland 41, 42
Lavizzari, Anna 158, 186
Lesbenorganisation Schweiz (LOS) (Switzerland) 42
Lesbian Avengers 23
lesbian feminism 7, 9, 11, 45; *see also* feminist movement
lesbians: coming out process 127–8; Dyke Marches and 23; gay men, discord and 10, 14, 89, 214, 215–16; LGBT organizations, membership of 106; LGBT strategies and **116**, 117; political engagement and 106, **107**; political orientations **113**; Pride parades and **100**, 106, 120; right-wing populist parties and 108

Lesbians and Gays Support the Miners (LGSM) 27, 157, 158, 165; National Union of Mineworkers and 165
Lesbisk Front (Lesbian Front) (Sweden) 31, 162
LGBT acronym 14n2
LGBT Christian Groups, European Forum of 72
LGBT community: class issue within (UK) 27; as a collective political actor 7; friends of 101; gender identities 99; "just like everybody else" 88, 90–102, 103, 117, 121; Pride parades, participation in 89, 120–1; socio-demographic composition of 90; stereotypes 106; visibility and 193, 194, **195**, 198
LGBT contexts: effects on Pride parades 213; friendly context 1, 81–3, 91, 117, 156, 157, 177, 180–3, 204; less friendly context 1, 78–81, 91, 92, 102, 103, 115, 177–80; unfriendly contexts 1, 13, 14, 76–8, 92, 103, 120, 136, 151, 178
LGBT individuals: harassment of 127; perception of 127
LGBT movements 5; basic rights and 2; categories within 22; coalitional nature of 176; collective identities and 2; conflicts and 14, 146; cultural goals 8; diversity within 146, 214; domination of US 4; equal rights 115; Europeanization/transnationalization, strategies and 4, 72; gender divisions 10; ideologies, rift in 11; influences on 3; modes of interaction 75; national/regional imprint 3; participation in parades 106; pedophile/pedosexual groups, repudiation of 145; political engagement and 103, **104–5**, **107**; political goals 8, 12, 89; political identities, creation of 3; political tension within 10, 11; politics, national contexts and 4; politics, shift in 12; post-Second World War 5; Pride parades as visible manifestations of 1, 224; public opinion and 203; as quintessential identity movement 9; similarities/differences 4; strategies 4, 72, 89, 115–17, **116**, **118–19**, 121; successes 2; tensions within 2, 89, 115, 214; transnational European 72, 220; two-level game concept 72

LGBT organizations: membership 89, 103, 106, 120, 131; Pride participants and 103, 120, 135
LGBT politics: coalitional nature of 7; globalization and 72, 73; national and local contexts 73–6
LGBT rights 194–5, 220; Application of International Human Rights Law in relation to Sexual Orientation and Gender Identity 221; autocracy and 222; Brazilian resolution and 220–1; Catholic Church and 81; Czech Republic and 81, 152; geopolitical divide 221; as human rights 221, 224; internationalization of 221; left-libertarian parties and 93, 109; left-wing parties and 82; liberal parties and 82; Poland and 57, 58; political parties and 39, 80, 82, 83, 93, 109, 112; radical right parties and 39; Rainbow Cities Network and 79; right wing parties and 108; social democratic parties and 93; Yogyakarta Principles and 221
LGBT youth: Pride parades and 127; stigma and 127
LGBTQI 22, 89
LGSM *see* Lesbians and Gays Support the Miners
liberal values 14, 222–3, 224
libertarian values 112, *114*
Liga Polskich Rodzin (League of Polish Families) (LPR) 56
Linden, A., and Klandermans, B. 127
Lithuania 223
Löfven, Stefan 128
London 1; Black Pride 29; Gay Pride parade (1984) 27; information channels 133; mid-1970s parade 7; miners, Gay Pride parade (1985) 27; Pride parade (1984) 27; WorldPride (2012) 24, 93, 125, 149, 164
London LGBT + Community Pride 28
London Mardi Gras 28
London Pride 146, 208–9; Act Up activists and 160; analysis of 219; carnivalesque nature of 183; commercialization of 28, 154, 157–8, 165, 183, 216; contextual factors **83**; costs and 219; female participants and 28; friends of Pride 148, 164; funding and 28; future development of 219–20; gay men, dominance of 149, 216; gender identities **98**;

gender of participants 97; information channels **134**; LGSM and 27, 157, 158, 165; non-LGBT participants 101; organizational friends 145; organizers' aims 148–9; orientation of 203; participants asked/asking 136, **137**, 138; participants **94–5**; participants' motives 14, **205**, 206, 207, 208, 213; perception of 215, 216; political engagement, participants and **104–5**; political orientations, participants and **110–11**, *114*, 115; political performance and 183; sexual orientations 99, **100**; sexually hedonistic theme, dominance of 28, 215; spectators (1972), aggression and 183; trade unions and 145, 157, 158, 165; UKIP and 159–60
London Pride week 26, 29
Long, S. 59, 60
LOS *see Lesbenorganisation Schweiz*
Los Angeles, California, US 2, 14, 18, 20–1
LPR *see Liga Polskich Rodzin* (League of Polish Families)
Lucerne, Switzerland 41, 42
Lundberg, A. 192
Luongo, M. 51

McCarthy, J.D., and Zald, M.N. 102
McFarland Bruce, Katherine 4, 5, 127, 177, 204; cultural challenge, Pride parades and 174–5, 193; exhibitionism, Pride parades and 178; fun, the element of 5; meanings of Pride 194, 203–4; participants' motives **195**, 196, 198; Pride events (1970) 20–1
Madrid 24, 147
Malagreca, M.A. 49
Malmö Pride 34, 35
Manchester, UK 7, 26, 27, 29
Manchester Mardi Gras 29
Manchester Pride 29
March on Washington for Lesbian, Gay and Bi Equal Rights and Liberation 22, 23
Markwell, K. 184
Mason, G., and Lo, G. 213
May Day marches 74, 83, 131, 213; choreographed ritual of 176; external orientation of 208; local/national traditions and 203; motivational differences 74;

participants' motives 193, 194, 202, 206, 208; political context 74; socio-demographic composition of 96; WUNC model and 176
Mellors, Bob 25
Mexican Constitution 48
Mexican Supreme Court 48
Mexico 79; age of consent, sexual acts and 79; Catholic Church in 79; CONAPRED 79; discrimination, constitutional prohibition of 79; homophobia 79, 80; homophobic violence 223; homosexuality, public opinion and 82; machismo culture 79, 179; Penal Code 79; Pride parades in 48–9; same-sex marriage and 48, 49, 79; Yogyakarta Principles and 221
Mexico City 1, 44–9; Catholic Church in 76; CGH 45–6; *Claustro de Sor Juana* 47; Corpus Christi massacre 45; FAHR 45; FNF marches 48; Gay, Lesbian, Bisexual and Transgender Pride Parade 47–8; hate crimes 79; HIV/AIDS crisis 46–7; homosexual organizations 45; homosexuals, arrests and 45; Lambda Group 45; Legislative Assembly 47, 48; lesbian and gay liberation 45–6; lesbian and gay movement 44–5; lesbian movement 47; Lesbian Pride March 48; LGBT legislation 79, 207; LGBT less friendly context 13, 79, 80; LGBT movement 46–9; *Movimiento de Liberación Homosexual* 45; Okiabeth 45; politics 47; post-war period, homophile organizations 1; PRI and 47; Rainbow Cities Network and 79; same-sex marriage, legalisation of 48, 49, 79; sexual diversity 47–8; Sexual Diversity Forum 47; student demonstrators, killing of 45; Tlatelolco massacre 45, 46
Mexico City Pride 48, 129, 135, 136, 145; commercialization and 155; contextual factors **83**; future development of 217, 218; gender identities **98**; general elections (2012) and 135, 141n1; history 44–5; information channels **134**, 135, 140; insider event 146; machismo culture and 179; municipal support and 156–7; participants **94–5**, 179; participants asked/asking 136, **137**, 138, 140; participants' motives 126, **205**, 206, 207; participants, number of 125; perception of 214; political agenda 163–4, 165; political engagement, participants and **104–5**; political orientations, participants and **110–11**, *114*, 115; political solidarity and 163–4; route, symbolic significance of 183, 184; single issue/multi-issue split 164; spectacular performance and 185–6; trans women and 179

Meyer, D.S., and Gamson, J. 150
Miami, Florida, US 21
Milwaukee, Wisconsin, US 21
mobilization 13, 124–9; action mobilization 125, 129; barriers for participation 126–7, 129; closed forms of 132; consensus mobilization 125; external events as catalysts 128–9, 132; information channels and 129–32, 140, 212; mobilizing contexts 2, 91–2, 125; motivation and 125–6, 201; multi-stage process 125; open mobilization 132; peace protests and 129, 131, 132; public opinion and 132, 133; SMOs and 131, 132; stigmatization, risk of 127; strategies 3
Modi, Narendra Damodardas 222
monogamy 101, 115, 116, **116**, 117, **118–19**
Montenegro 223
motivation 125–6; emotions, role of 192; external events and 128–9; identity logic and 192; Pride participants and 13–14, 190, 191–2, 194–200; process 126; for protest 191–2; types of motives 191–2, 194–200
motive types 194–200, 207; broader categorizations 199–200; celebration **195**, 197, 200, 203, 204, **205**, 208, 216; commemoration **195**, 198–9, 200, **205**; conviction/duty **195**, 196, 200, 201, **205**; curiosity **195**, 199, 201, **205**; entertainment/fun **195**, 197–8, 200, 204, **205**, 208, 216; external influence 200, 202, **205**, 206; feeling of community **195**, 199, 200, 201, **205**; meeting friends/co-members of organization **195**, 196–7, 200, 201, **205**, 206; minority identity **195**, 198, **205**; movement coherence 200,

202, **205**, 206; "out-group" motives 213; political motives 200, 204, **205**, 207, 208, 209, 213, 215; protest/fight for rights/tolerance 194–5, **195**, 200, 201, **205**, 207, 208, 213; representation of organization/group **195**, 197, 200, 201, **205**; show support **195**, 196, 200, 201, 204, **205**, 206; tradition **195**, 196, 200, **205**, 208; visibility/display identity/pride **195**, 198, 200, 201, 204, **205**, 206, 207, 208

motives: contextual variations 202–6; individual characteristics, effects of 200–1; non-normative gender identities 200–1; Pride participants and 13, 14, 190, 191, 192, 194; women and 200; younger age groups 201; *see also* motive types

Movimiento de Liberación Homosexual (Mexico) 45

Mucciaroni, Gary 75

Murray, S.O. 19

Muslims 108, 160; *see also* Islam; Islamophobia

Nagle, J. 29

NAL/GPC *see* National Association of Lesbian and Gay Pride Coordinators

Naples, Italy 50

Napoleonic Code 39

National Association of Lesbian and Gay Pride Coordinators (NAL/GPC) 23, 65n15

National Union of Mineworkers 165

Nazi/neo-Nazi movement 83, 158, 180

neoliberalism 12, 14, 158

Netherlands 1, 5; adoption rights 82; anti-discrimination legislation 82; CoC (Center for Recreation and Culture) 36–7, 38; Dutch Society for Homophiles 36; Dutch Society for the Integration of Homosexuals 36; Equal Treatment Law 37; external influence **205**, 206; Federation of Student Working Groups on Homosexuality 36; gay and lesbian Movement 37; Gay Pride parades, increase in 11; homosexual demonstrations 36; homosexual emancipation and 35–6; homosexuality, public opinion and 76; human rights and 36; ICSE and 36; International Liberation and Solidarity march (1978) 37; international solidarity 37; Lesbian Nation 36, 37; LGBT friendly context 13, 82–3, 156; LGBT movement, depoliticization of 160; LGBT rights 39, 82–3, 163; LGBT strategies **119**; Pink Front, The 37, 38; political parties, LGBT movement and 160, 163; political parties, LGBT rights and 82–3; politics, LGBT movement and 38–9; post-war period, homophile organizations 1; Pride parades 63; Pride parades, government support for 12, 83; Purple September 36; queer politics 163; radical gay liberation, decline of 11; radicalism, gay and lesbian movement 36; Red Faggots 36; right-wing populist parties 108; same-sex marriage 82; stigma, low levels of 133; *Wissenschaftlich-humanitäre Komitee* (Scientific Humanitarian Committee) 35–6; Yogyakarta Principles and 221; *see also* Amsterdam; Canal Pride; Haarlem Pink Saturday Parade; Pink Saturday parades

Network of European LGBT Families Associations 72

New Left 19, 162

New York City: Christopher Street Liberation parade 20; Dyke March (1993) 23; Gay Shame festival 23; Pride parade (1999) 22–3; Pride parades 2, 4, 14, 126, 128; Stonewall riots and 18–19; WorldPride (2019) 24

Newton, Esther 7

Niemiec, Szymon 55

Nieto, Enrique Peña 48

non-binary/intergender identities 97, **98**, **100**

non-gender conforming persons 22

non-LGBT Pride participants 99, 101–2, 120, 128, 151; de-gaying of Pride parades 150, 164, 166; discrimination and 101–2, 209n1; motives for participating 201, 207; perception of 164; Stockholm Pride and 149, 153, 214

Nordic Youth 180

North Western Homosexual Law Reform Committee (NWHLRC) 25

Northern Ireland 25, 29

NWHLRC *see* North Western Homosexual Law Reform Committee

Oakley-Melvin, Deborah 51
Obama administration 221
O'Dwyer, C. 60, 72
Oesch, Daniel 93, 121n1
Ohlsson, Birgitta 223
Okiabeth 45, 64n10
Orbán government 222, 224
Örebro, Sweden 30
Organization of American States (OAS) 220–1
Orlando, Florida, US 128, 129
other LGBT 106, 116; LGBT strategies and **116**; political engagement **107**; political orientations **113**, 121; socio-demographic characteristics **100**

Palestine 163; pro-Palestine groups 162, 181
pansexual **100**, 116, 121
Parada Równosìci (Poland) 54–5
Paris, France 42
partnerships (same-sex) 43, 60; civil 32, 77, 82; registered 2, 42, 54, 61, 78
Passy, F. 131; and Monsch, G.-A. 136
patriarchy: abolition of 116, **116**, 117, **118–19**; other genders and 117; struggle against 11, 115; women and 117
peace protests, mobilization and 129, 131, 132
pedophiles/pedosexuals 145, 161–2, 165
Perfekcyjność, Jej 58–9
Personal Rights in Defense and Education (PRIDE) 18
Peterson, A., et al. 193, 203
Petersson, Stig-Åke 31, 124–5
Pew Research Center 81, 82
Phelan, Shane 7
Philadelphia, Pennsylvania, US 19, 21
Pink Cross (Switzerland) 42, 80
Pink Front, The (Netherlands) 37, 38
Pink Saturday parades (Netherlands) 35–9, 148, 163, 216; de-politicization of 39; lesbians, family social outings 148, 164, 208; mobilization strategies 152; Muslims and 160; social aspects of 148, 164, 208; stage, spatial importance of 184; state sponsorship and 156; *see also* Haarlem Pink Saturday Parade
"pink washing" 156, 158
Plummer, Ken 71
Plymouth Pride 150, 166n3

Poland 1, 53–9, 161; abortion, partial criminalization of 54; AIDS, prevention of 54; Amnesty International and 77; Catholic Church in 53, 54, 72; Charter of Fundamental Rights of the European Union and 77; Communist regime 53; criminal code, hate crimes and 77; ECtHR and 57, 77; EU membership and 54, 56, 72, 77; gay men, repression of 53; hate crimes 77; homophobia 78, 222; homosexuality in 53; homosexuality, public opinion and 76, 77, *82*; ILGCN-Polska 54–5; information channels 133; KPH 54, 77; Lambda groups 53, 54, 55; Law and Justice Party (PiS) 77, 222; LGBT Business Forum Foundation 58; LGBT issues 56–7; LGBT legislation 77; LGBT movement 57–8, 72; LGBT organizations 54; LGBT rights 224; LGBT strategies **119**; LGBT unfriendly context 13, 14, 53–4, 56, 76–8, 120, 151, 157, 164, 177; LPR 56; *Młodziez Wszechpolska* (All-Polish Youth) 56; Operation Hyacinth 53; *Partia Zieloni* (The Greens) 58; patriarchy, abolition of 117; PiS party 56; PiS/LPR government 57; *Platforma Obywatelska* (Civic Platform) (PO) 58; post-socialist 53–4; post-war period 1; same-sex marriage and 77; SDPL (Social Democrats) 58; SLD party 54; Solidarity (trade union) 53; *Twój Ruch* (Your Movement) 55, 58, 218; WRH 53; Yogyakarta Principles and 221; *see also* Warsaw; Warsaw Equality Parade
political engagement: gender identities and 106; LGBT groups in Pride parades **107**; Pride participants and 102–6, **104–5**, 120; young gay men and 150
political orientations: conservative parties 112, 121; Feminist Initiative (Sweden) 109, 112; gender identity and 114; left-libertarian parties 109, 114, 120, 121; left-right divide 112; left-wing 108, 109; LGBT groups **113**, *114*, 121; Pride participants and 106, 108–15, **110–11**, **113**; right-wing populist parties 108, 112, 121
politics, national contexts and 4

Portugal 223
Poznan, Poland 56, 59
Prague, Czech Republic 59
Prague Pride 1, 59, 61, 62–3, 145, 152–3; commercialization and 154–5, 165, 212; contextual factors 83; exhibitionism and 178; future development of 217–18; gender identities **98**; inclusive strategy 152; information channels 133, **134**, 140; LGBT organizations, participants and 135; mobilization strategy 152, 153; participants **94–5**; participants asked/asking **137**, 138; participants' motives **205**, 206, 207; participants, number of 125; pedosexual group 161, 165; political engagement, participants and **104–5**; political orientations *114*; Pride Village 152; social networks 133
PRIDE *see* Personal Rights in Defense and Education
Pride celebrations/events: contexts and 12–13; cultural context 76; political context 76
Pride (film) 27
Pride parades 170–87; in 1970 2; alternative events and 23; annual ritual events 74, 174; carnivalesque and 6, 7, 12, 170–1, 172, 175–6, 177, 181; collective becoming, performances of 7–8; collective coming out 173; collective identities 3, 171–4; coming out and 6, 171, 172, 173; commercialization of 2, 12, 165, 212; contextual differences 84; contextual factors influencing **83**; contextual variations 74; cost of 185–6; cross-national similarities 71–3; cultural anchors 84; cultural challenge of 174–5, 193, 208, 212–13; de-gaying of 13, 144, 150, 152, 164, 212; depoliticization and 163, 194, 200; differences 3, 73, 203, 211; diffusion, similarities and 71–3; diversity 97–102, 176–7; existential meaning of 173; fiftieth anniversary (2020) 14; future development of 217–20, 224; gender identities 97, **98**, 99; geopolitics and 220–4; global cultural anchors 84; globalization and 73; government support for 12; identities, diversity of 97–102; inclusivity and 151–2, 212; information

channels, mobilizations and 132–5, **134**; internal tensions and 214–17; laughter, subversive role of 192; lesbians **100**, 106; LGBT friendly context 177, 180–3; LGBT groups, diversity of 97–102; LGBT less friendly context 177–80; local and national contexts 63–4; logic of numbers 124; meanings for participants 13–14, 190–209, 220; mobilizing contexts 2, 91–2, 125, 177; mobilizing participants 124–5; national contexts 211; non-participants 214, 216; organizers and 172, 176, 177, 178–9, 181–2, 202–3, 217–18; orientation of 202, 203, 206; origins of 24; political performances of 175–7; political protest 173, 174, 212–13; politicization of 2, 193, 208; politics of 3; polyvocal nature of 6, 176; sexual displays and 178; sexual orientations of participants 99, **100**, 120; similarities 3, 71–5; single issue/multi-issue split 11, 162–4; size of 212; socio-demographic characteristics **100**; socio-demographic composition of 89–97, **94–5**, 120; spatial location 183–5; spectacular performances, cost of 185–6; spectators/bystanders and 126, 185; stage, spatial importance of 183–5; symbol of modernity 223; symbol of Western liberal values 14, 222–3, 224; symbolic significance of route 183–4; tensions 2, 215–16; times/spaces and 184–5; traditions of 63–4; unity and 176–7; visibility and 1, 88–9, 184, 193; WUNC model and 176, 177; young people and 127; *see also* friends of Pride; Pride participants
Pride participants 2, 13, 88–21; age of 92, 216; asking/being asked 136, **137**, 138, **139**, 140; barriers, overcoming 136–8, 140; differences vis-à-vis general population 92, 103, 120; ethnic minorities 93; first-timers 138–9, **139**, 141, 172–3, 174, 201; gay men **100**, 106, 120, 216; gender identities 97, **98**, 99; heterosexual **100**, 102, 120; identity logic and 192; lesbians **100**, 106, 120; LGBT movement strategies 115–17; LGBT organizations and 135; loners 131, 133; meanings of Pride parades 13–14,

190–209; motives 13–14, 190, 191–2, 194, 200–6, 207; newcomers 138–40, 207; non-LGBT 99, 101–2, 120, 128, 164, 201; occupational class 93; political engagement 102–6, **104–5**, 120; political orientations 106, 108–15, **110–11**, **113**, 120; Pride parades and 2, 13, 88–121; returnees 138–40, **139**, 201; sexual orientations 99, **100**, 106, 115, 211–12, 215; social class 92–3; socio-demographic composition of 89–97, **94–5**, 211; stigmatization and 127, 128, 136, 138, 140; tensions, lesbians/gay men 215–16; tire watch and 130, 141n3; young people 127; *see also* friends of Pride
Pride Romandy 42–3, 88, 179
PrideRadar 48, 215
pro-Palestine groups 162
protests/protesters: anti-austerity 213; anti-war protests 213; motives for 191–2; normalization of 89–91, 103, 108, 117, 120; peace protests 129, 131, 132; protest campaigns 202; *see also* demonstrations; May Day marches
PROUD (Czech Republic) 63
Puar, J. 160
"puppies" and "handlers" 7
Putin, Vladimir 222
Putnam, R. 72

queer activists 7; boycott of Brooklyn Gay Pride (1998) 23; Gothenburg Pride parade (2010) 182–3; Poland and 54; radicalism (Queer fire) 36; rhetoric of hatred 182–3
Queer Institute 182
Queer parade, Brno (2008) 61
queer politics 1, 7, 11, 150; Netherlands 163
queers 22, **100**; European queers, Lady Gaga and 52; feminist queer groups in Brno 61; identity 97, **98**, 117; perception of 222

racism 158, 159, 222
radicalism 36, 221–2
Rainbow Cities Network 79
rainbow flag 24, 64, 72, 73, 186; as cultural anchor 84
rainbow imagery 148
RainbowRose 72

Regnbågsfestivalen (Rainbow Festival) (Sweden) 34
Regnbågsparaden (Rainbow Parade) *see* Gothenburg Rainbow Parade
Revolt mot sexuella fördomar (Revolt against sexual prejudices) 30, 31
RFSL *see Riksförbundet för homosexuellas, bisexuellas, transpersoners och queeras rättigheter* (Swedish Federation for Lesbian, Gay, Bisexual, Transgender and Queer Rights)
Richardson, Diane 12
right-wing populist parties 108; LGBT voters and 108, 121
Riksförbundet för homosexuellas, bisexuellas, transpersoners och queeras rättigheter (Swedish Federation for Lesbian, Gay, Bisexual, Transgender and Queer Rights) (RFSL) 30, 31, 32, 33, 35, 83, 128, 155; Sweden Democrats and 158–9
Riksförbundet för sexuellt likaberättigande see Riksförbundet för homosexuellas, bisexuellas, transpersoners och queeras rättigheter (Swedish Federation for Lesbian, Gay, Bisexual, Transgender and Queer Rights)
Rio de Janeiro 223
RIP Pride (2015) 216
Roman Catholic Church *see* Catholic Church
Romandy region, Switzerland 42–4, 179; *Dialogai* 43; *Pride romande, la* 42, 43, 44
Rome, Italy: *Circolo Mario Mieli* 49–50; EuroPride (2000) 50; EuroPride (2011) 52; Gay and Lesbian Pride 50; gay rights demonstration (1972) 49; WorldPride (2000) 24, 50, 51, 52
Romero, Óscar, Monsignor 46
Ross, B.L., and Landström, C. 5
Roth, A.L. 190
Rotterdam Pride 38
Rucht, Dieter 144
Russia 222; Anti-Homosexual Propaganda Law 221

Salt Lake City, Utah, US 4
same-sex marriage 2; Catholic Church and 75, 78; Czech support for 81; Italy and 78; Mexico and 48, 79; Netherlands and 82; Poland and 77; RFSL and 30; Sweden and 82; UK and 81

same-sex relationships, recognition of 2, 80
San Diego, California, US 4
San Francisco, California, US 21; Dyke March (1993) 23; Gay Shame 23; lesbian marches 23; marches (1990s) 22
San Jose, California, US 21
Santino, Jack 170, 176
São Paolo, Brazil 79, 223
Saunders, C., et al. 139
Schussman, A., and Soule, S.A. 102, 106
Schuyf, J., and Krouwel, A. 11
Schweizer Freundschaftsbund (The Swiss Friendship Association) 39
Schweizerische Organisation der Homophilen (Swiss Organization of Homophiles) (SOH) 40, 41, 42
Scotland 24, 25, 81
Sdružení organizací homosexuálních občanů (Association of Organizations of Homosexual Citizens) (SOHO) (Czech Republic) 60
secularity 75, 79, 81
Serbia 223
sexual fetishes 7
sexual identity: coming out and 6, 127; normalization of 6; open avowal of 6; public affirmation of 127
sexual liberation 30, 45, 49, 145, 146
Sexual Offences Act (1967) (UK) 25
sexual orientations: LGBT movement strategies and **118–19**; Pride parade participants 99, **100**, 106, 115, 120
sexual politics 221–2
SGL *see Stowarzyszenie Grup Lambda* (Association of Lambda Groups)
shame: coming out and 173; LGBT persons and 97, 192
Shepard, Benjamin 5, 22, 170, 170–1
Sion, Switzerland, Pride parade 42, 43, 179
Smith, M. 5
Snow, D.A., and McAdam, D. 192
social class, Pride participants and 92–3
social media 130, 132, 133, **134**, 140
social movement organizations (SMOs) 125, 140; information channels and 129, 139; mobilization and 131, 132
social movements: biographical availability and 102; the carnivalesque and 172; collective energy and 171; demonstrations and 120; mobilization potential of 125; socio-demographic composition of 120
socio-cultural values 112, 114
Socio-Therapeutic Club of Homosexuals (Czech Republic) 60
SOH *see Schweizerische Organisation der Homophilen* (Swiss Organization of Homophiles)
SOHO *see Sdružení organizací homosexuálních občanů* (Association of Organizations of Homosexual Citizens)
Sokolová, V. 59, 60
Solidarity (Polish trade union) 53
Spain 24, 48, 223
Sparkle Weekend 29
Starbucks 157, 158, 216
stereotypes, LGBT community and 106
stigma/stigmatization: barrier to Pride participation 127, 128, 136, 140–1; collective overcoming of 175; coming out and 140–1; commercial sponsors and 212; fear of 136, 138; first-time participants and 138; friends of Pride and 165; gay identity and 127; Netherlands, low levels of 133; non-LGBT Pride participants and 128; overcoming barrier of 201, 211, 212; risk of 127, 136, 165, 212
Stockholm Pride 12, 31, 32, 33–4, 92, 96–7, 146; broad political platform 147; carnivalesque elements 33; choreography 181–2; code of principles 161; commercial sponsors 145; commercialization and 155–6; contextual factors **83**; friends of Pride and 161, 214–15; gender identities **98**; gender of participants 97; goal of 147; high profile politics 180; identity for empowerment 154; identity as goal 154; identity strategy 181; inclusion, limits for 158–9; inclusivity and 147, 164, 181; information channels 133, **134**; LGBT organizations and 33; non-LGBT participants 101, 149, 153, 214; Nordic Youth and 180; organizational friends 145; parade (2014) 180–1; participants 92, **94–5**, 128, 136, **137**, 204; participants asked/asking **137**, 138; participants' motives **205**, 207, 209; participants, number of 125; "pink washing" 156;

political elite and 181; political engagement, participants and **104–5**; political motives, participants and 204; political orientations 109, 112, *114*; politics/politicians and 33, 34, 83, 147, 164–5; Pride House events 33, 156; Pride Park and 153–4, 156; pro-Palestine groups and 162; route, symbolic significance of 184; sexual orientation of participants 99, 216; sexual orientations **100**; single-issue/multi-issue split 162; stereotypes and 106; tensions 101, 115; trade unions and 145
Stockholm Pride Association 33, 96, 130, 147, 155–6, 159
Stockholm Pride Week 159
Stockholm, Sweden 1, 32–4; Anarcho-Pride 35; annual homosexual liberation demonstrations 31; Christopher Street Liberation Day 30–1, 124; EuroPride (1998) 32; *Homosexuella frigörelsedagen* (Homosexual Liberation Day) 31
Stockholms Homofestival (Stockholm's Homo Festival) 32
Stonewall myth, gay liberation and 18–24
Stonewall riot (1969): aftermath 63; commemoration, Sweden (1971) 30–1; commemoration, UK (1972) 25; commeration, Switzerland (1978) 40–1; fiftieth anniversary (2019) 24
Stowarzyszenie Grup Lambda (Association of Lambda Groups) (SGL) 53
structural availability 102; Pride participants and 103
Sundsvall, Sweden 34
Svenska Dagbladet (newspaper) 180
Svoboda, Bohuslav 62
Sweden 1, 4, 5, 29–35; adoption rights 82; Almedalen Week 33, 34; American Gay Liberation, influence of 30; AnarchoPride 35; anti-discrimination legislation 82; Christopher Street Liberation Day 30–1; decriminalization of homosexual acts (1944) 29; discrimination, constitutional prohibition of 79; Feminist Initiative 109, 112, 145; feminist movement 31, 117, 162; gay and lesbian activism 30–2; *Gaymoderaterna* (Gay Conservatives) 32; *HBT-festivalen* (the LGBT Festival) 34; HBTQ 14n2; homophobic public sentiments 29–30; homosexual divine service 32; Homosexual Liberation Day (1970s) 31–2, 33; Homosexual Liberation Week 32; homosexuality, public opinion and 76; *Homosexuella frigörelsedagen* (Homosexual Liberation Day) 31; *Homosexuella liberaler* (Homosexual Liberals) 32; *Homosexuella Socialister* (Homosexual Socialists) 31, 32; *Lesbisk Front* (Lesbian Front) 31, 162; LGBT friendly context 13, 82–3, 117, 156; LGBT movement 162–3, 209; LGBT organizations 30; LGBT rights, political support for 82, 83; Lutheran state church 32; May Day tradition 83; new left 162; Örebro demonstration 30; patriarchy, abolition of 117; political parties, gay and lesbian associations and 32; political parties, LGBT rights and 82, 83; post-war period, homophile organizations 1; Pride, history of 29–30; Pride parades, diffusion of 34–5, 63; Pride parades, government support for 12, 83; *Regnbågsfestivalen* (Rainbow Festival) 34; religious institutions 32; RFSL 30, 31, 32, 33, 35, 83, 128, 155; same-sex marriage 82; solidarity with LGBT people 128; Stonewall commemorative demonstration 30, 31; Yogyakarta Principles and 221; *see also* Gothenburg; Gothenburg Rainbow Parade; Stockholm; Stockholm Pride; West Pride
Sweden Democrats 83, 158–9, 166n2; Islamophobia and 158; RFSL and 158–9
Swedish Federation for Lesbian, Gay, Bisexual, Transgender and Queer Rights, The 30
Swedish Federation for Sexual Equality, The 30
Swedish Pride, political orientations 109
Switzerland 1, 39–44; adoption and 80; age of consent, sexual acts and 80; Catholic Church and 80; Christopher Street days 40–2; *Club68* 40; decriminalization of homosexual acts 39, 80; *Der Kreis*

(journal) 36, 39, 40; discrimination, constitutional prohibition of 79; *Freundschafts-Banner* 39; German influences 39; HACH 40, 42; HFG 40; homosexual activism 40; homosexuality, public opinion *82*; *Homosexuellen Arbeitsgruppen* (Homosexual Working Groups) 40; lesbian groups 42; LGBT less friendly context 13; LGBT rights, political parties and 80; LOS 42; Napoleonic Code, adoption of 39; Pink Cross 42, 80; political parties 80; post-war period, homophile organizations 1; Pride parades 42; referendums 43–4; Romandy region, Pride in 42–4, 179; *Schweizer Freundschaftsbund* (Swiss Friendship Association) 39; SOH 40, 41, 42; Stonewall commemorations 40–2; women's movement 40; see also Geneva; Geneva Pride; Zürich; Zürich Pride

Sydney Mardi Gras parade 55, 213

symbols: rainbow heart (Warsaw) 147; rainbow imagery 148; *see also* rainbow flag

Szulc, L. 77

Tabor, Czech Republic 61
Tatchell, Peter 25–6, 173, 183, 215, 219
Taylor, V., and Rupp, L.J. 127
terrorist attacks 128, 129
Thatcher Government 26, 27
Thatcher, Margaret 26, 27
Thor, Ebba Busch 128
Tilly, Charles 176, 177
tolerance 2, 35–6, 132; March of Tolerance, Cracow 56; promotion of 115, **116**
Toronto, Canada, WorldPride (2014) 24
trade unions: demonstrations 96, 120; London Pride and 145, 157, 158, 165; miners' unions (UK) 26, 27, 157; Pride parades and 145; Solidarity (Polish) 53
transgender people 22, 97, 116, 146; Czech Republic and 81; Gender Recognition Act (2004) (UK) 81–2; Italian legislation and 78; patriarchy and 117; political orientations 121; Pride parades and **100**; Sparkle Weekend 29; trans women, Mexico City Pride and 179
transnationalism 220–1
transsexuals, acceptance/inclusion 22
Tremblay, M., et al. 4
Trump, Donald 222
Turner, R.H., and Killian, L.M. 202

UK *see* United Kingdom
UKIP (UK Independence Party) 159–60, 216
United Kingdom (UK) 1, 24–9; adoption legislation 81; age of consent, sexual acts and 81; anti-gay law (Section 28) 27, 165; discrimination, legislation prohibiting 81; Gay Pride march (1972) 25; Gender Recognition Act (2004) 81–2; GLF 25; government funding, Pride events and 156; HIV epidemic 26; HLRS, lobbying activities 25; homosexuality, public opinion and 82, *82*; LBGT MPs 82; legislation, homosexuals and 25, 27, 165; LGBT friendly context 13, 81–2; LGBT movement 26, 27–8, 82; LGBT strategies **119**; mid-1970s parade 7; miners' unions, LGSM and 27; miners' unions, Thatcher government and 26, 27; post-war period, homophile organizations 1; Pride parades in 24–9, 63; Pride parades, proliferation of 29; Pride weekends 29; Pride-like events (1970s) 23; same-sex marriage 81; Sexual Offences Act (1967) 25; Yogyakarta Principles and 221; *see also* London; London Pride
United Nations (UN): Human Rights Council 221; ILGA sanctioned by 162; UN General Assembly 221; Yogyakarta Principles presented 221
United States (US): anti-homosexual campaign, Florida 37, 64n7; anti-war protesters (2003) 203; commercialization of Pride events 12, 154; domination in LGBT movements 4; Dyke Marches 23; gay hate crimes in 75; gay rights, perception of 75; homosexual repression 37; LGBT legislation and 76; LGBT movement, symbols/language of 4; LGBT movements, unity and 22; LGBT population 225n2; LGBT voters, Republican Party and 108; Pride

demonstrations (1970) 2; Pride parades 4; Pride parades, growth of 21–3; Pride parades, origins of 24; single/multi-issue split 162
Universal Declaration of Human Rights (1949) 36
Uppsala Pride 35
Uppsala, Sweden 30, 34
Uruguay 221
US *see* United States

van Delen, Frank 211
Van Laer, J. 130
van Stekelenburg, J., et al. 202
Venice, Italy 50
Verhulst, J., and Walgrave, S. 138, 140
Viking (magazine) 30
Village Charity 29
Village Voice 18
Vilnius, Lithuania 223
visibility: coming out performances and 6; LGBT community and 193, 194; Pride parades and 1, 88–9, 184, 193

Wahlström, M. 191–2, 193, 194, **195**, 196, 202, 206; and Wennerhag, M. 130–1, 133
Waites, Matthew 11
Wales 81
Walgrave, S.: et al. 203; and Klandermans, B. 129, 130, 131–2, 133; and Manssens, J. 130; and Verhulst, J. 90, 91, 211; and Wouters, R. 131, 136, 138
Walter, Aubrey 25
Warsaw Equality Parade 54–6, 58–9, 63, 133, 145; banning of 56–7; commercial sponsors and 165, 212; contextual factors **83**;Council of Europe grant and 151; external influence **205**, 206; friends of Pride, mobilization strategy 151; funding and 157; future development of 218; gay men, dominance of 216; gender identities, composition of **98**; inclusivity and 152, 164; inequality issues and 147; LGBT unfriendly context 177, 218; media and 148, 177; multi-issues of inequality/human rights 164; opposition to 77; organizers' framing of 146, 147–8, 149; orientation of 203; participants 92, **94–5**; participants, asked/asking 136, **137**; participants' motives **205**, 206, 207; participants, number of 125; political parties and 164; political engagement, participants and **104–5**; political orientations, participants and 109, **110–11**, *114*, 115; political parties and 164; politicized participants 204; sexual orientation of participants 99; sexual orientations **100**; symbol (rainbow heart) 147
Warsaw, Poland 1; Equality Foundation 55, 58; EuroPride (2010) 58, 77; information channels **134**; Lambda Warszawa 55; *Manifa* march (2001) 55; *Parada Równosìci* 54–5; Parade of Normality (2005) 56; Women's March (2001) 55; WRH 53
Warszawski Ruch Homoseksualny (Warsaw Homosexual Movement) (WRH) 53
Washington, D.C., US 21, 23, 146
Wasshede, Cathrin 182–3
Weber, M. 191
Weeks, J. 27
Weiss, Margot D. 11
West Germany 36
West Pride, Gothenburg 10, 34, 106, 147; code of principles 161; commercialization and 156; friends of Pride and 161; goal of 147; information channels 133, **134**; parade (2010) 182–3; parade participants 92; participants asked/asking **137**, 138; participants' motives 209; participants, number of 125; political orientations, participants and *114*; political parties and 164–5; Pride initiative, cultural institutions and 10; radical left in 35; state sponsorship and 156
Western Europe 23, 108, 109
Western liberal values 222–3
white gay men, dominance of 23
Wilson, Angelia 76, 77
Wissenschaftlich-humanitäre Komitee (Scientific Humanitarian Committee) 35–6
Women's Arcigay (Italy) 50
Women's movement *see* feminist movement
World Values Survey 79, 81

World War II, homosexual victims of 36, 163
WorldPride 24, 28; establishment of (2000) 63; Jerusalem (2006) 24; London (2012) 24, 93, 125, 145, 149, 164; Madrid (2017) 24; political agenda 51; Rome (2000) 24, 50, 51, 52; Toronto (2014) 24
worthiness, unity, numbers, commitment (WUNC) 176, 177
WRH *see Warszawski Ruch Homoseksualny* (Warsaw Homosexual Movement)
WUNC *see* worthiness, unity, numbers, commitment

Xalapa, Mexico 129

Yogyakarta Principles 221

Zürich Pride 41, 43, 44, *114*; commercial sponsors 145; contextual factors **83**; gender identities **98**; gender of participants 97; information channels **134**, 135; participants 92, **94–5**;participants asked/asking **137**; participants, number of 125; political engagement, participants and **104–5**, 204; political orientations, participants and **110–11**, 112, 115; tensions within 215
Zürich Pride Association 96
Zürich, Switzerland 1, 39, 40; CSD Gay Parade (1995) 41; CSD parades 41–2; CSD Zürich 41, 42; EuroPride (2009) 41; homosexuals, registration of 41; *Homosexuellen Arbeitsgruppen* (Homosexual Working Groups) 40